Congressional Procedures and the Policy Process

THIRD EDITION

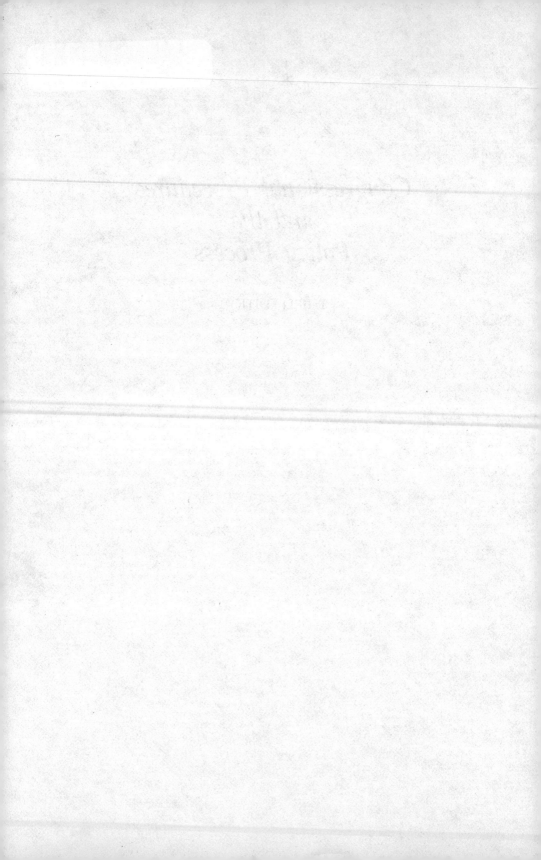

Congressional Procedures and the Policy Process

THIRD EDITION

Walter J. Oleszek

A Division of Congressional Quarterly Inc.
1414 22nd Street N.W., Washington, D.C. 20037

Printed in the United States of America

Library of Congress Cataloging-in-Publication Data

Oleszek, Walter J.
Congressional procedures and the policy process/Walter J. Oleszek.—3d ed.
p. cm.
Bibliography: p.
Includes index.
ISBN 0-87187-487-3 ISBN 0-87187-477-6 (pbk.)
1. United States. Congress. I. Title.
JK1096.043 1989
328.73—dc19 88-16132
CIP

For Janet, Mark, and Eric

Contents

TABLES

ILLUSTRATIONS

Preface

Congress is constantly adapting to change. New procedures, processes, and practices come about in response to developing conditions and circumstances. Some procedural innovations are incorporated formally in the rules of the House or Senate; others evolve informally. For all their variability over time, the rules of the House and Senate are constant in this sense: they establish the procedural context within which individual members and the two chambers raise issues and make (or avoid making) decisions. Members of Congress, in sum, must rely upon rules and procedures to expedite or delay legislation, to secure enactment, or to bring about the defeat of bills.

This book was first published in 1978, in the aftermath of momentous changes that affected legislative decision making and the political system. The result of many of these developments on Capitol Hill was to diffuse policy-making influence widely throughout Congress. The term often employed to describe this new environment was "subcommittee government." Six years later, when the second edition of *Congressional Procedures and the Policy Process* appeared, the House and Senate had undergone further procedural transformations. The House, for instance, began gavel-to-gavel television coverage of its floor proceedings. Since the second edition was published, there have been other important procedural and institutional developments that require discussion and analysis, including gavel-to-gavel television coverage in the Senate. Congress revamped its budgetary practices with the enactment of Gramm-Rudman-Hollings I and II; the House Rules Committee crafted unique new "rules" for regulating floor decision making; and greater use was made of comprehensive bills, or "packages," to process much of Congress's annual workload. Interestingly, one effect of these and other changes has been to recentralize authority in fewer legislative hands.

As Congress approaches the 1990s, it is emerging from a period that has witnessed the Iran-contra affair, the election of new congressional leaders, large budget and trade deficits, sharp controversy over the nature of the national agenda, and increased agitation in the House and Senate to improve the quality of life—changes that would streamline legislative scheduling and help members balance public and private pressures. That a great deal has occurred in Congress is beyond doubt. As a result, I have incorporated in this third edition discussion of new rules and procedures and new examples and materials that highlight how Congress changes its decision-making procedures.

The fundamental objective of the third edition of *Congressional Procedures and the Policy Process* is to discuss how the contemporary Congress makes laws and how its rules and procedures shape domestic and foreign policy. The theme of the book is that the interplay of rules, procedures, precedents, and strategies is vital to understanding how Congress works. I emphasize the rules and procedures most significant to congressional lawmaking; I do not attempt to survey all the rules and procedures used by Congress.

While the format and structure of the third edition closely follows that of the second, I have revised every chapter for the new edition. In Chapter 1, an overall view of the congressional process is presented. In Chapter 2, the focus shifts to the organizational setting and political environment of Congress to examine differences between the House and Senate; the leadership structure in Congress; pressures exerted on Congress; and recent changes in Congress's operations. Chapter 3 examines Congress's budget process, which shapes much of the legislative decision making.

Chapter 4 turns to the initial steps of the legislative process—the introduction and referral of bills to House and Senate committees, and committee action on measures. Chapter 5 explains how legislation that has emerged from committee is scheduled for floor action in the House. Chapter 6 then examines floor action in the House. In Chapter 7 the spotlight is put on the Senate, with discussion of how legislation is scheduled in that chamber. Senate floor action is the subject of Chapter 8.

Chapter 9 discusses the president's veto power and describes how House-Senate differences are reconciled when each chamber passes a different version of the same bill. Chapter 10 discusses how Congress monitors the implementation of the laws it has passed. The final chapter reexamines the legislative process, pulling together the major themes of this book.

There is no doubt that my intellectual indebtedness involves numerous scholars and colleagues, and I welcome the opportunity to acknowledge their generous assistance. My editor at CQ Press, Nola Healy Lynch, contributed greatly to the readability of this book. Noell Sottile and Nancy Lammers of CQ's Book Department skillfully steered (or "floor managed") the book through the production stages. My thanks, too, must go to David R. Tarr, director of CQ's Book Department, and Joanne D. Daniels, director of CQ Press, for their encouragement and support throughout this project.

Much credit for whatever understanding I have of the congressional process is due in large measure to my colleagues at the Congressional Research Service. Over the years I have learned the intricacies of the House and Senate from scores of CRS associates. That institution, I should note, bears no responsibility whatsoever for the views or interpretations expressed within these pages. I must also emphasize that whatever errors remain in this book are mine alone.

In addition to the colleagues I cite in footnotes or the selected bibliography, I want to thank Walter Kravitz, Louis Fisher, and Roger Davidson for their generous and constructive comments and suggestions about the workings of Congress. My sincere thanks extend also to CRS Director Joseph Ross and Government Division Chief Frederick Pauls for encouraging CRS employees—on their own time, of course—to teach, write, and lecture on Congress and the political system.

Finally, I dedicate this third edition (as I did the second) to my wife Janet, and my two sons, Mark and Eric. My greatest thanks go to them for all their love and encouragement.

Walter J. Oleszek

CHAPTER 1

Congress and Lawmaking

The bicentennial of the U.S. Constitution reminds us that Congress is one of the world's most prominent and durable lawmaking bodies. The framers intended this result. Over half of their time during the humid Philadelphia summer of 1787 was spent defining Congress's role and responsibilities. "In republican government," explained James Madison, "the legislative authority necessarily predominates." [1] And Madison, among others, tried to ensure that in the new United States government, Congress would emerge as the principal policy-making branch.

Lawmaking is Congress's most basic response to the entire range of national concerns, from agriculture to housing, environment to national defense, health to the economy. The process by which Congress transforms an idea into national policy is the subject of this book. This process is complicated and variable, but it is governed by rules, procedures, precedents, and customs, and it is open to the use of some generally predictable strategies and tactics.

Members of Congress have major responsibilities other than lawmaking—to represent their constituents and to review the implementation of laws. All these functions are integral parts of the congressional process.

This first chapter examines the constitutional foundation of congressional policy making, the functions of rules and procedures in organizations, the interaction of rules (formal and informal) and policy making in the congressional context, and the important features of congressional decision making.

THE CONSTITUTIONAL CONTEXT

Congress's central role in policy making can be traced to the writers of the Constitution. Madison, Alexander Hamilton, and the others developed a political system that established Congress as the lawmaking body and set out its relationship with the other branches of government and with the people. Several familiar basic principles underlie the specific provisions of the Constitution. These include limited government, separation of powers, checks and balances, and federalism. Each principle continues to shape lawmaking today despite the enormous changes that have transformed and enlarged the role of government in American society.

Limited Government

The framers of the Constitution wanted a strong and effective national government, but at the same time they wanted to avoid concentrating too much power in the central government lest it threaten personal and property rights. The Constitution is filled with implicit and explicit "auxiliary precautions" (Madison's phrase), such as checks and balances and a bill of rights. Limitation of government, the framers believed, could be achieved by dividing power among three branches of national government and between the nation and the states. The division of power ensured both policy conflicts and cooperation because it made officials in the several branches responsive to different constituencies, responsibilities, and perceptions of the public welfare.

The framers believed that the "accumulation of all powers, legislative, executive, and judiciary, in the same hands ... may justly be pronounced the very definition of tyranny."[2] As men of practical experience, they had witnessed firsthand the abuses of King George III and his royal governors. They also wanted to avoid the possible "elective despotism" of their own state legislatures.[3] Wary of excessive authority in either an executive or a legislative body, the framers also were familiar with the works of influential political theorists, particularly Locke and Montesquieu, who stressed such concepts as the separation of powers, checks and balances, and popular control of government.

Separation of Powers

The framers combined their practical experience with a theoretical outlook and established three independent branches of national government, none having a monopoly of governing power. Their objective was twofold. First, the separation of powers was designed to restrain the power of any one branch. Second, it was meant to ensure that cooperation would be necessary for effective government. As Supreme Court Justice Robert Jackson wrote in a 1952 case (*Youngstown Co. v. Sawyer*, 343 U.S. 579, 635): "While the Constitution diffuses power the better to secure liberty, it also contemplates that the practice will integrate the dispersed powers into a workable government."

The framers held a strong bias in favor of lawmaking by representative assemblies, and so viewed Congress as the prime national policy maker. The Constitution names Congress the first branch of government, assigns it "all legislative power," and grants it explicit and implied responsibilities through the so-called elastic clause (Section 8 of Article I). This clause empowers Congress to make "all Laws which shall be necessary and proper for carrying into Execution" its enumerated or specific powers.

In sharp contrast, Articles II and III, creating the executive and judicial branches, describe only briefly the framework and duties of these governmental units. Although separation of powers implies that Congress "enacts" the laws, the president "executes" them, and the Supreme Court "interprets" them, such a rigid division of labor was not intended by the framers. The Constitution, in short, creates a system not of separate institutions performing separate functions but of separate institutions sharing functions. The overlap of powers is fundamental to national decision making. The founders did grant certain unique responsibilities to each branch and ensured their separateness by, for example, prohibiting any officer from serving in more than one branch simultaneously. They linked the branches through a system of checks and balances.

Checks and Balances

An essential corollary of separation of powers is checks and balances. The framers realized that individuals in each branch might seek to aggrandize power at the expense of the other branches. Inevitably, conflicts would develop. In particular, the Constitution provides an open invitation to struggles for power by Congress and the president.

To restrain each branch, the framers devised a system of checks and balances. Congress's own legislative power was effectively "checked" by the establishment of a bicameral body consisting of the House of Representatives and the Senate. The laws Congress passes may be vetoed by the president. Treaties and high-level presidential appointments require the approval of the Senate. And many decisions and actions of Congress and the president are subject to review by the federal judiciary.

Checks and balances have a dual effect; they encourage cooperation and accommodation among the branches—particularly between the popularly elected Congress and the president—and they introduce the potential for conflict. Since 1789 Congress and the president have indeed cooperated with each other and protected their own powers. Each branch depends in various ways on the other. When conflicts occur, they are resolved most frequently by negotiation, bargaining, and compromise.

Federalism

Just as the three branches check each other, the state and federal governments also are countervailing forces. This division of power is another way to curb and control governing power. While the term "federalism" (like separation of powers or checks and balances) is not mentioned in the Constitution, the framers understood that federalism was a plan of government acceptable to the thirteen original states. The Constitution's "supremacy clause" makes national laws and treaties the "supreme Law of the Land"; however, powers not granted to the national government remain with the states and the people. The inevitable clashes that occur between levels of government are often arbitrated by the Supreme Court or worked out through practical accommodations or laws.

Federalism has infused "localism" into congressional proceedings. As a representative institution, Congress and its members respond to the needs and interests of states and congressional districts. The nation's diversity is given ample expression in Congress by legislators whose tenure rests on the continued support of their constituents.

Thus, the Constitution outlines a complicated system. Power is divided among the branches and between levels of government, and popular opinion is reflected differently in each. Both Congress and the president, each with different constituencies, terms of office, and times of election, can claim to represent majority sentiment on national issues. Given each branch's independence, formidable powers, different perspectives on many issues, and intricate mix of formal and informal relationships, it is apparent that important national policies reflect the judgment of both the legislative and the executive branches and the views of pressure groups and influential persons.

CONGRESS: AN INDEPENDENT POLICY MAKER

Much has been written about the growth of executive power in the twentieth century and the diminished role of Congress, but in fact there has been a dynamic, not static, pattern of activity between the legislative and executive branches. First one and then the other may be perceived as the predominant branch, and various periods are characterized as times of "congressional government" or "presidential government."[4] Such descriptions often underestimate the other branch's strategic importance, however. President John F. Kennedy, who served during a period regarded by some observers as one of presidential resurgence, observed that Congress "looks more powerful sitting here than it did when I was there." From his position in the White House, he looked at the collective power of Congress and found it "substantial." [5]

In short, the American political system is largely congressional *and* presidential government. Or, as British historian Paul Johnson put it, "We refer to the British constitution as a parliamentary democracy . . . [and] I would call yours a presidential and congressional democracy." [6]

The strength and independence of Congress contrast sharply with the position of legislatures in other democratic countries. In most, policy making is concentrated in the hands of a prime minister and cabinet who normally are elected members of the legislature and leaders of the majority party. As a result, the policy of the prime minister and his cabinet typically is approved by the legislature, with voting divided strictly along party lines. Conversely, if a prime minister loses a "vote of confidence" in parliament, he or she is expected to resign, and a general election is held to choose a successor government.

The U.S. Congress, by contrast, is elected separately from the president and has independent policy-making authority. As a result, a study of policy making in the United States requires a separate examination of the congressional process.

FUNCTIONS OF RULES AND PROCEDURES

Any decision-making body, Congress included, needs a set of rules, procedures, and conventions, formal and informal, in order to function. These rules and conventions establish the procedural context for both collective and individual policy-making action and behavior (see "Major Sources of House and Senate Rules").

In the case of Congress, the Constitution authorizes the House and Senate to formulate their own rules of procedure and also prescribes some basic procedures for both houses, such as overrides of presidential vetoes. Thomas Jefferson, who as vice president compiled the first parliamentary manual for the U.S. Senate, emphasized the importance of rules to any legislative body.

> It is much more material that there be a rule to go by, than what that rule is; that there may be a uniformity of proceeding in business not subject to the caprice of the Speaker or captiousness of the members. It is very material that order, decency, and regularity be preserved in a dignified public body.[7]

Rules and procedures in an organization serve many functions. Among them are to provide stability, legitimize decisions, divide responsibilities, reduce conflict, and distribute power. Each of these

Major Sources of House and Senate Rules

U.S. CONSTITUTION. Article I, Section 5, states: "Each House may determine the Rules of Its Proceedings." In addition, other procedures of Congress are addressed, such as quorums, adjournments, and roll calls.

STANDING RULES. The formal rules of the House are contained in the *Constitution, Jefferson's Manual,* and the *Rules of the House of Representatives.* The Senate's rules are in the *Senate Manual Containing the Standing Rules, Orders, Laws, and Resolutions Affecting the Business of the United States Senate.* Each chamber prints its rule book biennially as a House or Senate document.

PRECEDENTS. Each chamber, particularly the larger House, has scores of precedents, or "unwritten law," based upon past rulings of the Chair. The modern precedents of the Senate are compiled in one volume prepared by Floyd M. Riddick, parliamentarian emeritus. It is revised and updated periodically, printed as a Senate document, and entitled *Senate Procedure, Precedents and Practices.* House precedents are contained in several sources. Precedents from 1789 to 1936 are found in eleven volumes: *Hinds' Precedents of the House of Representatives* (from 1789 to 1907) and *Cannon's Precedents of the House of Representatives* (from 1908 to 1936). Precedents from 1936 through 1973 can be found in the multivolume series (not yet complete) entitled *Deschler's Precedents of the United States House of Representatives.* Hinds, Cannon, and Deschler were parliamentarians of the House. Further, the precedents now are updated every two years and published as *Procedure in the U.S. House of Representatives.* It is prepared by the House parliamentarian.

STATUTORY RULES. There are many public laws whose provisions have the force of congressional rules. Notable examples include the Legislative Reorganization Act of 1946 (PL 79-601), the Legislative Reorganization Act of 1970 (PL 91-510), and the Congressional Budget and Impoundment Control Act of 1974 (PL 93-344).

JEFFERSON'S MANUAL. When Thomas Jefferson was vice president (1797-1801) he prepared a manual of parliamentary procedure for the Senate. Ironically, the House in 1837 made it a formal part of its rules, but the Senate did not grant it such status. The provisions of his manual "govern the House in all cases to which they are applicable and in which they are not inconsistent with the standing rules and orders of the House."

PARTY RULES. Each of the two major political parties has its own set of party rules. Some of these party regulations directly affect legislative procedure. The House Democratic Caucus, for example, has a provision that affects the Speaker's use of the suspension of the rules procedure.

INFORMAL PRACTICES AND CUSTOMS. Each chamber develops its own informal traditions and customs. They can be uncovered by examining such sources as the *Congressional Record*—the substantially verbatim account of House and Senate floor debate—scholarly accounts, and other studies of Congress. Several committees and party groups also prepare manuals of legislative procedure and practice.

functions will be illustrated by examples drawn from a college or university setting and by parallel functions in Congress.

STABILITY

Rules provide stability and predictability in personal and organizational affairs. Individuals and institutions can conduct their day-to-day business without having to debate procedure. Universities, for example, have specific requirements for bachelor's, master's, and doctorate degrees. Students know that if they are to progress from one degree to the next they must comply with rules and requirements. Daily or weekly changes in those requirements would cause chaos on any campus. Similarly, legislators need not decide each day who can speak on the floor, offer amendments, or close debate. Such matters are governed by regularized procedures that continue from one Congress to the next and afford similar rights and privileges to every member.

To be sure, House and Senate rules change in response to new circumstances, needs, and demands. The history of Congress is reflected in the evolution of the House and Senate rules. Increases in the size of the House in the nineteenth century, for instance, produced limitations on debate for individual representatives. Explained Senate Democratic Leader Robert C. Byrd, W.Va., about Senate proceedings:

> The day-to-day functioning of the Senate has given rise to a set of traditions, rules, and practices with a life and history all its own. The body of principles and procedures governing many Senatorial obligations and routines ... is not so much the result of reasoned deliberations as the fruit of jousting and adjusting to circumstances in which the Senate found itself from time to time.[8]

LEGITIMACY

Students typically receive final course grades that are based on their classroom performance, examinations, and term papers. They accept the professors' evaluations if they believe in their fairness and legitimacy. If professors suddenly decided to use students' political opinions as the basis for final grades, there would be a storm of protest against such an arbitrary procedure. In a similar fashion, members of Congress and citizens accept legislative decisions when they believe the decisions have been approved according to orderly and fair procedures.

DIVISION OF LABOR

Any university requires a division of labor if it is to carry out its tasks effectively and responsibly, and rules establish the various jurisdictions.

Hence there are history, chemistry, and art departments; admissions officers and bursars; and food service and physical plant managers, all with specialized assignments. For Congress, committees are the heart of the legislative process. They provide the division of labor and specialization that Congress needs to handle about 15,000 measures that are introduced biennially, and to review the administration of scores of federal programs. Like specialized bodies in many organizations, committees do not make final policy decisions but initiate recommendations that are forwarded to their respective chambers.

The jurisdiction, or policy mandate, of Congress's standing (permanent) committees is outlined in the House and Senate rules. Legislation generally is referred to the committee that has authority over the subject matter. As a result, the rules generally determine which committee, and thus which members and their staffs, will exercise significant influence over a particular issue such as defense, taxes, health, or education.

Rules also prescribe the standards committees are expected to observe during their policy deliberations. These include quorum requirements, public notice of committee meetings and hearings, and the right to counsel for witnesses. These rules also allocate staff resources to committees and subcommittees.

Conflict Resolution

Rules reduce conflicts among members and units of organizations by distinguishing appropriate actions and behavior from the inappropriate. For example, universities have procedures by which students may drop or add classes. There are discussions with faculty advisers, completion of appropriate paperwork, and the approval of a dean. Students who informally attempt to drop or add classes may encounter conflicts with their professors as well as sanctions from the dean's office. Most of the conflicts can be avoided by observance of established procedures. Similarly, congressional rules reduce conflict by, for example, establishing procedures to fill vacancies on committees when several members are competing for the same position or to settle bicameral disputes on legislation.

As Rep. Clarence A. Cannon, D-Mo. (1923-1964), a former House parliamentarian and subsequently the chairman of the Appropriations Committee, explained:

> The time of the House is too valuable, the scope of its enactments too far-reaching, and the constantly increasing pressure of its business too great to justify lengthy and perhaps acrimonious discussion of questions of procedure which have been authoritatively decided in former sessions.[9]

Distribution of Power

A major consequence of rules is that they generally distribute power in any organization. Rules, therefore, often are a source of conflict themselves. During the 1960s, many campuses witnessed struggles among students, faculty, and administrators involving the curriculum. The charge of irrelevance in course work was a frequent criticism of many students. As a result, the "rules of the game" for curriculum development were changed on many campuses. Students, junior faculty, and even community groups became involved in reshaping the structure and content of the educational program.

Like universities, Congress distributes power according to its rules and customs. Informal party rules, for example, establish a hierarchy of leadership positions in both chambers. And House and Senate rules accord prerogatives to congressional committee chairmen that are unavailable to others. Rules, therefore, are not neutral devices. They help to shore up the more powerful members and influence the attainment of member goals such as winning reelection, gaining internal influence, or winning congressional passage of legislation. "The rules of the House are designed for a speaker with a strong personality and an agenda," said Republican representative Newt Gingrich of Georgia, on the elevation of Jim Wright, D-Texas, to the speakership.[10] Thus, attempts to change the rules almost invariably are efforts to redistribute power.

RULES AND POLICY MAKING IN CONGRESS

Rules play similar roles in most complex organizations. Congress has its own characteristics that affect the functions of the rules. First, members of Congress owe their positions to the electorate, not to their congressional peers or to influential congressional leaders. No one in Congress has authority over the other members comparable to that of university presidents and tenured faculty over junior faculty or to that of a corporation president over lower-level executives. Members cannot be fired except by their constituency. And each member has equal voting power in committees and on the floor of the House or Senate.

The rules of Congress, unlike those of many organizations, are especially sensitive to the rights of minorities, including the minority party, ideological minorities, and individual members. As the "resident expert at being in the minority," remarked Sen. Lowell P. Weicker, Jr., R-Conn., it is clear that "I do not have allies in terms of numbers either on my side of the aisle or on the Democratic side. My allies are the rules of the U.S. Senate." [11] Skillful use of the rules enables the minority to check majority action by delaying, defeating, or reshaping legislation.

Intensity often counts as much as numbers—an apathetic majority may find it difficult to prevail over a well-organized minority. Except in the few instances when extraordinary majorities are needed, such as overriding presidential vetoes (a two-thirds vote), Senate ratification of treaties (two-thirds), and ending extended debate (a filibuster) in the Senate (three-fifths), the rules of the House and Senate require a simple majority to decide public policies.

Congress also is different from other organizations in its degree of responsiveness to external groups and pressures. The legislative branch is not as self-contained an institution as a university or a corporation. Congress is involved with every significant national and international issue. Its agenda compels members to respond to changing constituent interests and needs. Congress also is subject to numerous other influences, particularly the president, pressure groups, political parties, and state and local officials.

Finally, Congress is a collegial, not hierarchical, body. Power flows not from the top down, as in a corporation, but in practically every direction. There is only minimal centralized authority at the top; congressional policies are not "announced" but "made" by shifting coalitions that vary from issue to issue. Congress's deliberations are more accessible to the public than those of perhaps any other kind of organization. These are some of the characteristics that set Congress apart from other bodies. Inevitably these differences affect the decision-making process.

Procedure and Policy

Legislative procedures and policy making are inextricably linked in at least four ways.

First, procedures affect policy outcomes. Congress processes legislation by complex rules and procedures that permeate the institution. Some matters are only gently brushed by the rules, while others become locked in their grip. Major civil rights legislation, for example, failed for decades to win congressional approval because southern senators used their chamber's rules and procedures to kill or modify such measures.

Congressional procedures are employed to define, restrict, or expand the policy options available to members during floor debate. They may prevent consideration of certain issues or presage policy outcomes. Such structured procedures enhance the policy influence of certain members, committees, or party leaders; facilitate expeditious treatment of issues; grant priority to some policy alternatives but not others; and determine, in general, the overall character of policy decisions.

A second point is that very often policy decisions are expressed as procedural moves. House Republican leader Robert H. Michel, Ill., frustrated with his party's minority status for more than three decades and the majority party's procedural control of that body, highlighted the procedure-substance linkage.

> Procedure hasn't simply become more important than substance—it has, through a strange alchemy, *become* the substance of our deliberations. Who rules House procedures rules the House—and to a great degree, rules the kind and scope of political debate in this country.[12]

Or as John D. Dingell, D-Mich., the chairman of the House Energy and Commerce Committee, phrased it, "If you let me write the procedure, and I let you write the substance, I'll [beat] you every time." [13]

Representatives and senators, on various occasions, prefer not to make clear-cut decisions on certain complex and far-reaching public issues. Should a major weapons system be continued or curtailed? Should the nation's energy production needs take precedence over environmental concerns? Should financial assistance for the elderly be reduced and priority given to aiding disadvantaged children? On questions like these, members may be "cross-pressured"—the president may exert influence one way while constituent interests dictate another approach. Legislators sometimes lack adequate information to make informed judgments. They may be reluctant to oppose powerful pressure groups. Or they may feel that an issue does not lend itself to a simple "yes" or "no" vote.

As a result, legislators employ various procedural devices to handle knotty problems. A matter may be postponed on the ground of insufficient study in committee. Congress may direct an agency to prepare a detailed report before an issue is considered. Or a measure may be "tabled" by the House or Senate, a procedural vote that effectively defeats a proposal without rendering a clear judgment on its substance.

Third, the nature of the policy can determine the use of certain procedures. The House and Senate generally consider noncontroversial measures under expeditious procedures, whereas controversial proposals normally involve lengthy deliberation. Extraordinary circumstances sometimes prompt Congress to use "fast track" procedures to pass legislation. When the 100th Congress convened, the new House Democratic leaders (Speaker Wright, Majority Leader Thomas S. Foley of Washington, and Majority Whip Tony Coelho of California) worked to ensure fast passage of legislation to aid the homeless. "During this critical winter period," said Majority Whip Coelho, it is imperative that the House move quickly to enact the homeless assistance legislation.[14] The measure was passed under suspension of the rules procedure (see Chapter 5), which limits debate to forty minutes and prohibits floor amendments.

Finally, policy outcomes are more likely to be influenced by members with procedural expertise. Members who are skilled parliamentarians are better prepared to gain approval of their proposals than those who are only vaguely familiar with the rules. Just as carpenters and lawyers must learn their trade, members of Congress need to understand the rules if they expect to perform effectively. Congressional procedures are confusing to members. "To table, to refer to committee, to amend—so many things come up," declared a junior senator. "You don't know whether you are coming or going." [15] House Speaker John W. McCormack of Massachusetts once advised House newcomers:

> Learn the rules and understand the precedents and procedures of the House. The congressman who knows how the House operates will soon be recognized for his parliamentary skills—and his prestige will rise among his colleagues, no matter what his party.[16]

Members who know the rules will always have the potential to shape legislation to their ends and to become key figures in coalitions trying to pass or defeat legislation. Those who do not understand the rules reduce their proficiency and influence as legislators. Some members even become parliamentary "watchdogs" or use "guerrilla warfare" tactics to harass the opposition. In the 1980s, Rep. Robert S. Walker, R-Pa., inherited the role of floor guardian against majority steamrollers. "So long as a floor watchdog exists," he wrote, "all members of the House are afforded some additional protection from precipitous actions." [17]

Members also learn the rules so they can better circumvent them for their own political and policy ends. There is, in brief, conventional and unconventional lawmaking. Conventional lawmaking involves the traditional parliamentary pathway of committee hearings, markups, and reports; floor consideration; conference committee deliberations; House and Senate approval of the conference reports; and presidential signature or veto (Figure 1.1).

Unconventional lawmaking follows a different procedural route. Typically, traditional lawmaking steps are bypassed in both chambers. Two examples will highlight the point.

Despite the constitutional requirement that the House must initiate revenue-raising measures, it was plain to members of both chambers that the Senate in 1982 initiated a tax increase of nearly $100 billion. To be sure, there was technical compliance with the Constitution. The GOP-led Senate took a minor House-passed tax bill (HR 4961) and added its tax package to it. Then the Democratic-controlled House voted to go directly to conference with the Senate and thus avoid taking any political blame for a tax increase during an election year—and in a recession, to boot. As a result, there were no House committee hearings, or a committee report, on the Senate's product; nor was there any House floor debate—except on the conference report—on one of the largest tax increases in American history.[18]

FIGURE 1-1 How a Bill Becomes Law

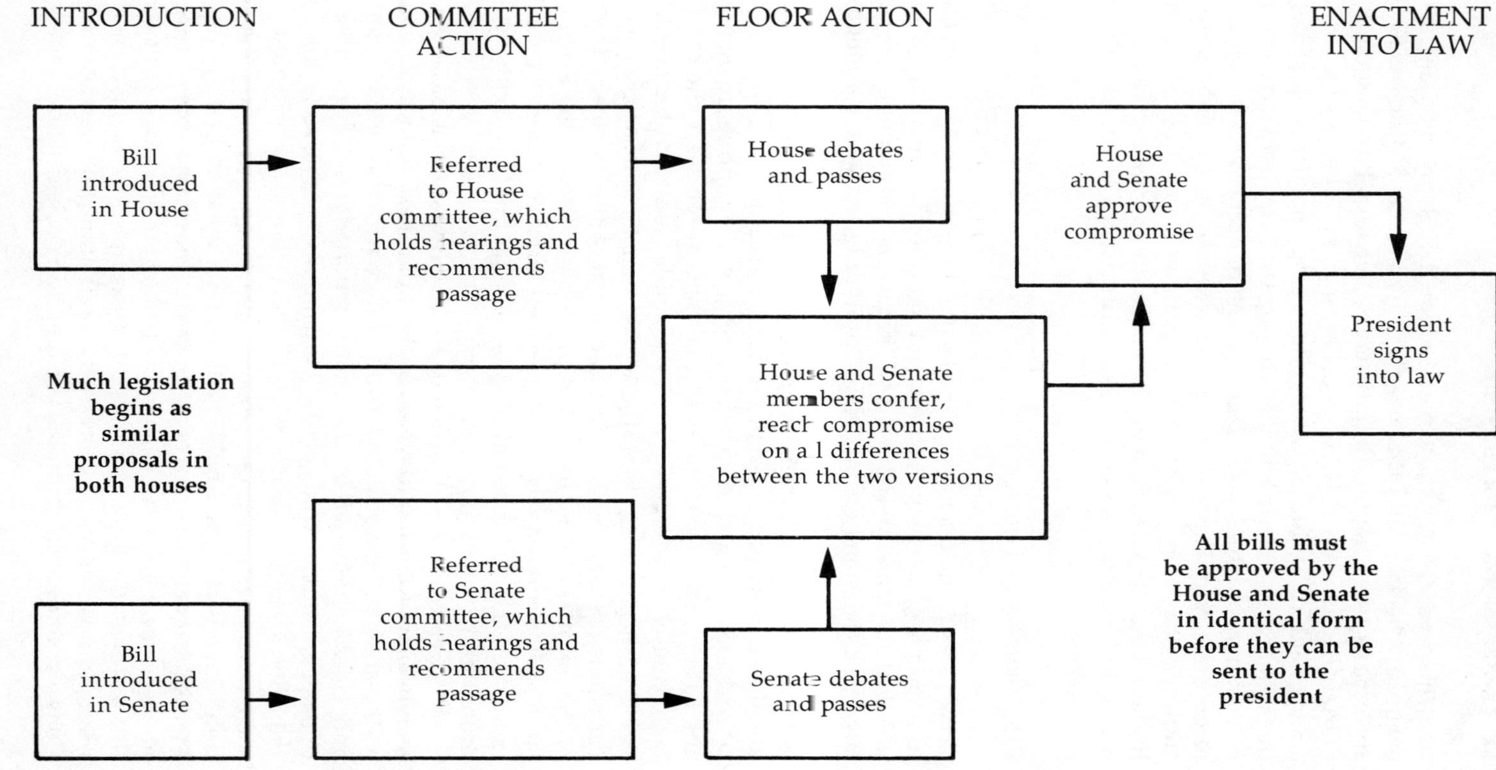
INTRODUCTION
COMMITTEE ACTION
FLOOR ACTION
ENACTMENT INTO LAW
Bill introduced in House
Referred to House committee, which holds hearings and recommends passage
House debates and passes
House and Senate approve compromise
President signs into law
Much legislation begins as similar proposals in both houses
House and Senate members confer, reach compromise on all differences between the two versions
Bill introduced in Senate
Referred to Senate committee, which holds hearings and recommends passage
Senate debates and passes
All bills must be approved by the House and Senate in identical form before they can be sent to the president

Three years later the Senate adopted a floor amendment (which eventually became law) that dramatically revamped Congress's budgetary process (see Chapter 3). Initiated by Senators Phil Gramm, R-Texas, Warren B. Rudman, R-N.H., and Ernest F. Hollings, D-S.C., as a floor amendment to a House-passed bill raising the national debt ceiling, their emergency deficit reduction proposal was never previously reviewed in committee or discussed on the floor. Because the House chose to go directly to conference with the Senate on the Gramm-Rudman-Hollings plan, it bypassed its own committee and floor stages as well. Initial House consideration of Gramm-Rudman-Hollings came at the *end* of the bill-enacting process, when representatives debated the conference report.

Precedents and Folkways

Congress is regulated not only by formal rules, but by informal ones that influence legislative procedure and member behavior. Two types of informal rules are precedents and "folkways." Precedents, the accumulated past decisions on matters of procedure, represent a blend of the formal and informal. They are the "common law" of Congress and govern many procedures not explicitly covered in the formal rules. As a noted House parliamentarian wrote, the great majority of the "rules of all parliamentary bodies are unwritten law; they spring up by precedent and custom; these precedents and customs are this day the chief law of both Houses of Congress." [19] For example, formal rules prescribe the order of business in the House and Senate, but precedents permit variations through the unanimous consent of the members. The rulings of the Speaker of the House and presiding officer of the Senate form a large body of precedents. They are given formal status by the parliamentarians in each chamber and then become part of the accepted rules and procedures.

Folkways, on the other hand, are unwritten norms of behavior that members are expected to observe. "Without these folkways," concluded a scholar, "the Senate could hardly operate with its present organization and rules." [20] Several of the more important are "legislative work" (members should concentrate on congressional duties and not be publicity seekers), "courtesy" (members should be solicitous toward their colleagues and avoid personal attacks on them), and "specialization" (members should master a few policy areas and not try to impress their colleagues as a "jack of all trades"). Those who abide by these and other norms, which can change over time, are rewarded with increased influence in the policy process, for example, by being appointed to prestigious committees. Conversely, legislators who persistently violate Congress's informal customs are apt to see legislation they support blocked in committee or on the floor. I'll "keep an eye on something he wants some day," said the Senate majority leader threateningly about a colleague who kept blocking action on a measure and who had even offered a motion to adjourn the body, a prerogative of the majority leader.[21] Congressional decision making, then, is shaped by each chamber's formal and informal structure of rules, precedents, and traditions.

CONGRESSIONAL DECISION MAKING

The congressional decision-making process is constantly evolving, but it has certain enduring features that affect consideration of all legislation. The first is the decentralized power structure of Congress, characterized by numerous specialized committees and a central party leadership that struggles to promote party and policy coherence. A second feature is the existence of multiple decision points for every piece of legislation. The many decision points mean that at each step of a bill's progress a majority coalition must be formed to move the measure along. This leads to the third important feature of the process: the need for bargaining and compromise at every juncture in order to form a winning coalition. And finally, each Congress has only a two-year life cycle in which to pass legislation once it has been introduced. The pressure of time is an ever present force underlying the process.

Decentralized Power Structure

Congress's decentralized character reflects both political and structural realities. Politically, legislators owe their reelection to voters in widely differing states and localities; structurally, the legislative branch has an elaborate division of labor to help it manage its immense workload. Responsibility for specific subject areas is dispersed among numerous committees, subcommittees, and task forces (more than 300 in the two chambers).

Structural decentralization means that policy making is subject to various disintegrative processes. Broad issues are divided into smaller subissues for consideration by the committees. Overlapping and fragmented committee responsibilities can impede the development of comprehensive and coordinated national policies. Many House and Senate committees, for example, consider some aspect of health, trade, or energy policy.[22] Jurisdictional controversies occur as committees fight to protect or expand their turf. Finally, committees develop special relationships with pressure groups, executive agencies, and scores of other interested participants. These alliances, often called "subgovernments," "issue networks," or "sloppy large hexagons," influence numerous policy areas. Committees, then, become advocates of policies and not simply impartial instruments of the House or Senate.[23]

In theory, political parties are supposed to provide the cohesive force to balance the centrifugal influences of a fragmented committee system. For the most part, the reality is much different. Parties serve to organize their members and elect the formal leaders of Congress. From time to time, Democrats and Republicans meet in policy committees and caucuses to discuss policy issues. Neither party, however, commands the consistent support of all its members. There is too great a spread of ideological convictions within each party. Too many countervailing pressures (constituency, region, individual conscience, career considerations, or committee loyalty) also influence the actions of representatives and senators. "I'll fight for my district even though it may be contrary to my national goals," declared the House majority whip.[24] As a result, public policies usually are enacted because diverse elements of both parties temporarily coalesce to achieve common goals.

The absence of disciplined parties, in or out of Congress, underscores the difficult and delicate role of congressional party leaders. They cannot dictate policy because they lack the means to force agreement among competing party factions or autonomous committees and subcommittees. "There are few rewards we may bestow," said Speaker Wright, and few "punishments we may inflict as inducements to follow the party line." [25] A number of legislators are not particularly dependent on their state or local parties for reelection. This means that party leaders cannot count on automatic party support but must rely heavily on their skills as bargainers and negotiators to influence legislative decisions. In addition, the power and style of any party leader depend on several factors, some outside the leader's control. Among them are personality, intellectual and political talent, the leader's view of the job, the size of the majority or minority party in the chamber, whether the White House is controlled by the opposition party, the expectations of colleagues, and the institutional complexion of the House or Senate during a particular historical era.

Multiple Decision Points

Although Congress can on occasion act quickly, normally legislation has to work its way slowly through multiple decision points. One congressional report identified more than a hundred specific steps that might mark a "bill's progress through the Congress from introduction to possible enactment into law." [26]

After a bill is introduced, it usually is referred to committee and then frequently to a subcommittee. The views of executive departments and agencies often are solicited. Hearings are held and reports on the bill are issued by the subcommittee and full committee. The bill then is "reported out" of the full committee and scheduled for consideration by the entire membership. After floor debate and final action in one chamber, the same steps generally are repeated in the other house. At any point in this sequential process, the bill is subject to delay, defeat, or modification. "It is very easy to defeat a bill in Congress," President Kennedy once noted. "It is much more difficult to pass one." [27]

Figure 1-1 outlines the major procedural steps in how a bill becomes law. Congressional procedures require bills to overcome numerous hurdles. At each stage, measures and procedures must receive majority approval. All along the procedural route, therefore, strategically located committees, groups, or individuals can delay, block, or change proposals if they can form majority coalitions. Bargaining may be necessary at each juncture in order to build the majority coalition that advances the bill to the next step in the legislative process. Thus, advocates of a piece of legislation must attract not just one majority but several successive majorities at each of the critical intersections along the legislative route.

Bargaining and Coalition Building

There are three principal forms of bargaining used to build majority coalitions: logrolling, compromise, and nonlegislative favors.

Logrolling is an exchange of voting support on different bills by different members of Congress. It is an effective means of coalition building because members rarely are equally concerned about all the measures before Congress. For example, representatives A, B, and C strongly support a bill that increases government aid to farmers. A, B, and C are indifferent toward a second bill that increases the minimum wage, which is strongly supported by representatives D, E, and F. Because D, E, and F do not have strong feelings about the farm bill, a bargain is struck: A, B, and C agree to vote for the minimum wage bill, and D, E, and F agree to vote for the farm bill. Thus both bills are helped on their way past the key decision points at which A, B, C, D, E, and F have influence.

Logrolling may be either explicit or implicit. A, B, and C may have negotiated directly with D, E, and F. Alternatively, A, B, and C may have voted for the minimum wage bill, letting it be known through the press or in other informal ways that they anticipate similar treatment on the farm bill from D, E, and F. The expectation is that D, E, and F will honor the tacit agreement since at a later date they may again need the support of A, B, and C.

Logrolling occurred when the House Agriculture chairman wrote a "Dear Colleague" letter to the more than a hundred representatives who belong to the Steel Caucus. This is an informal group of House members who have few farmers but heavy concentrations of steel workers in their districts. The chairman urged the caucus to support an extension of the sugar support program and stressed that domestic sugar and steel producers both faced unfair foreign competition. "I know that you, as a member of the Congressional steel caucus, are sympathetic to the [Agriculture] committee's commitment to protect American farmers and workers," he wrote.[28] When an attempt was made on the House floor to reduce funding for the sugar program, it was rejected by a 263-142 vote.

Compromise, unlike logrolling, builds coalitions through negotiation over the *content* of legislation. Each side agrees to modify policy goals on a given bill in a way that generally is acceptable to the other. A middle ground often is found—particularly with bills involving money. A, B, and C, for example, support a $50 million education bill; D, E, and F want to increase the funding to $100 million. The six meet and compromise on a $75 million bill they all can support.

Note the distinction between logrolling and compromise. In the logrolling example, the participants did not modify their objectives on the bills that mattered to them; each side traded voting support on a bill that meant little in return for support on a bill in which they were keenly interested. In a compromise, both sides modify their positions. "We have struck what we think is a fair bargain so that each achieves part of what" the two committees wanted, said Sen. Bob Packwood, R-Ore. "It was a perfect example of the art of compromise."[29]

Nonlegislative favors are useful because policy goals are only one of the many objectives of members of Congress. Other objectives include assignment to a prestigious committee, getting reelected, running for higher office, obtaining larger office space and staff, or even being selected to attend a conference abroad. The wide variety of these nonpolicy objectives creates numerous bargaining opportunities—particularly for party leaders, who can dispense many favors—from which coalitions can be built. As Senate majority leader from 1955 to 1961, Lyndon B. Johnson of Texas was known for his skill in using his powers to satisfy the personal needs of senators in order to build support for legislation Johnson wanted.

> For Johnson, each one of these assignments contained a potential opportunity for bargaining, for creating obligations, provided that he knew his fellow senators well enough to determine which invitations would matter the most to whom. If he knew that the wife of the senator from Idaho had been dreaming of a trip to Paris for ten years, or that the advisers to another senator had warned him about his slipping popularity with Italian voters, Johnson could increase the potential usefulness of assignments to the Parliamentary Conference in Paris or to the dedication of the cemeteries in Italy.[30]

In this way, Johnson made his colleagues understand that there was a debt to be repaid.

The Congressional Cycle

Every bill introduced in Congress faces the two-year deadline of the congressional term. (The term of the 101st Congress, elected in November 1988, begins at noon on January 3, 1989, and expires at noon on January 3, 1991.) Legislation introduced must be passed by both the House and the Senate in identical form within the two-year term in order to become law. And Congress normally adjourns prior to the end of the two-year term; thus bills usually have less than two full years. Bills that have not completed the required procedural journey prior to final adjournment of a Congress automatically die and must be reintroduced in a new Congress. Inaction or postponement at any stage of the process can mean the defeat of a bill. This book repeatedly focuses on the various delaying and expediting tactics available to members during the legislative process.

Many measures considered by Congress come up in cycles. Much of Congress's annual agenda is filled with legislation required each year to continue and finance the activities of federal agencies and programs. Generally, this kind of legislation appears regularly on the congressional agenda at about the same time each year. Other legislation comes up for renewal every few years.

Often, there are emergencies that demand immediate attention. Other issues become timely because public interest has focused on them; trade, child care, and AIDS in the 1980s are examples of such issues.

Complex legislation often is introduced early because it takes longer to process than a simple bill. A disproportionately large number of major bills are enacted during the last few weeks of a Congress. Compromises that were not possible in July can be made in December. By this time—with the two-year term about to expire—the pressures on members of the House and Senate are intense, and lawmaking can become frantic and furious. "It is a time when legislators pass dozens of bills without debate or recorded votes, a time when a canny legislator can slip in special favors for the folks back home or for special-interest lobbyists roaming Capitol corridors." [31]

Finally, many ideas require years or even decades of germination before they are enacted into law. Controversial proposals—reintroduced in successive Congresses—may need a four-, six-, or eight-year period before they win enactment. Many of the 1960s policies of Presidents Kennedy and Johnson, for example, first were considered during the Congresses of the 1950s. Landmark immigration reform legislation required the action of three 1980s Congresses before it eventually surmounted hurdles and roadblocks to become public law.

SUMMARY

Rules and procedures affect what Congress does and how it does it. They define the steps by which bills become law, decentralize authority among numerous specialized committees, distribute power among members, and permit orderly consideration of policies. Above all, the rules and organization of Congress create numerous decision points through which legislation must pass in order to become law. As a result, congressional decision making presents many opportunities for members to defeat bills they oppose. Proponents, by contrast, must win at every step of the way. At each procedural stage, they must assemble a majority coalition. Throughout the legislative process, time is a critical factor as members maneuver to enact or defeat legislation under the pressure of numerous scheduling deadlines and the two-year period of each Congress.

NOTES

1. Benjamin Fletcher Wright, ed., *The Federalist by Alexander Hamilton, James Madison, and John Jay* (Cambridge, Mass.: Belknap Press of Harvard University Press, 1961), 356 (Federalist No. 51).
2. Paul L. Ford, ed., *The Federalist: A Commentary on the Constitution of the United States by Alexander Hamilton, James Madison and John Jay* (New York: Henry Holt, 1898), 319 (Federalist No. 47). James Madison wrote this commentary on "Separation of the Departments of Power."
3. Thomas Jefferson, "Notes on Virginia" in *Free Government in the Making,* ed. Alpheus Thomas Mason (New York: Oxford University Press, 1965), 164.
4. See Woodrow Wilson, *Congressional Government* (Boston: Chapman, 1885), and James MacGregor Burns, *Presidential Government* (Boston: Houghton Mifflin, 1966).
5. Donald Bruce Johnson and Jack L. Walker, eds., "President John Kennedy Discusses the Presidency," in *The Dynamics of the American Presidency* (New York: John Wiley & Sons, 1964), 144.
6. *Washington Times,* June 4, 1987, 2B.
7. *Constitution, Jefferson's Manual and Rules of the House of Representatives,* 97th Cong., 2d sess., H. Doc. No. 97-271, 113-114.
8. *Congressional Record,* daily ed., April 8, 1981, S3615.
9. Clarence Cannon, *Cannon's Procedure in the House of Representatives,* 86th Cong., 1st sess., H. Doc. No. 86-122, iii.
10. John M. Barry, "The Man of the House," *New York Times Magazine,* Nov. 23, 1986, 109.
11. *Congressional Record,* daily ed., Feb. 26, 1986, S1663-S1664.
12. Testimony before the GOP Task Force on Congressional Reform, House Republican Research Committee, Dec. 16, 1987, 3.
13. *National Review,* Feb. 27, 1987, 24.
14. *Congressional Record,* daily ed., Jan. 27, 1987, H400.
15. *Los Angeles Times,* Feb. 7, 1977, sec. 1, 5.
16. *Congressional Record,* March 9, 1976, 5909.

17. Robert S. Walker, "Why House Republicans Need a Watchdog," *Roll Call*, Jan. 19, 1987, 10. See also Peter Carlson, "Is Bob Walker the Most Obnoxious Man in Congress?" *Washington Post Magazine*, Sept. 7, 1986, 59-65.
18. For a discussion of the House decision to send the tax bill to conference, see *Congressional Record*, daily ed., July 28, 1982, H4776-H4788. Several House members brought suit in federal district court challenging the constitutionality of the tax bill. The U.S. District Court for the District of Columbia dismissed the case because House plaintiffs lacked standing, and their grievance was with the House. See *Congressional Record*, daily ed., Dec. 20, 1982, E5362-E5364, and Jan. 27, 1983, S374.
19. Quoted in *Deschler's Precedents of the United States House of Representatives*, vol. 1, 94th Cong., 2d sess., H. Doc. No. 94-661, iv.
20. Donald Matthews, *U.S. Senators and Their World* (Chapel Hill: University of North Carolina Press, 1960), chap. 5. Several of the folkways described by Matthews have undergone considerable change. For example, the norm of "apprenticeship," specifying that new members should be seen and not heard, has all but disappeared in both chambers. See Norman J. Ornstein, Robert L. Peabody, and David W. Rohde, "The Contemporary Senate: Into the 1980s," in *Congress Reconsidered*, 2d ed., ed. Lawrence C. Dodd and Bruce I. Oppenheimer (Washington, D.C.: CQ Press, 1981), 16-19.
21. *New York Times*, March 11, 1986, A20.
22. During the 96th Congress (1979-1981), a House reorganization panel found that there were eighty-three committees and subcommittees in the House alone that exercised some jurisdiction over energy issues. See *Final Report of the Select Committee on Committees, U.S. House of Representatives*, 96th Cong., 2d sess., H. Rept. No. 96-866, 334-355.
23. Roger H. Davidson and Walter J. Oleszek, *Congress against Itself* (Bloomington: Indiana University Press, 1977), and Roger H. Davidson, "Breaking Up Those 'Cozy Triangles': An Impossible Dream?" in *Legislative Reform and Public Policy*, ed. Susan Welch and John G. Peters (New York: Praeger, 1977), 30-53; Hugh Heclo, "Issue Networks and the Executive Establishment," in *The New American Political System*, ed. Anthony King (Washington, D.C.: American Enterprise Institute for Public Policy Research, 1978), 87-124; and Charles O. Jones, *The United States Congress: People, Place, and Policy* (Homewood, Ill.: Dorsey Press, 1982), 360. "Sloppy large hexagons," a phrase coined by Jones, refers to the large number of participants who shape policy issues.
24. Jeff Rainmundo, "Cool Whip," *California Magazine*, April 1987, 64.
25. *Reflections of a Public Man* (Ft. Worth, Texas: Madison, 1984), 89.
26. *The Bill Status System for the United States House of Representatives*, Committee on House Administration, July 1, 1975, 19.
27. "President John Kennedy Discusses the Presidency," *The Dynamics of the American Presidency*, 144.
28. *New York Times*, Oct. 2, 1985, B6.
29. *Congressional Record*, daily ed., Oct. 22, 1985, S13780.
30. Doris Kearns, *Lyndon Johnson and the American Dream* (New York: Harper & Row, 1976), 119.
31. *Los Angeles Times*, Oct. 6, 1982, sec. 1, 1.

CHAPTER 2

The Congressional Environment

Congress is an independent policy maker. This does not mean that it is impermeable to outside influences; nor does it mean that each member operates independently of every other member. Rather, there is a tangled, multifaceted relationship between Congress and the other governmental and nongovernmental forces. Similarly, there are complicated internal hierarchies and networks that affect the way Congress goes about its business. This chapter will focus on some of the conditions that mold the congressional environment, including the bicameral nature of Congress, the key actors in the congressional leadership, the outside pressures on Congress, and the procedural changes that swept through the House and Senate during the past decade.

THE HOUSE AND SENATE COMPARED

The "House and Senate are naturally unlike," observed Woodrow Wilson.[1] Each chamber has its own rules, precedents, and customs; different terms of office; varying constitutional responsibilities; and differing constituencies. "We are constituted differently, we serve different purposes in the representative system, we operate differently, why should [the House and Senate] not have different rules," Sen. Wayne Morse (1945-1969) of Oregon once commented.[2] Table 2-1 lists the major differences between the chambers.

Probably the three most important differences between the two chambers are: (1) the House is more than four times the size of the Senate, (2) senators represent a broader constituency than do representatives, and (3) senators serve longer terms of office. These differences affect the way the two houses operate in a number of ways.

TABLE 2-1 Major Differences between the House and the Senate

House	*Senate*
Larger (435)	Smaller (100)
Shorter term of office (2 years)	Longer term of office (6 years)
More procedural restraints on members	Fewer procedural restraints on members
Narrower constituency	Broader, more varied constituency
Policy specialists	Policy generalists
Less press and media coverage	More press and media coverage
Power less evenly distributed	Power more evenly distributed
Less prestigious	More prestigious
More expeditious in floor debate	Less expeditious in floor debate
Less reliant on staff	More reliant on staff
More partisan	Less partisan

Complexity of the Rules

Certainly the factor of size explains much about why the two chambers differ. Because it is larger, the House is a more structured body than the Senate. The restraints imposed on representatives by rules and precedents are far more severe than those affecting senators. More than 650 pages are needed to describe the House rules for the 100th Congress, and its precedents from 1789 to 1936 are contained in eleven huge volumes; those from 1936 forward are recorded in the multivolume *Deschler's Precedents.* In contrast, the Senate's rules are contained in ninety pages and its precedents in one volume.

Whereas Senate rules maximize freedom of expression, House rules "show a constant subordination of the individual to the necessities of the whole House as the voice of the national will." [3] Furthermore, House and Senate rules differ fundamentally in their basic purpose. House rules are designed to permit a determined majority to work its will. Senate rules, on the other hand, are intended to slow down, or even defer, action on legislation by granting inordinate parliamentary power (through the filibuster, for example) to individual members and determined minorities. "Senate rules are tilted toward not doing things," remarked Speaker Wright. "House rules, if you know how to use them, are tilted toward allowing the majority to get its will done." [4] Ironically, it is easier to move legislation in the larger House than the smaller Senate because of differences in their rules. A simple majority is sufficient to pass major and controversial legislation in the House. In the Senate, at least sixty votes (necessary to break a filibuster) might be needed—sometimes more than once—to move legislation to final passage.

The Senate, as a result, is more personal and individualistic than the House. "The Senate is run for the convenience of one Senator, to the inconvenience of 99," said Sen. J. Bennett Johnston, D-La.[5] It functions to a large extent by unanimous consent, in effect adjusting or disregarding its rules as it goes along. It is not uncommon for votes on a bill to be rescheduled or delayed until an interested senator can be present. Senate party leaders are careful to consult all senators who have expressed an interest in the pending legislation, because "under the rules of the Senate any one Senator can hold up the works here," declared Democratic leader Byrd.[6] In the House, the leadership can consult only key members—usually committee leaders—about upcoming floor action.

Policy Incubation

Incubation entails "keeping a proposal alive, while it picks up support, or waits for a better climate, or while the problem to which it is addressed grows." [7] Both houses fulfill this role, but it is promoted in the Senate particularly because of that body's flexible rules, more varied constituent pressures on senators, and greater press and media coverage. As the chamber of greater prestige, lesser complexity, longer term of office, and smaller size, the Senate is simply easier for the media to cover than the House.[8] The Senate is more involved than the House with cultivating national constituencies, formulating questions for national debate, and gaining general public support for policy proposals. The policy-generating role is particularly characteristic of senators with presidential ambitions, who need to capture both headlines and national constituencies.[9]

However, when the House began televising its floor sessions in 1979 over C-SPAN (Cable Satellite Public Affairs Network)—the Senate began gavel-to-gavel coverage in mid-1986—many activist representatives recognized the technology's "bully pulpit" potential. Floor debates and speeches provided opportunities for members to promote ideas to the viewing national audience. House Republicans, in the minority for over three decades, especially sought to mobilize grassroots interest in their agenda through floor discussions. Their effort on behalf of the GOP even prompted Sen. Dan Quayle, R-Ind., to say: "There's much more idea work [in the House]. I wish we had the time for that over here." [10]

Specialists versus Generalists

Another difference between the chambers is that representatives tend to be known as subject matter "specialists" while senators tend to be "generalists." "If the Senate has been the nation's great forum," a representative said, then the "House has been its workshop."[11] Indeed its greater work force and division of labor facilitate policy specialization in the House. "Senators do not specialize as intensively or as exclusively in their committee work as House members do" because senators must spread their "efforts over a greater span of subjects than the average representative."[12] During the 100th Congress (1987-1989), for example, the average senator served on eleven committees and subcommittees, compared with six for the average representative.

One reason for the specialist-generalist distinction is that senators represent a broader constituency than House members. This compels the former to generalize as they attempt to be conversant on numerous national and international issues that affect their state. With their six-year term, senators are less vulnerable to immediate constituency pressures. Therefore, they can afford to be more cosmopolitan in their viewpoints than House members. Journalists, too, tend to expect senators, more than representatives, to have an informed opinion on almost every important public issue.

A result of the generalist role is greater reliance by senators on knowledgeable personal and committee staff aides for advice in decision making. A House member, on the other hand, is more likely to be an expert himself on particular policy issues. If not, he often relies on informed colleagues rather than staff aides for advice on legislation. "House members rely most heavily upon their colleagues for all information," one study concluded, while senators "will often turn to other sources, especially their own staffs, for their immediate information needs."[13] Consequently, Senate staff aides generally have more influence over the laws and programs of the nation than do their counterparts in the House.

There are senators, to be sure, who can hold their own with knowledgeable House members. And in some policy areas certain senators hold the specialization advantage over representatives. For instance, membership on the Senate Budget Committee is permanent, whereas the House Budget Committee has a limited-tenure (or rotational) system membership. This difference tilts the balance of expertise to the Senate during consideration of the annual concurrent budget resolution (see Chapter 3).

Distribution of Power

Another difference between the two chambers is that power to influence policy is more evenly distributed in the Senate than in the House. Unlike most representatives, senators can readily exercise initiative in legislation and oversight, get floor amendments incorporated in measures reported from committees on which they are not members, influence the scheduling of bills, and, in general, participate more widely and equally in all Senate and party activities. Witness junior senator Bill Bradley's, D-N.J., ability to become known as the "father" of the landmark tax reform package of 1986 even though the chamber was then in Republican hands. Every senator, too, of the majority party typically chairs at least one committee or subcommittee (the average in 1988 was 2.3 chairmanships).

This ability to make a difference quickly is one reason why the Senate is so politically attractive to House members. In the 100th Congress, thirty-nine senators were former House members; by contrast, only one representative (Claude Pepper, D-Fla.) served previously in the Senate. In the House, remarked Sen. Paul Simon, D-Ill., a former House member, "you are restricted by your committee. But in the Senate, you're not tied down. You have a lot more room to exert influence." [14] House procedures, in short, emphasize the mobilization of voting blocs to make policy; deference to individual prerogatives, including camaraderie across party lines, is the hallmark of senatorial decision making.

Similarities

There are many similarities between the House and Senate. Both chambers are essentially equal in power and share similar responsibilities in lawmaking, oversight, and representation. Both have heavy workloads, decentralized committee and party structures, and somewhat parallel committee jurisdictions. The roles and responsibilities of one chamber interact with those of the other. House and Senate party leaders often cooperate to coordinate action on legislation. Cooperation generally is made easier when both houses are controlled by the same party.

In recent years, the two chambers have become more similar in some unexpected areas. Today's House members are more dependent on staff than were their colleagues of a few decades ago, in part because issues are more complex and because more informed constituents look to Capitol Hill for assistance and information. And senators are much more involved in constituency service than ever before. Like House members, they travel frequently to their states to meet in diverse forums with their constituents. "I have averaged 48 weekends a year in going home to my State," remarked veteran Democratic senator Wendell Ford of Kentucky.[15]

Many senators, too, emulate their House colleagues by preparing to run for reelection almost immediately after being sworn into office. "When Republican Sen. Mitchell McConnell of Kentucky won an upset victory in 1984, he promptly set up a 'McConnell Senate Committee '90.' " [16] McConnell's action reflects contemporary electoral developments unforeseen by the framers—the huge costs of campaigns, the rise of campaign specialists, and the emphasis on videopolitics—that make senatorial races more competitive than most House contests.

House members enjoy more incumbent protection than senators, because they attract fewer effective challengers (in part by scaring off opponents with their money-raising ability), receive more favorable press and media attention, and court their constituents assiduously. Thus representatives are more likely than senators to survive periodic electoral tides that oust numerous incumbents. In the 1980 election, for example, Republicans won control of the Senate for the first time in twenty-six years; yet the House remained in Democratic hands, albeit with a diminished majority.

The House and Senate, in short, are separate yet interlocked bodies. A whole range of institutional, partisan, and policy connections makes bicameralism a force that shapes member behavior and policy outcomes. Recall the dual role of the GOP-controlled Senate from 1981 to 1987 in advancing the Republican administration's program through Congress and blocking unwanted initiatives from the Democratic-controlled House.

LEADERSHIP STRUCTURE OF CONGRESS

In both the House and the Senate, the party leadership is crucial to the smooth functioning of the legislative process. Leaders help to organize orderly consideration of legislative proposals, promote party support for or against legislation, attempt to reconcile differences that threaten to disrupt the chambers, plan strategy on important bills, consult with the president, and publicize legislative achievements (see Figure 2-1).

In the House, the formal leadership consists of the Speaker, who is both the chamber's presiding officer and the leader of the majority party; the majority and minority leaders; whips from each party; assistants to the whips; and various partisan (Democratic and Republican) committees that assist with party strategy, legislative scheduling, and the assignment of party members to the legislative committees.

In the Senate, there is no party official comparable to the Speaker. Under the Constitution, the vice president of the United States assumes the post of president of the Senate, and in his absence the president pro tempore or, more commonly, a temporary presiding officer, presides; none of these individuals, however, has political power comparable to that of the Speaker. The Senate also has majority and minority leaders, whips, assistant whips, and party committees.

The significance of leadership pressures on members of Congress was summed up succinctly years ago by Speaker Sam Rayburn of Texas,

FIGURE 2-1 Congressional Leadership

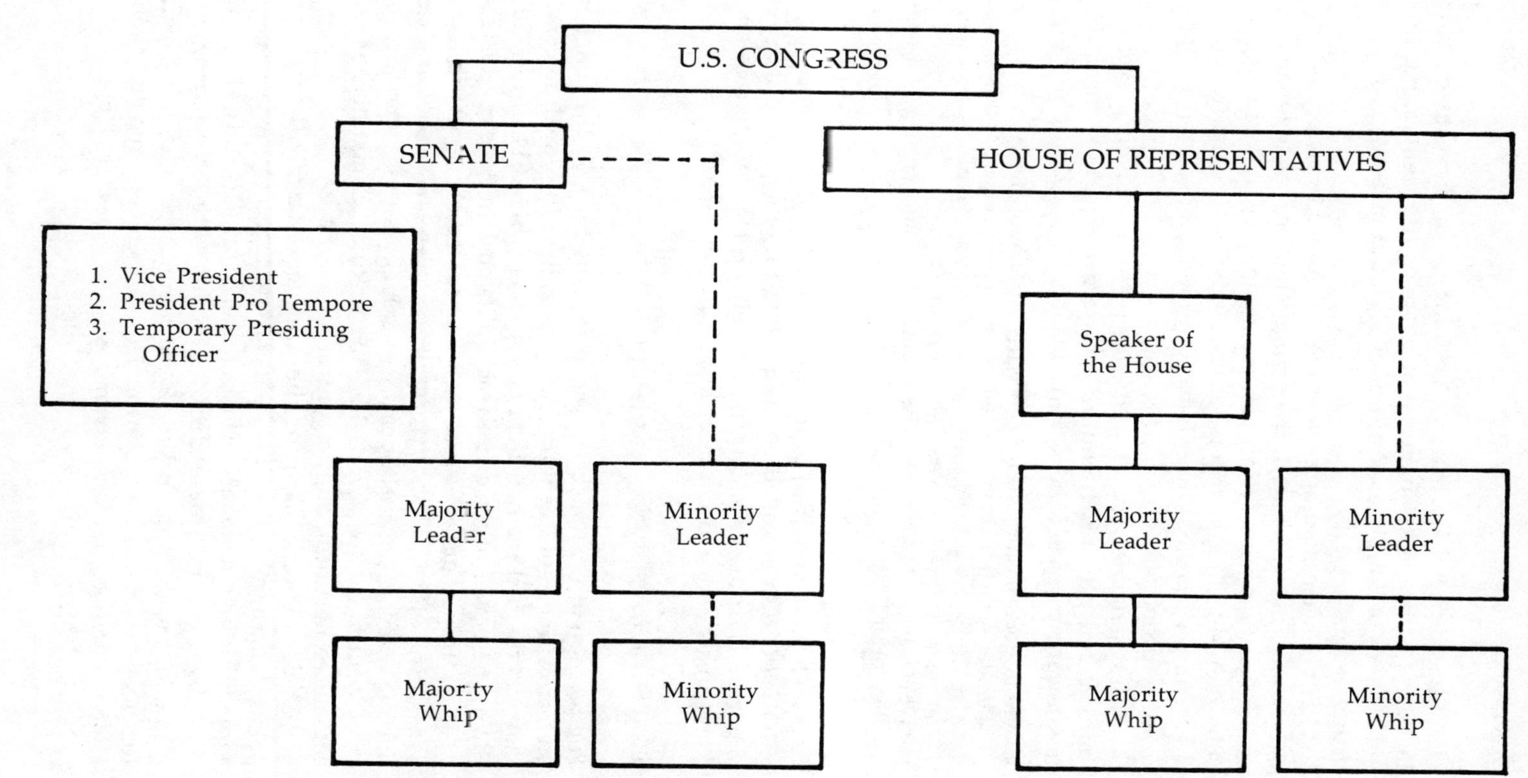

who advised members that "to get along, you have to go along."[17] Rayburn's advice is no longer as relevant as it once was, but the rules and customs of both houses still place significant resources in the hands of the leaders.

Party leaders may offer tangible incentives to shape the course of legislation. These include influencing committee assignments, sharing media attention with colleagues, raising money and campaigning for colleagues, selecting members to serve on special committees or panels, intervening with the White House, or mobilizing support or opposition to policy proposals.

A less tangible type of influence is the leadership's expression of approval and personal friendliness toward the party faithful and coolness toward party defectors. Party leaders in the House, for example,

> are in good position to influence the attitude of the House toward a member early in his career by telling other members what they think of him. There are also visible ways, such as the Speaker's selection of members to preside over the House or over the Committee of the Whole, by which party leaders indicate the younger members whom they regard highly."[18]

Most party leaders are eager to dispense favors to members (both of their own party and even of the opposition party) so as to create a stack of IOUs that can be called upon in the event of expected close votes on important measures. Leaders usually rely on tact and persuasion rather than threats or harsh criticism to win members' support.

Speaker of the House

The position of the Speaker is established by the Constitution, but until the early nineteenth century the Speaker had little real power. Henry Clay was the first really influential Speaker (1811-1814, 1815-1820, 1823-1825). The power of the office reached its peak in the early 1900s, under a series of Speakers who extended and sometimes abused the prerogatives of the office. Drastic reform of the rules came about as a result of the 1910 "revolt" against Speaker Joseph G. Cannon, who was stripped of his authority to sit on the House Rules Committee, to appoint committee members, and to control all floor action.

Modern Speakers achieve their influence largely through personal prestige, mastery of the art of persuasion, legislative expertise, and the support of the members. The Speaker's primary formal powers are presiding over the House, deciding points of order, referring bills and resolutions to the appropriate House committees, scheduling legislation for floor action, and appointing House members to select, joint, and House-Senate conference committees. As Speaker Thomas P. "Tip" O'Neill, D-Mass. (1977-1987), once remarked:

> You know, you ask me what are my powers and my authority around here. The power to recognize on the floor; little odds and ends—like men get pride out of the prestige of handling the Committee of the Whole, being named the Speaker for the day; those little trips that come along—like those trips to China, trips to Russia, things of that nature; or other ad hoc committees or special committees, which I have assignments to; plus the fact that there is a certain aura and respect that goes with the Speaker's office [second in succession to the White House].[19]

Although the Speaker may participate in debate he does so infrequently, and usually only when his remarks may affect the outcome of a crucial vote. He also may vote, but most recent Speakers seldom vote except to break a tie.

O'Neill's ten-year tenure as speaker transformed the post in an important respect. He elevated the national visibility of the speakership and thus the office's potential to articulate and establish the House's agenda. "[Speaker] Sam Rayburn could have walked down the streets of Spokane [Wash.] without anybody noticing him," said House Majority Leader Foley. "Tip O'Neill couldn't do that, and it is very unlikely that any future Speaker will be anonymous to the country."[20]

Although the Constitution does not specify that the Speaker must be a member of the House, no nonmember has ever been elected to the post. It has become common practice to elect the majority leader as Speaker when an opening occurs. Since the Civil War, neither party has ousted a sitting Speaker as long as his party remained in the majority.

Majority and Minority Leaders

Both the majority and minority parties of the House and Senate appoint officials to shape and direct strategy on the floor. These officials, elected by their respective party caucuses, try to hold together their parties' loose alliances in hopes of shaping them into voting majorities to pass or defeat bills and amendments. Majority leaders have considerable influence over the scheduling of bills. The majority leader in the House ranks just below the Speaker in importance. In the Senate, the majority leader is the most influential officer because neither the vice president nor the president pro tempore holds substantive powers over the chamber's proceedings. Like the Speaker, the majority and minority leaders in both chambers receive larger salaries than other members as well as additional staff resources and other perquisites.

Duties of the House majority and minority leaders are not spelled out in the standing rules of the House. In practice, the majority leader's job has been to formulate the party's legislative program in cooperation with the Speaker and other party leaders, steer the program through the House, work to ensure that committee chairmen take action on bills deemed of importance to the party, and act as party spokesman on the House floor.

Everyday duties of the minority leader correspond to those of the majority leader, except that the minority leader has no authority over scheduling legislation. The minority leader speaks for his party and acts as field general on the floor, promoting partisan cohesion and searching for votes on the majority side. It is the minority leader's duty to consult ranking minority members of House committees and encourage them to follow agreed-upon party positions. If the occupant of the White House is of the minority party, that party's leader in the House will be the president's spokesman. "It's a dual role," House Minority Leader Michel has noted. "On each decision, [the leader's job] makes you look at things from two perspectives—your own district's and the President's." [21]

The functions of the Senate majority leader are similar to those of his counterpart in the House. He can nominate members to party committees, influence the election of party officers, affect the assignment of members to committees, and appoint ad hoc party task forces to study and recommend substantive or procedural reforms. Traditionally, the "primary role of the majority leader remains similar to that at its inception, namely, to program and to expedite the flow of his party's legislation." [22] All Senate floor business essentially is scheduled by the majority leader in consultation with the minority leadership. Scheduling is the bedrock on which the majority leader's fundamental authority rests. The majority leader is aided in controlling scheduling by many parliamentary and procedural precedents, such as the priority given him (and the minority leader) when he seeks recognition on the floor, and the ability to set the times and dates the Senate recesses (or adjourns) and reconvenes. These informal prerogatives can be useful in deciding what tactics to employ against filibusters, for instance.

If used aggressively by the majority leader, scheduling, discussed in Chapter 7, can be transformed from a largely procedural responsibility to one with significant programmatic and political overtones. Legislation can be scheduled to suit party or White House interests; to facilitate comprehensive policy making through the sequential consideration of related topics; to expedite policies supported by the leadership; or to coordinate House-Senate decision making.

With the aid of the majority whip, the majority leader also is responsible for securing the attendance of party colleagues during important floor sessions and ascertaining in advance how senators are likely to vote on issues. Measures may be scheduled to maximize attendance by the bill's supporters and minimize attendance by the opponents. The leadership expends a great deal of effort to ensure that senators backing a measure favored by the party are on hand for important votes.

Occupying center stage in the Senate, the majority leader is best positioned institutionally to know the status of legislation, when a bill probably will be scheduled, how intensely committed its supporters and opponents are, what strategies are being formulated to pass or defeat it, and under what conditions the president will intervene to help secure the measure's enactment or defeat. A knowledgeable majority leader is in a good position to guide and advise his colleagues.

The minority leader in the Senate has important responsibilities, too. These include summarizing minority criticism of the majority party's legislation, mobilizing support for minority party positions, and acting as Senate spokesman for the president if both are of the same party.

Whips

Each party in the House and Senate elects a whip and usually appoints a number of deputy and assistant whips to aid the floor leader in implementing the party's legislative program. The principal jobs of the whips are to aid the party leadership in developing a program; transmit information to party members; check attendance before key votes; conduct counts of party members for and against major bills; assist the leaders in interpreting the counts and developing strategy; build coalitions to pass amendments and bills; oversee and expedite floor activity generally; and publicize the party's accomplishments.[23] In sum, their "first function is gathering intelligence, knowing where the votes are," observed Speaker Wright. "Their second function is persuasion, producing the votes."[24]

Congressional parties have expanded their whip structure over the years. In addition to the whip, House Democrats have a chief deputy whip, ten deputy whips, forty-four at-large whips, and twenty-two regional whips. The other congressional parties have somewhat similar whip organizations.

The increase in the number of whips reflects the important changes that have taken place in the House and Senate during the past two decades, particularly the diffusion of authority among subcommittees and the election of more and more independent-minded members. Such developments have made the task of leadership more difficult, precipitating the whip expansion. Additional whips provide greater geographical, ideological, and seniority balance in the party leadership structure.

Party Caucuses

Over the years, both parties have relied periodically on caucuses of party members (called "conferences" by Republicans in both houses and by

Senate Democrats) to adopt party positions on legislation, elect party leaders, approve committee assignments, and, on rare occasions, discipline party members. After relative inactivity during much of the twentieth century, party caucuses emerged in the late 1960s as important bodies. Caucuses now meet regularly to consider substantive and procedural matters. During the Reagan presidency, for example, the House Democratic Caucus appointed numerous task forces to formulate a party agenda for the 1980s and to highlight how Democrats differed from Republicans. Interestingly, the House leaders of these caucuses during all or part of the 100th Congress—Democrat Richard A. Gephardt of Missouri and Republican Jack F. Kemp of New York—attracted the standing and attention to campaign for their party's 1988 presidential nomination.

Party Committees

The parties have their own committees in each chamber to assist the party leadership and deal with related business. Steering committees recommend the order in which measures should be taken up and help with floor tactics, while policy committees research proposed legislation and recommend party positions. The two functions may be combined in a single committee, as happened in 1973 when the House Democratic Caucus voted to create a new Democratic Steering and Policy Committee, chaired by the Speaker, to give added coherence to the party's legislative strategy. In 1974 the committee was given the responsibility of assigning Democrats to House committees. Both parties in each chamber also have campaign committees, which help recruit candidates, raise funds, and craft campaign strategies.

Congressional Leaders and the President

Congressional leaders generally try to cooperate with a president of their own party and scrutinize programs put forth by a president of the opposing party. For example, when President Ronald Reagan took office in 1981, he faced a divided Congress: the Senate was in GOP hands and Democrats were in control of the House. Senate Majority Leader Howard H. Baker, Jr., Tenn. (1967-1985; majority leader 1981-1985), "quickly decided to mobilize the Senate into an instrument of the presidential party. Rather than establish an independent power center, Baker decided to cast his lot with the White House, helping to push the president's program through the Senate but also informing the president of the things that mattered to his colleagues." [25] As Baker expressed it, "I am the President's spear carrier in the Senate." [26] However, when Democrats recaptured control of the Senate in the aftermath of the

November 1986 elections, Senator Byrd, the incoming majority leader, declared: "The Senate will no longer be an agent of the White House. The people wanted checks and balances, and they're going to get them." [27]

Over the years, there have been important instances in which congressional leaders have resisted the program of a president of their own party or cooperated in a substantial way with an opposing party's president. Republican president Dwight D. Eisenhower, for example, said of Senate Majority Leader Johnson, a Democrat: "We had our differences . . . yet when put in perspective, he was far more often helpful than obstructive. . . ." [28] Congressional leaders also promote their own legislative program and seek to have it accepted by the White House. "Those who wrote the Constitution," said Speaker Wright, "intended the legislative branch not simply to react passively to recommendations from the President, but to take initiatives of their own." [29]

Other Groups

There are numerous informal organizations of senators and representatives that play a significant role in the legislative process. During the 100th Congress, there were more than 110 informal groups, many of them bipartisan and bicameral, serving multiple purposes: information clearinghouses, mobilizers of interests and votes on specific issues, advocates of certain issues, and contact points for executive officials.[30] Underlying all of these groups are the bonds of mutual interests and personal friendship that play such a large part in the functioning of Congress. Many of these groups were formed to represent specific interests, such as the Rural Caucus and the Congressional Black Caucus. Other informal groups, such as the House Democratic Study Group and the House Republican Wednesday Group, focus in part on procedural issues. Still other groups are composed of members who have similar outlooks on certain issues, such as the Competitiveness Caucus, which was created during the late 1980s to address the nation's economic problems. Some informal groups are aided by outside research institutes or foundations. There are also state delegations, such as that of Texas, whose members work together to advance the interests of their state or region.

PRESSURES ON MEMBERS

In making their legislative decisions, members of Congress are influenced by numerous pressures—from their constituents, the White

House, the news media, lobbyists and organized interest groups, and their own party leadership and colleagues on Capitol Hill. These pressures are a central feature of the congressional environment; they affect the formal procedures and rules of Congress. All of these pressures are present in varying degrees at every step of the legislative process. The interests and influence of groups and individuals outside Congress have a considerable impact on the fate of legislation. This section highlights some of the major influences on members.

The Executive Branch

The executive branch constitutes one of the most important sources of external pressure exerted on Congress. As noted in Chapter 1, there is an ongoing institutional struggle between the executive and legislative branches. Sometimes the rivalry is seen as no more than a means by which members of Congress develop public stature by demonstrating their ability to thwart the president's objectives. British political scientist Harold Laski subscribed to such a view when he wrote, "There can be no doubt that in its own eyes, Congress establishes its prestige when it either refuses to let the president have his own way, or compels him to compromise with it." [31]

Many of the president's legislative functions and activities are not mentioned in the Constitution. For example, the president is able to influence congressional action through the manipulation of patronage, the allocation of federal funds and projects that may be vital to the reelection of certain members of Congress, and the handling of constituents' cases in which senators and representatives are interested. As leader of the Democratic or Republican party, the president is his party's chief election campaigner. As the leading political figure, the president occupies a strategic position for promoting broad coalitions of social groups and interests. The president also has ready access to the news media for promoting his administration's policies and commanding headlines. This "bully pulpit" role, as Theodore Roosevelt described it, enables presidents to mold public opinion and build public backing for White House proposals.

The president's role as legislative leader, however, derives from the Constitution. While the Constitution vests "all legislative powers" in Congress, it also directs the president to "give to the Congress information of the state of the union and recommend to their consideration such measures as he shall judge necessary and expedient." This function has been broadened over the years. The president presents to Congress each year, in addition to his State of the Union message, two other general statements of presidential aims: an economic report, including proposals directed to the maintenance of maximum employment, and a budget message outlining his appropriations requests and policy proposals. And during a typical session, the president transmits to Congress scores of other legislative proposals, some on his own initiative or that of his cabinet officials and others in conformity with various statutes.

Another legislative vehicle for presidential leadership is the constitutional power to veto acts passed by Congress or to threaten to veto them. Because it is usually so difficult to override presidential vetoes—a two-thirds vote in each house is required—legislative-executive accommodations often occur when the White House sends veto signals on legislation. On the other hand, Congress can artfully package legislation so that presidents are reluctant to exercise their veto prerogative. In short, vetoes are employed to accomplish legislative and political (highlighting party differences, for instance) objectives and are a central feature of the Congress-White House tug-of-war.

To enhance the prospects for securing a good working relationship with Congress, presidents in recent years have established congressional liaison offices in the White House to keep tabs on legislative activities on Capitol Hill and to lobby on behalf of administration policies. In addition, all federal departments now have their own congressional liaison team. There are scores of executive branch officials charged with handling the administration's relations with Congress.

The Media

Of all the pressures on Congress, none is such a two-way proposition as the relationship between legislators and the media.

While senators and representatives must contend with the peculiarities of the news-gathering business, such as deadlines and limited space or time to describe events, and with constant media scrutiny of their actions, they also must rely on news organizations to inform the public of their legislative interests and accomplishments. At the same time, reporters must depend to some extent on "inside" information from members, a condition that makes many of them reluctant to displease their sources lest the pipeline of information be shut off.

But Congress basically is an open organization. Information flows freely on Capitol Hill and secrets rarely remain secret for long. It has always been the case that an enterprising reporter usually could find out what was newsworthy. Moreover, Congress has taken a variety of actions during the past two decades to further open its proceedings to public observation. Recall the nationwide, gavel-to-gavel coverage over C-SPAN of House and Senate floor proceedings. Instead of relying on press accounts of congressional actions, many citizens now have an opportunity to watch the floor sessions and make their own legislative judgments.

This new openness has created pressures on members that, although present before, were less intense. Members' actions are subject to closer scrutiny by the media and by constituents as well as by political opponents and interest groups. Members' fears of changing their positions once they have been expressed in public can make more difficult the process of arriving at necessary compromises.

Most House and Senate members, especially the younger legislators who were raised with television, are skilled in public relations. Whereas relatively few senators in the 1960s had a press secretary, nearly every senator today employs one. Many congressional offices are veritable publicity shops, sending out "electronic press releases" to local television studios, newsletters to constituents, articles to newspapers and magazines, and interviews over satellite to radio and television networks. Advances in political telecommunications not only enable incumbents to promote their careers and agendas; they are important in shaping strategies to move or delay legislation. In 1985, for example, the chairman of the tax-writing House Ways and Means Committee—Dan Rostenkowski, D-Ill.—made an eleven-minute nationally televised response to President Reagan's televised appeal for comprehensive tax reform. His "Write Rosty" address, urging voters to write letters backing tax revision, generated more than 75,000 responses and transformed Rostenkowski from the "consummate inside player of the dark, back corridors of the U.S. Congress" into a "kind of folk hero of federal taxation." [32] As former CBS Evening News anchorman Walter Cronkite once put it: "Politics and media are inseparable. It is only the politicians and the media that are incompatible." [33]

Constituent Pressures

Although there are many pressures competing for influence on Capitol Hill, it is still the constituents, not the president or the party or the congressional leadership, who grant and can take away a member's job.[34] A member who is popular back home can defy all three in a way unthinkable in a country like Great Britain, where the leadership of the legislature, the executive, and the party are the same.

The extent to which a member of Congress seeks to follow the wishes of his constituents is determined to a considerable extent by the issue at stake. Few members would actively oppose issues deemed vital by most constituents. A farm-state legislator, for instance, is unlikely to push policies designed to lower the price of foods grown by those who elect him. Likewise, few members would follow locally popular policies that would endanger the nation. Between these extremes lies a wide spectrum of different blends of pressure from constituents and from conscience. But it is in this gray area that members must make most of

Balancing Public and Private Pressures

Rep. Dennis E. Eckart was racing off the other day to spend the weekend in his Ohio district. When his four-year-old son, Eddie, spied the suitcase in his hand, the boy asked why he was going.

"To talk to people," replied Eckart.

"There are people here, Daddy," Eddie replied.

Eckart, a Democrat, tells that story with some sadness. But he is a thirty-three-year-old, second-term member of the House with high ambition and a new district, thanks to redistricting. So he goes back to Ohio many weekends, leaving his wife and son in suburban Virginia, and he knows he is paying a price for his political success.

"If you ask my son what I do for a living, he says campaigning," Eckart said with a wry laugh. "It's tough, extremely tough, to balance all the demands on you, and still be a father, a husband, a son, an uncle, a brother and a godfather."

This balancing act described by Eckart has always been a problem on Capitol Hill. The conflicts between a lawmaker's public and private lives were highlighted by the decision of the House in July 1983 to censure two members who engaged in sexual relations with teen-aged pages.

For most members of Congress, the conflicts are far less dramatic, much more on the order of Eckart's concern for his son. But all members share the strains and stresses of serving in what Rep. Newt Gingrich, R-Ga., calls "the most human institution in the Federal Government."

Indeed, some members have either forgotten, or never felt, the conflicting pressures described by Eckart. "I so completely submerged my private life into my public life, and I did so at such an early age, that I can't tell where one stops and the other starts," said Rep. Guy Vander Jagt, a Michigan Republican.

Still, the balancing act between public and private lives bothers most members. One of their biggest complaints is that even simple joys become "events," played out in the glaring eye of public notice.

Absent parents are an inevitable part of congressional life. Rep. Les AuCoin, an Oregon Democrat, says that in many congressional families "too many kids are almost strangers to their parents."

Time is the most precious commodity in any lawmaker's life, and its scarcity afflicts many congressional marriages. Eckart says he feels like a "guided missile," directed by his staff through remote control to attend this hearing or that fund-raiser. And that sort of life, he adds, "places added stress on any marriage. I can say that without equivocation." Eckart's wife, Sandy, left her job, her home, and her family to move to Washington with him, and she often feels left out of his work. "She's almost stopped calling and asking if I'll be home for dinner," Eckart said.

Source: Adapted from Steven V. Roberts, "Tales of Two Lives: One Public, the Other Private," *New York Times*, July 28, 1983, A20.

their decisions. (It is no coincidence that the committees on which senators and representatives seek membership often are determined by the type of constituency served.)

The growing sophistication of the electorate, combined with technological advances—easy airplane travel, polling, computer-generated letters, and so on—means that members face a deluge of constituent inquiries. For example, the House received 14.6 million pieces of mail in 1973, but nearly 225 million pieces in 1986.[35] Moreover, legislators understand the value of maintaining an effective two-way process of communication between themselves and their constituents. Legislators commute regularly (often weekly) to their states or districts, hold scores of "town meetings" with voters, employ mobile offices to travel throughout the constituency, keep full-time staff aides in their locale to assist constituents, and employ the latest technological devices to keep in touch with the folks back home. With 10,000 Russian-speaking constituents (Soviet emigrés) in his New York City district, Rep. Stephen J. Solarz "has begun putting out a Russian-language 'Special Washington Report' " for this sizable electoral group.[36]

Changes in the electorate, in brief, now oblige legislators to employ an "inside-outside" strategy to win major objectives on Capitol Hill. No longer is it sufficient for members to follow only the "inside" game: negotiating member-to-member behind the scenes to forge winning coalitions. Instead, constituents must be activated, public opinion galvanized, and public support organized—the "outside" game—to create the political climate necessary to win the "big votes" on controversial bills, treaties, or nominations.

Washington Lobbyists

Lobbyists and lobby groups play an active part in the legislative process. The corps of Washington lobbyists has grown markedly since the 1930s, in line with the expansion of federal authority into new areas and with the huge increase in federal spending. The federal government has become a tremendous force in the life of the nation, and the number of fields in which changes in federal policy may spell success or failure for special interest groups has been greatly enlarged. Thus commercial and industrial interests, labor unions, ethnic and racial groups, professional organizations, citizen groups, and representatives of foreign interests—all from time to time and some continuously—have sought by one method or another to exert pressure on Congress to attain their legislative goals.

Pressure groups, whether operating at the grass-roots level to influence public opinion or through direct contacts with members of Congress, perform some important and indispensable functions. These include helping to inform both Congress and the public about problems and issues, stimulating public debate, opening a path to Congress for the wronged and needy, and making known to Congress the practical aspects of proposed legislation: whom it would help, whom it would hurt, who is for it, and who is against it. Lobbyists also work closely with sympathetic legislators and their staffs. "Essentially, we operate as an extension of congressmen's staffs," said one consumer lobbyist. "Occasionally we come up with the legislation, or speeches—and questions [for lawmakers to ask at hearings] all the time. We look at it as providing staff work for allies." [37]

Interest groups may, in pursuing their own objectives, lead the legislature into decisions that benefit a particular pressure group but do not necessarily serve other segments of the public. A group's ability to influence legislation is based on a variety of factors: the quality of its arguments; the size, cohesion, and intensity of the organization's membership; the group's ability to augment its political power by forming ad hoc coalitions with other associations; its financial and staff resources; and the shrewdness of its leadership. There is little question that contemporary lobbying differs significantly from earlier forms. As Washington lawyer-lobbyist (and former Carter White House domestic aide) Stuart E. Eizenstat pointed out:

> Because of the increasing complexity of issues and increasing sophistication of [congressional] staff, you have to be armed with facts, precedents and legal points. Sure it's a political environment, but it's much more substantive. The old-style, pat-'em-on-the-back lobbyist is gone, or at least going.[38]

In recent years there has been a significant increase in the number of political action committees (PACs)—from 608 in 1974 to more than 4,100 in 1988. PACs are legal entities created by interest groups to raise and contribute money to election campaigns. With the rising costs of congressional campaigns (in 1986, the average campaign cost for the House was $500,000; for the Senate, $3 million), many members have become concerned about the influence of PAC money on legislative decisions. House Ways and Means Committee Chairman Rostenkowski, in discussing his panel's review of the landmark 1986 overhaul of the tax code, highlighted the money-lawmaking connection.

> There was on the part of three to five members, on both sides of the aisle, a definite string attached to some corporate lobbyist outside in the hall—in one instance a direct link with respect to how much money he could raise in a campaign. That got me nauseated. . . . There were two members in my opinion that flagrantly violated ethical codes.[39]

To be sure, other legislators deny that money influences decisions and emphasize the value of PACs as voluntary organizations that encourage and strengthen citizen participation in the electoral and legislative processes.

CONGRESS IN FLUX

The contemporary Congress is strikingly different from its predecessors in a variety of ways. For instance, the House and Senate have stripped away many vestiges of the secrecy that once cloaked their committee and floor activities; committee and member offices have been provided with modern technology; staff resources have been augmented; power has shifted from seniority leaders to subcommittee and individual leaders; party leaders have gained new authority, as the Speaker has in being able to appoint the Democratic members of the Rules Committee; and budgetary procedures have been revamped (see Chapter 3). These changes, in brief, have affected Congress's lawmaking processes, distribution of power, and policy-making capabilities.

External events and internal frustrations largely triggered these diverse developments. Congress began to change in the late 1960s and early 1970s. Of fundamental importance were the two overriding issues of the period: the Vietnam War and the Watergate scandal. Both forced Congress to reflect on the growing mistrust between the legislative and executive branches and to examine whether it had the tools, and the will, to handle those crises and others that might arise in the future. New members were coming to Congress—many brighter, more activist, and more ambitious than the people they replaced—determined to participate actively in legislative decision making and to restore Congress to a position equal with that of the presidency. "You don't have to wait around to have influence," noted Rep. Charles E. Schumer, D-N.Y., elected in 1981. "Entrepreneurs do very well," he added.[40]

A principal result of this era of change has been to reinforce the decentralized tendencies of Congress. Power has been diffused further throughout Congress's components—committees, subcommittees, party panels, task forces, staff aides, and informal groups—rather than concentrated (as during the 1950s) in a relatively few individuals. The object of the changes of the 1970s, said former Speaker O'Neill, "was to take power out of the hands of the few and give it to more people."[41] This development greatly increased the need for bargaining and coalition building to achieve legislative results.

Change, however, is an iron law of politics. The decentralizing developments of the past two decades have led in part to innovative lawmaking forms, such as "megabills" many hundreds or thousands of pages in length. Because so many of these comprehensive measures involve budgetary matters, they will be discussed in the next chapter.

Suffice it to say that one result of megabills is to recentralize authority in fewer hands—the legislators who directly assemble these massive packages.

SUMMARY

This chapter has discussed the general environment in which members of Congress operate, the many influences on congressional procedures and decision making, including the party leadership and outside pressures—from the executive branch, members' constituents, the news media, and lobbying groups. The chapter has also highlighted some of the similarities and differences in the House and Senate that affect the operations of the national legislature. This chapter completes a preliminary overview of Congress.

Chapter 3 turns to a detailed discussion of the congressional budget process. The power of the purse is one of Congress's fundamental constitutional prerogatives. Congress's revamped budgetary process has become an integrating mechanism in an institution that thrives on fragmented authority. Moreover, it imposes a web of relationships upon committees and members that affects action on almost all public policy. To examine the budget process at this stage should aid in understanding the fundamental thrust of the remaining chapters, which discuss what typically happens to bills as they follow the lawmaking route.

NOTES

1. Woodrow Wilson, *Constitutional Government in the United States* (New York: Columbia University Press, 1911), 87.
2. *Congressional Record,* Feb. 7, 1967, 2838.
3. Asher C. Hinds, *Hinds' Precedents of the House of Representatives,* vol. 1, v.
4. Janet Hook, "Speaker Jim Wright Takes Charge in the House," *Congressional Quarterly Weekly Report,* July 11, 1987, 1486.
5. *New York Times,* Nov. 22, 1985, B8.
6. *Congressional Record,* daily ed., Sept. 10, 1987, S11944.
7. Nelson W. Polsby, "Policy Analysis and Congress," *Public Policy* (Fall 1969): 67.
8. Michael Green, "Obstacles to Reform: Nobody Covers the House," *Washington Monthly,* June 1970, 62-70.
9. See Robert L. Peabody, Norman J. Ornstein, and David W. Rohde, "The United States Senate as a Presidential Incubator: Many Are Called but Few Are Chosen," *Political Science Quarterly* (Summer 1976): 236-258.
10. *Wall Street Journal,* May 1, 1985, 22.
11. Charles Clapp, *The Congressman* (Garden City, N.Y.: Doubleday, 1963), 39.
12. Richard F. Fenno, Jr., *Congressmen in Committees* (Boston: Little, Brown, 1973), 172.

13. Norman J. Ornstein, "Legislative Behavior and Legislative Structure: A Comparative Look at House and Senate Resource Utilization," in *Legislative Staffing,* ed. James J. Heaphey and Alan B. Balutis (New York: John Wiley & Sons, 1975), 175.
14. *Chicago Tribune,* July 21, 1983, 9.
15. *Congressional Record,* daily ed., Oct. 1, 1985, S12343.
16. *Wall Street Journal,* July 18, 1986, 10.
17. Richard W. Bolling, *House Out of Order* (New York: E. P. Dutton, 1965), 48.
18. Randall B. Ripley, *Party Leaders in the House of Representatives* (Washington, D.C.: Brookings Institution, 1967), 7.
19. Michael J. Malbin, "House Democrats Are Playing with a Strong Leadership Lineup," *National Journal,* June 18, 1977, 942.
20. *Los Angeles Times,* Oct. 19, 1986, sec. 1, 2.
21. *Chicago Tribune,* Aug. 16, 1982, 2.
22. Robert L. Peabody, *Leadership in Congress* (Boston: Little, Brown, 1976), 336.
23. Lawrence C. Dodd, "The Expanded Roles of the House Democratic Whip System: The 93rd and 94th Congresses," *Congressional Studies,* (Spring 1979): 27-56. See also Dodd and Terry Sullivan, "Majority Party Leadership and Partisan Vote Gathering: The House Democratic Whip System," in *Understanding Congressional Leadership,* ed. Frank H. Mackaman (Washington, D.C.: CQ Press, 1981), 227-260.
24. *New York Times,* Nov. 18, 1977, A18.
25. Allen Schick, "How the Budget Was Won and Lost," in *President and Congress, Assessing Reagan's First Year,* ed. Norman J. Ornstein (Washington, D.C.: American Enterprise Institute for Public Policy Research, 1982), 18.
26. *Congressional Record,* daily ed., July 28, 1983, S11029.
27. *New York Times,* Jan. 5, 1987, A13.
28. Dwight D. Eisenhower, *Waging the Peace, 1956-1961* (Garden City, N.Y.: Doubleday, 1965), 593.
29. John M. Barry, "The Man of the House," *New York Times Magazine,* Nov. 23, 1986, 54, 56.
30. See Arthur G. Stevens, Jr., Daniel P. Mulhollan, and Paul S. Rundquist, "U.S. Congressional Structure and Representation: The Role of Informal Groups," *Legislative Studies Quarterly* (August 1981): 415-438; Burdett A. Loomis, "Congressional Caucuses and the Politics of Representation," in *Congress Reconsidered,* 2d ed., ed. Lawrence C. Dodd and Bruce I. Oppenheimer (Washington, D.C.: CQ Press, 1981), 204-220; and Susan Webb Hammond, Arthur G. Stevens, Jr., and Daniel P. Mulhollan, "Congressional Caucuses: Legislators as Lobbyists," in *Interest Group Politics,* ed. Allan J. Cigler and Burdett A. Loomis (Washington, D.C.: CQ Press, 1983), 275-297.
31. Harold J. Laski, *The American Presidency: An Interpretation* (New York: Harper & Bros., 1940), 116.
32. Jeffrey H. Birnbaum and Alan S. Murray, *Showdown At Gucci Gulch* (New York: Random House, 1987), 100.
33. Doris A. Graber, *Mass Media and American Politics* (Washington, D.C.: CQ Press, 1980), 193. Also see Dom Bonafede, "The Washington Press—Competing for Power with the Federal Government"; "The Washington Press—An Interpreter or a Participant in Policy Making?"; and "The Washington Press—It Magnifies the President's Flaws and Blemishes," *National Journal,* April 17, April 24, and May 1, 1982, 664-674, 716-721, and 767-771.
34. For a valuable discussion of constituent pressures, see David Mayhew, *The Electoral Connection* (New Haven: Yale University Press, 1974).
35. *Washington Post,* Aug. 15, 1986, A15.

36. *New York Times,* Dec. 15, 1987, B8.
37. *Wall Street Journal,* Oct. 5, 1987, 54.
38. Kirk Victor, "New Kids on the Block," *National Journal,* Oct. 31, 1987, 2727. Also see Burt Solomon, "Clout Merchants," *National Journal,* March 21, 1987, 662-666.
39. *Wall Street Journal,* July 18, 1986, 10.
40. *Wall Street Journal,* June 29, 1987, 54.
41. *U.S. News & World Report,* Aug. 11, 1980, 24.

CHAPTER 3

The Congressional Budget Process

The framers of the Constitution deliberately lodged the power of the purse in Congress. Only Congress can authorize the government to collect taxes, borrow money, and make expenditures. The executive branch can spend funds only for the purposes and in the amounts specified by Congress. As Article I, Section 9, proclaims: "No Money shall be drawn from the Treasury, but in Consequence of Appropriations made by Law."

These words have not been amended since they were written into the Constitution. But the framers would wonder about the effectiveness of the congressional purse strings today when over 75 percent of federal expenditures is relatively uncontrollable under existing law. This means that the national government is required to spend money automatically for certain purposes because of laws previously enacted by Congress. "Uncontrollables" include interest on the public debt (the debt currently is over $2 trillion); entitlements (laws that require benefit payments to all eligible individuals, such as Social Security, Medicare, and black lung benefits programs); and contract obligations that must be paid when due (the Defense Department's procurement arrangements with the Lockheed Corporation, for example).

One consequence of uncontrollables is clear. On the day the 100th Congress convened (January 6, 1987), it could have adjourned the session immediately, without passing any laws, and spending by the federal government for 1987 still would have been in the range of $500 billion. Further, spending each year thereafter would continue—and increase—because many federal programs are indexed to the cost of living. In short, large portions of the federal budget operate on "automatic pilot."

Interestingly, Congress in the early 1970s indexed Social Security as a cost-saving measure. Before it made this change Congress regularly granted recipients of Social Security, a well-organized and potent electoral group, benefits that far exceeded inflation. No one at the time of the change, however, foresaw either the tremendous inflationary surge of the 1970s or the growth in the number of elderly. Both developments increased dramatically the cost of COLAs (cost-of-living adjustments). Today, attempts to reduce or freeze COLAs are fraught with electoral danger, because recipients "consider COLAs as much a part of the entitlement as the benefit itself."[1] Changes in the fiscal environment, however, could make indexation adjustments politically palatable.

Congress, of course, can convert uncontrollables into controllables by changing the basic law that authorizes automatic funding without regular legislative review. (There are different degrees of controllability, however. Interest on the national debt and the interest rates to finance that debt are largely beyond Congress's control.) But there are serious political risks for members who want to subject uncontrollables to annual budgetary scrutiny. The elderly, for example, are sensitive to any changes in Social Security and have the clout to quickly mobilize against legislators who arouse their ire.

Congress chooses to place programs in the uncontrollable category for a variety of reasons. Stability, certainty, and preferred status are among the values that accrue to such programs. Retired persons, for instance, would have "to live under a great deal of financial uncertainty" if Congress subjected Social Security to annual review.[2]

Budgetary decisions of Congress profoundly affect the taxpaying electorate, the national and international economy, and the volume and variety of federal programs and activities. The federal budget itself (prepared annually by the president as directed by the Budget and Accounting Act of 1921) reflects key choices among competing national priorities and identifies where the nation has been, where it is now, and where the administration plans to make future fiscal as well as policy commitments. Thus the nation's budget is both an economic and a political document.

It is hardly surprising that Congress devotes a large percentage of its time to spending and taxing issues. This is particularly true during periods of fiscal scarcity and economic hardship, when the pressure and competition for funds are greatest.

In broad terms, federal budgeting is composed of four phases:

1. Preparation and submission of the budget by the president to Congress.
2. Congressional action on the president's budget proposals.
3. Execution of budget-related laws by federal departments and agencies.
4. Audits of agency spending.

The first and third steps are controlled primarily by the executive branch; the fourth is conducted largely by the General Accounting Office (GAO), a legislative support agency of Congress. The focus of this chapter is on the second stage, the basic elements and features of Congress's budgetary process. The first part of the chapter examines traditional procedures; the second discusses exceptions to the routine.

AUTHORIZATION-APPROPRIATIONS PROCESS

Fundamental to the congressional budget process is the distinction between authorizations and appropriations. This two-step, sequential procedure is intended to work as follows. Congress first passes an authorization bill that establishes or continues an agency or program and provides it with the legal authority to operate. Authorizations may be for one or more years, and such legislation may recommend funding levels for programs and agencies. Authorizations also make possible later consideration of appropriations.

Authorization bills must be approved by each house and submitted to the president for his signature or veto. Before any money can be withdrawn from the Treasury, however, a separate appropriations law must be enacted. "I think most people realize," stated Sen. Mark O. Hatfield, R-Ore., that an authorization "is only a hunting license for an appropriation." [3]

Today, much of the federal government is funded through the annual enactment of thirteen general appropriations bills. About one-half of federal spending each year is subject to the congressional authorization-appropriations process. The other half gets its legal basis from laws that provide spending authority automatically, such as the entitlement programs just referred to.

Appropriations approved by Congress provide "budget authority"; this allows government agencies to make financial commitments, up to a specified amount, that eventually result in the spending of dollars. As one budget analyst explains it:

> Congress does not directly control the level of federal spending that will occur in a particular year. Rather, it grants the executive branch authority (referred to as *budget authority*) to enter into *obligations*, which are legally binding agreements with suppliers of goods or services or with a beneficiary. When those obligations come due, the Treasury Department issues a payment. The amount of payments, called *outlays*, over an accounting period called the fiscal year (running from October 1 to September 30) equals federal expenditures for that fiscal year. Federal spending (outlays) in any given year, therefore, results from the spending authority (budget authority) granted by Congress in the current and in prior fiscal years.[4]

Or, as Rep. Les Aspin, D-Wis., put it, "Budget authority is permission to spend; outlays are actual spending."[5]

Legislators are particularly sensitive to budget authority figures, for these—rather than the outlay numbers—are the better predictors of an agency's growth or decline. Outlays, however, are reflected in each year's national deficit levels. With the escalation of annual deficits from about $75 billion at the start of the 1980s into the $200 billion range a few years later, outlays have loomed large in legislative-executive efforts to constrain federal spending.

Authorizing and Appropriating Committees

Whether agencies receive all the budget authority they request depends in part on the recommendations of the authorizing and appropriating committees. Each chamber has authorizing committees (Agriculture, Banking, Armed Services, Energy, and many others), which have responsibilities that differ from those of the two appropriating committees—the House and Senate Appropriations committees. The authorizing committees are the policy-making centers on Capitol Hill. As the substantive legislative panels, they propose solutions to public problems and advocate what they believe to be the necessary level of appropriations for new and existing federal programs.

The two Appropriations committees and their thirteen subcommittees have the job of recommending how much federal agencies and programs will receive in relation to available fiscal resources and economic conditions.

For each program and agency subject to the annual appropriations process, these committees have three main options: (1) provide all the funds recommended in the previously approved authorization bill; (2) propose reductions in the amounts already authorized; or (3) refuse to provide any funds.[6]

The following table provides a brief illustration of some of the key participants who influence a particular agency's level of funding.

Federal Agency	*Authorization Committees*	*Appropriations Committees*
Park Service, U.S. Department of the Interior	House Interior and Insular Affairs; Senate Energy and Natural Resources	House Subcommittee on Interior; Senate Subcommittee on Interior. Submitted to full committee in each house and reported.

To recapitulate, Congress requires authorizations to precede appropriations to ensure that substantive and financial issues are subject to separate and independent analysis. This procedure also permits almost every member and committee to participate in Congress's constitutional power of the purse. There are, to be sure, numerous exceptions to this two-step model, despite House and Senate rules that encourage separation of the authorization-appropriations stages. (See subsection "Exceptions to the Rules.")

Constitutional Underpinning

The authorization-appropriation dichotomy is not required by the Constitution. Rather, it is a process that has been institutionalized by the rules of the House and Senate and in some cases by statute. Of the two steps, the appropriations stage appears to be on firmer legal ground because it is rooted in the Constitution. An appropriations measure, which provides departments and agencies with authority to commit funds, may be approved even if the authorization bill has not been enacted. As long as "appropriations are enacted," wrote a budget scholar, "funds may be obligated by agencies, regardless of whether . . . authorizations have been enacted." [7]

Informally, Congress has employed this division of labor since the beginning of the Republic, as did the British Parliament in 1789 as well as the colonial legislatures. As Sen. William Plumer of New Hampshire noted in 1806: "Tis a good provision in the constitution of Maryland that prohibits their Legislature from adding any thing to an appropriation law." [8] Generally called "supply bills" in the early Congresses, appropriations measures had narrow purposes: to provide specific sums of money for fixed periods and stated objectives. Such bills were not to contain matters of policy.

There were exceptions to this informal rule even during the early days, but the practice of adding "riders," or extraneous policy provisos, to appropriations bills mushroomed in the 1830s. This practice often provoked sharp controversy in Congress and delayed the enactment of supply bills. "By 1835," wrote a parliamentary expert, the "delays caused by injecting legislation [policy] into these [appropriations] bills had become serious, and John Quincy Adams . . . suggested that they be stripped of everything save appropriations." [9] Two years later the House adopted a rule requiring authorization bills to precede appropriations. The Senate later followed suit.

Separate Policy and Fiscal Decisions

There are several major implications that flow from Congress's efforts to separate policy from fiscal decision making.

FLEXIBILITY. The authorization-appropriations rules, like almost all congressional rules, are not self-enforcing. Either chamber can choose to waive, ignore, or circumvent them or establish precedents and practices that obviate distinctions between the two. As one scholar has written:

> The real world of the legislative process differs considerably from the idealized model of the two-step authorization-appropriation procedure. Authorization bills contain appropriations, appropriation bills contain authorizations, and the order of their enactment is sometimes reversed. The Appropriations Committees, acting through various kinds of limitations, riders, and nonstatutory controls, are able to establish policy and act in a substantive manner. Authorization committees have considerable power to force the hand of the Appropriations Committees and, in some cases, even to appropriate.[10]

Recent Congresses, operating in a period of fiscal austerity, have witnessed an increase in unauthorized appropriations and in legislation in appropriations measures.

In short, there is flexibility in the authorization-appropriations procedure that allows it to accommodate stresses and strains. For example, a failure to enact authorization bills does not bring the appropriations process to a halt, though on occasion it does cause serious program dislocations.

BICAMERAL DIFFERENCES. Because the House and Senate are dissimilar, they have different rules governing the authorization-appropriations process. These differences are described in Table 3-1 and reflect each chamber's fundamental nature: the smaller Senate permits greater procedural flexibility than the larger House.

The dissimilar rules of the House and Senate affect each chamber's legislative behavior and policy deliberations. The Senate, for example, often gets off to a slower start on appropriations measures since it customarily waits for the House to originate those bills. Moreover, the multistage process creates numerous opportunities to shape issues. Policy debates may be resurrected again and again in different contexts in either chamber.

Exceptions to the Rules

There are many exceptions to the authorization-appropriations rules. For instance, the House rule that forbids legislation in any general appropriations bill explicitly permits such policy making if it is a retrenchment (reduction) and if it is "germane to the subject matter of the bill." The ostensible purpose of this rule (called the Holman rule after Rep. William S. Holman of Indiana, who formulated it in 1876) is to encourage economy in government. Over the years members seldom

TABLE 3-1 Authorization-Appropriations Rules Compared

House	*Senate*
No unauthorized appropriations are permitted except for public works in progress. The Appropriations Committee generally cannot report a general appropriations bill unless there is an authorization law.	Unauthorized appropriations are not permitted. There are exceptions: if the Senate has passed an authorization during that session; if an authorization is reported by any Senate standing committee, including Appropriations; or if an authorization is requested in the president's annual budget.
No legislation (policy) is permitted in an appropriations bill.	No legislation is permitted in an appropriations bill unless it is germane to the House-passed bill.
No appropriation is permitted in an authorization bill; floor amendments that propose appropriations are not in order in authorization bills.	There is no equivalent rule. By custom, the House initiates appropriations bills and objects to Senate efforts aimed at circumventing this arrangement.

have used the Holman rule to make policy. Instead, they have relied heavily on "limitation" riders.

Legislative provisions find their way into appropriations bills notwithstanding the strictures of the rules—for instance, if no member raises a point of order against the practice. Members of authorizing committees sometimes request that policy provisos be included in appropriations bills. The House also permits, by precedent, that unauthorized programs can be included in continuing resolutions (see "Government by Continuing Resolutions," later in this chapter) that provide interim funding for agencies whose general appropriations bills have not been enacted by the start of the fiscal year.

LIMITATION RIDERS. Limitations are provisions in general appropriations bills or floor amendments to those measures that prohibit the spending of funds for specific purposes. Always phrased in the negative ("None of the funds provided in this Act shall be used for . . ."), limitations are based on scores of House precedents that collectively uphold the position that because the House can refuse to appropriate funds for programs that have been authorized, it also can prohibit the use of funds for any part of a program or activity.

House members and staff aides devote endless hours to carefully drafting provisions that make policy in the guise of limitations. For guidance they turn to the House rule book, which is replete with precedents that have interpreted permissible from impermissible limitations. There are three basic criteria. Limitations cannot (1) impose additional duties or burdens on executive branch officials; (2) interfere with these officials' discretionary authority; or (3) require officials to make judgments or determinations not required by existing law.

The 1977 anti-abortion amendment is a classic example of a limitation and the impact procedure can exert on policy. The Labor-Health Education and Welfare (now Health and Human Services) appropriations bill for that year contained a limitation on the use of funds "to perform abortions except where the life of the mother would be endangered if the fetus were carried to term." A point of order was raised and sustained against that amendment on the ground that it was legislation in an appropriations bill. The limitation required officials in the executive branch to determine when the life of a pregnant woman would be endangered. The language then was amended to read: "None of the funds appropriated by this Act shall be used to pay for abortions or to promote or encourage abortions, except when a physician has certified the abortion is necessary to save the life of the mother." Again, a point of order was raised that the amendment was legislation in an appropriations bill. And again the chair ruled in favor of the parliamentary objection, this time on the ground that the federal government employed many physicians and that they would be required to make "life-deciding" judgments.

Finally, the sponsor of the proposal, Rep. Henry J. Hyde, R-Ill., said he had no choice but to offer the following language: "None of the funds appropriated under this Act shall be used to pay for abortions or to promote or encourage abortions." There was no point of order because the amendment required no judgments by executive officials. The Hyde amendment then was adopted.[11]

When the Labor-HEW bill, now containing the Hyde amendment, reached the Senate, Sen. Edward W. Brooke, R-Mass. (1967-1979), offered an amendment that permitted abortions "where the life of the mother would be endangered if the fetus were carried to term, or where medically necessary, or for the treatment of rape or incest." Sen. Barry Goldwater, R-Ariz. (1953-1965, 1969-1987), said the amendment was legislation in an appropriations bill and raised a point of order. The Senate has its own procedural devices to obviate such points of order, however, and Senator Brooke used them successfully on the abortion issue. He raised what is called a "question of germaneness" before the presiding officer had ruled on the Goldwater point of order.

DECIDING GERMANENESS QUESTIONS. Senate rules require that amendments be germane to general appropriations bills. And once the question of germaneness is raised, those rules require that the issue be submitted to the entire membership for resolution by majority vote and without debate. If the Senate decides that the proposed amendment is germane, the point of order automatically falls. In the abortion case described above, the Senate declared Senator Brooke's amendment germane by a 74-21 vote. To be sure, in such situations senators typically vote on the policy issue and not on the procedural question. There is a tendency in these cases, said Sen. Brock Adams, D-Wash., "to view the rules primarily as a technical obstacle and translate a procedural vote into the underlying substantive issue." [12]

In recent years, the House experienced a rapid increase in the number of limitation amendments—from eleven in 1965 to eighty-six in 1980. Many of these dealt with so-called social issues, particularly school busing, school prayer, and abortion. These controversial issues were repeatedly bottled up in the authorizing committees, and members wanting action on them turned increasingly to limitations as a vehicle to force House consideration. Frustrated by the sharp controversies and long delays these limitations were causing, the House changed its rules in 1983 to restrict the opportunities for members to offer limitation riders to appropriations bills.[13]

The new procedure prohibits members, with some exceptions, from proposing limitation amendments on the House floor. Only if the motion to have the Committee of the Whole rise is defeated may members offer a limitation proposal. To be sure, the Rules Committee may waive the limitation rule and permit such amendments to be offered on the floor, or floor leaders may choose not to challenge them by offering the motion to rise. (See Chapter 6 on floor procedures.)

The new procedure was applied for the first time on June 2, 1983, when a clean air rider was added to a Housing and Urban Development Department appropriations bill. "This one [rider] was just intriguing to members," said Representative Foley. "They obviously wanted to cast a vote on it." [14] The number of limitation amendments has decreased substantially since the rules change.

The House adopted another new rule in 1983, one that forbids any committee except Ways and Means from reporting tax or tariff proposals. This rule was first used on October 27, 1983, when Ways and Means Chairman Rostenkowski raised a point of order against a proposition in a general appropriations bill that concerned the duty-free entry of certain products from the Caribbean countries. The Chair sustained the point of order by ruling that the provision "is a tariff measure in violation" of House rules. Just as authorizing committees may not report appropriations, appropriating and authorizing panels may not report tax and tariff proposals.

Committee Rivalries

Another consequence of the two-step system is that it breeds continuing conflict between the authorizing and appropriating committees. Predictably, the authorizing committees generally support high levels of spending for the programs they recommend and seek ways to bypass Appropriations Committee domination. The appropriating panels, on the other hand, often view themselves as "guardians of the purse." It is their job, they believe, to say no to many funding requests. There are occasions, however, when maximum funding is the preferred objective of the Appropriations committees.

LOOSENING THE PURSE STRINGS

Tensions between the two types of committees led to procedural strategies by the authorizing committees—especially from the 1950s to the mid-1970s—that tended to erode the Appropriations committees' authority. The two major ones were (1) use of annual or short-term authorizations and (2) "backdoor" spending.

Permanent and Annual Authorizations

Until the 1950s, most federal programs were permanently authorized.[15] Permanent authorizations remain in effect until changed by Congress and provide continuing statutory authority for ongoing federal programs. Unlike the present custom, authorizations in the past usually did not recommend an amount of money to be appropriated each year to operate the programs. Instead, the Appropriations committees made these funding decisions on an annual basis. The appropriating panels, as a result, exercised more influence over agency activities than did the authorizing committees. This situation began to change after World War II. The authorizing committees won enactment of laws that converted many permanent authorizations into short-term or annual authorizations. As Sen. Sam Nunn, D-Ga., chairman of the Armed Services Committee, pointed out:

> The requirement for Congress to enact annual authorizations of Defense programs dates back to the legislation passed in 1959 which required annual congressional authorization of appropriations for the procurement of aircraft, missiles, and naval vessels. This requirement for annual authorization of national defense appropriations has been amended and expanded since 1959, so that now virtually the entire Defense budget requires annual authorization.[16]

Beginning in 1987, significant portions of the Pentagon's budget were shifted from annual to biennial authorization.

Several factors have influenced the trend toward short-term authorizations, but two have been critical. First, the authorizing committees wanted greater control and oversight of executive and presidential activities. Annual authorizations are a "relatively effective oversight device," two political scientists have written, "allowing for increased involvement of legislative committees in policymaking and surveillance, providing increased access to agency bases of information, improving the ability of Congress to focus attention on crucial programs, and producing an increased knowledge base from which to examine agency activity." [17]

Second, annual authorizations put pressure on the appropriating committees to fund programs at levels recommended by the authorizing panels. Under an annual cycle, appropriations bills often are "taken up only weeks after passage of the companion authorization. As a result, the authorization is likely to exert a direct influence on the subsequent appropriation. For most annual authorization bills the amount appropriated is more than 90 percent of the authorized level." [18] The funding gap is wider for programs authorized on a multiyear basis.

Types of Backdoor Spending

Another factor that has blurred the distinction between authorizations and appropriations has been the growth of backdoor spending. The objective of backdoor authorization measures is to circumvent the annual appropriations process yet permit the spending of federal monies.

The three basic forms of backdoor spending are borrowing authority, contract authority, and entitlements. Each is discussed below.

Under borrowing authority, a federal agency legally is authorized to borrow a specified amount of money from the Treasury or the public, through commercial channels, to finance activities such as building low-cost houses or making student loans.

Congress also authorizes annually millions of dollars in contract authority. An example of this type of financing arrangement would be a federal agency that is statutorily permitted to enter into contractual agreements with private firms for the construction of municipal sewage treatment plants. Appropriations must be provided in the future to honor these commitments.

Entitlements require the federal government to make payments to all eligible beneficiaries. Social Security, Medicare, veterans' pensions, and federal retirement benefits are examples of entitlement programs. Most entitlements are funded automatically through authority granted in permanent laws. They constitute one of the fastest growing parts of the federal budget.

> From a budgetary point of view, the significance of such programs is that, at least in the short run, their costs cannot be controlled. If the Congress appropriates $2 billion to build a dam or a highway, it can be confident that no more that $2 billion may be legally spent. But when it authorizes extended unemployment benefits, or a different reimbursement formula under Medicare, it can set no limit on the money that will ultimately flow from the Treasury, since the government is legally obligated to provide benefits to anyone who can prove that he is eligible.[19]

The escalation of entitlement expenditures has occurred in part because of demographic factors—the aging of the population, for example—and actions of Congress to ensure that payments to eligible citizens keep pace with inflation.

PRELUDE TO BUDGET REFORM

By 1973 less than half of federal spending was controlled by the congressional Appropriations committees. These panels gradually lost overall control of budget expenditures as the legislative, or authorizing, committees turned to backdoor financing and permanent appropriations to accomplish their policy objectives. The result was that Congress lacked a central body to coordinate budgetary decisions, relate government revenue to expenditures, or calculate the effect of individual spending actions on the national economy. Federal expenditures skyrocketed and national fiscal policy reflected whatever emerged from Congress's haphazard and decentralized budget process.

Presidents, to be sure, took advantage of the piecemeal process. President Richard Nixon, in particular, clashed with Congress over national spending priorities and frequently impounded (refused to spend) monies for programs sponsored by Democrats in Congress. During the 1972 presidential campaign, Nixon charged Congress with being spendthrift and financially irresponsible. He told a nationwide radio audience:

> But, let's face it, the Congress suffers from institutional faults when it comes to Federal spending. In our economy, the President is required by law to operate within the discipline of his budget, just as most American families must operate within the discipline of their budget. . . .
>
> Both the President and a family must consider total income and total out-go when they take a look at some new item which would involve spending additional money. They must take into account their financial situation as they make each and every spending decision. . . .
>
> In the Congress, however, it is vastly different. Congress not only does not consider the total financial picture when it votes on a particular spending bill, it does not even contain a mechanism to do so if it wished.[20]

Despite this partisan critique, many members of Congress recognized that excessive fragmentation epitomized the weakness of the legislative budget process. Congress appropriates for different programs, such as defense, education, housing, and so on, with little effort to operate within an overall budget or to determine priorities among programs. "[W]e are still practicing this outdated and fragmented congressional appropriations process," declared Sen. Alan Cranston, D-Calif., in 1973. "There can be no doubt of the need for a solution to this problem."[21] Further, conflict raged between the Nixon White House and Congress over the president's impoundment of appropriated funds. "Far from administrative routine," wrote a budget expert, "Nixon's impoundments in late 1972 and 1973 were designed to rewrite national policy at the expense of congressional power and intent."[22]

The erosion of Congress's control of the purse strings, budgetary clashes with presidents, sharp internal conflicts among the appropriating, authorizing, and taxing committees, and public concern about the state of the national economy provided the impetus that led to enactment of a landmark procedural measure: the Congressional Budget and Impoundment Control Act of 1974. That act established a congressional budget process that encouraged coordination and centralization. However, it did not institute this fiscal reorganization by abolishing the traditional authorization-appropriations process. Such an attempt would have pitted the most powerful committees and members against one another and jeopardized any chance of realizing substantive budgetary changes. Instead, Congress added another budget procedure to "the existing revenue and appropriations process" of the House and Senate.[23] In brief, the act was a "shotgun marriage"—an effort to accommodate Congress's chronic fragmentation with its felt need for budgetary integration.

THE 1974 BUDGET ACT

Passage of the 1974 budget act had a major institutional and procedural impact on the legislative branch. Not unexpectedly, many of the original requirements of the act have been modified in response to new developments. It is worthwhile to describe the main features of the 1974 act, because they remain fundamentally intact—the institutional entities, the concurrent budget resolution, controls on backdoors and entitlements, and reconciliation—despite today's changed legislative budgeting process.

The act created three new entities: the House Budget Committee, the Senate Budget Committee, and the Congressional Budget Office (CBO). The two budget committees have essentially the same functions, which include: (1) preparing annually at least two concurrent budget resolutions; (2) reviewing the impact of existing or proposed legislation on federal expenditures; (3) overseeing the Congressional Budget Office; and (4) monitoring throughout the year the revenue and spending actions of the House and Senate. The last function listed here is called "scorekeeping" and is shared with the CBO.

The two panels, however, are constituted differently. The House Budget Committee is required to have a rotating membership: most members may not serve more than six years during the same decade. The committee must be composed of members drawn mainly from other standing committees, as follows: five each from Appropriations and Ways and Means, twenty-three from other committees, and a nonrotating leadership member from each of the two parties. The chairman may be elected to serve for eight years. Rotation has the effect of sometimes making it difficult for committee members to reach consensus on issues, because their task is limited to one critical, visible, and often partisan function: producing a budget resolution.

By contrast, the Senate Budget Committee has no restrictions on tenure, nor are its members required to come from other designated committees. A consequence of the membership difference is that key career-oriented senators have become more knowledgeable about budgetary matters than their House Budget counterparts and, therefore, are better equipped to shape conference committee deliberations to their own liking. (See Chapter 9 on conference committees.)

The Congressional Budget Office is Congress's principal informational and analytical resource for budget, tax, and spending proposals. With about 230 aides, CBO performs important services for the House and Senate Budget committees and other congressional panels. As a Senate Budget Committee chairman, Pete V. Domenici, R-N.M., put it:

> The core services which we in Congress have come to expect of CBO have been the provision of cost estimates of bills, scorekeeping reports, economic forecasts and 5-year projections, the analysis of the president's budget in its session review, alternative budget reduction strategies, and more detailed analysis of particular problems and Federal activities.[24]

Procedurally, the 1974 act established a rigorous timetable for Congress and its committees to consider the annual appropriations bills. The timetable for budgetary action was seldom met, largely because of conflicts within Congress and between Congress and the White House. (See Table 3-2 for the current timetable.) Enforcement of the act's objectives—relating revenues to spending decisions and setting priorities among competing national programs—occurred mainly through a limited number of points of order against bills, amendments, or confer-

TABLE 3-2 Congressional Budget Timetable

Deadline	*Action to be Completed*
First Monday after January 3	President submits budget to Congress.
February 25	Committees submit views and estimates to Budget committees.
April 15	Congress completes action on the concurrent budget resolution.
May 15	Annual appropriations bills may be considered in the House.
June 10	House Appropriations Committee reports last annual appropriations bill.
June 15	Congress completes reconciliation.
June 30	House completes action on annual appropriations bill.
October 1	Fiscal year begins.

Note: It is not uncommon for Congress to miss or modify some of these deadlines.

ence reports that violated the budgetary totals specified in the concurrent budget resolution and through information, such as scorekeeping reports, that identified the fiscal consequences of legislative decisions.

Concurrent Budget Resolutions

The core of Congress's annual budget process centers today on the adoption of a concurrent budget resolution. This resolution is formulated by the Budget committees and is composed of two basic parts. The first deals with fiscal aggregates: total federal spending (budget authority and outlays), total federal revenue, and the public debt (or surplus) for the upcoming fiscal year (October 1 through September 30). The second part subdivides the spending aggregates into twenty-one functional categories, such as national defense, energy, and agriculture. This fiscal blueprint, in brief, establishes the context of congressional budgeting; guides the budgetary actions of the authorizing, appropriating, and taxing committees; and represents Congress's spending priorities.

The 1974 act originally required the adoption of at least two concurrent budget resolutions—one in the spring (by May 15) that served as a guidepost or target for committee actions and one in the fall (by September 15) that was binding on Congress. "Reconciliation" legislation was to follow if Congress's individual fiscal decisions—made during the rest of spring, summer, and early autumn—did not match the budgetary totals agreed to in the second budget resolution. Reconciliation directed appropriate committees to report additional savings or revenues to meet the fiscal requirements of the second resolution. Congress informally abandoned the second resolution in the early 1980s when it became clear that the first was the fundamental vehicle of congressional budgeting. This informal change was later embodied in law (now April 15 for passage of the budget resolution) when Congress passed its most significant revision of the 1974 act—the Balanced Budget and Emergency Deficit Reduction Act of 1985 (or Gramm-Rudman-Hollings, after the measure's sponsors). Detailed discussion of Gramm-Rudman-Hollings will follow.

Because of its importance to congressional policy making, the budget resolution is considered in the House and Senate under special procedures that expedite its consideration. The 1974 act changed traditional Senate procedures in two fundamental ways. First, budget resolutions carry a fifty-hour statutory debate limitation, which means that they cannot be filibustered to death. Second, the 1974 act imposes a germaneness (somewhat akin to a relevancy) requirement on amendments to budget resolutions. The Senate, unlike the House, has no general germaneness rule.

The budget resolution is not submitted to the president. It is a concurrent resolution. Hence, it cannot be vetoed; nor does it carry legal effect. Presidents, of course, may veto tax or appropriations bills that follow the guidelines established in the budget resolutions.

To assemble the resolution, the budget panels employ several sources: annual February 25 reports from the other standing committees outlining each panel's fiscal plans for programs under its jurisdiction; the president's annual budget; informal consultations with members and staff; CBO analyses; and assessments of what the national interest and the economy require.

When the House and Senate pass budget resolutions that contain different aggregate and functional totals, which is normal practice, the disagreements usually have to be resolved by a conference committee. The conferees prepare a report that provides a "bank account" for the various House and Senate committees. This account distributes the total agreed-upon spending for the year among twenty-one functional categories.

This allocation procedure, called a "budget crosswalk," involves two steps. First, section 302 of the budget act requires the conference report to subdivide the congressionally agreed-upon spending levels for all twenty-one functional categories among the legislative committees having jurisdiction over these categories.

In the second step in the crosswalk, the committees subdivide their spending allocations among the appropriate subcommittees or programs. As explained by a member of the House Appropriations Committee:

> Under the Budget Act we are assigned a lump sum of funds to be appropriated by the Appropriations Committee. Under section 302 we in the Appropriations Committee allocate that [lump sum] among our subcommittees, and our subcommittees have been scrupulous in staying within those section 302 limits.[25]

The crosswalk procedure is necessary because Congress chooses to employ functional category designations developed by the Office of Management and Budget (OMB). These designations do not correspond exactly to many House and Senate committees, with their overlapping jurisdictional mandates.

Until Congress adopts its budget resolution for a fiscal year, it may not take up any spending, revenue, entitlement, or debt legislation affecting that year unless this prohibition is waived by the House and the Senate. The 1974 act also specified reporting deadlines for authorization measures to prevent delays in considering appropriations bills. Congress, as noted earlier, finds it difficult to meet such deadlines.

Reconciliation

Reconciliation is a two-step process designed to bring existing law into conformity with current budget plans. In practice, reconciliation is used to reduce spending, primarily through entitlement savings, and to increase revenues. It does not address funding that is established in annual appropriations bills.

Although it was intended to be employed at the end of Congress's budget cycle, the two-step reconciliation procedure has been moved since 1980 to the front of the cycle, where it has proved to be an effective device for making budgetary savings. "The first budget resolution has been the place where the important decisions are made," stated Alice Rivlin, the first CBO director, "and reconciling the parts with the whole has been moved into the first resolution."[26]

The first step in reconciliation calls for congressional approval of a budget resolution that instructs House and Senate committees to propose cuts in spending (and/or increases in revenue) on programs and agency operations by a certain date. The panels' recommended budget savings, which are supposed to meet or exceed the amounts designated for each committee in the resolution, are transmitted to the respective House and Senate Budget committees.

The second step involves the packaging of the recommendations into an omnibus reconciliation bill, followed by floor action in each chamber. The Budget committees cannot make substantive changes in the savings proposals received from each instructed committee.

In 1981 President Ronald Reagan persuaded Congress to employ reconciliation to achieve massive cuts in domestic programs (totaling about $130 billion over three years). Never before had reconciliation been employed on such a grand scale. The entire two-step process was put on a "fast track" that short-circuited regular legislative procedures. A highly charged atmosphere produced a legislative result, wrote Senate Majority Leader Baker, "that would have been impossible to achieve if each committee had reported an individual bill on subject matter solely within its jurisdiction."[27] In short, reconciliation forced nearly all House and Senate committees to make unwanted cuts in programs under their jurisdiction.

After enactment of the 1981 reconciliation bill, many members wondered whether Congress could reconcile itself ever again to such a drastic exercise. Rep. Richard W. Bolling, D-Mo., who at the time was the chairman of the Rules Committee, charged that exploitation of the reconciliation process "enabled the Executive to unilaterally impose its will in near totality on Congress."[28] The irony was that Congress's budget process, designed in 1974 to advance and reassert the legislative branch's power of the purse, was captured by the White House in 1981 and used to achieve President Reagan's objectives. Nonetheless, reconciliation's proven effectiveness in compelling fiscal retrenchment has made it a vital and regular part of the budget process.

Controls on Backdoors and Impoundments

The 1974 act tightened control over some types of backdoor financing methods, although the changes applied only to new backdoor schemes, not to any in effect at the time the 1974 measure was enacted. Legislation providing new contract or borrowing authority must indicate that the authority becomes effective only to the extent provided in appropriations acts. Members can raise points of order against such legislation, including amendments and conference reports, to enforce this requirement.

New entitlements are also subject to procedural constraints. Entitlement measures that are reported in excess of a committee's crosswalk allocation must be referred to the House and Senate Appropriations committees. These panels have the authority to recommend modifications of the proposed entitlements.

Title X of the 1974 act permits Congress to review executive impoundments of appropriated funds. Under the act, impoundments are divided into two categories—deferrals (a temporary delay in the expenditure of funds) and rescissions (the permanent cancellation of budget authority)—and considered under separate procedures. Presidents are obligated to inform Congress of their proposed deferrals and rescissions in special messages to Congress that explain why they are making those decisions. The General Accounting Office (GAO), a legislative support agency of Congress, is authorized to review these messages to insure that impoundments are not misclassified and to challenge misclassifications in federal court.

The rescission procedure, according to House Appropriations Chairman Jamie Whitten, D-Miss. (who helped write the 1974 act), has largely "worked as intended." [29] When presidents send rescission messages to Congress, a forty-five-day, continuous-session clock starts ticking. Unless *both* the House and Senate enact rescission legislation during this legislative time period, the president must spend the funds appropriated by Congress.

The deferral procedure originally provided that *either* chamber could overturn delays in spending of any length up to one year by passing a resolution of disapproval. This one-house veto, however, was declared unconstitutional by the Supreme Court in 1983 in *Immigration and Naturalization Service v. Chadha* (see Chapter 10). Now the question became whether the president had unilateral authority to defer or whether the deferral authority of the 1974 act was itself invalid because Congress would not have granted such authority to the president without the check of the one-house veto. In the wake of legislative-executive struggles over the deferral process, a federal court in 1987 *(City of New Haven v. United States)* declared the deferral procedure invalid. Two legal scholars noted: "While Congress has lost its power to veto deferrals . . . the president no longer has any general statutory authority for policy deferrals. Judicial precedent would seem to allow him little maneuvering room to find impoundment authority in general appropriation laws.[30]

The court distinguished between policy deferrals (which negate Congress's will) and programmatic deferrals (which achieve efficiency and budgetary savings). In rejecting the former, the court supported the latter. As a result of *City of New Haven v. United States,* the president is limited to recommending deferrals only for routine matters. The budget deferral process, in brief, remains an arena of struggle between the branches. Unless it is revised, Congress will remain able to overturn deferrals by passing a law, which the president may veto.

EVOLUTION OF THE BUDGET PROCESS

Change is ever present in congressional procedures and politics. This is certainly the case with the congressional budget process. The 1974 act even contains an "elastic clause" that permits Congress to include in its budget resolution "any other procedure which is considered appropriate to carry out the purposes of this Act." Dropping the requirement for a second budget resolution, moving reconciliation into the first budget resolution, and expanding the scope of the budget resolution to include such matters as federal credit activities are examples of how the 1974 act was changed informally in some fundamental ways. In the mid-1980s, however, Congress enacted significant statutory changes to its budget process. These changes emerged from a new political climate: the politics of deficit reduction.

When Ronald Reagan began his tenure as president in 1981, his principal objectives were threefold: slash domestic spending, increase defense expenditures, and cut taxes. Congress, with the Senate (at that point in GOP hands) spearheading the effort, generally went along with the Reagan initiatives. Major problems soon arose, however. The revenue losses caused by the tax cuts, combined with rising defense spending and insufficient funding reductions in other areas, soon produced annual budget deficits in the $200 billion range. Never before had the nation seen such huge deficits during peacetime and during an economic expansion (following the 1982 recession).

Federal outlays were also being driven upward by entitlements. Not surprisingly, in just six years the total national debt more than doubled from about $1 trillion to over $2 trillion (Table 3-3). "Borrow and spend" or "debt and consumption" were the catchwords of this period. Citizens decried deficit financing, but objected to tax increases or cuts in favorite programs. "Congress wants to control the budget, but it also wants to meet people's demands for spending," remarked Rep. Lee H. Hamilton, D-Ind. "This is the dilemma." [31]

Concern with growing deficits mounted, but there was no consensus between the branches on how to address the problem. Many Democrats and Republicans in Congress wanted no further cuts in domestic programs, favored defense reductions, and argued for more revenues. President Reagan vigorously opposed defense cuts and tax hikes ("over my dead body," he said) and insisted on further domestic cuts. Congress and the President each favored spending, but for different priorities. "Heck, the Republicans and Democrats all want a trillion dollar budget," said Senator Hollings, "it's just a matter of where to squeeze the sack" to come up with budgetary savings.[32] In short, sharp disputes over spending priorities between the branches, chambers, and parties, plus intraparty disagreements, led to little progress in reducing the budgetary deficit. Legislative-executive deadlock characterized much of the fiscal politics of this period.

It was this political and economic environment that prompted passage in late 1985 of the Gramm-Rudman-Hollings (GRH) deficit-reduction plan (the Balanced Budget and Emergency Deficit Control Act). Introduced on the Senate floor without any prior committee hearings or floor debate as an amendment to a "must pass" bill raising

TABLE 3-3 Total Public Debt

Fiscal Year	*Gross Federal Debt*
1970	$ 382.6 billion
1975	544.1
1980	914.3
1981	1,003.9
1982	1,146.9
1983	1,381.8
1984	1,576.7
1985	1,827.4
1986	2,130.0
1987	2,355.2
1988	2,581.5

Source: Office of Management and Budget, Historical Tables, Fiscal Year 1988.

the national debt ceiling, the amendment became law in less than three months. By comparison, the 1974 act took nearly two years to become law. GRH was passed to force a specific objective: deficit reduction.

GRH established a statutory pathway to "zero out" deficits and have a balanced federal budget after six years, by 1991. It mandated that a set amount—$36 billion—must be chopped yearly from the allowable deficit ceilings established in GRH. For instance, the allowable deficit for fiscal 1987 was $144 billion, for fiscal 1988 was $108 billion, and so on down to the zero deficit of fiscal 1991. To ensure that Congress and the president met the successive installment payments on the deficit, GRH included an automatic deficit reduction mechanism called "sequestration."

Sequestration is the core concept of GRH. Its objective was to change the political dynamics between the branches. If there is no legislative-executive success in meeting the deficit target, then the President must make across-the-board spending cuts (sequestration), evenly divided between domestic and defense programs, to achieve the prescribed GRH target. No further action is required of Congress. In effect, inaction produces action. "Without an automatic spending cut, you don't guarantee an outcome," noted Representative Gephardt. "And that's what [GRH] is all about, guaranteeing an outcome." [33]

To be sure, the operative assumption of those who advocated the sequestration mechanism was that it would never be used. As Senate Budget Chairman Lawton Chiles, D-Fla., explained: "The whole idea behind sequester was to force Congress and the President to work together and find a responsible way to reduce the Federal deficit. Sequester was intended to be the price we would have to pay for failure."[34] The threat of sequestration loomed over both branches as a contrived crisis to force concessions from each: consideration of more revenues and a defense slowdown from the president's side in exchange for deeper cuts in domestic social programs from Congress. Unless a fiscal accord was reached between the branches, sequestration would indiscriminately cut defense and domestic programs.

GRH exempted nearly 70 percent of federal spending from the sequestration procedure. This meant that the remaining 30 percent of defense and domestic spending would bear the brunt of deficit reduction. To prevent the defense sector from being cut, the theory went, the president would support revenue increases. GRH contained provisions for its suspension in the event of war or economic recession; it also provided a $10 billion "fudge factor" for technical and economic errors in estimating the deficit.

Under GRH, the sequester "trigger" would be pulled by the comptroller general of the GAO. Based on a joint report he received from CBO and OMB, the comptroller general was authorized to draft his own report making the necessary cuts if Congress failed to meet the annual deficit target. The president was required to issue the GAO report under his own name without change.

In passing GRH, Congress was unwilling to entrust the triggering responsibility to anyone in the executive branch. So it gave that responsibility to the GAO, an entity known for its independence. However, the constitutionality of this provision was suspect from the start; as a result, GRH contained a fallback procedure—a special joint budget committee would issue a joint resolution making the necessary cuts—if the comptroller's role was declared unconstitutional.

On July 7, 1986, the Supreme Court ruled in *Bowsher v. Synar* that the automatic sequestration process *was* unconstitutional. The reason: it violated the Constitution's separation of powers. "The structure of the Constitution," wrote the chief justice, "does not permit Congress to execute the laws; it follows that Congress cannot grant to an officer [the Comptroller General] under its control what it does not possess." Because an $11.7 billion sequestration order had already taken effect in March 1986, Congress employed its fallback procedure to certify those cuts.

Quickly, Congress's attention focused on ways to fix GRH's constitutional defect. Many legislators, to be sure, argued against fixing GRH on the ground that Congress should make the hard choices in determining program reduction. A majority in both chambers, however, supported restoration of the automatic trigger as the only way in the face of rising deficits to force the president to negotiate with Congress in producing acceptable deficit reduction plans. "For 6 years, the Congress and the President have been at odds on how to reduce the deficit without crippling America's future," stated Senate Democratic Leader Byrd. "Those differences, and the resulting inaction, have been at the root of this country's major domestic problem—the budget deficit."[35] The threat of automatic budget cuts, in short, was designed to produce legislative-executive agreement on deficit-cutting plans; otherwise sequestration took effect automatically.

In September 1987, Congress passed GRH II. Its major objectives were twofold: restore automatic cuts through a constitutional sequestration procedure (GRH II directed an executive agency, the OMB, to issue the sequestration report that triggered the across-the-board cuts) and delay for two years—from 1991 to 1993—the timetable for eliminating the deficit (see Table 3-4). These twin objectives facilitated enactment of GRH II, for many members would not vote for one without the other.

Despite the specter of sequestration, Congress and the president remained at loggerheads in the aftermath of GRH II. President Reagan renewed his threat to veto any tax increases. Congress objected to further cuts in domestic discretionary programs. There was little incentive in either branch to cut defense after two years of little real growth. And neither branch wanted to address cuts in entitlement programs.

What finally forced the long-awaited Congress-White House fiscal summit was a calamitous outside event, the October 19, 1987, stock market crash. An economic crisis changed the political climate. "The crash did what Gramm-Rudman was supposed to do but never did, force everyone to negotiate," remarked Rep. Barney Frank, D-Mass.[36]

Negotiators from the House and Senate soon met in a budget summit with President Reagan's top aides. After intense and difficult negotiations, these bipartisan leaders finally agreed on November 20 to a package of reductions that totaled $76 billion over two years. If enacted by Congress and signed into law by the president, the summit agreement would obviate the $23 billion in sequestration cuts that had already taken effect automatically under GRH II's timetable (see Table 3-5). Combining tax increases and spending cuts, the summit plan was designed to bolster confidence in world financial markets and demonstrate that Congress and the president could work together to reduce the deficit.

Despite opposition to the summit agreement, it was implemented in two massive bills just a few days before Christmas. Tax increases and spending reductions were achieved in reconciliation legislation along with separate enactment of additional spending cuts in the continuing resolution. As House Majority Leader Foley put it: "For the first time in recent years, an unprecedented, and unparalleled budget agreement was reached by the two political parties, both bodies of the Congress, and the President and his administration even though the parties to the agree-

TABLE 3-4 Taming the Deficit

	Actual deficit	*Original Gramm-Rudman target*	*Revised Gramm-Rudman target*
1981	$ 74		
1982	120		
1983	208		
1984	186		
1985	222		
1986	237	$180	
1987	157[a]	144[b]	
1988	183[a]	108	$144[b]
1989		72	136[b]
1990		36	100
1991		0	64
1992		0	28
1993		0	0

[a] Congressional Budget Office's estimate, based on policies now in effect.
[b] For 1988 and 1989, the deficit could be higher than the targets shown. For these two years, the reductions are limited to $23 billion and $38 billion, respectively, even if that is insufficient to reach the targets. In future years, the new Gramm-Rudman bill requires deficit reductions sufficient to reach the targets.

Source: Los Angeles Times, Sept. 24, 1987, sec. 1, 26.

ment were deeply divided over budget priorities."[37] The intense lobbying effort by party leaders and White House officials, combined with members' desire to go home for Christmas, led to successful enactment of the two budget measures.

GRH put Congress on a glide path toward deficit reduction, and compelled the legislative and executive branches to struggle with fundamental questions: how much to spend on defense, how much to spend on domestic programs, and how and where to get revenues. These issues will shape political debate for the foreseeable future as Congress and the president strive to maintain a healthy economy amid national and international economic uncertainty.

ASSESSMENT AND OUTLOOK

The 1974 act worked reasonably well until the 1980s. Its procedures took root and the three-step process—adoption of the budget resolution followed by authorization and then appropriations—was followed, albeit with modifications and difficulties. Members did not always agree with the results of the process; they complained about delays, missed

TABLE 3-5 Sequestration Timetable, 1988-1993

Date	*Action*
August 15	Initial OMB/CBO snapshot.
August 25	OMB issues its initial sequestration report to the president and Congress.
Within fifteen days after the initial order is issued	President transmits to Congress a detailed message regarding the order.
October 1	Fiscal year begins and initial order becomes effective.
October 15	OMB issues its revised sequestration report to the president and Congress.
October 15	President issues final sequestration order, which becomes effective immediately.
Within ten days of revised OMB report	Majority leaders of each house may introduce a joint resolution modifying the final sequestration order.

deadlines, partisanship, and fiscal impasses. Still, the 1974 act provided members and committees with better information about the financial implications of their policy decisions and made them much less dependent on the White House and OMB for financial data and advice. Congress now had the fiscal tools to challenge and compete with the executive branch.

The fiscal landscape changed in the 1980s when "sharing budgetary pain" replaced "sharing budgetary gain" as the legislative imperative. As one House member explained:

> The financial stringency heightens the necessity to view these issues in [a broad] framework because it just isn't as easy as it once was to say, "Ah-ha, there's a problem, let's put some more money into it." Now the question is, "Ah-ha, there's a problem, now how can we redeploy the funds that are available to try to deal fairly with all these groups that are involved?" [38]

This redeployment task is made arduous not only by the constraints of large deficits but by shifts in the composition of the budget itself (Figure 3-1).

Four general items—defense, entitlements, discretionary domestic, and interest on the national debt—comprise all federal spending. Entitlements are politically difficult to cut (the elderly, for example, support well-organized lobbying groups); interest on the national debt must be paid to avoid financial chaos and default; and an adequate

FIGURE 3-1 Changing Composition of the Budget

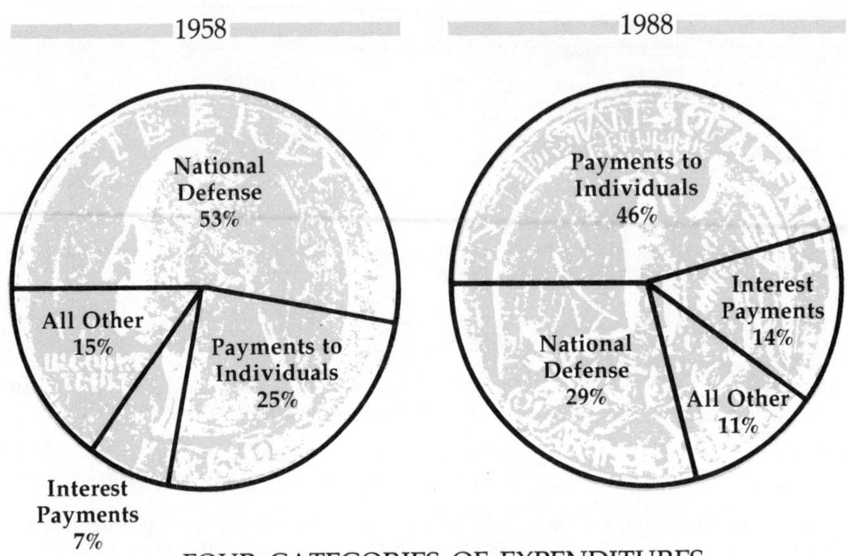

FOUR CATEGORIES OF EXPENDITURES

As a share of total federal spending
1987 figures are projected; 1988 figures are proposed

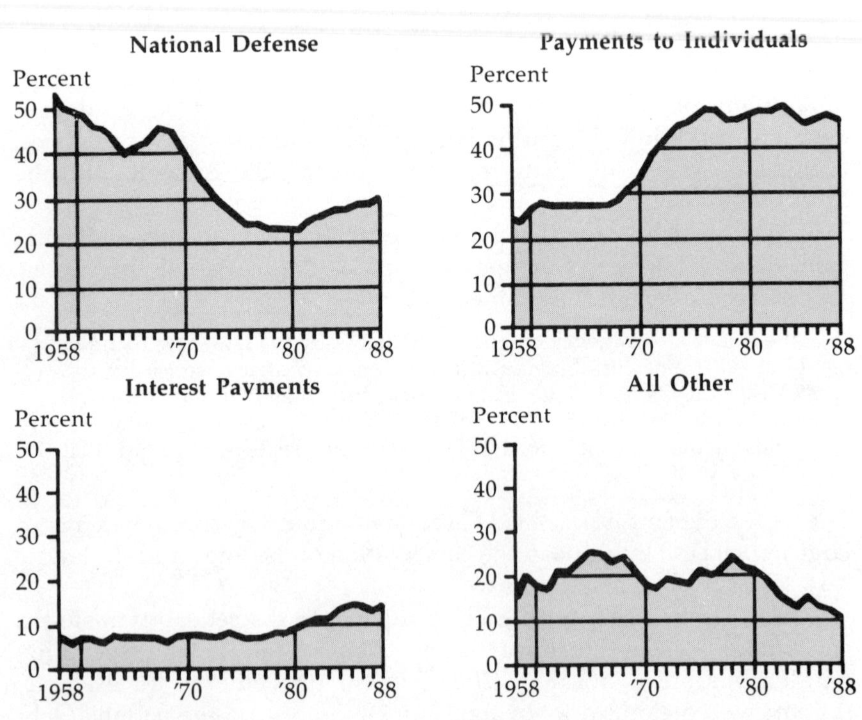

Source: Los Angeles Times, Jan. 6, 1987, sec. 1, 11.

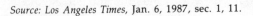

defense (how much defense is debatable, of course) is essential to national security. Congress's ability to maneuver in cutting the deficit is severely circumscribed when so much federal spending is fenced off from review for political and policy reasons.

In an era of cutback budgeting, Congress and the White House struggled to define the nation's priorities. The struggling process produced significant developments—GRH, government by continuing resolution, and new roles for committees—that merit review.

Gramm-Rudman-Hollings

As a blueprint for deficit reduction, GRH has had mixed results. Its advocates claim that spending is lower than it would have been without the law. While that claim is difficult to prove, there seems little question that the fiscal discipline of GRH has at least slowed the rate of growth of federal spending. "Congress means they're spending less than they would have spent when it talks of budget cuts," remarked Senator Gramm, one of the principal sponsors of the deficit reduction law.[39]

The procedures of GRH, especially its "deficit neutrality" requirement, have had a noticeable impact on lawmaking. Deficit neutrality means that when legislators propose spending more in one area they have to cut somewhere else or find new revenues to offset the proposed increase. Costly measures or amendments, in brief, need offsets to make them deficit neutral or GRH's requirements must be waived.

For instance, Senator Weicker offered an amendment to provide an additional $600 million for energy assistance to low-income families unable to heat their homes in winter or cool them in summer. The Senate Budget chairman raised a point of order against the amendment, because under GRH it is not in order for an Appropriations subcommittee to exceed its budgetary allocation. Senator Weicker's amendment would push the pending appropriations bill over the Labor-HHS Subcommittee's allocation; each of the thirteen Appropriations subcommittees must adhere to its fiscal allotment under GRH.

To permit consideration of his amendment, Senator Weicker offered a motion to waive this feature of GRH. By design, such waivers are not easy to obtain. They require a supermajority of sixty votes. Senator Weicker's waiver motion failed by a 47-50 vote, and his amendment was ruled out of order by the presiding officer.[40] GRH is filled with a variety of comparable points of order to enforce its requirements.

There are, in some estimations, two major weaknesses in GRH. First, the act exempts most of the budget from sequestration. While defense and many domestic programs are subject to automatic cuts, popular entitlement programs are exempt from reduction. Yet payments "to individuals constituted more than forty cents of every dollar of federal expenditure in 1986—compared to less than thirty cents of every federal dollar spent on national defense."[41] Deficit reduction is difficult to achieve when so much of the budget is excluded from cutbacks.

Second, GRH is inextricably linked to economic forecasts. Whether sequestration is triggered depends on economic projections made months in advance of the annual October trigger date. Given volatile economic conditions and faulty economic assumptions about inflation, employment, or interest rates, GRH's deficit targets may never be fully realized. The Gramm-Rudman "scheme does not work to reduce deficits," declared Sen. James Exon, D-Neb., "it works to reduce deficit projections."[42] With rosy economic scenarios, fiscal gimmicks, and unrealistic revenue proposals (such as selling the Postal Service or the National Institutes of Health to the private sector, so-called privatization), GRH's deficit levels can be met on paper with "blue smoke and mirrors" while the actual deficit continues to grow far beyond expectations.

In sum, GRH's lasting effect on Capitol Hill may be to change the fiscal dialogue. With spending austerity looming for years to come, a test that might be utilized to assess whether programs should be continued or terminated, suggests Senator Domenici is, "If the program didn't already exist, would we spend the money to start it?"[43] With huge deficits putting a damper on new program initiatives, legislators are exploring that question and considering policy innovations that neither cost much nor add more bureaucrats to the government.

Government by Continuing Resolution

Whenever Congress cannot complete action on one or more of the thirteen regular appropriations bills by the start of the fiscal year, it provides temporary emergency funding for the affected federal agencies through a continuing resolution (a joint resolution). Traditionally, continuing resolutions were employed to keep a few government agencies in operation for short periods, typically one to three months. Continuing resolutions today are major policy-making instruments of massive size and scope. They authorize *and* appropriate money each year for much of the federal government and make national policy in areas as diverse as defense, foreign policy, and public works. The surge in the use of continuing resolutions is attributed in part to Congress's inability to meet the budgetary timetable, the strife engendered by rising deficits, and also to sharp legislative-executive and bicameral conflicts over budget priorities.

"Government by continuing resolution" is a 1980s development that is unique in congressional history. In 1986 and 1987, for example, Congress packaged all thirteen regular appropriations bills into continuing resolutions, making them the largest spending measures in Congress's history. These "megabills," widely lambasted as a perversion of the lawmaking process by many Democrats and Republicans, are employed because of advantages associated with their use. At least five merit some mention.

One advantage is the political leverage omnibus measures give Congress over the president. Bundling all appropriations bills into a continuing resolution presents the president with a "take it or leave it" dilemma. He can veto a continuing resolution, but that action will shut down the government. Omnibus measures, in brief, have the effect of undercutting the potency of the president's veto power. "Since I, as president, do not have a line-item veto," said Ronald Reagan, "I had to ignore the many objectionable features of the omnibus appropriations legislation and sign it to avoid a Federal funding crisis."[44]

Megabills also strengthen the influence of the legislators who put these packages together—members of the key committees and party leaders. In an era of heightened decentralization in Congress, continuing resolutions have the indirect effect of recentralizing authority in fewer hands. Conferees on the continuing resolution "are beginning to be known as 'super Congresspeople,'" exclaimed Rep. Dan Glickman, D-Kan.[45] Dissatisfaction with the continuing resolution process is mounting on Capitol Hill, and changes in the process are likely to occur before the next decade.

A third advantage of continuing resolutions is the "last train out of the station" attitude. Members understand that these measures must be passed before Congress can adjourn. Hence they are attractive vehicles for unrelated policy "riders." These extraneous issues, which would not pass if considered separately on the floor, are sometimes buried deep in the interstices of these massive bills and pass unnoticed during the hectic days or hours before adjournment.

Continuing resolutions also reflect a form of "hostage politics" on Capitol Hill. Congress may take the entire budget hostage to compel White House compromises on national priorities. Deadline pressures will then force some type of legislative-executive resolution. Members and committees, too, sometimes prefer to hold all fiscal action to the end so they can review spending issues in their entirety and ensure that cuts are equitably distributed among various programs. As Bill Green, R-N.Y., a senior member of House Appropriations, explained:

> None of us wanted to give up what we were interested in . . . unless we saw that everyone else was doing the same. The only way we could really see that . . . that would happen was to have this kind of [continuing resolution] conference at the end of the Congress where we could see that everyone was giving up the same amount that we were giving up.[46]

Finally, omnibus money bills minimize the unfavorable political consequences often associated with cutting programs backed by powerful groups. Omnibus bills, explained Rep. Leon E. Panetta, D-Calif., can be used as a way "to avoid hard votes that Members would have to account for at election time, as a way to avoid angering special-interest groups that use votes [to decide] contributions to campaigns. . . ."[47] Packages provide political cover to members. They enable legislators to tell constituent groups whose programs are being cut that the omnibus measure was considered under procedures that permitted only an up-or-down vote and that amendments to any part could undermine the integrity of the whole bill.

New Roles for Committees

"There's been a tremendous change in the way things are supposed to operate," said Representative Panetta.[48] Among the changes is a breakdown in the authorization process. The contemporary climate of fiscal austerity means that authorizing panels infrequently report new programs or policies. Instead, their primary focus is often on protecting favorite programs from drastic spending cuts. As one House member stated: "It's no fun to be an authorization committee chairman anymore. They can't get new programs passed. The best they can do is preserve their most beloved programs at some level that makes sense."[49]

Squeezed between the budget resolution and appropriations stages, there is little time left for debating the recommendations of the authorization committees. As a result, these panels have lost influence to the Appropriations and Budget committees. In recognition of their waning authority, these panels are moving away from annual to multiyear authorizations as one means to promote stability in the programs they oversee and to reduce Congress's annual workload. Authorizers are also emphasizing new objectives. "Rather than solely proposing programs to meet social needs, as they did when money was plentiful, they are now also proposing ways to save money in existing programs or to create new ones that don't cost anything."[50]

The difficulty of legislating has made appropriations bills—such as continuing resolutions—and the reconciliation process attractive policy-making vehicles. Reconciliation, intended to be used by the authorizing panels to reduce spending as directed by the budget resolution, has been a primary procedure for reauthorizing existing programs and initiating new ones. Reconciliation bills are considered in both bodies under expedited procedures that limit debate and inhibit opportunities for reviewing these policy proposals on the floor. As Rep. Trent Lott, R-Miss., noted:

> Some committees see [the reconciliation bill] as a convenient vehicle for attaching their favorite reauthorization bills and even some new goodies. The bill is not subject to the same scrutiny and amendment as bills brought up individually. These tend to be relatively closed rules, and relatively veto-proof. So the temptation is there to catch a free ride.[51]

Concern about the addition of extraneous policy issues to reconciliation measures prompted the Senate in 1985 to change its rules to permit points of order to be raised against extraneous matter contained in the reconciliation bill, floor amendments, or the reconciliation conference report. This rule can be waived, but it requires a three-fifths majority to set it aside.

Still another major change involves the Appropriations committees. Long regarded as protectors of the purse, they are now "claimants whose striving for higher spending is to be policed by budget controls."[52] These panels spend money in accordance with the dictates of the budget resolution. Appropriations subcommittees even battle now over how their overall budget allocation will be divided into thirteen parts. Moreover, the Appropriations committees face greater challenges from rank-and-file members. Given members' reluctance to cut entitlements or increase taxes, they focus their deficit-reduction efforts on appropriations bills. "Many younger members," one study noted, "will no longer settle for what comes out of the money committees, or bow to an establishment that excludes them from fiscal-policy decisions."[53]

Finally, legislative budgetary procedures are increasingly being criticized as too complex and confusing to members and citizens alike, as well as too time consuming. Congress annually debates endless budget issues to the exclusion of nearly everything else. Numerous proposals for change have been made over the years to simplify procedures and eliminate at least one of the budget-making stages. Whether fiscal impasses are the result of ineffective procedures or policy disagreements, or some mix of the two, is the question. "Budget reform," said one House member, "is an attempt to correct a problem which is basically caused by policy disagreements, not process weaknesses."[54] How, when, or whether Congress can establish a consensus to "reform" its budget process is uncertain.

SUMMARY

Legislative changes are notable for producing mixed results and unexpected consequences. The budget process has been no exception to these conditions. Its procedures, and those applicable generally to congressional policy making, can produce whatever can attract a majority or, in some cases, an extraordinary majority. Legislative procedures, in short, define the context in which policies are made and influence the choice of strategies to advance or frustrate legislation, including budget resolutions.

Chapter 4 turns to the initial steps of the legislative process: the introduction and referral of bills to House and Senate committees and committee action on legislation. The executive branch and pressure groups usually are given most of the credit for initiating ideas that Congress eventually formulates and passes in legislative form. But Congress also initiates numerous proposals. And ideas for legislation frequently are discussed in academic circles, private associations, federal advisory committees, national commissions, citizens' groups, professional societies, and by knowledgeable individuals.

In essence, legislation "is an aggregate, not a simple production," Woodrow Wilson once wrote. "It is impossible to tell how many persons, opinions and influences have entered into its composition."[55]

NOTES

1. Jonathan Rauch, "Congress, Worried about Huge Budget Deficits, Eyes an UNCOLA Strategy," *National Journal,* Jan. 19, 1985, 153.
2. *Congressional Control of Expenditures,* House Committee on the Budget, January 1977, 6. The study was prepared by Allen Schick.
3. *Congressional Record,* daily ed., April 9, 1987, S4919.
4. John William Ellwood, ed., *Reductions in U.S. Domestic Spending* (New Brunswick, N.J.: Transaction Books, 1982), 21.
5. *Congressional Record,* daily ed., Nov. 2, 1987, E4279.
6. Absent an authorization law, the Appropriations committees typically base their financial recommendations on the president's budget requests.
7. Roy T. Meyers, "Biennial Budgeting," Staff Working Paper, Congressional Budget Office, November 1987, 42.
8. Everett Somerville Brown, ed., *William Plumer's Memorandum of Proceedings in the United States Senate, 1803-1807* (New York: Macmillan, 1923), 490.
9. Robert Luce, *Legislative Problems* (Boston: Houghton Mifflin, 1935), 425-426.
10. Louis Fisher, "The Authorization-Appropriation Process in Congress: Formal Rules and Informal Practices," *Catholic University Law Review* (Fall 1979): 53.
11. Ibid., 74-75. The House considered the issue on June 17, 1977, and the Senate on June 29, 1977. See Roger H. Davidson, "Procedures and Politics in Congress," in *The Abortion Dispute and the American System,* ed. Gilbert Y. Steiner (Washington, D.C.: Brookings Institution, 1982), 30-46.
12. *Congressional Record,* daily ed., Nov. 4, 1987, S15754.
13. *Congressional Record,* daily ed., Jan. 3, 1983, H5-H22.
14. Joseph A. Davis and Susan Smith, "EPA Funding Raised: $54.4 Billion HUD Bill Passed after Test of New Rider Rule," *Congressional Quarterly Weekly Report,* June 4, 1983, 1125. Ironically, in the wake of the June 1983 Supreme

Court decision declaring legislative vetoes unconstitutional, some representatives wanted to again revise House rules to allow use of the old procedure permitting any member to offer limitation riders on appropriations bills. See *Congressional Record*, daily ed., June 28, 1983, H4504.

15. Authorizations and appropriations come in several forms: annual, multiyear, and permanent. For example, permanent authorizations "last for an indefinite period of time, until altered or terminated by Congress; multiyear authorizations last for a specified period of time, usually two to five years; and annual authorizations last for one year and must be renewed each year if the particular program is to be continued." However, "an authorization could lapse and the program continue through an unauthorized appropriation." See Michael D. Margeson, "The Use of Annual Authorizations, 94th-96th Congresses," Paper prepared by the Congressional Budget Office, March 25, 1982, 2. Today, appropriations seldom are approved for other than on an annual basis.
16. *Congressional Record*, daily ed., May 15, 1987, S6546.
17. Lawrence C. Dodd and Richard L. Schott, *Congress and the Administrative State* (New York: John Wiley & Sons, 1979), 236.
18. Allen Schick, *Congress and Money* (Washington, D.C.: Urban Institute, 1980), 175.
19. James Fallows, "Entitlements," *Atlantic*, November 1982, 52.
20. "Federal Spending," the President's Address on Nationwide Radio from Camp David, Oct. 7, 1972, *Weekly Compilation of Presidential Documents*, vol. 8, no. 41, 1497-1499.
21. *Congressional Record*, 93d Cong., 1st sess., Feb. 8, 1973, 4015.
22. Schick, *Congress and Money*, 46.
23. Ibid., 59.
24. *Congressional Budget Office Oversight*, Hearing before the Senate Committee on the Budget, 97th Cong., 2d sess., Feb. 5, 1982, 1.
25. *Congressional Record*, daily ed., July 30, 1981, H5403. The budget act requires the House and Senate Appropriations committees to divide the lump sum among its subcommittees; the other panels do it by custom.
26. *Washington Post*, July 10, 1983, G3.
27. Howard H. Baker, Jr., "Essay, An Introduction to the Politics of Reconciliation," *Harvard Journal on Legislation* (Winter 1983): 2.
28. *Review of the Congressional Budget and Impoundment Control Act of 1974*, Hearings before the Senate Committee on Governmental Affairs, 97th Cong., 1st sess. (Washington, D.C.: Government Printing Office, 1982), 8. Also see John William Ellwood, "Congress Cuts the Budget: The Omnibus Reconciliation Act of 1981," *Public Budgeting and Finance* (Spring 1982): 50-64; Allen Schick, *Reconciliation and the Congressional Budget Process* (Washington, D.C.: American Enterprise Institute for Public Policy Research, 1982); Robert A. Keith, "Budget Reconciliation in 1981," *Public Budgeting and Finance* (Winter 1981): 37-47; Steven S. Smith, "Budget Battles of 1981: The Role of the Majority Party Leadership," in *American Politics and Public Policy*, ed. Allan P. Sindler (Washington, D.C.: CQ Press, 1982), 43-78; and Lance T. LeLoup, "After the Blitz: Reagan and the U.S. Congressional Budget Process," *Legislative Studies Quarterly* (August 1982): 321-339.
29. *The Deferral Process after Chadha*, Hearing before the House Committee on Rules, April 9, 1986, 6.
30. Richard Ehlke and Morton Rosenberg, "Lines Blurred Again in Continuing Debate over Spending Power," *Legal Times*, June 8, 1987, 17. See Jonathan Rauch, "Power of the Purse," *National Journal*, May 24, 1986, 1259-1261;

and Elizabeth Wehr, "Court Rejects Administration Deferral Authority," *Congressional Quarterly Weekly Report*, Jan. 24, 1987, 145-147.

31. *Congressional Record*, daily ed., Oct. 26, 1987, E5121.
32. *Washington Post*, May 1, 1987, A3.
33. *New York Times*, Oct. 16, 1985, A22.
34. *Congressional Record*, daily ed., Oct. 14, 1987, S14257. See, for example, Harry S. Havens, "Gramm-Rudman-Hollings: Origins and Implementation," *Public Budgeting and Finance* (Autumn 1986): 4-24; and Lance T. LeLoup, Barbara Luck Graham, and Stacey Barwick, "Deficit Politics and Constitutional Government: The Impact of Gramm-Rudman-Hollings," *Public Budgeting and Finance* (Spring 1987): 83-103.
35. *Congressional Record*, daily ed., Dec. 10, 1987, S17603.
36. *Christian Science Monitor*, Oct. 30, 1987, 6.
37. *Congressional Record*, daily ed., Dec. 21, 1987, H11984.
38. Jeffrey Finn, "Gradison Challenges Trustees to Delve Deeper into Critical Issues," *Trustee*, July 1987, 12.
39. *Washington Post*, Jan. 4, 1988, A5.
40. *Congressional Record*, daily ed., Oct. 14, 1987, S14229-S14239.
41. R. Kent Weaver, "Social Policy in the Reagan Era," in B. B. Kymlicka and Jean V. Matthews, eds., *The Reagan Revolution?* (Chicago: Dorsey Press, 1988), 146.
42. *Congressional Record*, daily ed., April 10, 1987, S5169.
43. Jonathan Rauch, "The Fiscal Ice Age," *National Journal*, Jan. 10, 1987, 59.
44. Budget of the United States Government, Fiscal Year 1988, Executive Office of the President, Office of Management and Budget, Jan. 5 1987, M-13.
45. *Congressional Record*, daily ed., Dec. 21, 1987, H11918.
46. *Congressional Record*, daily ed., Dec. 21, 1987, H11995.
47. Haas, "Unauthorized Action," *National Journal*, Jan. 2, 1988, 20.
48. Ibid., 17.
49. *Wall Street Journal*, April 16, 1985, 64.
50. Lawrence J. Haas, "Unauthorized Action," *National Journal*, Jan. 2, 1988, 18.
51. *Congressional Record*, daily ed., Oct. 23, 1985, H9011.
52. Allen Schick, "The Three-Ring Budget Process: The Appropriations, Tax, and Budget Committees in Congress," in *The New Congress*, ed. Thomas E. Mann and Norman J. Ornstein (Washington, D.C.: American Enterprise Institute for Public Policy Research, 1981), 313.
53. *Congressional Quarterly Weekly Report*, July 18, 1987, 1573.
54. *Washington Post*, June 16, 1987, A7.
55. Woodrow Wilson, *Congressional Government* (Boston: Houghton Mifflin, 1885), 320.

CHAPTER 4

Preliminary Legislative Action

The introduction of a bill in the House or Senate is a simple procedure. In the House, members just drop their bills into the "hopper," a mahogany box near the clerk's desk at the front of the chamber. In the Senate, members usually submit their proposals and accompanying statements to clerks, or they may introduce their bills from the floor. Measures may be introduced only when the chamber is in session. All House and Senate bills are printed and made available to members and the public.

The simple act of introducing a bill sets off a complex and variable chain of events that may or may not result in the final passage of a bill by Congress. Most bills follow a path in which the various steps, governed by rules and convention, are fairly predictable, but the outcome usually is uncertain. This chapter considers some of the factors that affect the probable route a bill will take and focuses on the early stages in the life of a bill: its referral to committee and, of utmost importance, its consideration in committee.

Although thousands of pieces of legislation are introduced in every Congress, a relatively small number become law. Figure 4-1 shows that of the roughly 10,000 measures introduced during the 99th Congress (1985-1987), 1,512 were reported from committee and only 663 became public law. Of the 13,000 to 29,000 measures that have been introduced in each Congress since 1965, the number emerging from committee in any one Congress never exceeded 4,200 and the number that became law never exceeded 810. Committees clearly are the primary graveyard for most bills that die in Congress. Stated positively, committees select from the vast number of bills introduced those that they feel merit further consideration.

Quantitative data on legislative output require careful interpretation. Although the number of laws that Congress enacts annually has

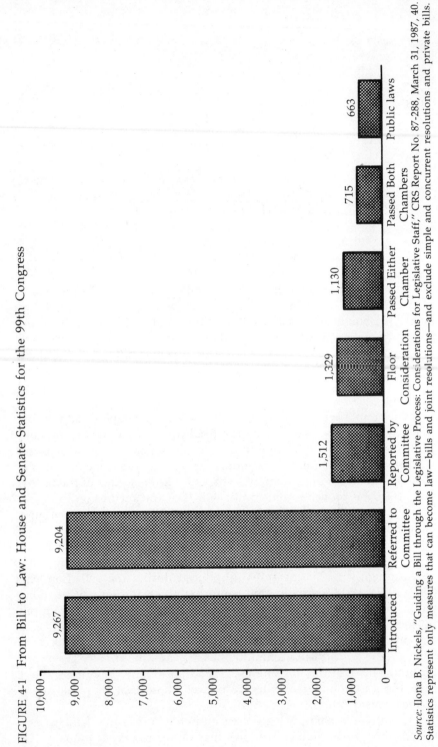

FIGURE 4-1 From Bill to Law: House and Senate Statistics for the 99th Congress

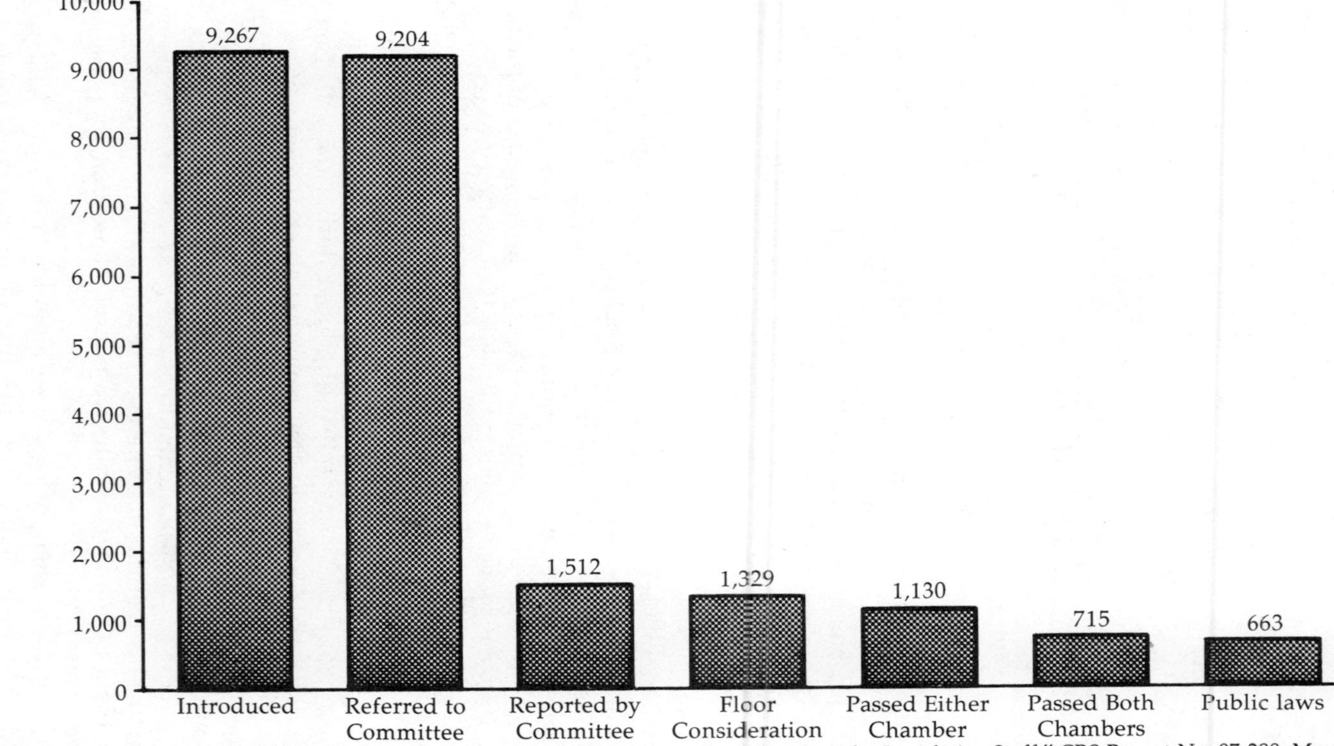

Source: Ilona B. Nickels, "Guiding a Bill through the Legislative Process: Considerations for Legislative Staff," CRS Report No. 87-288, March 31, 1987, 40. Statistics represent only measures that can become law—bills and joint resolutions—and exclude simple and concurrent resolutions and private bills.

dropped in recent years, the number of pages per law has increased significantly (from 2.5 pages on average in the 1950s to over 9 pages in the early 1980s), a reflection of wider use of megabills. The contemporary Congress may pass fewer laws than before, but they are, on average, about four times longer.

The productivity of Congress cannot be measured only by the number of laws it enacts annually. Today Congress devotes considerably more time and effort to its other principal functions: representation and oversight. The surge of legislative activity in both areas is considerable. Finally, the very complexity and interconnectedness of many contemporary issues slows down the law-enacting process.

CATEGORIES OF LEGISLATION

The winnowing process that occurs in committee suggests that the thousands of bills introduced in each Congress may be broken down roughly into three categories: bills having so little support that they are ignored and die in committee; noncontroversial bills that are expedited through Congress; and finally, major bills that are generally so controversial that they occupy the major portion of Congress's time.

Bills Lacking Wide Support

Bills having little support usually are introduced with no expectation that they will be enacted into law. Members introduce such bills for a variety of reasons: to go on record in support of a given proposal, to satisfy individual constituents or interest groups from the member's district or state, to convey a message to executive agencies, to publicize an issue, to attract media attention, or to fend off criticism during political campaigns. Once a member has introduced a bill, he or she can claim "action" on the issue and can blame the committee to which the bill has been referred for its failure to win enactment. These bills make up a majority of the large number introduced in each Congress.

Noncontroversial Bills

Noncontroversial bills make up another large segment of the measures introduced. Examples of such legislation are bills that authorize construction of statues of public figures, establish university programs in the memory of a senator, rename a national park, or name federal buildings after former members of Congress. Committees in both chambers have developed rapid procedures for dealing with such measures. As shown in Chapters 6 and 8, these bills generally are passed on the floor without debate in a matter of minutes.

MAJOR LEGISLATION

Bills taking up the largest percentage of a committee's time have some or all of the following characteristics: they are prepared and drafted by executive agencies or by major pressure groups; they are introduced by committee chairmen or other influential members of Congress; they are supported by the majority party leadership; or they deal with issues on which a significant segment of public opinion and the membership of Congress believe some sort of legislation is necessary.

Bills having such characteristics do not necessarily become law; nor is there any assurance that they will become law in the form in which they originally were introduced. Indeed, sentiment may be so sharply divided that they do not even emerge from committee. Nevertheless, these are the major bills before Congress each year. They may affect the wage earner's paycheck (taxes and Social Security) and the consumer's pocketbook (health insurance and natural gas deregulation); they may be brought up repeatedly at presidential news conferences and covered in the electronic and print media. In short, they are the bills on which Congress devotes the largest portion of its committee and floor time. These bills account for perhaps only a hundred or so of the thousands introduced in each Congress.

EXECUTIVE BRANCH BILLS. The president's leadership in the initial stages of the legislative process is pronounced. The administration's major legislative proposals are outlined in the president's annual State of the Union address, nowadays televised nationally and delivered before a joint session of Congress. In the weeks and months following the address, the president sends to Congress special messages detailing his proposals in specific areas, such as energy, welfare, and health. Bills containing the administration's programs are drafted in the executive agencies, and members of Congress, usually committee chairmen, are asked to introduce them simultaneously as "companion" bills in both chambers. Only representatives and senators, not the president or executive officials, may introduce legislation in Congress.

INFLUENTIAL MEMBERS' BILLS. Bills supported by influential members stand a good chance of receiving attention in committee. During 1981-1986, for example, the House and Senate on several occasions debated immigration reform bills. Because of the mounting public concern about the flood of illegal aliens into the country, two key members, Sen. Alan

K. Simpson, R-Wyo., and Rep. Romano L. Mazzoli, D-Ky., sponsored companion bills to revamp the nation's immigration laws. Simpson and Mazzoli each chaired his chamber's Judiciary subcommittee that handled immigration measures. Because of their strategic leadership posts, the two members were successful in advancing the legislation to the House and Senate floor during the 97th and 98th Congresses. Finally, after being given up for dead several times, the landmark measure became law at the end of the 99th Congress. Simpson and Mazzoli had worked diligently to develop tradeoffs and compromises among colleagues and lobbyists to enhance the measure's prospects for passage.

"MUST" LEGISLATION. As legislators, members of Congress may not want to deal with controversial "no-win" public issues such as abortion or gun control. As politicians answering constituent mail, responding to inquiring journalists, and, of course, facing reelection, they may not be able to ignore them. Hence, it frequently occurs that members are in basic agreement that legislation must be enacted to deal with a given problem but are in sharp disagreement over the solution. Under these circumstances, most members work hard to compromise their differences because they realize that some type of legislation is desirable or unavoidable. Money bills, to be sure, fall into the category of "must pass" legislation.

Many of the factors determining the probable route a bill will take are apparent, therefore, by the time the legislation is introduced. Bills having little support will be buried in committee; noncontroversial legislation will move quickly through Congress; major bills may or may not become law but in any case will command the greatest portion of Congress's time.

BILL REFERRAL PROCEDURE

Once a bill is introduced it receives an identifying number. Measures introduced in the House are identified by the letters "HR" and an accompanying number; Senate bills are identified by the letter "S" and a number. Usually, bills are assigned numbers according to the sequence in which they are introduced. Occasionally, however, members will request the bill clerk to reserve a particular number. During consideration of statehood for Alaska and Hawaii, various bills were introduced as S 49 or HR 50, representing the new states. Bill numbers also may be assigned for political and symbolic purposes. At the start of the 100th Congress, Democratic leaders of the House and Senate reserved the first several numbers for measures that were important party initiatives. Speaker Wright even organized his nationally televised remarks in response to the president's 1988 State of the Union message around the first five measures introduced ("House bill number 1, our first legislative act, was the clean water bill . . ."). Because 1988 was also the year for the Olympic games, a House member introduced HR 1988, a measure to aid young men and women "who dream of being Olympic athletes one day." [1] Some measures are assigned the same number for several Congresses. This is done to avoid confusion among legislators and others who have grown accustomed to referring to a proposal by its bill number. Informally, many bills also come to be known by the names of their sponsors, such as Gramm-Rudman-Hollings, discussed in Chapter 3.

With few exceptions, bills are referred to the appropriate standing committees.[2] The job of referral formally is the responsibility of the Speaker of the House and the presiding officer of the Senate,[3] but usually this task is carried out on their behalf by the parliamentarians of the House and Senate.[4] Precedent, public laws, and the jurisdictional mandates of the committees as set forth in the rules of the House and Senate determine which committees receive what kinds of bills. For example, the jurisdiction of the House Education and Labor Committee is listed in Table 4-1.

The vast majority of referrals are routine. Bills dealing with farm crops are sent to the House Agriculture Committee and the Senate Agriculture, Nutrition and Forestry Committee; tax bills are sent to the House Ways and Means Committee and the Senate Finance Committee; and bills dealing with veterans' benefits are sent to the Veterans' Affairs committees of each chamber.[5] Thus, referrals generally are cut-and-dried decisions. (House and Senate standing committees are listed in the box on page 88.)

In the House, a member is not permitted to appeal referral decisions to the entire membership except in rare instances of erroneous referral. In the Senate, the rules do permit an appeal to the full Senate by majority vote, but in practice such appeals do not take place. Disputes over referral in the Senate are resolved informally through negotiation prior to the introduction of the bill in question.

Legislative Drafting, Referral Strategy

Occasionally, a bill's sponsors may have the opportunity to draft legislation in such a fashion that it will be referred to a committee likely to act favorably on it rather than one where members are known to be less sympathetic. One technique is to draft the measure ambiguously so that it can legitimately fall within the jurisdiction of more than one committee, thus presenting the Speaker or the presiding officer with some options in making the referral. The classic example of this

TABLE 4-1 Jurisdiction of House Committee on Education and Labor

1. Measures relating to education and labor generally.
2. Child labor.
3. Columbia Institution for the Deaf, Dumb, and Blind; Howard University; Freedmen's Hospital [institutions in the District of Columbia].
4. Convict labor and the entry of goods made by convicts into interstate commerce.
5. Labor standards.
6. Labor statistics.
7. Mediation and arbitration of labor disputes.
8. Regulation or prevention of importation of foreign laborers under contract.
9. Food programs for children in schools.
10. United States Employees' Compensation Commission.
11. Vocational rehabilitation.
12. Wages and hours of labor.
13. Welfare of miners.
14. Work incentive programs.

Source: Constitution, Jefferson's Manual and Rules of the House of Representatives, H. Doc. No. 99-279, 99th Cong., 2d sess., 357-358.

involved the 1963 civil rights bill, which was drafted somewhat differently for each chamber so that it could be referred to the Judiciary Committee in the House and the Commerce Committee in the Senate. The two committees were chaired respectively by Rep. Emanuel Celler, D-N.Y. (1923-1973), and Sen. Warren G. Magnuson, D-Wash. (1944-1981), strong proponents of the legislation. Opposed to the legislation were Rep. Oren Harris, D-Ark. (1941-1966), and Sen. James O. Eastland, D-Miss. (1941, 1943-1978), chairmen respectively of the House Interstate and Foreign Commerce Committee and the Senate Judiciary Committee. Careful drafting, therefore, coupled with favorable referral decisions in the House and Senate prevented the bill from being bogged down in hostile committees.

Another drafting technique by members is to introduce legislation that amends statutes over which their committees have jurisdiction. Noted Rep. Bob Eckhardt, D-Texas (1967-1981):

> You can phrase your new bill as an amendment to some Act that the Committee has previously dealt with, and then the bill will go to that Committee. For instance, I had the Open Beaches Bill. I had a strong interest in it. By phrasing it as an amendment to certain legislation involving estuarine matters, I could get my bill referred to Merchant Marine and Fisheries, because that Committee had previously processed the statute my bill amended. Had I amended certain bills dealing with land use, I could have got it referred to the Interior Committee.[6]

Other examples of bill drafting that resulted in a favorable referral could be cited. Nevertheless, it is important to understand that these are

Standing Committees of Congress

SENATE

Agriculture, Nutrition and Forestry	Finance
Appropriations	Foreign Relations
Armed Services	Governmental Affairs
Banking, Housing and Urban Affairs	Labor and Human Resources
Budget	Judiciary
Commerce, Science and Transportation	Rules and Administration
Energy and Natural Resources	Small Business
Environment and Public Works	Veterans' Affairs

HOUSE

Agriculture	Judiciary
Appropriations	Merchant Marine and Fisheries
Armed Services	Post Office and Civil Service
Banking, Finance and Urban Affairs	Public Works and Transportation
Budget	Rules
District of Columbia	Science, Space and Technology
Education and Labor	Small Business
Energy and Commerce	Standards of Official Conduct
Foreign Affairs	Veterans' Affairs
Government Operations	Ways and Means
House Administration	

the exceptions and not the rule. Committees guard their jurisdictional turfs closely, and the parliamentarians know and follow the precedents. Only instances of genuine jurisdictional ambiguity provide opportunities for the legislative draftsman and referral options for the Speaker and the presiding officer of the Senate to bypass one committee in favor of another.

REFERRAL TO SEVERAL COMMITTEES

Many bills obviously cut across the jurisdiction of several committees so that it sometimes is difficult for the Speaker or the presiding officer of the Senate to decide where to refer a bill. Particular sections of a bill, for example, may fall outside the main jurisdiction of the committee. Other committees may assert their jurisdiction over those bills, refusing to be bypassed on referrals. The jurisdictional mandates of committees are ambiguous or overlap in various issue areas. For example, rules of the

House assign the Committee on Foreign Affairs jurisdiction over "international economic policy"; Energy and Commerce handles "foreign commerce generally"; and Ways and Means considers "reciprocal trade agreements." Committees, in brief, often share jurisdiction—formally or informally. As House Agriculture Chairman E. "Kika" de la Garza, D-Texas, observed in regard to forestry matters:

> Jurisdiction for legislation designating wilderness in the national forests is shared by the Committee on Agriculture and the Committee on Interior and Insular Affairs. However, by prior agreement between the Committees, the Committee on Interior . . . has maintained primary jurisdiction over the designation of wilderness in forest reserves created from the public domain, while the Committee on Agriculture and the Committee on Interior have shared responsibility for designating wilderness on acquired forest lands. This has meant that wilderness bills in the eastern States have been reviewed by both committees prior to their consideration by the House. . . . Jurisdiction over forestry and forest management throughout the National Forest System remains primarily with the Committee on Agriculture.[7]

This type of intercommittee referral agreement will be honored by the parliamentarian.

The Senate has long permitted the practice of multiple referral, referring legislation to two or more committees. There are three types of multiple referral: joint referral of a bill concurrently to two or more committees; sequential referral of a bill successively to one committee, then a second, and so on; and split referral of various parts of a bill to different committees for consideration of each part.

In the Senate, multiple referral can be implemented either by unanimous consent or upon a joint motion made by the majority and minority leaders (to date never employed). An example of the former method occurred on March 3, 1987, upon a request made by the majority leader:

> Mr. President, I ask unanimous consent that the bill S. 610 be jointly referred to the Committees on Governmental Affairs and Finance and, provided that a concurrent sequential referral take place at the time both committees report, to the Committees on Agriculture, Nutrition and Forestry; Banking, Housing and Urban Affairs; and Labor and Human Resources for a period not to exceed 15 days of session.

No senator objected to this request. Such requests normally are granted by the Senate because senators who offer them usually have worked out an agreement previously with all interested parties—committee chairmen, party leaders, and other members concerned about the bill. By the time the bill is introduced the appropriate bases have been touched; thus no senator is likely to object to the multiple referral.

In the House, the precedents until 1975 dictated that the Speaker could refer a bill to only one committee. That year, flexibility was injected into the bill referral process by two changes in the rules. First, the Speaker was permitted to refer a bill to more than one committee through joint, sequential, or split referral. Second, the Speaker, subject to approval of the House, was permitted to create ad hoc committees to consider measures that overlap the jurisdictions of several committees.

Speaker O'Neill exercised this ad hoc committee option in 1977 by creating an Ad Hoc Energy Committee to expedite action on the Carter administration's complex energy proposals. The ad hoc committee was composed of members selected from the five committees to which various parts of the energy proposal initially had been referred.[8] In the Senate, the administration's 1977 energy proposals were referred to the Finance Committee and the Energy and Natural Resources Committee. There is no Senate provision for the creation of ad hoc committees by party leaders.

In 1977 House rules were amended to permit the Speaker to impose committee reporting deadlines during the initial referral of measures. Further, the Speaker announced on January 3, 1983, his intention "in particular situations to designate a primary committee among those to whom a bill may be jointly referred, and may impose time limits on committees having a secondary interest following the report of the primary committee."

Several observations may be made about multiple referral. First, contemporary problems tend to have repercussions in many areas; thus more and more of the major bills coming before Congress—particularly those in new problem areas—will be candidates for multiple referral. Second, to the extent that multiple referral is chosen as an option, the decentralized nature of congressional decision making is reinforced. Third, every time another committee is added to the legislative process there is one more hurdle for a bill to overcome and additional opportunities for delay, negotiation, compromise, and bargaining. Fourth, multiple referrals may promote effective problem solving as several committees bring their expertise to bear on complex issues. Finally, multiple referrals are a growth area in the House. From 6 percent of all House measures introduced during the 94th Congress (1975-1977), multiple referrals climbed to 14 percent of all measures introduced by the 99th Congress (1985-1987). "One bill, one committee" no longer applies to the same extent as it once did. With growing frequency, the processing of legislation has become "one bill, many committees," including multiple subcommittee review within the parent committees.

CONSIDERATION IN COMMITTEE

Once a bill has been referred to a committee, the committee has several options. It may consider and report (approve) the bill, with or without amendments or recommendation, and send it to the House or Senate. It may rewrite the bill entirely, reject it, or simply refuse to consider it. Failure of a committee to act on a bill usually is equivalent to killing it. When a committee does report a bill, the House or Senate often accepts its main thrust even when they amend the bill on the floor.

There are several reasons for this deference to the decisions of the committee, a practice one scholar has referred to as the "sanctity of committee decisions." [9] Committee members and their staffs have a high degree of expertise on the subjects within their jurisdiction, and it is at the committee stage that a bill comes under its sharpest congressional scrutiny. It is understandable, therefore, that a bill that has survived the scrutiny of the experts will be given serious consideration on the floor by the generalists of the House and Senate.

Recent Congresses, however, have seen more floor challenges to some committee-reported measures. Defense bills, for instance, have been subject to extensive floor "markups" in both chambers. Hundreds of amendments are sometimes offered to these measures. "[W]e have had 118 amendments on this bill," said Senate Armed Services Chairman Nunn. "That is more amendments than any Department of Defense authorization bill since the Senate first started the [Pentagon] authorizing process." [10] Contrast this development with the situation a few decades ago when legislation reported by the Armed Services committees was enacted in each house within a day or so and with few amendments proposed from the floor. Today's consideration of military measures often stretches over several weeks.

Several factors account for this development. First, military bills are attractive vehicles for floor amendments, because they involve jobs, public works, and large sums of money. "At $20,000 per taxpayer per year, the defense budget is something people get into," stated Rep. Patricia Schroeder, D-Colo.[11] Second, deference to committee prerogatives has been weakened with the influx of many activist and independent legislators who are not reluctant to challenge seniority leaders. Third, members who disagree with the administration's defense objectives, such as the Strategic Defense Initiative (SDI), use floor amendments to push the administration in the direction of arms control. Fourth, the Armed Services committees are often more pro-defense than their respective chambers. Hence, rank-and-file members propose changes in the committees' handiwork. Finally, the increase in floor amendments reflects legislative mistrust of the executive. Many amendments are written in great detail to limit or define executive behavior and activity.

It is true that a committee's decision not to report a bill generally will be respected by the chamber as a whole. After all, if the experts have decided not to approve a bill, why should their decision be second-guessed? Furthermore, since all members of Congress are members of committees, and do not wish the decisions of their own committees to be overturned, they normally will reciprocate by not undermining the actions of another committee. Finally, the general impact of the rules in both chambers—particularly those of the House—is to "protect the power and prerogatives of the . . . committees . . . by making it very difficult for a bill that does not have committee approval to come to the floor."[12]

There are procedures, to be examined in Chapters 5 and 8, for overturning committee decisions or even bypassing committees, but these procedures are employed infrequently and are rarely successful.

When a committee decides to take up a major bill, it may be considered immediately by the full committee, but more often the committee chairman assigns the bill to a subcommittee for study and hearings. (Subcommittees of the House Energy and Commerce Committee are listed in the box on page 93.)

The subcommittee usually schedules public hearings on the measure, inviting testimony from interested public and private witnesses. Or the subcommittee may decide not to schedule hearings if there is strong opposition from executive branch officials or interest groups. After the hearings have concluded, the subcommittee meets to "mark up" the bill—that is, to consider line by line and section by section the specific language of the legislation before sending the bill to the full committee. The subcommittee may approve the bill unaltered, amend it, rewrite it, or block it altogether. It then reports its recommendations to the full committee.

When the full committee receives the bill, it may repeat the subcommittee's procedures, in whole or in part, or it may simply ratify the action of the subcommittee. If the committee decides to send the bill to the House or Senate, it justifies its actions in a written statement called a report, which must accompany the bill.[13]

On a major legislative proposal the entire committee process may stretch over several Congresses, with a new bill (containing identical or similar provisions) introduced at the beginning of each Congress. For example, the struggle to enact the aforementioned immigration reform measure took several consecutive Congresses. Indeed, decades may pass before some bills become public law.

On the other hand, the process can be compressed into a very short period of time. The House acted with uncharacteristic speed in 1983 when it passed a controversial bill to revise the Social Security system and to provide funds for unemployment compensation and jobs programs. The start of a new Congress usually is marked by a slow legislative pace while committee and party leaders attend to matters such as filling vacancies on the committees.

House Energy and Commerce Subcommittees

Oversight and Investigations
Energy and Power
Health and the Environment
Telecommunications and Finance
Transportation, Tourism and Hazardous Materials
Commerce, Consumer Protection and Competitiveness

The remainder of this chapter will focus on the key steps in committee consideration of a major bill: hearings, the markup, and the report. To simplify the discussion, assume, as sometimes happens, that the committee chairman is also the chairman of the subcommittee to which the bill is referred, and assume further that the full committee merely ratifies the subcommittee decisions. Because the committee chairman is a central figure in the legislative process, it is first necessary to focus on the chairman's role.

THE COMMITTEE CHAIRMAN'S ROLE

To a large extent, the options available to a committee in dealing with a bill are exercised by the chairman, who has wide discretion in establishing the legislative priorities of the committee. The sources of the chairman's authority are many. They include: (1) control of the committee's legislative agenda, (2) control over referral of legislation to the subcommittees, (3) management of committee funds, and (4) control of the committee staff.

The chairman usually has had a long period of service on the committee and is likely to be better informed than most other members on the myriad of issues coming before the committee. The chairman often is privy to the leadership's plans and policies, especially the Speaker's or the senate majority leader's legislative objectives. Chairmen can use these and other resources to delay, expedite, or modify legislation.

A chairman who opposes a bill may simply refuse to schedule hearings on it until it is too late to finish action on the bill during the session. The same result can be achieved by allowing the hearings to drag on interminably. A chairman having strong negative feelings about a bill can instruct the committee staff to "stack" the witnesses testifying on it. He may, for example, ask witnesses holding favorable views to submit statements rather than appear in person.[14] Committee members who are likely to raise dilatory questions or employ obstructive tactics may be recognized before others. And through his control of committee funds and the power to hire and fire most committee staffers, the chairman can effectively block action on a bill by directing the staff to disregard it.[15]

A chairman who favors a bill can give it top priority by mobilizing staff resources, compressing the time for hearings and markups, and, in general, encouraging expeditious action by committee members. In sum, chairmen are the chief "agenda setters" of committees and employ this prerogative to powerfully influence the form in which bills are reported to the House or Senate as well as the timing of floor action on their bills.

Recent Restraints on Chairmen

The general picture of a committee chairman as an almost omnipotent figure underwent modification during the 1970s. Until then, the chairmen were the central figures in the legislative process, holding power equaled only by a few party leaders of great influence such as House Speaker Sam Rayburn, D-Texas (1913-1961; Speaker 1940-1947, 1949-1953, 1955-1961), or Senate Majority Leader Lyndon B. Johnson, D-Texas (1937-1961; majority leader 1955-1961). Beginning about 1970, however, the chairmen's power was gradually trimmed under pressure from newly elected members and from some senior members who wanted to equalize the distribution of power. During that decade, Congress approved several fundamental changes that ended the nearly absolute authority enjoyed by committee chairmen.

The most significant change in the status of chairmen came when both parties modified the seniority system, specifically the practice of automatically selecting as the committee chairman the member of the majority party with the longest continuous service on the committee. Seniority meant that chairmen normally came from safe congressional districts, were repeatedly reelected, and served until their retirement or death. Because many safe districts during the 1950s and 1960s were in the conservative Democratic South, chairmen often were sharply at odds with Democratic presidents, congressional leaders, and northern Democrats. Nevertheless, as seniority then was practiced, the chairmen could not be removed. They were able to use their entrenched positions to block civil rights and social welfare legislation proposed by Democratic administrations.

HOUSE CHANGES IN SENIORITY. In 1971 members of the minority party in the House, the Republican party, made the first assault on the old order when they adopted a policy declaration stating that seniority need not be followed in making committee assignments and requiring a secret ballot to elect the ranking minority member of the committee. The ranking member is the most influential member of the minority party in a Senate or House committee. This member's powers include appointment of minority members to subcommittees and control of the committee's minority funds and staff. Generally, under seniority the ranking minority member became committee chairman when there was a shift in party control of the chamber, as occurred in 1981, when the GOP took control of the Senate for the first time in twenty-six years.

Democrats in 1971 also established the policy that seniority need not be followed in naming committee chairmen, permitting party members to challenge any nominee for chairman through a separate ballot in their party caucus (the party organization of House Democrats). This change dramatized the accountability of the chairmen to the caucus. Democrats also adopted party rules specifying that no member could head more than one subcommittee, and that committee chairmen could head no more than one subcommittee within their own committees. Both provisions were designed to create additional committee leadership opportunities for relatively junior members.

House Democrats adopted a subcommittee "bill of rights" in 1973. Powers that had been exercised exclusively by committee chairmen were assigned to all Democrats on committees. Thus committee Democratic caucuses were given the power to select subcommittee chairmen, determine subcommittee jurisdictions, ensure that each subcommittee had an adequate budget, and guarantee each Democrat at least one major subcommittee assignment. Chairmen also were required to refer legislation to subcommittees within two weeks of receiving it unless the full committee determined otherwise.

In 1975 House Democrats further democratized their procedures for appointing committee chairmen. They required all committee chairmen, and even the subcommittee chairmen of the powerful Appropriations Committee, to be elected by secret ballot. In a dramatic move, the Democrats deposed three incumbent committee chairmen. This act demonstrated that chairmen who lost the support of their party colleagues risked losing their coveted posts. Two years later, Democrats voted to oust the incumbent chairman of the House Appropriations Committee's Military Construction Subcommittee.

In January 1985, the Democratic Caucus voted to oust the chairman of the House Armed Services Committee—octogenarian Melvin Price, Ill., who was in frail health—and replaced him with the seventh-ranking Democrat on the panel—Les Aspin of Wisconsin. Because Chairman Aspin took several controversial positions during the 99th Congress (on the MX missile, aid to the Nicaraguan Contras, and defense spending, for instance), he antagonized many of his former allies within the Democratic Caucus. As a result, several Armed Services Democrats challenged Aspin for the Chairmanship at the start of the 100th Congress. Aspin withstood the multiple challenges and retained his chairmanship. However, the message of these Caucus challenges has not been lost on the Democratic chairmen. "I have to have loyalty to the Democratic Caucus," stated Veterans' Affairs Chairman G. V. "Sonny" Montgomery, Miss. "They gave me a chairmanship." [16]

SENATE CHANGES IN SENIORITY. Reforms since 1970 also reduced the authority of Senate committee chairmen. While there were no dramatic dismissals of sitting Democratic or Republican chairmen, as occurred in the House, both parties dropped the rigid adherence to seniority as a basis for automatically determining committee chairmen. In 1975 the majority Democrats adopted a rule (which took effect in 1977) requiring a secret ballot on any nominee for a chairmanship if one-fifth of the party members in the Senate requested it. In 1973 the minority Republicans had adopted a rule authorizing Republican members of each committee to elect their "ranking member," subject to ratification by all Senate Republicans. This GOP rule was invoked at the start of the 100th Congress when Senators Richard G. Lugar, Ind., and Jesse Helms, N.C., both claimed the ranking minority post on Foreign Relations. Lugar had headed the panel when Republicans controlled the Senate during the previous Congress, but Helms had more seniority. Lugar won the initial balloting of the GOP members of Foreign Relations, but Helms prevailed when the entire Republican membership chose between the two in their party conference.

In other important changes in committee practices since 1970, the Senate, or each of the parties individually through their own conferences, generally restricted the opportunities for senior members to monopolize key positions. In 1970 members were limited to service on only one of the four so-called elite committees: Appropriations, Armed Services, Finance, and Foreign Relations. In 1971 the Republicans adopted a party rule permitting a GOP senator to be a ranking minority member of only one committee. And in 1977 the Senate adopted a rule, which became effective in 1979, prohibiting a committee chairman from serving as chairman of more than two subcommittees of any committee.

These changes were designed to give junior members an opportunity to obtain leadership positions on important subcommittees. And they reinforced a characteristic of the Senate that was stressed in Chapter 1: power always has been more evenly distributed in the Senate than in the House. The institutional trends of the 1970s and 1980s reflected a further diffusion of power from committee chairmen to subcommittees and to individual members of the Senate. "It's every man for himself," said one member. "Every senator is a baron. He has his own principality. Once you adopt that as a means of doing business, it's hard to establish any cohesion." [17]

The Chairman in Perspective

Changes in the structure of congressional committees in the 1970s have clearly chipped away at the power base of both House and Senate committee chairmen. By and large, one-person rule has been replaced by bargaining and negotiation between the chairman and the other members of his committee, particularly the subcommittee chairmen. In short, "subcommittee government" rather than "committee government," more accurately characterizes the contemporary House (and the Senate to a lesser extent). This shift in the locus of decision making limits the chairmen's prerogatives.

Nevertheless, committee chairmen remain crucial figures in the legislative process. It is true that congressional decision making has become increasingly decentralized within the committee structure. But as long as Congress functions primarily through its committees the person who heads one has considerable influence over the advancement or defeat of legislation. For example, Chairman John D. Dingell, D-Mich., of the House Energy and Commerce Committee, is recognized as one of the most powerful chairmen on Capitol Hill. Called "Big John" by members, Dingell is known for the skill, intensity, and determination he brings to issues. A GOP committee colleague, Edward R. Madigan, Ill., has identified some of the sources of Dingell's authority:

> Sometimes I think he is an arbitrary and capricious [person], and other times I think he is a great parliamentarian. At all times I'd much rather have him on my side than against me. Dingell is formidable not because he has more friends than anyone else, nor because he is more skilled—there are others as skilled as he is. His strength comes because he takes the skill he has and combines it with good staff work, a thorough knowledge of the issues and bulldog determination not to let go. He is the most tenacious member of Congress.[18]

HEARINGS

Ostensibly, hearings are important primarily as fact-finding instruments. Witnesses from the executive branch, concerned members of Congress, interest group spokesmen, academic experts, and knowledgeable citizens appear before the committee to give it their opinions as to the merits or pitfalls of a given piece of legislation. From this encounter the committee members gather the information needed to act as informed lawmakers. Hearings also aid members in determining whether new laws are needed or whether changes in the administration of existing laws will be sufficient to resolve problems. "Legislation need not always be the answer," remarked Sen. Albert Gore, Jr., D-Tenn. "In many areas, the most important missing ingredient is attention, and an elevated awareness of the problem can be a very successful outcome of hearings."[19]

Much information is available to committee members long before the hearings take place. Major bills have usually been the subject of public debate and coverage in the media. The positions of the administration and the special interest groups are well known, and, in all likelihood, executive branch officials and pressure group lobbyists have already presented their views to committee members and staff aides well in advance of the hearings. The members themselves often have strong partisan positions on the legislation and thus may have little interest in whatever additional information emerges from the hearings.[20] Hearings often are poorly attended by committee members, and interruptions are common because of floor votes or quorum calls.

Hearings Format

Staff research and preparatory work precede committee hearings. Committee aides, for example, may interview witnesses in advance of hearings, compile research and documentary materials, and prepare notebooks for committee members to use at the hearings. These notebooks may list questions—and the answers—used in probing the witnesses. Explained a committee staff director:

> We write the question. Under the question we write the answer. This is the answer we expect to get on the basis of the staff research that has gone before. The Member who asks the question knows what the witness has told us in the weeks and weeks of preparation; and he knows he should get the same information. If he does not get that information, then he has the answer in front of him and he can ad lib the questions that solicit that information or refute it.[21]

Hearings can be perfunctory, particularly where similar legislation has been before the committee for several years in succession. Witnesses usually read from prepared texts, while the committee members present often feign interest or simply look bored until the statement has been read. Once the formal testimony is completed, each committee member, usually in order of seniority, will ask the witness questions. House rules allot at least five minutes per member to question witnesses. Senate rules have no such provision. Instead, each committee establishes its own rules governing internal procedures. For example, the rules of the Senate Energy and Natural Resources Committee give each member five minutes to question witnesses until all members have had an opportunity to ask questions.

The traditional format for questioning witnesses in the House and Senate does not lend itself to opportunities for extended exchanges between members and witnesses, for analysis of different points of view, or for in-depth probing of one witness's views by another. "I've testified before Congress several times," said an automotive executive, "and I've always come away a little frustrated by the limits on the dialogue."[22] However, this is changing as numerous committees today structure their hearings to ensure that conflicting viewpoints are heard. Committees often hold panel sessions where members and witnesses of different persuasions sit in roundtable fashion to discuss the merits of particular policies.

Committees also conduct joint hearings (with other panels or with the "other body") or "field" hearings (away from Capitol Hill). The House Budget Committee, for example, has held annual field hearings in major cities across the country to focus public attention on the president's budget. Committees even hold "prehearings" to assess issues in private that will be discussed later by witnesses during the public sessions.

Purposes of Hearings

Despite their limitations, hearings remain an integral part of the legislative process. They provide a permanent public record of the position of committee members and the various interested groups on a legislative proposal. Preparation of congressional testimony is regarded as an important function by executive agencies and interest groups. Above all, hearings are important because members of Congress believe them to be important. The decision to hold hearings is a critical point in the life of a bill. Seldom is a measure considered on the floor without first being the subject of hearings. The sanctity of the committee stage is based on the assumption that the experts—the committee members—carefully scrutinize a proposal, and hearings provide a demonstrable record of that scrutiny.

Hearings are part of any overall strategy to get bills enacted into law. Committee members and staff typically plan with care who should testify, when, and on what issues. Ralph Nader's testimony before several congressional committees on his 1965 best-selling book, *Unsafe at Any Speed,* led to passage of the Traffic Safety Act of 1966. The testimony of celebrity witnesses, such as actors and actresses, is a sure-fire way to attract national attention to issues. "I haven't seen anything like this in the 30 days we have had hearings," declared a Senate subcommittee chairman about the extensive press coverage when Elizabeth Taylor testified on the need for more money for AIDS research.[23] Committees, in brief, often want witnesses who will provide a broad coalition of endorsements for their predetermined position and promote political and public support for this course of action.

Hearings serve other functions as well. They may be used to assess the intensity of support or opposition to a bill, to gauge the capabilities of an executive agency official, to publicize the role of politically ambitious committee chairmen and members, to allow citizens to express their views to their representatives, and to promote new ideas or agendas. The Senate's constitutional duties mean that it holds hearings on advising and consenting to treaties and nominations. The Judiciary Committee's televised hearings on the controversial nomination of Robert H. Bork to the Supreme Court dominated the headlines in 1987, as did hearings the following year of the Foreign Relations Committee on the INF (intermediate nuclear forces) treaty signed by President Reagan and Soviet leader Mikhail Gorbachev.

Congress also uses investigative hearings to explore problems and issues. These hearings serve several purposes. They promote efficient program administration, secure information needed to legislate, and inform public opinion. Millions of American households watched on television the unfolding drama of the 1954 Army-McCarthy hearings, the 1957 hearings into corruption of the Teamsters union, the Senate Foreign Relations Committee's hearings during the 1960s on the Vietnam War, the Watergate hearings of the 1970s, and the 1987 Iran-Contra hearings. These investigative hearings often prompted the drafting of legislation to deal with the problems that were uncovered and subsequently led to more hearings on the legislation itself. On occasion, individual members conduct ad hoc, or "informal," investigative hearings of their own.

Importance of Timing

The chairman's control over the timing and duration of the hearings is an important factor in deciding the fate of a bill. Postponing or dragging out hearings is an obvious ploy if the chairman is opposed to a bill or wants it extensively modified. There are times, too, when a delay in the hearings will help the bill's chances. This might be true if sentiment in favor of the bill is much stronger in the other chamber than in the chairman's. Another possibility is that both House and Senate chairmen supporting a bill may want to expedite hearings because of time pressures.

In short, committee chairmen take into account a variety of factors when scheduling hearings. Among the more important are the positions of the White House, pressure groups, executive agencies, the other chamber, and key legislators; the climate of public opinion; the intensity of feeling of the principal participants; and the mix of witnesses that can create momentum and support for legislation.

THE MARKUP

Sometime after the conclusion of the hearings, the committee or subcommittee meets to mark up the bill. Here committee members decide whether the legislation should be rewritten, either in whole or in part. The chairman's task is to keep the committee moving, getting unanimous agreement on as many sections of the bill as possible, trying to resolve differences through compromise, and sensing when to delay or expedite matters. The chairman may line up leadership backing for the committee's bill, insert special provisions in legislation to win members' support, or accommodate interest group or agency officials by permitting them to make presentations during the committee's markup. Chairmen may even collect "proxy" votes to win key issues. Proxy voting permits a committee member to cast a vote for an absent colleague. (Regulated by congressional and committee rules, proxy voting is prohibited on the House or Senate floor.) As one account of a Senate markup noted:

> [Subcommittee Chairman Frank] Lautenberg's [D-N.J.] preparation paid off. The committee had been in session for more than five hours and about half the members had left. But when the vote was taken, Lautenberg could supplement the eight votes he had in the room with nine proxies. The vote was 17-12.[24]

Because the chairman is likely to be responsible for managing the bill on the floor, he or she will try throughout the markup to gather as much support within the committee as possible. A sharp split among the committee members will seriously damage chances of passing the bill in the House or Senate.

Chairmen may schedule pre-markup sessions to discuss possible revisions of the legislation and to develop a consensus on the bill. On the Clean Air Act, for instance, the Senate chairman of the Environment and Public Works Committee, "scheduled several seminars prior to formal markup, to educate the members on the major issues and to try to develop a consensus among the members on the issues."[25] The chairmen also usually decide which vehicle will be used for markup purposes: the bill as introduced, a related proposal drafted by the chair, a staff proposal, or the administration's plan. Tactically, it often is easier to retain something already in a bill than to add it by amendment.

The markup, then, is where committee members redraft portions of the bill, attempt to insert new provisions and delete others, bargain over final language, and generally determine the final committee product.

With the movement in the 1970s to open to the public more committee meetings, most markups today are conducted in open session. However, important measures (tax, defense, and appropriations, for example) are still marked up in private without much protest from the press, media, or others. Even proponents of openness admit that members can reach compromises and make tough decisions more easily when they are away from the glare of lobbyists sitting in the audience. Moreover, with scores of journalists and media representatives covering Capitol Hill, the results of "closed" sessions become quickly known once the committee opens its doors. "Closed sessions don't necessarily mean bad legislation and sunshine doesn't guarantee good laws," remarked a journalist. "Openness just makes the process and the results slightly easier to discern."[26]

Strategies During Markup

Members use various strategies during the markup. One ploy, sometimes used by opponents of a bill, is to add amendments to strengthen the measure. During markup of a gun control measure by the House Judiciary Committee, the National Rifle Association, the major lobbying group opposed to gun control, told its supporters in Congress that it would be easier to defeat a strong firearms proposal. "The way we look at it," said an NRA lobbyist, "the stronger the bill that comes out of committee, the less chance it has of passing on the floor."[27] Conversely, proponents of a strong bill might try to weaken it in committee so that it stands a better chance of winning majority support on the floor. Supporters then can try to persuade the other chamber or the House-Senate conference committee to strengthen the measure.

Another approach used by a bill's opponent is to offer a flurry of amendments to make a bill complicated, confusing, and unworkable for the executive branch agencies that will have responsibility for administering the law. Moreover, offering scores of amendments, or offering one huge amendment and insisting that it be read—slowly—in full, may stall the markup and grant opponents additional time to lobby against the legislation. Mobilizing grass-roots support and targeting the states or districts of key committee members is often critical to the outcome of markups. During markup by Congress's tax-writing panels, special interests work diligently to shape the thinking of these committees.

> For several months, the lobbyists have been working behind the scenes trying to influence the outcome by personally talking with members and aides of the tax committees in both chambers and getting members of their lobbying coalitions to write and phone their Congressmen. To bolster their arguments, the lobbyists have hired independent research firms to produce analyses that show the impact of the proposed tax

changes, and they have tried to mold public opinion through press releases and advertising campaigns.[28]

To win over opponents or skeptics, chairmen often willingly accept numerous amendments from their committee colleagues. In this way, these members develop a stake in the legislation and may stand united behind it on the House or Senate floor. The reverse strategy is to load down a bill with scores of "add-ons" so the legislation might sink of its own weight. "I've seen bills killed around here before, even though there were the votes [to pass them] . . . by loading them down," observed Sen. Russell B. Long, D-La.[29]

An important factor affecting markup strategies in the Senate is the smaller size of its panels. "To get an amendment adopted [on my Senate subcommittee]," wrote Sen. Paul Simon, D-Ill., "I need only two other votes of the five-member subcommittee. In the House, subcommittees with more than 20 members are common," which means greater effort in forging winning coalitions.[30]

Equally significant is that Senate rules permit legislation that has been blocked in committee to be considered on the floor. Senators can offer to pending legislation nongermane amendments that embody bills pigeonholed in committee. The opportunity to offer such amendments on the Senate floor indicates a significant difference between House and Senate committee procedures: efforts to block legislation in committee are less successful in the Senate than in the House. Senate floor procedures provide various ways to bypass committees if they refuse to report measures (Chapter 8).

Nevertheless, bypassing a Senate committee occurs infrequently. All senators have an interest in seeing that the prerogatives of their own committees are respected. Thus they will make every effort to resolve their differences within the committee.

Compromise during the committee markup—indeed, at any stage of the legislative process—is more likely when the members recognize that some sort of legislation is necessary. The outcome of markups, with their tradeoffs, compromises, and complexities, may not represent perfection, but it does reflect what attracted at least a majority vote of the panel members. As Ways and Means Chairman Rostenkowski said after a tax markup: "We have not written perfect law. Perhaps a faculty of scholars could do a better job. A group of ideologues could have provided greater consistency. But politics is an imperfect process." [31] Rep. Barney Frank, D-Mass., emphasized this point in describing coalition building on a controversial measure: "Our goal is to find something that's 60 percent acceptable to 52 percent of the members and I think we have a 75 percent chance of doing that." [32]

Table 4-2 lists several major House-Senate differences regarding the introduction, referral, and committee consideration of legislation.

THE REPORT

Assuming that major differences have been ironed out in the markup, the committee then meets to vote on reporting the bill out of committee. House and Senate rules require a committee majority to be present for this purpose; otherwise, a point of order may be made on the floor that will force the bill to be returned to committee. Bills voted out of committee unanimously stand a good chance on the floor. A sharply divided committee vote presages an equally sharp dispute on the floor. A bill is rejected if the committee vote is a tie. (See "Point of Order" box.)

Committees have several options when they vote to report, or approve, a bill. They may report the bill without any changes or with various amendments. Or a committee that has extensively amended a bill may instruct the chairman to incorporate the modifications in a new measure, known as a "clean bill." This bill will be reintroduced, assigned a new bill number, referred back to the committee, and

TABLE 4-2 Procedural Differences at Preliminary Stages

House	*Senate*
Bills are usually introduced before committee or floor action can proceed.	Bills may originate from the floor.
No effective way to challenge the Speaker's (parliamentarian's) referral decisions.	Referrals are subject to appeals from the floor.
The Speaker is granted authority by House rules to refer bills to more than one committee.	Multiple referrals occur by unanimous consent, although the majority leader and minority leader can jointly offer a motion to that effect.
The Speaker is authorized, subject to House approval, to create ad hoc panels to consider legislation.	Neither the majority leader nor the presiding officer has authority to create ad hoc panels to process legislation.
Difficult to bypass committee consideration of measures.	Bypassing committee consideration of measures occurs more easily.
Floor action is somewhat less important for policy making than committees.	Floor action is as important as committee action in decision making.

Point of Order

When Senate Labor and Human Resources Committee Chairman Edward M. Kennedy, D-Mass., sought to bring a bilingual education measure to the Senate floor, Majority Leader Robert C. Byrd, D-W.Va., raised a point of order. The bill had been reported from committee through a telephone poll of committee members, which is contrary to Senate rules.

> Mr. BYRD. Mr. President, the rule requires that before any measure or matter is reported from a committee there must be a majority of the members of that committee present and voting to report such matter. It is my understanding that this measure does not meet that requirement because it was polled out of the committee. If that is the case, then it does not meet the requirement because a majority of the members were not physically present at the time that measure was reported out. If the point of order stands, the measure goes back to the committee. I make that point of order.
>
> The PRESIDING OFFICER. The Chair will first state that the matter would go back to the committee. The Chair would inquire of the chairman of the committee, was a quorum physically present to report the matter?
>
> Mr. KENNEDY. Mr. President, the point of order is well stated. There had been a request by Members to poll this particular measure, and to accommodate some of the Members that process was taken. The majority leader is exactly correct.
>
> The PRESIDING OFFICER. The point of order is then well taken. S. 857 will be returned to the committee.

Source: Congressional Record, daily ed., May 15, 1987, S6553.

reported by the panel. Only the full House or Senate, of course, can amend legislation; committees formally recommend revisions to measures.

The clean bill procedure is employed for various reasons, such as expediting floor consideration of legislation. Another factor involves germaneness. Provisions already in a bill are ipso facto considered to be germane; hence they are protected against points of order (germaneness rules apply to proposed floor amendments and not to provisions in the bill itself). Finally, a clean bill may reflect negotiated agreements between key committee members and executive officials.

Committees may take other actions besides favorably reporting a bill. They may report out a bill adversely (unfavorably), recommending that the bill not be passed by the full chamber, or they may report legislation without a formal recommendation, allowing the chamber to decide the bill's merits. In either case, though, the bill may be sent to the full chamber and scheduled for floor action. Committees adamantly opposed to a measure may decide, of course, not to take any action at all, thus blocking further consideration except through special procedures (see Chapters 5 and 8).

After the bill is reported favorably, or unfavorably, the chairman instructs the staff to prepare a written report. (House rules require a written report to accompany legislation; Senate rules do not impose that requirement, but it is informally observed in most cases.) The report will describe the purposes and scope of the bill, explain the committee revisions, note proposed changes in existing law, and, usually, include the views of the executive branch agencies consulted. Committee members opposing the bill often will submit dissenting, or minority, views. Any committee member may file minority, supplemental, or additional views, which are printed in the committee report. House and Senate rules also require committee reports to contain certain information, such as five-year cost estimates, oversight findings, and regulatory impact statements. Measures are open to points of order on the floor if their committee report fails to contain this material. A report may be more than a thousand pages long.

Reports are directed primarily at members of the House and Senate and seek to persuade the membership to endorse the committee's recommendations when it comes up for a vote on the floor. They are the principal official means of communicating a committee decision to the entire chamber. Committee reports are also used by executive officials to fathom legislative intent when they are interpreting ambiguous statutory phrases. Federal judges, too, examine committee reports and other aspects of legislative history (hearings, floor debates, and conference reports) when laws are challenged in court.

Reports are numbered, by Congress and chamber, in the order in which they are filed with the clerk of the House or Senate. (Thus, in the 100th Congress the first House report was designated H Rept 100-1 and the first Senate report as S Rept 100-1.) Both the committee-reported bill and its accompanying report are then assigned to the appropriate House or Senate calendar to await scheduling for floor action. Once committees conclude their markups, members often mobilize to achieve their objectives, such as lobbying colleagues and organizing pep rallies on Capitol Hill. Chapters 5 and 7 discuss the House and Senate calendars and scheduling legislation for floor action in each chamber.

SUMMARY

Of the thousands of bills introduced in each Congress, the vast majority have little support and provoke little controversy. Congress routinely either ignores these measures or rushes them through the legislative process, reserving the bulk of its time for the relatively small number of bills that deal with the nation's major problems and programs.

Once a bill is introduced, it usually is referred to a single committee, the one having jurisdiction over its subject area. In cases of overlapping jurisdiction, a bill may be referred to several committees.

In committee the critical decision is made either to ignore, expedite, or carefully examine a legislative proposal. Since committee members and their staffs have more expertise on matters within their jurisdiction than members of Congress as a whole, the fundamental outlines of committee decisions generally will be accepted. As one senator explained in objecting to a pending bill on the floor:

> [This bill] did not emerge from the crucible of the committee process, tempered by the heat of debate. The committees are important because, like them or not, they do provide a means by which legislation can be carefully considered, can be exposed to public view and public discussion by calling witnesses before the committee.[33]

The rules and precedents of both chambers reinforce committee prerogatives. Exceptions to these rules exist, but members of Congress generally are reluctant to see the committee system weakened by frequent recourse to extraordinary procedures. Hence, members are encouraged to resolve their differences within the committees.

The key stages in committee consideration of a bill are hearings, the markup, voting, and the report. This process is controlled largely by the subcommittee and committee chairmen, who have many resources at their disposal to expedite, delay, or modify legislation. Chairmen choose tactics on the basis of their assessment of the many political and legislative factors present and their long-range objectives for the bill. Opportunities for a chairman to act arbitrarily have been trimmed somewhat by recent procedural reforms, particularly the abandonment of seniority as an automatic system for choosing chairmen.

When a bill has been reported from committee, it is ready to be scheduled for floor action. Like the winnowing process that occurs in committee, scheduling involves the budgeting of congressional time. Important political choices must be made in determining the order in which bills will be considered on the floor, how much time will be devoted to each measure, and to what extent the full chamber will be permitted to re-examine a committee decision. House scheduling of legislation is discussed in the next chapter and Senate scheduling in Chapter 7.

NOTES

1. *Congressional Record,* daily ed., April 8, 1987, E1362.
2. On rare occasions a member introducing a bill may ask unanimous consent that it be passed. Unanimous consent is more likely to be granted in the Senate than in the House and only on a noncontroversial measure or one on which all members agree that immediate action is required.
3. Article I, Section 3, of the Constitution provides that the vice president is president of the Senate, but he infrequently presides over that body. The Constitution also provides for a president pro tempore, a largely honorary position elected by the majority party. By custom, that position nowadays is held by the most senior member of the majority party. Usually, however, junior members designated by the majority leader preside over the daily sessions of the Senate.
4. Each chamber has a parliamentarian, who is an expert on rules of procedure. During a session, the parliamentarians or one of their assistants always are present to advise the chair on all points of order and parliamentary inquiries. They also provide technical assistance to members in drafting bills or motions.
5. Committee structure and jurisdiction are not identical in the House and Senate. There are twenty-two standing (permanent) committees in the House and sixteen in the Senate.
6. Bob Eckhardt and Charles L. Black, Jr., *The Tides of Power* (New Haven: Yale University Press, 1976), 146.
7. *Congressional Record,* daily ed., Oct. 13, 1987, H8550-H8551.
8. See Bruce I. Oppenheimer, "Policy Effects of U.S. House Reform: Decentralization and the Capacity to Resolve Energy Issues," *Legislative Studies Quarterly* (February 1980): 5-30; and David J. Vogler, "Ad Hoc Committees in the House of Representatives and Purposive Models of Legislative Behavior," *Polity* (Fall 1981): 89-109.
9. Randall B. Ripley, *Congress: Process and Policy* (New York: W. W. Norton, 1975), 75. Also see the third edition (1983) of this book.
10. *Congressional Record,* daily ed., Oct. 2, 1987, S13438.
11. *New York Times,* May 13, 1987, B12.
12. Ripley, *Congress,* 75.
13. There is no formal requirement in the Senate for written reports to accompany legislation voted out of committee.
14. "Stacking" was modified somewhat by the Legislative Reorganization Act of 1970, which gives the minority party on a committee at least one day in which to call witnesses. However, on issues where the committee members of both parties share similar views, the opportunities to testify for witnesses who oppose those views is limited.
15. Members of Congress rely heavily on committee staff for assistance in organizing hearings, selecting witnesses, and drafting bills, as well as for many other key support functions. The chairman's control of committee staff therefore is an important resource in his control of the legislative process.
16. *Congressional Quarterly Weekly Report,* Aug. 1, 1987, 1700.
17. Alan Ehrenhalt, "Special Report: The Individualist Senate," *Congressional Quarterly Weekly Report,* Sept. 4, 1982, 2181.
18. *Washington Post,* May 15, 1983, A14.
19. *Wall Street Journal,* April 11, 1986, 54.
20. Members unable to attend a committee session frequently assign committee staffers to attend the meeting and brief them later. Staff aides can ask questions of witnesses if authorized by committee rules or by the chairman.

21. *Workshop on Congressional Oversight and Investigations,* 96th Cong., 1st sess., H. Doc. No. 96-217, 25.
22. *Congressional Record,* daily ed., May 7, 1987, E1789.
23. *Washington Post,* May 9, 1986, D8.
24. *Congressional Quarterly Weekly Report,* Oct. 3, 1987, 2409.
25. *State Government News,* April 1982, 4.
26. *Washington Post,* May 6, 1984, F5. See Jacqueline Calmes, "Few Complaints Are Voiced as Doors Close on Capitol Hill," *Congressional Quarterly Weekly Report,* May 23, 1987, 1059-1060.
27. *Washington Post,* Feb. 6, 1976, A6.
28. *New York Times,* Oct. 15, 1985, D25.
29. Pamela Fessler, "'Christmas Tree' Ornaments?" *Congressional Quarterly Weekly Report,* May 28, 1983, 1068.
30. Paul Simon, "Trying on the Senate for Size," *Chicago,* November 1985, 150.
31. *Washington Post,* Nov. 25, 1985, A4.
32. *Washington Post,* Feb. 24, 1988, A22.
33. *Congressional Record,* daily ed., Sept. 26, 1986, S13769.

CHAPTER 5

Scheduling Legislation in the House

Scheduling legislation for floor debate in the House may be simple or complex. As we have seen, relatively few bills are reported from committee. For those that are, priorities for floor consideration are established by the majority leadership (the Speaker, the majority leader, and the majority whip), sometimes in consultation with the minority leader. Numerous factors influence their decisions: House rules, budgetary timetables, bicameral considerations, election-year activities, the pressure of national and international events, the administration's programs, the leadership's policy and political preferences, and the actions of the Rules Committee. All these elements interact as legislators, pressure groups, and executive agencies maneuver to get favored legislation on the floor.

Scheduling involves many considerations: advance planning of annual recesses and adjournments, coordinating committee and floor action, providing a steady and predictable weekly agenda of business, and regulating the flow of bills to the floor during slack or peak periods. Even some "mystery" is involved in scheduling as majority party leaders assess the political climate. As Speaker Wright once noted:

> In scheduling the program for the Congress one must be constantly aware of the importance of maintaining a little suspense. I learned this from Agatha Christie. Always hold something back and keep people guessing a little bit. And that is what we are doing with this bill, quite frankly. We are maintaining a little suspense in the schedule [while we determine the best time for taking up this legislation].[1]

The procedures for managing the flow of bills to the floor have evolved throughout the history of Congress and still undergo frequent change. At first glance, they may appear needlessly complex and cumbersome, but they have an internal logic and over the years have served the needs of the House.

The focus in this chapter is on how bills reach the floor through one of three basic scheduling procedures: (1) special calendar days for speedy action on minor and noncontroversial legislation; (2) privileges (facilitated access to the floor) for certain categories of important legislation; and (3) actions of the Rules Committee, which is charged with the responsibility of scheduling most major legislation.

THE HOUSE LEGISLATIVE CALENDARS

Measures reported from committee are assigned by the clerk of the House to one of four regularly used "calendars." These list bills in the chronological order in which they are reported from the various committees. The calendars are: Union, House, Consent, and Private.

Legislation dealing with raising, authorizing, or spending money is assigned to the Union Calendar. Non-money measures of major importance are put on the House Calendar. Noncontroversial measures are assigned to the Consent Calendar. Bills of a private nature ("for the relief of"), those not of general application and usually dealing with individuals or small groups, are assigned to the Private Calendar.

In addition, there is a Discharge Calendar, which lists bills removed from committees through special, and infrequently successful, procedures. All of these are discussed below.

MINOR AND NONCONTROVERSIAL BILLS

Legislation on the Consent and Private calendars is in order only during special calendar days. The House also processes noncontroversial measures that are on the Union, House, or Consent calendars under procedures that grant them privileged access to the floor during certain designated days of the month. These include bills dealing with the District of Columbia and measures brought to the floor under the suspension of the rules procedure. Each of these expedited procedures for processing relatively minor legislation also is discussed in this chapter.

When the House is in session, members receive a daily document, the *Calendars of the United States House of Representatives and History of Legislation* (page 113), which lists all House as well as Senate measures that have been reported from committee. The document is a handy reference source, but not every measure listed is called up and considered by the House.

ONE HUNDREDTH CONGRESS

FIRST SESSION { CONVENED JANUARY 6, 1987
ADJOURNED DEC. 22 *(Legislative day of Dec. 21)*, 1987

SECOND SESSION { CONVENED JANUARY 25, 1988

CALENDARS
OF THE UNITED STATES HOUSE OF REPRESENTATIVES
AND
HISTORY OF LEGISLATION

LEGISLATIVE DAY 39 CALENDAR DAY 39

Wednesday, April 13, 1988

HOUSE MEETS AT 2 P.M.

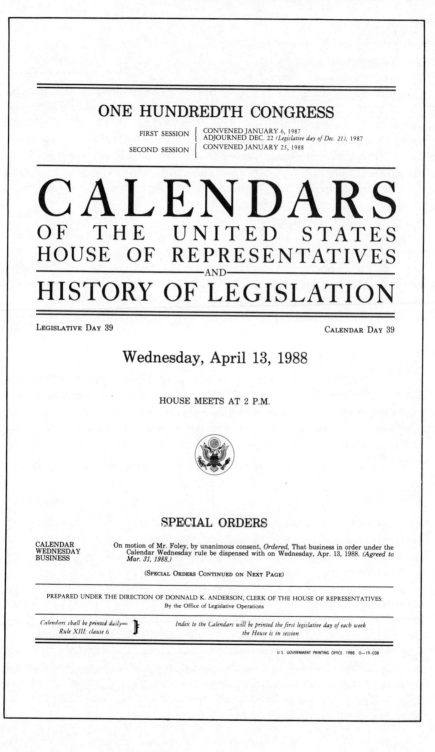

SPECIAL ORDERS

CALENDAR WEDNESDAY BUSINESS

On motion of Mr. Foley, by unanimous consent, *Ordered*, That business in order under the Calendar Wednesday rule be dispensed with on Wednesday, Apr. 13, 1988. *(Agreed to Mar. 31, 1988.)*

(SPECIAL ORDERS CONTINUED ON NEXT PAGE)

PREPARED UNDER THE DIRECTION OF DONNALD K. ANDERSON, CLERK OF THE HOUSE OF REPRESENTATIVES:
By the Office of Legislative Operations

Calendars shall be printed daily—Rule XIII: clause 6

Index to the Calendars will be printed the first legislative day of each week the House is in session

U.S. GOVERNMENT PRINTING OFFICE : 1988 0—19-038

THE CONSENT CALENDAR

Noncontroversial measures, such as the provision of a staff assistant for the chief justice of the United States, are assigned to the Consent Calendar. A bill assigned to the House or Union calendars also may be placed on the Consent Calendar at the request of the member who introduced it. The first and third Mondays of the month are Consent Calendar days. Measures must be entered on the Consent Calendar at least three days before they can be considered by the House. Bills brought up from the Consent Calendar by unanimous consent almost invariably are passed without debate or further amendment. The first time a bill is called, a single objection prevents its consideration. In such cases, the bill is returned to the Consent Calendar for possible consideration the next time such legislation is in order. If three or more members object when the bill is called a second time, the bill is stricken from the Consent Calendar for the rest of the congressional session. If members anticipate that objections will be made, they may secure unanimous consent that the bill be "passed over without prejudice" and remain on the Consent Calendar.

The Consent Calendar is supervised by six official "objectors," three members from each party, appointed by the majority and minority leaders. As a matter of policy, the objectors will prevent consideration of bills from the Consent Calendar if they: (1) involve expenditures of more than $1 million; (2) make changes in domestic or international policy; or (3) appear to be sufficiently controversial or substantive enough to provoke floor debate. Sponsors of Consent Calendar bills are asked to contact the objectors at least twenty-four hours before Consent Day to clear up any questions the objectors may have and to expedite the legislation.[2]

SUSPENSION OF THE RULES

Another legislative shortcut, which may be used for both important and minor public bills, resolutions, and conference reports, is through suspension of the rules. By a two-thirds majority vote, the House may suspend its regular procedures for any bill.

A vote to suspend the rules is simultaneously a vote to pass the measure in question. Before the vote, debate is limited to forty minutes, evenly divided between proponents and opponents. The motion to suspend the rules and pass a bill may include committee amendments, if they are stipulated in the motion, but floor amendments are not permitted. Bills that fail to gain the necessary two-thirds support may be considered again under regular House procedures. The House rules that govern legislation considered under the Consent Calendar and suspension procedure are listed in Table 5-1.

TABLE 5-1 The Consent Calendar and Suspension of the Rules

Consent Calendar	*Suspension of the Rules*
First and third Mondays	Every Monday and Tuesday, and during the last six days of the session
Bills must be placed on Consent Calendar three days before House consideration	No deadline
Bills may be amended	No floor amendments; 40 minutes of debate
Official party objectors	No objectors
Ground rules on types of bills allowed	No restrictions on substance of bills ($100 million limit established by Democratic Caucus)
Unanimous consent required for passage	Two-thirds of the members voting, a quorum being present, is required for passage

Until the 94th Congress (1975-1977), motions to suspend the rules were in order only during the first and third Mondays of the month (following the call of the Consent Calendar) and during the last six days of a session when the backlog of bills awaiting floor debate is heavy. In 1975 the number of days for suspension of the rules was doubled by adding the first and third Tuesdays. In addition, the House instituted "cluster" voting to save more time. Under the most recent version of the "cluster" voting rule, the Speaker announces that recorded votes on a group of bills considered under the suspension procedure will be postponed until later that day or until sometime within the next two days. The bills then are brought up in sequence and disposed of without further debate. On the first clustered vote in a series, members have a minimum of fifteen minutes in which to vote; on the remaining votes the Speaker may reduce the time on each one to a minimum of five minutes.

In 1977 the suspension rule was changed again—over the objections of many Republicans—to permit the Speaker to entertain motions to suspend the rules every Monday and Tuesday. The Republican minority saw this as an effort by Democrats to steamroll legislation through the House. Democrats argued that the change facilitated action on the House's business.

The Speaker is in complete charge of the measures considered under the suspension procedure. The Speaker "has the discretion whom to recognize for a motion to suspend the rules," the Chair noted in response to a question about "why it is impossible to proceed with a suspension bill." I am "exercising that discretion" on this bill, declared the Speaker.[3] Committee chairmen, usually with the concurrence of their ranking minority colleagues, write the Speaker requesting that certain bills be taken up via the suspension route. Typically, these are bills that have not been reported by committee. But any measure—reported or not, previously introduced or not—can be brought to the floor under suspension of the rules if the Speaker chooses to recognize the representative offering the suspension motion.

In 1979 the Democratic Caucus adopted guidelines governing the consideration of measures under the suspension method. The Speaker, for instance, is directed not to schedule measures if they exceed $100 million in any fiscal year unless authorized to do so by the Democratic Steering and Policy Committee, the party caucus's executive committee, which the Speaker chairs. Committee chairmen are mindful of this party rule. As Interior Chairman Morris K. Udall, D-Ariz., noted: "H.R. 4600 was specifically developed as a suspension vehicle in order to accommodate members who felt that this important legislation should be expedited. In order to qualify for consideration under suspension, the total cost of that bill was reduced below $100,000,000."[4]

The suspension procedure enables the House to bypass normal floor procedures and quickly pass legislation that can attract an overwhelming voting majority. Committee chairmen generally support the suspension of the rules because they can bring measures to the floor under a procedure that protects their bills from floor amendments and points of order. Party leaders, too, use the suspension route to "fast track" emergency legislation, such as providing shelter to the homeless.

During the hectic last days of a congressional session, suspension of the rules is used more frequently than merely on Mondays and Tuesdays. The parliamentary situation also is somewhat different during this period. Members who at an earlier time in the session might vote against a bill brought up under suspension because they had no opportunity to offer amendments to it or because it was a major bill, might vote for the legislation during the end-of-the-session crunch on the argument that it was that version or nothing.

In summary, it should be noted that the great bulk of legislation that comes before the House is passed by means of either the Consent Calendar or the suspension procedure.

District of Columbia Legislation

The federal capital is a unique governmental unit. Residents of the District of Columbia have no voting representation in Congress. (They have a nonvoting delegate in the House and no representation in the Senate.)

Despite "home rule" for the capital, the House exercises control over the District principally through its standing Committee on the District of Columbia and the Appropriations Committee's Subcommittee on the District of Columbia. House rules set aside the second and fourth Mondays of each month for legislation reported by the District of Columbia Committee. However, appropriations bills for the District do not come up during those special days. Instead, they are considered under the privilege given all legislation reported by the Appropriations Committee (see "Privileged Legislation").

The Private Calendar

Private bills cover a range of purposes, such as authorizing reimbursement to the family of a CIA agent who died while testing LSD for the agency, waiving immigration requirements so a Philadelphia woman could marry a Greek man, and granting citizenship to a 111-year-old Albanian woman so she could vote in one free election before she died. Under House procedures, the Speaker is required to call private bills on the first Tuesday of each month (unless the rule is dispensed with by a two-thirds vote or unanimous consent is obtained to transfer the call to some other day of the month) and, at his discretion, on the third Tuesday as well.

Few members have the time to review carefully all the private bills reported in each session. That job is done by a committee of "official objectors" composed of three members from each party appointed by the majority and minority leaders (but note that these are not the same objectors who review the Consent Calendar). Bills must be placed on the Private Calendar seven days before being called up to give the objectors time to screen them for controversial provisions. (Committee reports on private measures must also be available to the objectors for three calendar days.) The objectors attend House sessions on Private Calendar days to answer any questions about the pending measures. If two or more members of the House object to a bill on the first Tuesday, it automatically is sent back to the committee that reported it, although at the request of a member it may at this time be "passed over without prejudice" for later consideration.

Private bills that are not opposed are considered in "the House as in Committee of the Whole." This is a special forum into which the House transforms itself to consider private bills and some public bills. Here, general debate on legislation is not permitted and amendments are considered under expedited procedures.

On the third Tuesday of the month, the Speaker gives preference to omnibus bills—those containing several previously rejected private measures. These measures are in order even if they were objected to earlier. Omnibus bills also are considered in "the House as in Committee of the Whole." As Rep. Edward P. Boland, D-Mass., a longtime member of the Private Calendar objectors, has pointed out:

> Such omnibus bills are read by paragraph, and no amendments are entertained except to strike out or reduce amounts or provide limitations. Matter so stricken out shall not be again included in an omnibus bill during that session. Debate is limited to motions allowable under the rule and does not admit motions to strike out the last word [see Chapter 6] or reservations of objections. The rules prohibit the Speaker from recognizing Members for statements or for requests for unanimous consent for debate.[5]

Immigration matters and claims against the government constitute the bulk of the private bills. These are referred to the Judiciary Committee of each chamber for consideration. To limit the introduction of private bills, these subcommittees have established strict procedural rules for considering such measures.[6] An objective of these rules, along with enactment of new immigration laws that assign additional responsibilities to executive agencies in handling immigration and alien issues, is to keep the "number of private bills introduced yearly to fewer than 300." [7] Private bills are submitted to the president for signature or veto.

"PRIVILEGED" LEGISLATION

Under House rules, six standing committees have direct access to the floor for selected bills. The committees and the types of legislation eligible to be called up for immediate debate are listed in Table 5-2. Despite this privilege, most of these bills must observe a waiting period of at least three days to give members time to read the committee reports. Special rules from the Rules Committee, however, must lay over only one day, while reports on budget resolutions must be available to members for ten days before those resolutions can come to the floor. (See also "Types of Special Rules.")

Privileged measures are matters of special import to the House as an institution or to the federal government. The Appropriations, Ways and Means, and Budget panels report measures to finance the operations of the government; the Standards of Official Conduct Committee is concerned with matters involving the public reputation of the House; the House Administration panel handles necessary housekeeping proposals; and the Rules Committee plays a major role in determining which measures the House considers.

TABLE 5-2 Committees With Direct Access to the Floor for Selected Legislation

Committee	*Legislation*
Appropriations	General appropriations bills; continuing appropriations resolutions if reported after Sept. 15
Budget	Budget resolutions under the Congressional Budget and Impoundment Control Act of 1974
House Administration	Printing resolutions and expenditures of the House contingent fund
Rules	Rules and the order of business
Standards of Official Conduct	Resolutions recommending action with respect to the conduct of a member, officer or employee of the House
Ways and Means[a]	Revenue-raising bills

[a] House precedents appear to indicate that the Ways and Means Committee has less privilege than the other committees because of an ambiguity in House rules. See the commentary that follows House Rule XVI, clause nine, of the rules of the House of Representatives in H. Doc. No. 97-271.

Before 1974, the Interior and Insular Affairs, Public Works, and Veterans' Affairs committees also had privileged access to the floor. This was eliminated as part of changes in committee procedures adopted that year. The purpose was to narrow the range of bills with a "green light" to the floor.

Even privileged measures are subject to points of order (parliamentary objections that any member may raise at an appropriate time) on the ground that they violate certain rules of the House. If upheld, such points of order return the measure to the committee that considered it. Frequently, therefore, committees with privileged access will ask the Rules Committee to waive points of order against their bills. The Appropriations Committee, for example, occasionally violates the House rule banning policy language (authorization legislation) in general appropriations bills and protects such language from points of order by persuading the Rules Committee to issue waivers.

MAJOR LEGISLATION

Most major bills, particularly controversial ones, do not go directly from committee to a calendar and then to the floor of the House. Instead, such measures are given special treatment by the Rules Committee.

The Rules Committee is among the oldest of House panels. The First Congress in April 1789 appointed an eleven-member rules body to draw up its procedures. With a few early exceptions, each succeeding Congress has done the same, although for nearly a century the Rules panel was a select (temporary) committee that prepared procedures for the incoming Congress and then went out of existence.

In 1858 the Speaker became a member of the Rules Committee and, shortly thereafter, chairman of the panel. In 1880 the Rules Committee became a standing (permanent) committee, and in 1883 it initiated the practice of reporting special orders, or rules, which, when agreed to by majority votes of the House, controlled the amount of time allowed for debate on major bills and the extent to which they could be amended from the floor.

From 1858 to 1910 the Speaker determined which bills reached the House floor. He also appointed the other members of the Rules Committee and thus ensured a favorable attitude toward his policy preferences. Speakers during this period permitted the Rules Committee to acquire overwhelming authority over the House's agenda and the order of business. Speaker Joseph G. Cannon, a Republican from Illinois who was Speaker from 1903 to 1911, abused these and other powers, with the result that the House "revolted" in 1910 and removed the Speaker from the Rules Committee. The House leadership, however, retained—and still retains, in cooperation with the Rules Committee—considerable control over the flow of legislation reaching the floor.

The power of the Rules Committee lies in its scheduling responsibilities: its "traffic cop" or even "police chief" role. As public bills are reported out of committee, they are entered in chronological order on one of two calendars, the Union Calendar (technically, the Calendar of the Committee of the Whole House on the State of the Union) or the House Calendar. On the former are placed all revenue bills, general appropriations bills, and measures that directly or indirectly appropriate money or property (including all authorization measures); all remaining public bills, which generally deal with administrative and procedural matters, go on the latter.

If all measures had to be taken up in the order in which they were listed on the calendars, as was the practice in the early nineteenth century, many major bills would not reach the House floor before Congress adjourned. Instead, major legislation reaches the floor in most instances by being granted precedence through a special order (rule) obtained from the Rules Committee. A rule is really a simple resolution (H Res). A request for a rule usually is made by the chairman of the committee reporting the bill.

The Rules Committee holds a hearing on the request and debates it in the same manner other committees consider legislative matters. The rule, if granted, then is considered on the House floor and voted on in the same fashion as regular bills.

A rule serves two principal purposes:

1. It bumps a bill up the ladder of precedence, eliminating the waiting time that would be necessary if chronological order were observed. The Rules Committee, in effect, shuffles the Union and House calendars by holding back rules for some bills and reporting them for others.

2. It governs the length of debate permitted once the bill reaches the floor and the extent to which a measure can be amended.

In blocking or delaying legislation from reaching the floor, the Rules Committee is not necessarily playing an obstructionist role. It actually may be drawing fire away from the leadership, certain committees, and individual members. It is not uncommon for representatives to request the Rules Committee to prevent unwanted bills from reaching the floor. Speaker O'Neill, a former member of the committee, once said, "It takes the heat for the rest of the Congress, there is no question about that." [8]

The committee also acts as an informal arbiter of disputes among other House committees. Because of overlapping jurisdictions, one committee may report a measure that trespasses on the authority of another. In such a case, the Rules Committee may resolve the dispute by authorizing the second committee to offer amendments or by refusing to waive points of order on the floor, thus giving members of the second committee an opportunity to attempt to delete the offending matter.

Rules also plays a jurisdictional arbitration role on multiply referred legislation. As a precondition for a "rule," the Rules Committee may urge or require committees to agree on the vehicle—one of the committee's reported bills, some consensus product, or something else—for floor debate and amendment. "Prior to the Rules Committee consideration" of the water resources bill, stated Rules member Joe Moakley, D-Mass., "the four committees responsible for this bill negotiated a substitute text to be used as the basis for [floor] consideration." [9]

This practice limits fights on the floor among rival committees, simplifies floor decision making, and avoids putting Rules in the position of deciding that one panel's bill rather than another's will be the vehicle for floor discussion.

ROLE OF THE RULES COMMITTEE

As the previous discussion demonstrates, few pieces of major legislation would reach the House floor without a rule. Thus, action, or lack of it, by the Rules Committee generally determines whether a bill is considered at all. The chairman of the committee has wide discretion in scheduling the panel's order of business. By not setting a hearing on a rule for a particular bill, the chairman can, in most cases, kill the measure. Alternatively, the Rules chairman and members of the panel are well positioned to attach their favorite proposals to virtually any measure needing a rule (see "Rules Members Gain by Helping Others").

Once hearings are under way, two common delaying techniques have been used:

1. Preventing quorums in the committee
2. Scheduling a parade of witnesses to testify against issuing a rule for the bill

House rules require committees to have a specific number of members present (a quorum) before they officially can conduct business. One-third of a committee's membership constitutes a quorum for the purpose of marking up legislation; however, a majority of the committee must be present when the panel votes on reporting a bill to the House.

The first technique involves manipulation of the rules governing a quorum. Opponents of a bill may persuade sympathetic Rules Committee members not to attend committee meetings on the bill. The Rules chairman also may either strictly observe or ignore the rules for a quorum. Strict observance of the rules can be an effective delaying tactic. For example, in 1971 Rules Chairman William M. Colmer, D-Miss. (1933-1973), and several Republican members opposed a Civil Service pay bill. During a committee meeting on the bill, committee member Ray Madden, D-Ind. (1943-1977), left the session briefly to greet a visiting constituent. A Republican member observed that a quorum was not present. Chairman Colmer did not send for Madden, "who was within voice range in the adjoining hallway," but "promptly adjourned the meeting for lack of a quorum." [10]

In the second strategy, opponents of a bill line up a series of witnesses to testify against it. Executive agency officials and pressure group witnesses do not testify at hearings of the Rules Committee that involve the granting of rules. The witness list is confined to legislators interested in the measure, usually the chairman and members of the committee reporting the bill, legislators opposing it, and members who desire to offer certain amendments during floor consideration. Committee rules state that all members "will be provided a reasonable opportunity to testify." This provision, when honored to the extreme, can open the way to a time-consuming flood of testimony. Rules hearings also function as a "dress rehearsal"—previewing in advance for a bill's proponents and opponents the issues and amendments that will be raised during the House debate.[11]

After holding hearings, the Rules Committee can refuse to grant a rule, thus preventing the measure from reaching the floor. In short, it is possible to keep from the floor bills that are poorly conceived, technically deficient, inimical to majority party interests, or whose jurisdiction is hotly contested by several committees.

Even on the vote to approve a rule, there is room for maneuver. The chairman may unexpectedly schedule the vote when certain committee members cannot attend. The Consumer Protection Act of 1970 failed to obtain a rule on a 7-7 tie because Rep. Richard W. Bolling, D-Mo. (1949-1983), a supporter of the measure, was out of town. The vote was scheduled on only one day's notice, leaving little or no time for Bolling to return. The vote killed further action on consumer legislation in the 91st Congress, and there was a two-year delay before the House finally passed the consumer agency bill.

In 1968 the Rules Committee set a specific cutoff date after which no requests for rules would be heard. The policy was initiated by Rules Chairman Colmer and has been followed by successive committee chairmen, subject to the Speaker's scheduling and deadline-making prerogatives. Its purpose is to prevent logjams at the end of each session, albeit not with much success. Emergency and procedural measures, such as stopgap funding bills, are excluded from the cutoff dictum.

Types of Special Rules

The Rules Committee traditionally grants three basic kinds of rules: open, closed, and modified. The distinction between them goes solely to the question of the amendment process. All three types almost always provide a fixed number of hours for general debate. In addition, any of these types also may contain waivers of points of order. A rule from the Rules Committee is reproduced on page 146.

OPEN RULE. The majority of bills are considered under an open rule (see Table 5-3). Under an open rule, any germane amendment may be offered from the floor. Amendments may be simple or complex. For example, an amendment may simply extend the funding of a program from two to four years or it may rewrite whole sections of a bill.

Rules Members Gain . . .

Serving on the House Rules Committee is generally a profitable experience.

The committee can be a springboard to House leadership posts; Speaker Thomas P. O'Neill Jr., D-Mass., for example, was a member of Rules when he helped make a name for himself in a 1970 House reorganization. And Trent Lott, R-Miss., named to Rules in 1975 at the start of his second House term, by 1981 had become minority whip, the No. 2 GOP leadership job.

"You get to do things for other members," says David E. Bonior, D-Mich., a Rules member who hopes to become chairman of the Democratic Caucus if Richard A. Gephardt, D-Mo., decides to give up the chairmanship in 1987 to run for the presidency. "You can get to be a patron saint."

Beyond institutional gains, committee members also can affect substantive issues they care about. Butler Derrick, D-S.C., for example, has used his position on Rules to shape legislation on nuclear-waste disposal that is vital to South Carolina. Bonior has been a key player on foreign policy issues. And Martin Frost, D-Texas, has been at the center of tax and budget issues, running briefly last year for the chairmanship of the Budget Committee before withdrawing.

Rules Committee service also gives members an opportunity to funnel dollars into their districts. Knowing that their bills must win Rules' approval to reach the House floor, the leaders of other committees are anxious to accommodate the needs of Rules members. "You have leverage with the committee chairmen," says Bonior. "Those guys are always looking to please us."

Members do not have to be particularly senior to partake of the bounty. As a freshman member of Rules in the last Congress, Alan Wheat, D-Mo., won funding for a flood control project that will cost the federal government about $128 million when completed at the end of the decade.

"Membership on Rules should not be a disadvantage," says Wheat.

In preparing the fiscal 1985 supplemental appropriations bill (HR 2577—PL 99-88), the Appropriations Committee kept Rules firmly in mind. The spending measure was loaded with water projects, including several for key Rules members.

Of particular importance to Rules Chairman Claude Pepper, D-Fla., was the bill's authorization of part of a Miami park that includes the Mildred and Claude Pepper fountain. The measure also provided both authorization and funding for major improvements to the Gulfport, Miss., harbor located in Lott's district; expansion of the lake and recreational facilities at Sepulveda Dam in the Los Angeles district of Rules

. . . by Helping Others

Democrat Anthony C. Beilenson; and a water main in the Tennessee district of James H. Quillen, the senior Republican on Rules.

When the Public Works and Transportation Committee objected to Appropriations' inclusion of unauthorized projects in the spending package, Rules issued a rule that left a number of them vulnerable to a point of order when the bill reached the floor. But the rule protected most of the projects sought by Rules members, including those of Pepper, Beilenson and Quillen.

Lott was furious that his harbor was not similarly protected, and consequently was among the projects stricken on the floor. But it was included by the Senate and stayed in the final version of the bill, as did the projects of the other Rules members.

In a private caucus of Rules Democrats before the committee's consideration of the rule for the supplemental, Pepper had made no bones about his insistence that the Miami project stay in the bill.

In an interview, he said that most of the federal involvement in the 40-acre Bayfront Park renovation was taken care of in other bills and that the supplemental merely contained authorization of a promenade connecting the park to a main street.

Pepper, who led ground-breaking ceremonies on the $21 million project Aug. 10, has worked for years on securing more than $13 million in federal funding for the park. The project is to be built by the Army Corps of Engineers, and will also get funding from the state of Florida and private donors.

Pepper says he told Rules Democrats that three of the four pieces of the project were already authorized and that he did not want the rest held up "for one little pavilion. I didn't think it was fair to deprive me on that."

Quillen acknowledges that being ranking Republican on the Rules Committee may have helped him secure $5 million in the bill for an eight-mile water transmission line for the city of Bristol, the kind of water main normally built and paid for by local governments.

The bill provides the money to the Tennessee Valley Authority, which has built many reservoirs but never this kind of water main, according to TVA officials. According to Jerry Pulliam, acting city manager of Bristol, the city did not have the money for the project.

Pulliam said the city now uses a 40-year-old water line that is generally sufficient for current needs but not for economic growth.

Source: Andy Plattner, "Rules Members Gain by Helping Others," *Congressional Quarterly Weekly Report,* Aug. 24, 1985, 1673.

CLOSED RULE. A closed rule prohibits floor amendments, but rarely are such "pure" closed rules reported by the Rules Committee. Instead, closed rules in the contemporary House forbid floor amendments except those offered by the reporting committee or committees. Critics say closed rules (also called "gag" rules) hamper the legislative process and violate democratic norms. Rep. Charles W. Stenholm, D-Texas, put it this way:

> In most cases, closed rules say that we as individual Members are willing to allow a small portion of the whole decide what information we need to consider, what complexities our minds are able to master, and from what alternatives we should choose. Furthermore, many times closed rules indicate either an arrogance on the part of the proponents of a bill or an insecurity about the bill's merits or abilities to stand up against competing ideas.[12]

Supporters of closed rules say they are necessary in the case of very complex measures subject to intense lobbying. In addition, national emergency legislation sometimes needs to be expedited by the closed rule procedure.

Tax bills provide a good illustration of the pressures surrounding closed rules. For decades the House considered tax measures under closed rules, agreeing with the argument of Wilbur D. Mills, D-Ark. (1939-1977), chairman of the Ways and Means Committee from 1959 to 1974, that tax legislation was too complex and technical to be tampered with on the floor. If unlimited floor amendments were allowed, Mills argued, the internal revenue code soon would be in shambles and at the mercy of pressure groups.

For years House members trusted the judgment of the Ways and Means Committee, but in the 1970s disenchantment began to set in. In 1973 the Democratic Caucus approved a change in committee procedures requiring a chairman to give advance notice in the *Congressional Record* of his intention to request a closed rule. After such notice is made, a party caucus may be called at the request of fifty House Democrats. The caucus discusses the support in the party for particular amendments to the bill and may instruct Democrats on the Rules Committee to make those amendments "in order" in the House debate on the legislation.[13]

MODIFIED RULE. A third category of special orders is the modified rule. These rules typically impose a rigorous structure on the amendment process, specifying the number and types of amendments that will be in order on the floor. A main feature of modified rules is that some parts of the bill will be open to amendment and some parts will not be.

WAIVER RULES. Finally, there are rules waiving points of order. Under these rules, which appear in open, closed, and modified rules, specific House procedures may be temporarily set aside. Without such waivers, measures in technical violation of House procedures could not be dealt with rapidly, and important parts of bills could be deleted for technical reasons during floor debate. "If we went strictly by the House rules," remarked a House member, "I am sure this body would have a very difficult time operating." [14] Waivers permit timely floor action on those measures.

Generally, waivers are confined to temporary exemptions from *specific* House rules and procedures. In recent Congresses, Rules has granted *blanket* waivers of all points of order against pending legislation. The minority party has objected strenuously to this development. As Rules member Trent Lott stated:

> The number of Rules Committee resolutions in which all House rules have been waived against a bill or conference report has increased from 2 percent in the 98th Congress to 25.5 percent in the 1st session of [the 100th] Congress. Blanket waivers are indicative of the leadership's willingness to permit committees to circumvent and violate House rules in order to advance their legislative agenda.[15]

There are occasions, however, when blanket waivers are essential to lawmaking. "Under the circumstances in which this bill is brought to the floor," exclaimed Rules Republican Delbert L. Latta, Ohio, "I do not see how we could possibly proceed without the [blanket] waivers that are being asked for." [16]

Creative "Rules" for the House

With activism and visibility highlighting contemporary floor decision making, the Rules Committee has employed its procedural imagination to produce innovative rules. These rules often structure the floor amendment process to provide advantages to the majority party. They seek to impose predictability in an environment grown more conflict-ridden and unpredictable. Generally, these creative rules are more complex variations of modified rules. "Structured," "self-executing," and "king-of-the-hill" rules are examples of these ingenious procedures. All three, which may overlap one another, are designed to achieve policy, political, and parliamentary objectives.

STRUCTURED RULES. The structured rules limit the number of floor amendments, establish a specific order in which those amendments are to be offered, frequently identifying the member who can offer each amendment, and typically prohibit any change in the amendments made in order. These rules may also prescribe debate limits on the entire amendment process or on each amendment made in order. Structured rules may require that all amendments be printed in the *Congressional Record* prior to floor action on the legislation. This requirement aids the

TABLE 5-3 Open and Restrictive Rules, 95th-100th Congresses

Congress	*Open Rules*		*Restrictive Rules*		Total
	Number	Percent	Number	Percent	
95th	213	88	28	12	241
96th	161	81	37	19	198
97th	90	80	22	20	112
98th	105	72	40	28	145
99th	65	64	36	36	101
100th, 1st sess.	42	55	34	45	76

Source: Congressional Record, daily ed., Dec. 22, 1987, E4981.

floor managers. "Newer chairmen are kind of unsure of themselves," said Rules member Joe Moakley. "They ask for amendments to be printed [in advance, in the *Record*] so they can be ready for anything." [17]

On the one hand, the thrust of these rules is to restrict members' general right to offer floor amendments. This result frequently arouses the ire of minority party members and even rank-and-file Democrats. As Table 5-3 indicates, most rules permit an open floor amendment process, but measures that dominate the nation's and House's attention are common recipients of restrictive floor procedures. The objectives of these restrictive rules are to expedite floor decision making, focus member attention on the major policy alternatives, enhance partisan goals, and strengthen committee prerogatives.

On the other hand, structured rules can expand the range of policy options put before the membership. Issues that are not eligible under normal parliamentary procedures can be made in order. The Rules Committee can make in order nongermane amendments, legislation stuck in committee, or even measures that have never been introduced.

Whether restrictive, expansive, or both, a fundamental thrust of structured rules is to define the sequence in which specific amendments are to be voted upon. Sometimes the purpose is to benefit the committee that reported the legislation; sometimes it grants other members an opportunity to revamp the reporting committee's priorities. There is little question, however, that the Rules Committee's ability to determine the sequence of action can influence the ultimate outcome.

For example, the majority leadership may support an expensive initiative over a less costly one advocated by the minority leadership. The Rules Committee could fashion a rule that permits votes on only three policy alternatives: the costly version; the less costly version; and a compromise midway between the other two, advanced by the majority leadership and designed to attract broad support. Members can then explain to constituents who opposed both the "budget-buster" and "inadequate" alternatives that they voted for the "reasonable" option.

SELF-EXECUTING RULES. Self-executing rules stipulate a two-for-one procedure: adoption of the rule simultaneously enacts another measure, amendment, or both. The House, in short, is deemed to have passed a separate proposition when it adopts the rule. Traditionally used to expedite consideration of Senate amendments to House-passed legislation, self-executing rules now appear in more complex guises. "Back in the old days, the Rules Committee only used this unusual procedure for making technical or minor and noncontroversial amendments to a bill," remarked Representative Lott. "But this procedure is being used more and more lately for the automatic adoption of substantive and controversial provisions." [18]

A rule on a continuing resolution, for instance, provided that an amendment to provide $3.5 million in assistance to Nicaraguan Contras was automatically agreed to by the House upon adoption of the special order. The bipartisan House leadership supported the self-executing rule because it facilitated House passage of the controversial plan by precluding a direct vote on it.[19]

KING-OF-THE-HILL RULES. Completely new to Capitol Hill are king-of-the-hill (or king-of-the-mountain) rules. "As far as I know," said Rules Chairman Bolling during May 1982 debate on a rule governing consideration of the concurrent budget resolution, this procedure is "unique." [20] The rule is unusual in a parliamentary sense for two major reasons. First, it permits the House to vote on an array of major policy alternatives—so-called substitutes that are the equal of new bills—one after the other. Significantly, no matter the outcome—yea or nay—on any of the substitutes, the king-of-the-hill rule typically stipulates that the vote on the last substitute is the only one that counts for purposes of accepting or rejecting a national policy. As Rules member Butler Derrick, D-S.C., explained in describing a rule on a concurrent budget resolution to which major alternatives would be proposed:

> Each substitute will be in order notwithstanding the prior disposition of any one of them. The amendments will be considered under the so-called king-of-the-mountain procedure whereby the last amendment . . . will be considered to have been finally adopted in the Committee of the Whole and reported back to the House.[21]

One advantage of this approach is that it provides "political cover" to legislators who can cast votes on several budgetary plans and explain their actions to constituents in any manner they choose.

Second, the king-of-the-hill rule waives scores of procedures and precedents. For instance, parliamentary principles state that once part of a bill is amended, it is not in order to vote on that part unless another amendment, broader in scope, changes the part plus a "bigger bite" of the legislation. The massive substitutes made in order by the king-of-the-hill rule amend literally everything in the pending legislation. Technically, nothing is left to be changed and the amending process automatically terminates under traditional House procedures. Traditional procedures, however, are not followed when this type of rule is used, because political and policy objectives are of overriding concern.

Adoption of the Rule

All rules must be approved by a majority of the House. Rules are reported to the House by the Rules Committee and are debated for a maximum of one hour, with the time equally divided by custom between the Rules chairman, or his designee, and the ranking minority member of the committee, or a designee. The "hour rule" is the basic rule of floor debate in the House. Theoretically, it permits each member one hour of debate on any question, including the rules approved by the Rules Committee. The hour rule is never followed in practice, however. A member who controls the debate time under the hour rule, in this case the Rules chairman or his designee, always moves the "previous question" at the end of this hour (or before the full hour is used if no member seeks time for debate). Adoption of this motion by majority vote stops all debate, prevents the offering of amendments, and brings the House to an immediate vote on the main question, the rule itself in this context.

The main strategy, then, for a member wishing to amend a rule is to defeat the previous question. "I am urging my colleagues to vote against the previous question on this rule so that we can offer a substitute rule" is a common refrain from members who oppose the rule. Under House precedents, the member who led the fight against approval of the previous question is recognized by the Speaker to propose a substitute rule. In short, the key vote here often is not on adoption of the rule but on approval of the previous question.

If there is no controversy, rules are adopted routinely by voice vote after a brief discussion. Under a 1977 procedural change, the Speaker may postpone votes on rules and permit them to be voted on at five-minute intervals later in the day or anytime within the next two days. The procedure is similar to cluster voting under suspension of the rules.

The House seldom rejects a rule proposed by the Rules Committee. Speaker O'Neill once remarked, "Defeat of the rule on the House floor is considered an affront both to the Committee and to the Speaker." [22] The Rules Committee generally understands the conditions the House will accept for debating and amending important bills.

To be sure, there are always a few rules on major bills that the House turns down every year. House Republicans, for instance, successfully led the effort to vote down the initial rule on the landmark overhaul of the internal revenue code that eventually became law at the end of the 99th Congress. During the next Congress the House rejected a rule on reconciliation legislation in part because it contained a major welfare reform proposal. Undeterred, Speaker Wright adjourned the House for one minute, reconvened it immediately, and took up another rule on the measure (minus the welfare plan), which the House adopted. (House rules stipulate that a special order cannot be taken up on the same day it is reported unless it attracts a two-thirds vote.) Lacking the two-thirds support and with many legislators slated to return to their districts the next day, Speaker Wright employed this unusual and controversial procedure. House Republicans railed against the Speaker's parliamentary end run. "The House is convinced the sun rises and sets over it, but this is the first time I've ever seen us readjust the sun," stated Rep. Hank Brown, R-Colo.[23]

Recent Rules Committee Changes

The Rules Committee is "specifically designed to function as the responsible agent of the majority party, using its great discretionary authority over pending legislation to facilitate the consideration and adoption of the majority party's program," Representative Bolling asserted many years before he became the committee's chairman (1979-1983).[24] As the agent of the majority party, the committee today generally is under the influence of the Speaker of the House.

It has not always worked that way, however. There have been maverick Rules chairmen. One of the best known was Rep. Howard W. Smith, D-Va. (1931-1967), who presided over the committee with an iron hand from 1955 to 1967. Smith was no traffic cop simply regulating the flow of bills to the floor. He firmly believed the committee should "consider the substance and merits of the bills," and he often blocked measures he disapproved of and advanced those he favored, sometimes thwarting the will of the majority.[25]

The Rules Committee lacks authority to amend bills, but it can bargain for changes in return for granting rules. Smith frequently did this. In an attempt to lessen the power of the conservative coalition of southern Democrats and Republicans that controlled the committee from the mid-1930s to the early 1960s, House liberals succeeded in adopting a series of rules changes beginning in the late 1940s. These included several versions of the "twenty-one-day rule." But the independent power of the chairman was not effectively curbed until the membership of the committee was expanded in 1961.[26] The committee's present composition is nine Democrats and four Republicans. Traditionally, the panel has had a disproportionate party ratio to ensure majority control.

Since the early 1970s, the House Democratic leadership has relied on the Rules Committee to deal with the recent changes that have affected the House as an institution, such as wider use of multiple referrals of legislation and the rise of subcommittee government. Today, this committee is one of the few centralizing panels in a greatly decentralized House. Hence the importance of its rule-writing responsibilities.

The Rules Committee also has substantive responsibilities. It reported out such major measures as the Legislative Reorganization Act of 1970, the Congressional Budget and Impoundment Control Act of 1974, and resolutions providing for the creation of a permanent Select Intelligence Committee and the televising of House floor sessions.

The Speaker and the Rules Committee

By the 95th Congress, the Rules Committee had become closely linked to the Speaker and the Democratic Caucus. Dormant for decades, the Democratic Caucus began to stir at the end of the 1960s. Beginning in 1971, the caucus initiated procedures for using secret ballots to elect committee chairmen, including the chairman of the Rules Committee. In 1975 the Speaker was authorized to appoint, subject to caucus ratification, all majority party members of the Rules Committee.

The institutional changes adopted in the 1970s reduced the Rules panel's independence. The committee can still oppose the Speaker, but this seldom happens. As Speaker Wright stated:

> The Rules Committee is an agent of the leadership. It is what distinguishes us from the Senate, where the rules deliberately favor those who would delay. The rules of the House, if one understands how to employ them, permit a majority to work its will on legislation rather than allow it to be bottled up and stymied.[27]

The Speaker's influence over the Rules Committee enables him, on occasion, to challenge the prerogatives of committee chairmen.

Still, the power of the Rules Committee should not be underestimated. The Speaker cannot track every major and minor bill. The caucus cannot convene every week to issue instructions to the committee. The history of the Rules Committee is "one of the committee's accommodating the leadership on the one hand and seeking independent status on the other." [28] For the time being, at least, the emphasis is on sharing power with the Speaker.

In summary, the Rules Committee performs the critical task of assuring the orderly consideration of legislation. Although it generally works in harmony with the majority leadership today, the committee can and sometimes does act contrary to the leadership's wishes and to the will of the House. Its actions in preventing or delaying certain bills from reaching the floor, or in negotiating changes in legislation in return for a rule, led to periodic efforts, particularly in the 1950s and 1960s, to curb the committee's power. But the House is unlikely to endorse another mechanism to perform its functions.

LEGISLATION BLOCKED IN COMMITTEE

What happens when a standing committee refuses to report a bill that many members support, or when the Rules Committee fails to grant a rule to legislation with substantial support? Several procedures are available to bring legislation to the floor that had been stalled in committee.

Which procedure to use depends on the nature of the legislation. Suspension of the rules, discussed earlier, is appropriate if the measure is relatively noncontroversial or minor. If a major bill is being blocked by a standing committee or the Rules Committee, there are extraordinary procedures that can be employed to "spring" the bill from committee. These procedures are difficult to implement, but if the House is determined, committees can be compelled to yield legislation.

The Discharge Petition

The discharge procedure, adopted in 1910, provides that if a bill has been before a standing committee for thirty days, any member can introduce a motion to relieve the panel of the measure. A clerk of the House then prepares a discharge petition, which is made available for members to sign when the House is in session. The names are not disclosed until the required 218 signatures (a majority of the 435-member House) are obtained. The names then are published in the *Congressional Record*. A member may withdraw his or her signature until a majority is secured.

When 218 members have signed the petition, the motion to discharge is put on the Discharge Calendar. After seven days on the calendar, it becomes privileged business on the second and fourth Mondays of the month (but not during the last six days of a session). Any member who signed the petition may be recognized to offer the discharge motion. When the motion is called up, debate is limited to twenty minutes, divided between proponents and opponents. If the discharge motion is rejected, the bill is not eligible again for discharge during that session. If the discharge motion prevails, any member who signed the petition can make a motion to call up the bill for immediate consideration. It then becomes the business of the House until it is disposed of. A vote against immediate consideration assigns the bill to the appropriate calendar, with the same rights as any bill reported from committee.

Few measures are ever discharged from committee. From 1937 through 1986 (approximately the period during which the modern version of the rule has been in effect), 393 discharge petitions were filed; but only 19 measures actually were discharged.[29] Of those, 17 were passed by the House, but only 2 of these became law: the Fair Labor Standards Act of 1938 and the Federal Pay Raise Act of 1960. Several factors account for this. Members are reluctant to second-guess a committee's right to consider a bill. The discharge rule violates normal legislative routine, and even members who support a bill blocked in committee may refuse to sign a discharge petition for this reason.

Legislators also are reluctant to write legislation on the floor of the House, without the guidance and information provided in committee hearings and reports. Particularly in the case of complicated legislation, many members feel the need for committee interpretation. Then, too, it is not easy to obtain 218 signatures. Attempts to reduce the present requirement occasionally are made, but none has been successful. Finally, members are hesitant to employ a procedure that one day may be used against committees on which they serve.

For all its limitations, the discharge rule serves important purposes. It focuses attention on particular legislative issues, and the threat of using it may stimulate a committee to hold hearings or report a bill. During the 99th Congress, for example, the House Judiciary Committee had bottled up a Senate-passed measure that weakened the 1968 gun control law. Rep. Harold L. Volkmer, D-Mo., introduced a discharge petition to bring the legislation to the floor. With the aid of other legislators and the National Rifle Association, Representative Volkmer obtained the necessary 218 signatures. However, when the number went over 200 signatures, the Judiciary Committee met and voted to report gun legislation. To better control the parliamentary process, the majority leadership then brought the measure to the floor under regular procedures (a "rule" from the Rules Committee) rather than under those procedures specified by the discharge calendar rule.[30] The threat and reality of discharge, in sum, triggered fast action by the Judiciary Committee and subsequent enactment of the gun bill.

Rules Committee's Extraction Power

The Rules Committee has an extraordinary authority that it rarely exercises: it can introduce rules for bills that the committee of jurisdiction does not want to report. The power of extraction is based on an 1895 precedent, which the committee has invoked rarely. Extraction is a highly controversial procedure and evokes charges of usurpation of other committees' rights. As Energy and Commerce Chairman Dingell declaimed: the Rules Committee, "in a very high-handed and arrogant fashion [is placing] before this body a piece of legislation which has never been properly or fairly considered in a committee of proper jurisdiction." [31]

One of the rare occasions when extraction was used occurred on February 9, 1972. The Education and Labor Committee refused to approve a dock strike measure, but the Rules Committee went ahead and reported a rule for floor action on the bill. Despite the vigorous opposition of Speaker Carl Albert, D-Okla. (1947-1977), the House adopted the rule by a 203-170 vote, thus springing the bill from the committee. The House then proceeded to pass the bill.

The threat of extraction by the Rules panel in itself can break legislative logjams. In 1967 the Judiciary Committee balked at reporting an anti-riot bill. Rules Chairman Colmer announced that his committee would soon hold hearings on a rule for the bill. This was enough to prompt the Judiciary Committee to report the bill.[32] Or a Rules Chairman, such as Claude Pepper, can try to make any measure in order for floor action, whether it has received committee consideration or not. Chairman Pepper "used his position to circumvent Ways and Means and clear his home-care health bill for floor action without hearings, debate, or markup in the committee of jurisdiction—a rare use of the Rules Committee's chairman's power." [33]

Discharging the Rules Committee

The discharge rule, with several variations, also applies to the Rules Committee, with one significant difference: a motion to discharge the committee is in order seven days, rather than thirty days, after a measure has been before that panel. Any member may enter the motion, which is handled like any other discharge petition in the House.

Since the Rules Committee reports "rules" as a matter of original jurisdiction, members who wish to discharge a special rule must introduce one of their own so there will be something to discharge. For example, on July 12, 1982, Barber B. Conable, Jr., R-N.Y. (1965-1985), filed "a petition to discharge from the Rules Committee, House Resolution 450, which will provide 10 hours of debate and consideration" of a constitutional amendment to balance the federal budget. House Resolution 450 was the rule introduced earlier by Representative Conable and referred to the Rules Committee.

Once a rule has been pending before the Rules Committee for seven legislative days, House precedents state, it is in order to bring before the House "a measure pending before a standing committee for 30 legislative days." In the example discussed above, the House Judiciary Committee had refused to take action on a constitutional balanced budget amendment for more than a year.

Proponents of the constitutional amendment worked diligently to obtain the 218 signatures for the White House-backed measure, which already had been passed by the Senate.

> As the petition neared the required number of signatures, the Democratic leadership persuaded some members to remove their names. So amendment backers and Republicans devised a new strategy. They worked intensely to gather the last 13 needed. Once they had them, the group marched en masse onto the House floor, signed the petition, and put it over the top. So organized was the "coup" that Vice President George Bush was on hand to greet the 13 in a Capitol meeting room.[34]

In the end, the required two-thirds of the House failed to support the proposed constitutional amendment. Until 1982, the last time the discharge procedure had been used successfully against the Rules Committee was in 1965. (See "Long-Shot Legislative Strategy" for a 1986 attempt to discharge Rules.)

In summation, when the Rules panel is discharged from a special rule, the bill to which it applies automatically is discharged from the legislative committee that is blocking it.

Calendar Wednesday

Under House procedures, every Wednesday is reserved for standing committees to call up measures (except privileged bills) that have been reported but not granted rules by the Rules Committee. The Speaker calls the roll of standing committees in alphabetical order. Each chairman (or designated committee member) either passes or brings up for House debate a measure pending on the House or Union calendars. The rule may be dispensed with by unanimous consent, that is, without objection, or by a two-thirds vote of the House. The Rules Committee may not report a rule setting aside Calendar Wednesday.

The Calendar Wednesday rule was adopted in 1909 in an attempt to circumvent Speaker Cannon's control of the legislative agenda. Today it is seldom employed and usually is dispensed with by unanimous consent. During the 98th Congress (1983-1985), however, a group of Republicans came to object regularly to dispensing with Calendar Wednesday proceedings. Their purpose was to generate political heat on the majority leadership to schedule nonprivileged measures (a constitutional balanced budget amendment, school prayer measures, criminal code reform, and so on) pending on the Union or House Calendars for floor action. Republicans called their list of priority measures "the Agenda of the American People." The House even adopted an agricul-

Long-Shot Legislative Strategy

Republicans on April 23 began implementing their high-risk strategy to force the House leadership to allow new action on President Reagan's request for $100 million in aid for the Nicaraguan "contras."

Democratic leaders have not yet responded officially to the Republican challenge, but they are expected to offer a plan soon for the House to reconsider contra aid next month.

Leadership sources said Speaker Thomas P. O'Neill Jr., D-Mass., will meet the week of April 28 with conservative and moderate Democrats who support Reagan's request but who want to impose some conditions on the aid. O'Neill already has said he will allow the House to act again on contra aid, possibly on one of several Defense Department funding bills now being written.

The House in March rejected Reagan's original request for military and logistical aid. When the House debated the matter again on April 16, Republicans rebelled at the Democrats' ground rules, thus forcing a postponement.

The Republicans now are trying to get 218 House members — a majority — to sign a petition to force action under terms likely to give Reagan the House victory he so far has been unable to obtain. They hope to reach the goal by the end of April, allowing time for a House vote by mid-May.

Although publicly professing optimism about gaining the 218 signatures, GOP leaders privately acknowledge that doing so will be almost impossible. To reach that goal, they will have to attract about 40 Democrats. So far, even Democrats who back Reagan on contra aid have been reluctant to support the Republican ploy—largely because doing so would challenge the Democratic leadership. Majority Whip Thomas S. Foley, D-Wash., said the leaders will ask Democrats not to sign.

But just getting close to the 218 figure might force O'Neill to allow a vote on Reagan's request, some Republicans have said. "It might be like horseshoes: Close is enough," said Robert J. Lagomarsino, R-Calif.

To force new House action on contra aid, Republicans on April 14 introduced their own proposed rule (H Res 419) for considering it. The Republicans on April 23 filed a motion to "discharge" that rule from the Rules Committee and began rounding up 218 signatures on their petition to force the issue to the House floor.

If Republicans get the 218 names, House rules require delays. First, the matter must be held for seven legislative days, to give the Rules Committee time to act. Second, discharge petitions can be considered only on the second and fourth Mondays of each month. That means the earliest the GOP measure could reach the floor is May 12. The next day would be June 9 since the House will be in recess on May 26, the fourth Monday in May. [The GOP strategy was unsuccessful.]

Source: John Felton, "Long-Shot Legislative Strategy: House Republicans Launch Bid for Reagan's 'Contra' Program," *Congressional Quarterly Weekly Report*, April 26, 1986, 919.

ture bill under its Calendar Wednesday procedure.[35] Objections to dispensing with Calendar Wednesday gradually diminished because of inherent limitations with the procedure.

Since 1943, fewer than fifteen measures have become law under Calendar Wednesday proceedings.[36] House consideration of the aforementioned 1984 agricultural measure was the first time the procedure had been used in a quarter-century. Five factors account for the limited use of this procedure: (1) Only two hours of debate are permitted, one for proponents and one for opponents. This may not be enough to debate complex bills. (2) A committee far down in the alphabet may have to wait weeks before its turn is reached. (3) A bill that is not completed on one Wednesday is not in order the following Wednesday, unless two-thirds of the members agree. (4) The procedure is subject to dilatory tactics precisely because the House must complete action on the same day. (5) Only the chairman or a member authorized by the committee may bring up a bill under Calendar Wednesday. This requirement limits use of the procedure.

FINAL SCHEDULING STEPS

After a bill has been granted a rule, the final decision on when the measure is to be debated is made by the majority party leaders. The leadership prepares daily and weekly schedules of floor business and adjusts them according to shifting legislative situations and demands. A bill the majority has scheduled for consideration may be withdrawn if it appears to lack sufficient support. Or measures may be put on a fast track by the leadership. Some statutes, too, provide expedited procedures for processing certain measures. (Timetables established in law commonly provide for committee review for a specified time followed by an up-or-down vote—no amendments are permitted—on the floor, again within a specified time following committee consideration.)

Nothing in the House rules requires the majority leadership to provide advance notice of the daily or weekly legislative program. This is done as a matter of longstanding custom in two principal ways. Announcements about floor action are made by majority party leaders, often in response to a query from the minority leader. The legislative program for the following day for both chambers also is printed in each issue of the *Congressional Record*, in a section called the Daily Digest. The Friday *Record* contains a section called the Congressional Program Ahead, which lists the following week's legislative agenda and the dates on which floor action has been scheduled.

The majority leadership also sends "whip notices" to its members at the end of each week, or more frequently, if necessary. The whip notices

TONY COELHO
CALIFORNIA
MAJORITY WHIP

Congress of the United States
House of Representatives
Office of the Majority Whip
Washington, D.C. 20515

October 30, 1987

WHIP NOTICE INFORMATION

Legislative Program -- 51600
Floor Information -- 57400
Whip Information -- 53130

My dear Colleague:

The program for the House of Representatives for the week of November 2, 1987 is as follows:

MONDAY, NOVEMBER 2

HOUSE MEETS AT NOON
PRO FORMA SESSION

TUESDAY, NOVEMBER 3

HOUSE MEETS AT NOON
SUSPENSIONS
(4 Bills)
RECORDED VOTES ON SUSPENSIONS WILL BE POSTPONED UNTIL THE END OF THE DAY

1. S. 1158 -- Omnibus Health Amendments
2. H.R. 3235 -- Health Maintenance Organization Amendments of 1987
3. H.R. 3108 -- FIFRA Scientific Advisory Panel Reauthorization Act
4. H.R. 1517 -- Aircraft Collision Avoidance Act of 1987

H.R. 3479 -- Notice To Lessees No. 5 (NTL-5) Gas Royalty Act of 1987
(Open rule, one hour of debate)

WEDNESDAY AND THE BALANCE OF THE WEEK, NOVEMBER 4, 5 AND 6

HOUSE MEETS AT 10 A.M.

H.R. 1212 -- Employee Polygraph Protection Act
(Open rule, one hour of debate)

H. J. Res. 395 -- Continuing Resolution, Fiscal 1988
(Subject to a rule)

Conference Reports may be brought up at any time. Any further program will be announced later.

Sincerely,

Tony Coelho

Tony Coelho
Majority Whip

contain information concerning the daily program for the following week. Although sent under the majority whip's signature, they are prepared mainly by the Speaker and majority leader. The schedule often is changed in response to unforeseen events or new circumstances. A whip notice is reproduced on page 139.

The majority (and minority) whip's office has several phone recordings that announce the daily and weekly programs, legislative actions taken on the floor, and changes in the schedule. Democratic and Republican members obtain similar information from their respective cloakrooms (located just off the chamber floor). The majority whip prepares one-page summaries of pending bills, called "Whip Advisories," and publishes "Whip Issues Papers," which describes activities of the House on one or more major issues. The minority whip prepares a weekly notice of floor business for all members. The GOP party conference publishes each week summaries of bills to be considered on the floor, and the minority leader prepares "Legislative Alerts" for party colleagues that highlight measures reported from the committees.

SUMMARY

Scheduling is a party function that the House majority leadership shares with the Rules Committee. Bills reported from committees are assigned to one of several calendars. (Committee reports on measures must also meet appropriate "layover" requirements—three calendar days excluding Saturdays, Sundays, and legal holidays in most cases—before legislation can be scheduled for floor action. To be sure, the Rules Committee can waive the layover requirement.) If measures are not brought up under the suspension of the rules procedure, most bills must receive a special rule, granted by the Rules Committee, giving the bill a green light to the floor and specifying the conditions under which it will be considered.

Although they are seldom employed, there are special procedures to dislodge bills that are stalled either by a standing committee or the Rules Committee.

Outside events and pressures often influence the timing of floor action on a particular bill. Upcoming congressional elections can be a critical factor in scheduling controversial bills. And the congressional work load must be taken into account.

Bargaining and compromise are necessary at each stage of the scheduling process. Members, pressure groups, and executive officials all try to influence the shaping of the House agenda. Their efforts are directed principally at the Rules Committee and the majority leadership. Once an important proposal is granted a rule and placed on the House schedule by the Speaker, the focus shifts to the intricacies of floor procedure.

NOTES

1. *Congressional Record,* daily ed., July 2, 1980, H6106.
2. The objectors' criteria can be found in the *Congressional Record,* daily ed., March 4, 1987, H960.
3. *Congressional Record,* daily ed., Sept. 22, 1986, H7893.
4. *Congressional Record,* daily ed., Sept. 18, 1986, H7339.
5. *Congressional Record,* daily ed., March 4, 1987, H960.
6. *Congressional Record,* daily ed., May 28, 1987, H4048-H4051. See Joe Morehead, "Private Bills and Private Laws: A Guide to the Legislative Process," *Technical Services Quarterly* (Spring-Summer 1986): 173-184.
7. *New York Times,* April 11, 1986, A18.
8. Spark M. Matsunaga and Ping Chen, *Rulemakers of the House* (Urbana: University of Illinois Press, 1976), 21.
9. *Congressional Record,* daily ed., Nov. 5, 1985, H9681.
10. Matsunaga and Chen, *Rulemakers of the House,* 98.
11. Bruce I. Oppenheimer, "The Rules Committee: New Arm of Leadership in a Decentralized House," in *Congress Reconsidered,* ed. Lawrence C. Dodd and Bruce I. Oppenheimer (New York: Praeger, 1977), 105-113.
12. *Congressional Record,* daily ed., Dec. 15, 1987, H11436.
13. For an example of the use of this party procedure, see Catherine E. Rudder, "Committee Reform and the Revenue Process," in *Congress Reconsidered,* 126-128.
14. *Congressional Record,* daily ed., July 14, 1987, H6282.
15. *Congressional Record,* daily ed., Dec. 22, 1987, E4981.
16. *Congressional Record,* daily ed., Dec. 21, 1987, H11956. Implicitly, all special rules waive certain House rules and therefore potential points of order under them, such as the daily order of business rule. Explicitly, waivers are generally of two kinds: those waiving points of order that would prevent consideration of a bill and those waiving points of order against specific provisions in a bill or amendments to the bill that otherwise might be ruled out of order.
17. Janet Hook, "GOP Chafes under Restrictive House Rules," *Congressional Quarterly Weekly Report,* Oct. 10, 1987, 2452.
18. *Congressional Record,* daily ed., Oct. 29, 1987, H9131.
19. *Congressional Record,* daily ed., Sept. 23, 1987, 1987, H7814-H7822. See Steven Pressman, "Wright Steers Middle Course on Contra Aid," *Congressional Quarterly Weekly Report,* Sept. 19, 1987, 2255.
20. *Congressional Record,* daily ed., May 21, 1982, H2519.
21. *Congressional Record,* daily ed., Nov. 4, 1987, H1867.
22. *Congressional Quarterly Weekly Report,* Feb. 14, 1976, 313.
23. *Washington Post,* Oct. 30, 1987, A16. The unusual proceedings can be found in the Oct. 29, 1987, *Congressional Record.*
24. Richard W. Bolling, "The House Rules Committee," *Business and Government Review,* University of Missouri (September-October 1961): 39.
25. *Nation's Business,* February 1956, 103.
26. See, for example, James A. Robinson, *The House Rules Committee* (Indianapolis: Bobbs-Merrill, 1963); Charles O. Jones, "Joseph G. Cannon and Howard W. Smith: An Essay on the Limits of Leadership in the House of Representatives," *Journal of Politics* (September 1968): 617-646; and Robert L. Peabody, "The Enlarged Rules Committee," in *New Perspectives on the House of Representatives,* 2d ed., ed. Robert L. Peabody and Nelson W. Polsby (Chicago: Rand McNally, 1969).

27. *New York Times,* Dec. 18, 1987, A34.
28. Matsunaga and Chen, *Rulemakers of the House,* 143. Also see *A History of the Committee on Rules,* 97th Cong., 2d sess. (Washington, D.C.: Government Printing Office, 1983); and Alan Ehrenhalt, "The Unfashionable House Rules Committee," *Congressional Quarterly Weekly Report,* Jan. 15, 1983, 151.
29. Figures were made available to the author by Richard Beth, Government Division, Congressional Research Service, Library of Congress.
30. Nadine Cohodas, "House Votes to Weaken U.S. Gun Control Law," *Congressional Quarterly Weekly Report,* April 12, 1986, 783-785.
31. *Congressional Record,* daily ed., July 13, 1987, H6228.
32. Matsunaga and Chen, *Rulemakers of the House,* 25.
33. Julie Kosterlitz, "Still Going Strong," *National Journal,* Jan. 2, 1988, 15.
34. *Christian Science Monitor,* Oct. 4, 1982, 4.
35. *Congressional Record,* daily ed., Jan. 25, 1984, H126-H139.
36. Information compiled by Richard Beth, Government Division, Congressional Research Service, Library of Congress.

CHAPTER 6

House Floor Procedure

To a casual observer, the House floor may appear hopelessly disorganized. Legislators talk in small groups or read newspapers while a colleague drones on. People come and go in an endless stream. Motions are offered, amendments proposed, points of order raised—all evoking little apparent interest from the members present. The scene may not make much sense to visitors in the gallery.

If the visitors are there to see their representatives in action, they are likely to be disappointed. Attendance is often sparse during floor debates. Members may be in committee sessions, meeting with constituents, or attending to numerous other tasks. Members can reach the floor quickly, however, to respond to quorum calls, participate in debate, or vote.

The House chamber has two levels. Above the floor itself are the galleries for visitors, diplomats, the media, and other observers. Visitors sit on either side or facing the Speaker's rostrum; the press sits above and behind the rostrum. Unlike senators, representatives have no desks in the chamber. Their seats, which are unassigned, are arranged in semicircular rows in front of the Speaker. Aisles divide groups of seats, and a broad center aisle divides the majority and minority parties. Traditionally, the Democrats sit to the Speaker's right, the Republicans to the left. When a majority of the 435 members are present, for a recorded vote, for instance, the floor becomes alive with activity.

Normally, the House convenes daily at noon.[1] Buzzers ring in committee rooms, members' offices, and in the Capitol, summoning representatives to the floor. Rules and informal practices set the daily order of business: an opening prayer, approval of the *Journal* (a record of the previous day's proceedings), receipt of messages from the Senate or the president, one-minute speeches and insertions in the *Congressional Record*, and other routine business.

Under the rules, a majority of the House (218 members) must be present for business to be conducted. Whether or not a quorum has been established, it is assumed to be present unless officially discovered otherwise. A member may ask for a quorum call provided he or she is recognized for that purpose by the Speaker. Any member, however, may make a point of no quorum whenever a vote is pending. Informally, the House frequently operates with far fewer members.

The House usually is in session Monday through Friday. Mondays are reserved mainly for routine legislation. The workload on Fridays generally is light because many members want to return to their home districts on weekends. Most major proposals are taken up Tuesday through Thursday.

The previous chapter outlined the normal procedure by which major legislation reported by standing committees is routed to the House floor through the Rules Committee, as well as certain legislative shortcuts to the floor, such as the Consent Calendar, Private Calendar, and suspension of the rules. This chapter will focus on major bills, the most common route by which they reach the House floor—via a special "rule" granted by the Rules Committee—and basic floor procedures in the Committee of the Whole.

The basic steps in floor consideration for these bills are:

1. Adoption of the rule granted by the Rules Committee
2. The act of resolving the House into the Committee of the Whole
3. General debate
4. The amending process
5. Final action by the full House

Along the way we shall examine some of the strategies used by proponents of bills to secure passage of legislation and by opponents to defeat or modify bills, as well as examples of how the rules can be used to delay or expedite the proceedings.

ADOPTION OF THE "RULE"

As was noted in Chapter 5, the first step in bringing a major bill to the floor is to adopt the special rule issued by the Rules Committee. A rule, or special order, sets the conditions under which the measure is to be considered, decreeing whether floor amendments will be permitted and how much debate will be allowed.

Rules are infrequently rejected by the House. Challenging the Rules Committee is an uninviting task; House members realize that at some future time they will need a rule from the committee for their own bills. Rejection of a rule usually reflects sharp divisions in the House; heavy lobbying by pressure groups, the president, or federal agency officials; or general agreement that the reporting committee did a poor job of drafting the bill.

Voting down a rule is often a "procedural kill." During the 99th Congress, for example, Republicans organized to defeat the rule on the landmark tax reform bill.

> The rule was a tempting target for the Republicans. Members were hesitant to vote against the bill itself, fearing they might be straddled with the blame for killing reform, but the rule offered a chance, as [GOP Whip Trent] Lott put it, for members "to get rid of the bill without putting their fingerprints on the trigger." [2]

The defeat of the rule launched an intensive round of negotiations among the Speaker, party leaders, the treasury secretary, and White House officials, including the president meeting privately with all House Republicans, to bring a second rule on the tax bill to the floor. Speaker O'Neill even took the floor and urged members in a moving speech to vote for the second rule, which the House agreed to. This example shows how procedural matters can have a critical impact on policy making. Without favorable action on the second rule, tax reform would have been dead.

A typical rule from the Rules Committee is reproduced on page 146. This is an open rule for a bill concerning rehiring of former air traffic controllers. The decision-making process it outlines is used in the House for most major bills.

After the House votes to adopt the rule, the Speaker declares the House resolved into the Committee of the Whole. Under most rules, there is an hour of general debate, after which the bill is open to amendment under the five-minute rule. In other instances, a rule may permit more debate, restrict amendments, waive points of order, or grant priority to certain amendments. After all amendments are dealt with, the Committee of the Whole is directed to report the bill back to the House. There, after voting on any amendments reported (adopted) by the Committee of the Whole and on engrossment (printing the bill as revised by any changes made during floor consideration) and third reading (by title only), the House turns to a motion to recommit—returning the bill to the legislative committee that handled it, with or without instructions to revise the measure. Finally, the bill is voted on in its entirety. If the bill is passed, there also occurs an automatic pro forma motion to reconsider, which invariably is rejected ("laid on the table").

In the rule for the air traffic controllers bill, the five principal procedural steps governing House consideration of major legislation are spelled out. These are:

IV

House Calendar No. 126

100TH CONGRESS
2D SESSION

H. RES. 360

[Report No. 100–502]

Providing for the consideration of the bill (H.R. 3396) to provide for the rehiring of certain former air traffic controllers.

IN THE HOUSE OF REPRESENTATIVES

FEBRUARY 4, 1988

Mr. GORDON, from the Committee on Rules, reported the following resolution; which was referred to the House Calendar and ordered to be printed

---

RESOLUTION

Providing for the consideration of the bill (H.R. 3396) to provide for the rehiring of certain former air traffic controllers.

Resolved, That at any time after the adoption of this resolution the Speaker may, pursuant to clause 1(b) of rule XXIII, declare the House resolved into the Committee of the Whole House on the State of the Union for the consideration of the bill (H.R. 3396) to provide for the rehiring of certain former air traffic controllers, and the first reading of the bill shall be dispensed with. After general debate, which shall be confined to the bill and which shall not exceed one hour, to

This sheet has an adhesive backing. Remove the backing and attach the errata sheet to page 146. Please note the page number corrections elsewhere in your copy.

Errata

The concluding section of H.Res.360, as reproduced in its original form on p. 146, was inadvertently omitted. The full text is as follows:

Resolved, That at any time after the adoption of this resolution the Speaker may, pursuant to clause 1(b) of rule XXIII, declare the House resolved into the Committee of the Whole House on the State of the Union for the consideration of the bill (H.R. 3396) to provide for the rehiring of certain former air traffic controllers, and the first reading of the bill shall be dispensed with. After general debate, which shall be confined to the bill and which shall not exceed one hour, to be equally divided and controlled by the chairman and ranking minority member of the Committee on Post Office and Civil Service, the bill shall be considered for amendment under the five-minute rule and each section shall be considered as having been read. At the conclusion of the consideration of the bill for amendment, the Committee shall rise and report the bill to the House with such amendments as may have been adopted, and the previous question shall be considered as ordered on the bill and amendments thereto to final passage without intervening motion except one motion to recommit.

Page	*For*	*Read*
242, para. 1, line 6	p. 243	p. 259
253, para. 1, line 6	p. 254	p. 243
258, para. 5, line 7	p. 259	p. 254

1. Resolving the House into the Committee of the Whole
2. General debate
3. Consideration of amendments under the five-minute rule
4. A recommittal motion
5. Vote on final passage

Roadblocks usually occur during the amending stage in the Committee of the Whole.

COMMITTEE OF THE WHOLE

The Committee of the Whole is simply the House in another form. Every legislator is a member. House rules require all revenue raising or appropriations bills to be considered first in the Committee of the Whole. Technically, there are two such bodies. One is the "Committee of the Whole House," which debates private bills. The other and more important is the "Committee of the Whole House on the State of the Union," commonly shortened to Committee of the Whole, which considers public measures. (Further references to the Committee of the Whole in this chapter are to its meaning as the Committee of the Whole on the State of the Union.)

The rules used in the Committee of the Whole are designed to speed up floor action. Four rules or customs distinguish the conduct of business in the full House from proceedings in the Committee of the Whole.

First, a quorum is only 100 members in the Committee of the Whole (218 constitute a quorum in the House). Second, the Speaker does not preside over the Committee of the Whole but appoints a colleague, who is a member of his own party, to chair it (a practice that can be traced to English precedent). The Speaker is permitted to remain in the chamber and take part in debate, but he rarely participates except to make closing remarks on closely contested major bills. By tradition, the Speaker seldom votes, except to break a tie. Third, it is in order to close or limit debate on sections of the bill by unanimous consent or majority vote of the members present. The "previous question" motion is not permitted in the Committee of the Whole. Finally, amendments to bills are introduced and debated under the five-minute rule (discussed in this chapter under "the amending process") rather than under the hour rule (Table 6-1).[3]

Visitors in the gallery can tell whether the House is in the Committee of the Whole by noting the position of the mace, a 46-inch column of ebony rods bound together by silver and topped by a silver eagle. The mace, symbol of the authority of the Sergeant at Arms, is

TABLE 6-1 Major House-Committee of the Whole Characteristics

House	*Committee of the Whole*
Mace raised	Mace lowered
Speaker presides	Chairman presides
More than half the House (218) is a quorum	100 is a quorum
One-hour rule for amendments	Five-minute rule for amendments
Previous question in order	Motion to limit debate on amendments, but not the previous question motion, in order
Forty-four members or one-fifth of the House trigger a recorded vote	Twenty-five members trigger a recorded vote
Motion to recommit in order	Motion to recommit not in order

Source: Adapted from *Manual on Legislative Procedure in the U.S. House of Representatives,* 6th ed., prepared under the auspices of the House Republican Leader, May 1986.

carried by him, if called upon, to enforce order on the floor. It rests on a pedestal on a table at the right of the Speaker's podium. It is taken down from the table when the Speaker hands the gavel to the chairman of the Committee of the Whole. When the committee rises and the Speaker resumes the chair, the mace is returned to its place.[4]

GENERAL DEBATE

The first order of business in the Committee of the Whole is general debate on the entire bill under consideration.[5] One hour of debate usually is allowed, equally divided between the minority and majority parties. In the rule on the air traffic controllers bill, one hour was authorized; for very complex legislation, as many as ten hours may be scheduled.

Each party has a floor manager from the committee of original jurisdiction who controls time, allotting segments to supporters or opponents, as the case may be. Almost without exception, the floor manager for the majority party is the spokesman for the bill. Sometimes both sides favor passage of a bill, and both floor managers rise in support. During debate on controversial legislation, both floor managers may declare their support for the bill's aims, but reflect differences of opinion on specific sections or amendments.

The term "general debate" can be misleading, as most members deliver set speeches and engage in a minimum of give-and-take. Because committees and subcommittees shape the fundamental character of most legislation, only a limited number of representatives actually participate in debate, and those who do usually are members of the committee that drafted the legislation. Yet general debate has an intrinsic value that is recognized by most House members and experts on the legislative process.

Purposes of General Debate

General debate is both symbolic and practical. It assures both legislators and the public that the House makes its decisions in a democratic fashion, with due respect for majority and minority opinion. "Congress is the only branch of government that can argue publicly," noted a House Republican. "Debate appropriately tests the conclusions of the majority."[6] General debate forces members to come to grips with the issues at hand; difficult and controversial sections of the bill are explained; constituents and interest groups are alerted to a measure's purpose through press coverage of the debate; member sentiment can be assessed by the floor leaders; a public record, or legislative history, for administrative agencies and the courts is built, revealing the intentions of proponents and opponents alike; legislators may take positions for reelection purposes; and, occasionally, fence-sitters may be influenced.

Not all legislators agree on the last point. Some doubt that debate can really change views or affect the outcome of a vote. But debate, especially by party leaders just before a key vote, can change opinion. Speaker O'Neill's "speech on Lebanon," said a House Democrat, "was one of the few times on the House floor when a speech changed a lot of votes."[7]

In sum, reasoned deliberation is important in decision making. Lawmaking consists of more than log rolling, compromises, or power plays. General debate enables members to gain a better understanding of complex issues, and it may influence the collective decisions of the House. The dilemma members often face, explained Representative Udall, "is to know what is right, and to make the right decisions" based upon skimpy, incomplete, or unavailable information.[8]

Floor Managers' Role

Longstanding customs govern much of the action on the floor. But the floor managers direct the course of debate on each bill. The manager for the majority side often is the chairman of the committee that reported the bill, or an appointed committee colleague. The ranking minority committee member, or an appointed surrogate, usually is the floor manager for the minority party. Many committees routinely name subcommittee chairmen to manage the bills reported from their subcommittees. The floor managers are centrally located during debate at long tables near the center of the chamber, with the main aisle separating the Democratic from the Republican side.

The floor managers guide their bills through final disposition by the House. Their duties are varied. They must:

1. Plan strategy and parliamentary maneuvers to meet changing floor situations
2. Respond to points of order
3. Attempt to protect the bill from amendments the majority considers undesirable
4. Alert supporters to be on the floor to vote for or against closely contested amendments
5. Advise colleagues on the meaning and importance of the amendments
6. Judge when amendments of committee members should be offered or deferred
7. Inform party leaders of member sentiment and the mood of the House toward their bill
8. Control the time for general debate and, if necessary, act to limit debate on amendments, sections or titles of the bill, or on the entire measure
9. Arrange the sequence of speakers on major amendments to insure that the best supporting orators are matched against those of the opposition
10. Mobilize outside support to build winning coalitions on the floor

The fate of much legislation depends on the skill of the floor managers. Effective floor management increases the chances for smooth passage of legislation. The enactment of the landmark Congressional Budget and Impoundment Control Act of 1974 was credited in large part to its skillful floor manager, Representative Bolling.

Floor managers are given several advantages over their colleagues. They customarily lead off debate in the Committee of the Whole and have the first opportunity to appeal for support. During debate they receive priority recognition from the chair. A floor manager may take the floor at critical moments ahead of other legislators to defend or rebut attacks on the bill, or they may offer amendments to coalesce support for the measure. The floor manager also is entitled, by custom, to close the debate on an amendment, thus having the last chance to influence sentiment.

Floor managers generally can count on support from their party leadership. They also are permitted to have up to five of their committee's staff members on the floor during debate, ready to research rules and precedents, draft amendments, answer technical questions about the bill, or prepare statements. Finally, as a result of committee hearings, discussion, and markup, the managers have a reservoir of knowledge about the technical details of a measure and are in a good position to judge which amendments to accept and reject, and the best arguments to employ for or against them.

Delaying Tactics

Despite the generally tighter rules on debate in the House than in the Senate, there are many ways to prolong or delay proceedings. Members may raise numerous points of order, make scores of parliamentary inquiries, or offer trivial amendments. For example, during consideration of a bill creating the Department of Education, a member opposed to the legislation offered two unsuccessful but dilatory amendments. One would have changed the department's name to the Department of Public Education (DOPE), the other to the Department of Public Education and Youth (DOPEY).[9] Members may also demand recorded votes on every amendment, ask unanimous consent to speak for additional minutes on each amendment, make certain that all time for general debate is used, or, if the chair declares their amendments nongermane, appeal the ruling and demand recorded votes on each appeal.

Until a 1971 rules change, a reading of the *Journal* was used as a delaying tactic. Before that time, the reading could be dispensed with only by unanimous consent or by a motion to suspend the rules, requiring a two-thirds vote. Since then, the Speaker has been authorized to examine the *Journal*, although a vote may be demanded on its approval. That often happens at the start of every day for various reasons: to determine which members are present, to break up committee meetings, or simply to vent partisan frustrations. Rules changes in 1974 and 1977 drastically reduced demands for quorum calls as a dilatory device.

The purpose of delaying tactics is often to stall action on a measure in order to allow more time to gather support (if those using such tactics favor the bill) or to kill it (if they are opposed). Delay is intended sometimes to force action and other times to prevent it. Or delay may be employed to protest actions of the majority. Republicans used obstructionist tactics in the aftermath of a one-vote victory engineered, the GOP argued, by the unwarranted actions of Speaker Wright in permitting an extra ten minutes on a vote so that Democrats could lobby a partisan colleague to change his vote. To vent their anger and forge greater party rapport, Republicans retaliated by tying up the House for the next three days. The House, for example, found itself without a quorum (many legislators were in their districts) and could not conduct any business. The Majority Leader several times tried to adjourn the House but, because of Democratic absentees, Republicans kept voting against adjournment. Several hours elapsed before Democratic leaders rounded up enough partisan colleagues to adjourn the House.[10]

THE AMENDING PROCESS

The amending process is the heart of decision making on the floor. Under an open rule, amendments determine the final shape of bills passed by the House. At times, amendments become more important or controversial than the bills themselves. A good example is the 1974 Jackson-Vanik amendment—named for its sponsors, Sen. Henry M. Jackson, D-Wash. (1953-1983), and Rep. Charles A. Vanik, D-Ohio (1955-1981). The amendment was tacked on to a 1974 trade act after prolonged controversy in each house. It limited trade with the Soviet Union until that country lifted its restrictions on Jewish emigration.

The Five-Minute Rule

House rules require all bills and joint resolutions to be "read" three times to give members every opportunity to become familiar with the measures they are considering. In practice, bills are not read word for word. Verbatim readings generally are dispensed with by unanimous consent, or by a rule that stipulates that each section of the bill is considered to have been read.

The first "reading" occurs when a measure is introduced and referred to committee. The bill is not read aloud; the bill's number and title are printed in the *Congressional Record*. The second reading occurs in the Committee of the Whole. The third occurs by title (the name of the bill only) just before the vote on final passage.

Bills are considered, or "read," as specified in the rule from the Rules Committee, usually section by section. The Rules Committee might specify a reading by title rather than by section, to permit larger, interrelated parts of the measure to be open to amendment.

At the end of general debate, a bill is "read" for amendment under the five-minute rule. Under this rule, "any Member shall be allowed five minutes to explain any amendment he may offer, after which the Member who shall first obtain the floor shall be allowed to speak five minutes in opposition to it, and there shall be no further debate thereon."[11]

Actual practice differs from the rule. Amendments are regularly debated for more than the ten minutes allowed. Members gain the floor by offering pro forma amendments, moving "to strike the last word," or "to strike the requisite number of words." Technically, these also are amendments, although no alteration of the bill is contemplated by the sponsors; their purpose is to extend the debate. (Pro forma amendments are not in order under a "closed" rule.) In addition, members may ask unanimous consent to speak longer than five minutes, and may yield part of their time to other legislators. Debate on amendments cannot extend forever, however, since the floor manager can move that discussion be terminated at a specified time. Time limits on amendments can be critical at times to the fate of legislation. On the Labor-HHS appropriations bill, for example,

> a time limit on debate engineered by William H. Natcher, D-Ky., the chairman of the Appropriations Subcommittee on Labor, HHS, and Education, effectively prevented amendments from being offered on sensitive social topics [abortion, for example] that in years past have mired the funding bill in controversy.[12]

The box on pp. 154-155 illustrates how Representative Natcher gained the time agreement.

Amendments are in order as soon as the section to which they apply has been read, but they must be proposed before the clerk starts to read the next section. If the clerk has passed on to a succeeding section, a member must be granted unanimous consent to offer an amendment to the previous section. In addition to being timely, amendments must be germane to the bill and section under consideration. Reading by section or title helps structure rational consideration of complex bills, but on noncontroversial measures it is common for the floor manager to ask unanimous consent that the entire bill be considered as read. In that case, the entire measure is open to amendment at any point.

Reading amendments can be used to delay or prolong proceedings. Any member can object to a unanimous consent request to dispense with the reading of amendments. Opponents of a bill may draft lengthy amendments, perhaps the size of the Manhattan telephone directory, not with the expectation that they will be adopted, but to cause delays by having them read in their entirety.

House rules, however, permit a nondebatable motion to be made in Committee of the Whole to dispense with the reading of an amendment if it was either printed in the *Congressional Record* or provided to the reporting committee at least one day prior to floor action on the bill. The Rules Committee, too, can obviate the reading requirement by requiring that amendments be printed in advance in the *Record* or by specifying in its rules that amendments meet the terms of the aforementioned House rule that dispenses with the reading of amendments. Opportunities for dilatory tactics, in brief, can be short-circuited by other actions. More-

Limiting Debate in the Committee of the Whole . . .

Mr. NATCHER: Mr. Chairman, I ask unanimous consent that all debate on this bill and all amendments thereto conclude no later than 4 o'clock.

The CHAIRMAN: Is there objection to the request of the gentleman from Kentucky?

Mr. TAUKE: Mr. Chairman, I object.

The CHAIRMAN: Objection is heard.

Mr. NATCHER: Mr. Chairman, I renew my request.

Mr. TAUKE: Instead of objection, if I could, I would reserve the right to object, Mr. Chairman.

The CHAIRMAN: Objection was heard; however, as the Chair understands, the gentleman from Kentucky [Mr. NATCHER] renews his unanimous-consent request that all debate end at 4 o'clock, and the gentleman from Iowa has reserved an objection.

Mr. NATCHER: Mr. Chairman, will the gentleman yield to me on his reservation of objection?

Mr. TAUKE: I am pleased to yield to the gentleman from Kentucky.

Mr. NATCHER: Mr. Chairman, let me say to the gentleman from Iowa we understand on this side that there are three or four amendments pertaining to reductions in this bill. It is our intention that every Member that has an amendment to offer, that that amendment be heard and properly heard and voted upon. That is our intention. We have no intention on this side, and my friend, the gentleman from Massachusetts [Mr. CONTE], has no intention on his side to cut any Member off.

Mr. TAUKE: I appreciate the chairman's characterization of the request, and I certainly understand that there is no intent to cut anyone off.

Mr. NATCHER: Mr. Chairman, at this time I ask unanimous consent that all debate on this bill and all amendments thereto conclude no later than 4:30.

The CHAIRMAN: The Chair must indicate that we have a pending unanimous-consent request of the gentleman from Kentucky to end debate at 4 o'clock on which discussion was occurring on a reservation by the gentleman from Iowa.

Is there objection or does the gentleman from Kentucky wish to modify his unanimous-consent request?

Mr. NATCHER: Mr. Chairman, at this time I would like to maintain the hour of 4 o'clock.

The CHAIRMAN: Is there objection to the request of the gentleman from Kentucky?

Mr. TAUKE: Mr. Chairman, reserving the right to object, I do not want to be difficult, but at this juncture I probably will object to any limitation

. . . on the Labor-HHS Appropriations Bill

until we have an opportunity to get a better handle on what amendments may be offered.

The CHAIRMAN: Objection is heard.

Mr. NATCHER: Mr. Chairman, at this time I ask unanimous consent that all debate on the bill and all amendments thereto conclude no later than 4:30.

The CHAIRMAN: Is there objection to the request of the gentleman from Kentucky?

Mr. TAUKE: Mr. Chairman, reserving the right to object, perhaps the Chair and the gentleman from Kentucky, I would say, could perhaps reach a limitation on individual amendments, but I am reluctant without knowing how many amendments are out there to limit debate on the total bill. So I will object.

The CHAIRMAN: Objection is heard.

Mr. NATCHER: Mr. Chairman, at this time I ask unanimous consent that all debate on the bill and all amendments thereto conclude not later than 5 o'clock.

The CHAIRMAN: Is there objection to the request of the gentleman from Kentucky?

Mr. TAUKE: Mr. Chairman, reserving the right to object, again, I do not mean to be difficult, but I intend to object to any limitation on the total amount of debate on the bill until we have a better handle on how many amendments are available.

Mr. Chairman, I would not oppose a limitation on individual amendments, but I do on the whole bill, so I do object.

The CHAIRMAN: Objection is heard.

Mr. NATCHER: Mr. Chairman, I move that all debate on this bill and all amendments thereto conclude no later than 5 p.m.

The CHAIRMAN: The question is on the motion offered by the gentleman from Kentucky [Mr. NATCHER].

The question was taken; and the Chairman announced that the ayes appeared to have it.

RECORDED VOTE

Mr. TAUKE: Mr. Chairman, I demand a recorded vote.

A recorded vote was ordered.

The vote was taken by electronic device, and there were—ayes 262, noes 159, not voting 12.

Source: Excerpted from *Congressional Record,* daily ed., Aug. 5, 1987, H7123.

over, the rules of the game and the expectation of retaliation in kind encourage moderation in the use of dilatory tactics.

RATIONALE FOR AMENDMENTS

Amendments serve diverse objectives. Some are offered in deference to pressure groups, executive branch officials, or constituents; others are designed to attract public notice, to stall the legislative process, to demonstrate concern for an issue, or to test sentiment for or against a bill. Some amendments are more technical than substantive; they may renumber sections of a bill or correct typographical errors. One common strategy is to load down a bill with so many objectionable amendments that it will sink of its own weight. Declared Speaker Wright to proponents of an amendment he strongly opposed: "If that is your goal, if you just want to find a cynical way to burden down the committee bill and make it unpassable, then you might want to vote for this [amendment]." [13] Committee members themselves may vote against a bill they originally reported if objectionable or "irresistable," but inappropriate, amendments are added on the floor.

Four types of amendments are worthy of special attention: committee amendments, "riders," substitutes, and "previously noticed" amendments. These different amendments all propose to do one of three things: add or insert something into a bill, strike something from a bill, or both strike out and insert something that isn't already in the measure.

COMMITTEE AND FLOOR AMENDMENTS. House precedents grant priority to amendments recommended by the reporting committee(s). "Committee amendments to a pending section," these precedents state, "are normally considered prior to amendments offered from the floor." [14] This condition is another example of the parliamentary advantage accorded committees by House rules and precedents. Recall, for instance, that committees receive most of the bills introduced in the House, influence the kind of "rule" their bills receive from the Rules Committee, and control general debate on the floor.

In the past, the House was inclined to defer to the committees' recommendations. That is changing. "When I came here . . . [in 1965]," reflected Majority Leader Foley, "most of the Members would follow the committee. Now partly because of the . . . breakdown of the legitimacy of leadership, the committee's 'aye' or 'nay' isn't enough." [15] With most committees being open to greater challenges on the floor (subject, of course, to the character of the "rule"), it is no surprise that chairmen sometimes look to the suspension procedure as a way to protect their measures from floor amendments. Or the Rules Committee will make clear that if legislation gets bogged down during an open amendment

Some Tests of Germaneness

When a Representative raises a germaneness point of order, the burden of proof rests with the sponsor of the amendment to establish its germaneness.

1. *Fundamental Purpose.* A basic test of germaneness is that the fundamental purpose of an amendment must be germane to the fundamental purpose of the bill. In determining this purpose, substantial reliance should not be placed upon the title of the bill as the title need not state the fundamental purpose of the bill, either as introduced or later amended. One must look rather to the text of the bill as the principal tool in determining purpose.

2. *Subject Matter.* The amendment must relate to the subject matter under consideration. One must determine "what is the subject matter under consideration?" Once it is clear just what the subject matter is, the next element . . . is whether or not the amendment relates to that subject matter.

3. *Committee Jurisdiction.* The jurisdiction of a committee is not necessarily controlling as to the germaneness of an amendment. When an argument has been advanced that the subject matter of an amendment lies within the jurisdiction of a committee other than the committee reporting the bill, the Chair has ruled that the germaneness of an amendment is based upon its relation to the bill in its amended form. In short, the subject matter of the bill is the controlling factor, not the description in the Rules of the House of the various committees' jurisdiction.

Source: Excerpted from *Manual on Legislative Procedure in the U.S. House of Representatives,* 6th ed., 99th Cong. Prepared under the auspices of the Republican leader.

process, the panel will reconvene and report another "follow-on rule" that limits amendments and expedites action on the bill.

RIDERS. Riders are amendments that are extraneous to the subject matter of the bill. They are more common in the Senate because House rules, in theory at least, require amendments to be germane or relevant to the bill itself. Any member can question the relevance of a proposed amendment by raising a point of order, on which the chair must rule. Such questions are not always raised, however, either becaue the rule from the Rules Committee may waive them, through oversight, or because members are in general agreement with the provision. "I don't make points of order on all [riders]," a member once observed, "because some may be necessary due to changing conditions." [16] In short, the

House's strict rule requiring the germaneness of amendments is not self-enforcing (see box on germaneness tests).

Riders often encompass proposals that are less likely to become law on their own merits (as separate bills), either because of resistance in the Senate or the probability of a presidential veto. The strategy on such issues is to draft them as riders to important legislation—"must" bills that are almost certain to be enacted—such as appropriations measures funding the federal government or bills to raise the federal debt ceiling. If the House is tenacious enough in clinging to its rider, the chances are good that it will be accepted—grudgingly—by the Senate and the president.

SUBSTITUTE AMENDMENTS. There are two kinds of substitutes: a "substitute amendment" and "an amendment in the nature of a substitute." The first type is an amendment that deals with *part* of a bill. When there is a proposal to change a section of a bill, a substitute amendment offers alternative language for that pending proposal. The second kind recommends new language for the *entire* bill. Amendments in the nature of substitutes have increased in importance in recent years, in part because of the complexity of contemporary issues and also because of the greater use of multiple referrals.

For example, committees that consider the same bill may report dissimilar versions of it. Sometimes, such differences are resolved through intercommittee cooperation. Members and staff from each panel might blend their products into a consensus bill that will be offered on the House floor as an amendment in the nature of a substitute for the bill as originally introduced. Usually, the Rules Committee will accommodate the committees by giving such an amendment special status by making it, rather than the original bill, the vehicle for House debate and amendment. The rule typically states that the consensus or substitute text will be considered an "original bill for the purpose of amendment."

PREVIOUSLY NOTICED AMENDMENTS. All amendments must be offered from the floor, but in the House there is no requirement that they be submitted in advance ("previously noticed") to all members. Most amendments are in printed form when they are offered, but they need not be distributed ahead of time for review by members or staff. However, the Legislative Reorganization Act of 1970 provided that amendments printed in the *Congressional Record* at least one day prior to their consideration in the Committee of the Whole are guaranteed ten minutes of debate time, regardless of any House agreements to end debate on the bill. The objective is to prevent arbitrary closing of debate when important amendments are pending, but the rule can be used also as a stalling device. For example, a member once sponsored 682 prenoticed amendments to signal his dissatisfaction with an endangered species act. If each had been considered, more than two weeks of the House's time would have been consumed. On another occasion, members who opposed a military draft registration measure introduced prenoticed amendments to require coal-fired attack submarines, solar-powered cruise missiles, and transcendental meditation courses for armed forces personnel.

Advance notice of amendments in the *Congressional Record* is sometimes required by a rule from the Rules Committee. (Rules, on occasion, even notifies the House that any member wishing to offer amendments to a bill must submit those proposals to the committee by a certain date and time.) The advance notice requirement strengthens the reporting committee's role on the floor by enabling it to prepare advance arguments, alternatives, or modifications to each prenoticed change. The prenotice requirement also provides some degree of predictability in floor decision making, an objective favored by the floor managers and the majority leadership. Rank-and-file members may object to the advance notice provision in rules if they are given inadequate time to prepare their amendments.

Degrees of Amendments

A basic parliamentary principle permits only two degrees of amendments: an amendment and the amendment to it. Any further motion to amend is a third-degree proposal (an amendment to an amendment to an amendment) and is out of order. "The line must be drawn somewhere," Thomas Jefferson wrote, "and usage has drawn it after the amendment to the amendment." [17]

When a bill is open to revision in the House, only four forms of amendments can be pending simultaneously. The four forms are:

1. An amendment to the bill itself
2. An amendment to the first amendment
3. A substitute amendment
4. An amendment to the substitute amendment

Once an amendment to a bill has been offered (the first degree), either an amendment to that amendment (the second degree), or a substitute amendment (another first degree proposal under House rules) is in order.[18] Assuming that an amendment to the original amendment is offered, then members still may offer a substitute as well as an amendment to the substitute (second degree). A substitute amendment seeks not merely to modify the original first degree amendment but to substitute entirely new language for it. If a substitute is adopted, it in ef-

FIGURE 6-1 The Basic Amendment Tree

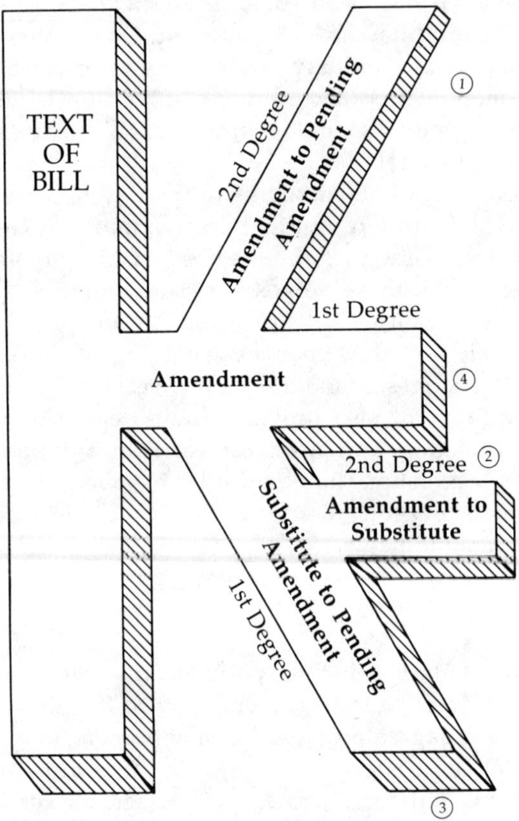

Note: Circled numbers indicate order of voting on amendments.

fect replaces the language of the original first degree proposal and the second degree amendment to it, if one has been adopted.

The four amendments, with the degrees that are permissible and the order of voting on each, are shown in Figure 6-1.

The voting sequence reveals that second degree amendments are voted on first, and that the second degree amendment to the original amendment to the bill is voted on before the second degree amendment to the substitute. After consideration of the second degree amendments, members then face a choice between two policy alternatives, with voting occurring first on the perfected substitute and then on the perfected original amendment. (Perfected amendments in this context are amendments that themselves have been amended by the second degree proposals.) In sum, the final vote occurs on the originally offered amendment as modified by any of the subsequent amendments.

Strategically, the amendment procedure can be critical to policy formulation. Either side of an issue may be aided by the voting sequence: whether the amendment—a policy alternative—is voted upon first or last. During House consideration of a nuclear freeze proposal in 1983, the proponents wanted the House to vote first on their policy recommendation. As a result, they waited for opponents to offer a first-degree amendment before they countered with a second-degree amendment to their liking. This approach gave backers of the freeze the opportunity "to formulate the final version of any amendment." [19] The first vote, therefore, was on the freeze backers' alternative amendment to the opponents' amendment revising the text of the freeze resolution.

The amending strategy on the 1987 defense authorization bill was designed to give an advantage to Democratic critics of White House policies.

> The major arms control amendments were brought up at three points during the nearly two weeks of debate on the bill. This allowed members who voted against Reagan on important amendments to follow those with "pro-Reagan" votes on other amendments, in order to assuage conservative sentiment in their districts.[20]

The amendment process was also structured to ensure that any Republican substitute was superseded by a final vote on a liberal-moderate amendment.

Maneuvering for Advantage: Common Tactics

Proponents and opponents of bills constantly seek to advance their policy objectives through the amending process. Skillful use of various motions, dilatory tactics, or shrewd drafting of the wording of amendments can influence which side carries the day. Customarily, the minority party has self-appointed "floor watchdogs" who seek to protect party interests and stymie majority steamrollers by raising points of order or making parliamentary inquiries. Timing, too, is all important to the success of many floor maneuvers, especially preferential motions and amendments to "sweeten" bills. Even television can be a factor in prompting amendment activity.

"STRIKE THE ENACTING CLAUSE." Certain motions from the floor take preference over other House business. One is the motion to "strike the enacting clause." This clause is the opening phrase of every House and Senate bill and makes it an operative law once the bill is approved by Congress and signed by the president: "Be it enacted by the Senate and House of Representatives of the United States of America in Congress assembled, . . ." Under House rules, approval of a motion to strike the enacting clause is equivalent to rejecting the measure. A motion to strike the clause is in order at any time during the amending process. (The phrasing of the preferential motion is as follows: "I move that the Committee do now rise and report the bill to the House with the recommendation that the enacting clause be stricken out.") It is a privileged motion that must be disposed of before the House takes up any further business on the bill. The motion is in order only once, unless the bill is materially changed by adoption of major amendments, an interpretation made by the chair if a point of order is raised against a second motion to strike.

A motion to strike the enacting clause may cause considerable excitement in the chamber, and it may be used for psychological purposes by either opponents or proponents of a measure.[21] In 1974, for example, Representative Bolling, floor manager of the bitterly contested House committee reorganization bill, surprised foes of the plan by inviting them to offer a motion to strike the enacting clause. Bolling's plan was to defeat such a motion so resoundingly that it would be clear to all members that the so-called committee reform was going to be considered in its entirety and adopted by the House.

Bolling gained an immediate psychological advantage when Rep. Joe D. Waggonner, D-La. (1961-1979), one of the opposition leaders, observed that his side did not have the votes to pass the motion. It might be made, he said, "at a point in time when we think there is a chance for it to succeed." Ironically, a supporter of committee reorganization, disappointed by the course of the debate on the floor, later offered a motion to strike. It was turned down overwhelmingly because most members did not want the measure abruptly killed.

"SWEETENERS." Measures considered unpalatable can be made more acceptable, or "sweetened," by proposing changes to attract broader support. These might include amendments granting members more staff or additional office allowances, or "pork barrel" provisions providing for construction of dams, highways, port facilities, airports, and the like, in various congressional districts.

Pot-sweetening is the opposite of a technique mentioned earlier, loading down a bill with enough unattractive amendments to kill it. There also are amendments that political scientists call "saving" and "killer" amendments. The first is essentially a compromise amendment that, if adopted, enhances prospects for the measure's enactment. The second type deliberately strengthens a bill too much and turns a majority against the legislation.[22] Adoption of an amendment to include primaries in a congressional public financing bill, for example, is almost certain to kill the legislation because many House incumbents, particularly those from safe and one-party districts, oppose any measure that aids party challengers.

Television and Amendments

Videopolitics has an effect on the amendment process. With the House in the television age, members sometimes craft amendments with the viewing public—or at least the voters in their districts—in mind. Proposing or debating amendments on the floor provides exposure for members and their ideas. Members who make articulate and forceful arguments may even find the footage of the House debates used on the national networks' evening news programs. Television and strategy are also linked. Representative Gephardt was the chief sponsor of a tough trade amendment in the 100th Congress. "He fought for his amendment on the House floor, where proceedings are televised, rather than in the Ways and Means Committee," which considered trade legislation in closed session.[23] Members and staff can also monitor the rhythm and pace of the amending process from their offices, which have television monitors to carry the proceedings.

Importance of the Amending Process

Attempts are almost always made to amend controversial bills when they are considered in the Committee of the Whole. The amending process is a critical stage for any bill and, as has been seen, quite complex. Some of the main features of the process are noted below:

- Amendments in the Committee of the Whole are usually offered section by section under the five-minute rule.
- All amendments must be offered from the floor in written form.
- Amendments may not be repetitious. When an amendment is rejected, a member may not offer exactly the same proposal later.
- Any amendment may be challenged on a point of order before debate on the amendment has begun.
- Committee amendments are considered before those introduced by other legislators.
- Pro forma amendments enable members to discuss the bill under consideration for five minutes, even though no change is intended.
- Amendments must be germane to the subject under consideration. Occasionally, nongermane amendments may slip by, either because members generally are agreed on their intent or because the Rules Committee has barred points of order against them.

VOTING IN COMMITTEE OF THE WHOLE

Until 1971 there were three methods of voting in the Committee of the Whole: voice, standing (division), and teller. *Voice* voting is based on the volume of sound of members responding yea or nay. If the chair is in doubt about the result, or if any member requests it, a *standing* vote is called for. First those in favor and then those opposed are asked to stand while a head count is taken.

Any member dissatisfied with the result as announced by the chair may say, "Mr. Chairman, I demand tellers." To hold a *teller* vote, the member's demand has to be supported by one-fifth of a quorum (twenty members). If that requirement is met, the chair then appoints members, usually one from each side of the question, to act as tellers (vote counters). Members file up the center aisle toward the rear of the House—the yeas first, followed by the nays—between the two tellers, who count them. Tellers then report their results to the chair, for example: "200 for and 100 against."

None of these three methods provides a public record of who voted, how they voted, or even whether they voted. Often crucial amendments were adopted in the Committee of the Whole before 1971 without recorded votes. Traditional arguments for this procedure were that it facilitated compromise and permitted members to vote the national interest against regional or local interests. Secrecy was not absolute since reporters often monitored the voting, but they found it difficult to identify members whose backs were turned as they passed between the two tellers.

Many members, nonetheless, supported the addition of recorded teller voting in the Committee of the Whole. Secret voting, they argued, had enabled legislators to duck issues or vote contrary to publicly stated positions. Constituents could not trace their representatives' voting records and hold them accountable. "A member can vote for any number of amendments which may cripple a water pollution bill or render ineffective a civil rights bill or fail to provide adequate funding for hospital construction or programs for the elderly," Rep. David R. Obey, D-Wis., had noted, "and then he can turn around on final passage and vote for the bill he has just voted to emasculate by amendment." [24] (Unlike voting in the Committee of the Whole, votes on passage of major bills usually were recorded.)

Change to Recorded Teller Votes

Frustration with secret voting in the Committee of the Whole mounted in the late 1960s. Some members felt they were coming under increasing pressure from committee chairmen and party leaders to vote the party's position, whereas with recorded voting they could argue that their reelection depended on voting as their constituents wished. In 1970 the movement for instituting *recorded teller* votes succeeded.

Members of the Democratic Study Group (DSG), the largest ad hoc group in the House, with about 235 moderate and liberal members by the late 1970s, were the driving force in the campaign to revise the teller voting procedure. Attendance by members of the DSG during Committee of the Whole proceedings had sometimes been poor. The DSG reasoned that if votes were recorded publicly, attendance would improve markedly since excessive absences could be used against legislators in future reelection campaigns.

To avoid a partisan label, the DSG joined forces with reform-minded Republicans and developed a bipartisan package of amendments to a proposed legislative reorganization act. The coalition developed an antisecrecy strategy to build public support for allowing teller votes to be recorded. Thousands of letters were mailed to newspaper editors. Editorials soon began appearing across the nation in support of recorded teller voting. Public attention helped persuade formerly hostile members to support the change.

The campaign was helped—perhaps inadvertently—by the activities of "gallery spotters," observers, often members of Vietnam antiwar groups in the late 1960s, who sat in the visitors' gallery trying to recognize and record members as they walked up the center aisle to cast their teller votes on war-related issues. The information was shared with reporters and others. Sometimes the spotters made mistakes, provoking protests from members who were identified in news reports as voting one way when they had actually voted another. Through a confluence of factors—public pressure, members' dissatisfaction with the spotting system, and bipartisan backing—an amendment was added to the Legislative Reorganization Act of 1970 permitting votes to be recorded in the Committee of the Whole.

Recorded teller voting compelled members to take public stands on controversial issues. Under the new procedure, which took effect at the beginning of the 1971 session, members had to sign and deposit green or red cards, signifying yea or nay, in ballot boxes in full view of the House and the galleries. That simple procedure was thought by many observers to have changed the outcome almost immediately on many controversial issues, including a bill providing for federal financing of a commercial supersonic transport (SST). For months before the vote on the plane, environmental groups had been generating strong opposition to the SST, and public opinion appeared to be swinging to their position. In Congress, however, sentiment seemingly leaned toward approval of the plane. Then, on March 18, 1971, Rep. Sidney R. Yates, D-Ill., stood and said, "Mr. Chairman, I demand tellers with clerks" (now called a recorded vote by clerks). Knowing that their votes would be recorded in the *Congressional Record* and widely publicized, members voted 217-204 to cut off funds for the proposed SST.

ELECTRONIC VOTING. Electronic voting, also authorized by the 1970 Legislative Reorganization Act, began in 1973, largely superseding the recorded teller voting procedure. Members insert a personalized card about the size of a credit card into one of the more than 40 voting stations located on the House floor, and press one of three buttons: Yea, Nay, or Present. Each member's vote is displayed on panels above the Speaker's desk and also on the walls of the House behind the press gallery. The system also is used to establish quorums. If electronic voting malfunctions, traditional methods are used.

NEW RECORDED VOTE REQUIREMENT. Beginning in 1979, the number of members needed to obtain a recorded vote in the Committee of the Whole was increased to one-fourth of a quorum (twenty-five) instead of one-fifth. (The one-fifth requirement was kept for recorded votes during other sessions of the House.)

Table 6-2 shows the impact that recorded teller votes and the electronic voting procedure has had on House voting since 1971.

The increase in the number of recorded votes caused scheduling conflicts and kept legislators running from committee meetings to the House floor to cast their votes. Many members complained that too many recorded votes were being taken on frivolous or unnecessary amendments.

In recent years there has been a downward trend in the number of recorded votes. This development reflects such factors as greater use of omnibus bills (combining separate measures into one big package) and divided control of Congress. Split party control no doubt accentuated bicameral conflicts on policy priorities and contributed to the slower lawmaking pace of recent Congresses.

The voting changes placed additional pressures on the floor managers. Electronic voting cut balloting time in half, from about thirty minutes under the traditional roll-call method, to no less than fifteen minutes. Further, recent changes in the rules have permitted the Speaker to postpone votes and schedule votes in clusters on matters such as passing bills or agreeing to suspension of the rules motions. The time allowed for each vote in this procedure may be reduced to five minutes by the Speaker.

Managers today have less time to coordinate floor activities during a vote. Members can enter the chamber through numerous doors, insert their cards and vote, leaving before the leadership has a chance to talk to them. As a result, both parties station monitors at all the doors to advise their colleagues when they enter and urge them to support the position of the floor manager or the party leadership.

From the floor managers' standpoint, there are advantages and disadvantages to the modern system. Managers have computer display

TABLE 6-2 Recorded Votes in the House

Year	*Number of Recorded Votes*	*Year*	*Number of Recorded Votes*
1970	266	1978	834
1971 (Recorded teller voting first used)	320	1979	672
		1980	604
1972	329	1981	353
1973 (Electronic voting first used)	541	1982	459
		1983	498
1974	537	1984	408
1975	612	1985	439
1976	661	1986	451
1977	706	1987	488

terminals that show a continuous and changing record of the progress of a vote. However, there is less time to evaluate opposition to proposals and line up votes. Thus, floor managers today must work harder to build support before bills reach the floor. On the other hand, problems such as the absence of one member or the unexpected switch on a vote by another can be spotted quickly on the computer consoles. Absent members can be summoned to the floor, and vote-switchers can be approached by persuasive members of the party.

"PAIRS" IN COMMITTEE OF THE WHOLE. One other voting change is worth noting. On January 14, 1975, the House amended its rules to permit "pairs" in the Committee of the Whole. "Pairing" previously was limited to the House. Pairing is a voluntary arrangement between any two representatives on opposite sides of an issue. Wrote a noted House parliamentarian:

> A pair is essentially a "gentlemen's agreement," and the construction and interpretation of the terms, provisions, and conditions of a pair rests exclusively with the contracting Members. The rules do not specifically authorize them and the House does not interpret or construe them or consider questions or complaints arising out of their violation. Such questions must be determined by the interested Members themselves individually.[25]

Pairs are not counted in tabulating the final results of recorded votes.

Pairs take three forms:

1. A *general* pair means that two members are listed without any indication as to how either might have voted.
2. A *specific* pair indicates how the two absent legislators would have voted, one for and the other against.
3. A *live* pair matches two members, one present and one absent.

In a live pair, the member in attendance casts a vote, but then withdraws it and votes "present," announcing that he or she has a live pair with a colleague and identifying how each would have voted on the issue. A live pair subtracts one vote, yea or nay, from the final tally and can influence the outcome of closely contested issues. Both parties have pair clerks to help arrange these informal agreements.

Factors in Voting

On any given day, legislators may be required to vote on measures ranging from foreign aid to abortion, from maritime subsidies to tax reform. It is nearly impossible for a member to be fully informed on every issue before the House. Noted Rep. Dick Cheney, R-Wyo., "The sheer volume of votes is so great that there's no way you can weigh each and every issue." [26] As a result, many lawmakers rely on "cue-givers" for guidance on matters beyond their special competence. These may be committee or party leaders, members of the state congressional delegation, trusted colleagues, staff aides, or floor managers.[27] "You want to know how Members are voting on an issue," a House Democrat said, "you want to know how Members from your delegation vote, and you want to know how Members who always vote the opposite of you are voting." [28] Party loyalty, constituency interests, and individual conscience are primary factors in determining a member's vote on any issue, but they are not the only factors. It is not unusual for members to vote for proposals they actually oppose in order to prevent enactment of something worse, or in the expectation that somewhere along the line the proposal will go down to defeat. Members, too, might vote one way on an authorization bill and another on the corresponding appropriations measure.

To mobilize winning coalitions behind issues is no easy task on divisive issues. The art of vote counting can be crucial to policy outcomes (see box on pp. 170-171). Members use their votes, too, as trading material. In exchange for voting yea or nay on an issue, they may receive some project or favor that benefits their district.

Finally, the voting records of members can become a campaign issue. Representatives who miss numerous votes might find their congressional attendance record an issue during the next campaign. Many interest groups contribute campaign funds to legislators whose votes are in accord with the groups' views. "If I cast a vote, I might have to answer for it," said Rep. Philip R. Sharp, D-Ind. "It may be an issue in the next campaign. Over and over I have to have a response to the question: Why did you do that?" [29]

When voting on all amendments has been concluded, the Committee of the Whole "rises" (dissolves) and reports the bill back to the full

House. The chairman of the Committee of the Whole hands the gavel back to the Speaker, who resumes his place at the podium. The mace is returned to its pedestal on the table next to the podium, and a quorum becomes 218 members (a majority of the House). As prescribed in the rule, there is a standard sequence of events that takes place prior to the vote on final passage of a bill.

FINAL PROCEDURAL STEPS

After taking the chair, the Speaker announces that "under the rule, the previous question is ordered." This means that no further debate is permitted on the measure or on amendments, no amendments other than those reported by the Committee of the Whole may be considered, and previously adopted amendments are not subject to further amendment. Then members, sitting as the House, consider the decisions taken in the Committee of the Whole. The Speaker asks all the members to identify amendments on which they want separate recorded ballots. The remaining amendments are decided *en bloc* by voice vote, after which the contested amendments are voted on individually. Except for motions to send a measure back to the reporting committee with instructions, only first-degree amendments adopted in the Committee of the Whole can now be considered. Separate recorded votes are not usually requested on amendments previously adopted in the Committee of the Whole unless the earlier votes were very close and the amendments highly controversial. On occasion, amendments adopted in Committee of the Whole are rejected by the House.[30]

After all floor amendments are disposed of, there are two more steps before the final vote on passage. The first is *engrossment* and *third reading*. "The question is on engrossment and third reading of the bill," the Speaker declares. This is a pro forma question, which is approved automatically by unanimous consent. House rules provide that the bill be read by its title. (Before 1965 any legislator could demand that the bill be read in full, but the rules were changed to prevent this dilatory tactic.)

Engrossment is the preparation of a final and accurate version of the bill by an enrolling clerk, for transmission to the Senate. This can be a complicated process, particularly if numerous amendments were adopted.

The second step is the *recommittal motion*, provided for in the rule from the Rules Committee. This is a privileged motion, protected and guaranteed by the rules, that gives the opponents one last chance to obtain a recorded vote on their own proposals. Recommittal is a motion to return the bill to the committee that reported it; it is always made by a

The Art of Vote Counting . . .

Smack in the middle of debate on a foreign aid bill Dec. 9, all the members of the House were summoned to the floor for an unexpected quorum call.

For Democratic leaders, the point of the roll call had nothing to do with foreign aid; it was an opportunity for leadership lieutenants, stationed around the floor, to check Democrats' views of a controversial welfare bill (HR 1720) scheduled to go to the floor the next day. When they found the welfare bill was in trouble, it was abruptly dropped from the schedule.

Taking a head count of the 257-member Democratic Caucus before key votes is an unwieldy job, unseen by the casual observer, but it is an essential part of leadership strategy.

An unfavorable "whip count" can force the leadership to postpone action on a bill or seek major modifications before bringing it to the floor.

That happened more than once on the welfare bill. Three times it was put on the schedule and later pulled for lack of votes.

On one of the last big votes of the year, "you don't want to take a chance," said Tony Coelho, D-Calif., who as majority whip is chief Democratic vote-counter.

The 89-member whip organization overseen by Coelho is a two-way communications device: It lets the leadership know what the rank and file is thinking, and it helps the leadership communicate its position and enforce party discipline.

Focusing on the South

The leadership had been counting heads on the welfare bill for weeks, since before it was first brought to the floor Oct. 29 as part of the budget reconciliation bill (HR 3545). The welfare provisions were stripped out of that package after the House defeated a rule to govern floor debate, partly because some Southern Democrats opposed the juxtaposition of welfare and taxes in the same measure.

By the week of Dec. 7, a task force named to handle the bill, headed by Steny H. Hoyer, D-Md., was meeting as often as twice a day to update the count. Members took the membership's pulse both on the bill itself and the rule governing floor debate, which many Democrats thought was too restrictive in shutting out amendments.

In the final days, the whips were focusing on key votes in Deep South states such as Louisiana. A concerted effort was made to ensure the presence of Buddy Roemer, an influential Louisiana Democrat who has spent little time in Washington since he became the state's governor-elect Oct. 24. He returned to support the bill, and helped bring along the rest of the Louisiana Democrats.

"Roemer's presence is needed and appreciated," said Thomas J. Downey, D-N.Y., chief sponsor of the bill.

. . . Crucial to Leadership Success

MORE ART THAN SCIENCE

While Majority Whip Coelho prides himself on the precision of his whip checks, vote-counting is in some ways more an art than a science. It requires an ability to read colleagues that comes more readily to some members than others; it is an aptitude that improves with experience.

"It takes the ability to look into someone's eyes and see they mean 'no' when they say 'maybe,' " said Pat Williams, D-Mont., a deputy whip.

In the House, the vote-counting system has been expanded so much that about one-third of the Democratic caucus are members of the whip organization.

The best whips are those who can not only count noses, but twist arms. They don't just tally votes, they deliver them.

Among the House members best known for their whipping talents is John P. Murtha, D-Pa.

He is the ultimate insider, and has endeared himself to colleagues for taking on the politically sensitive cause of advocating increases in members' salaries and outside-earnings limits. Members don't run away when they see him approaching.

"He does a lot of things for people in the House," said Hoyer, adding that Murtha's persuasive powers are augmented by his willingness to help members from his seat on the Appropriations Committee.

However, one leadership source said Murtha's reach was largely limited to his colleagues from Pennsylvania, West Virginia and Ohio and questioned his vote-counting acumen in light of the recent defeat, by a surprisingly large margin, of a Murtha amendment postponing pollution-control deadlines.

Another member well-known for his whipping talents is Marty Russo, D-Ill. He has both persistence and a seat on the tax-writing Ways and Means Committee that gives him leverage with members looking for favors.

Standing well over six feet, Russo can be physically intimidating. "He just stands there, right up close and says '*Look*, we *need* you on this thing,' " said one Democrat.

In a legendary incident, Russo in 1984 literally carried Daniel K. Akaka, D-Hawaii, from the cloakroom to the House floor to get him to reverse his vote.

"He'll embarrass you on the floor" during a roll-call vote, said Robert T. Matsui, D-Calif. "He'll point and say, 'Look at that vote—why don't you start being a Democrat?' "

Source: Janet Hook, "The Art of Vote-Counting Proved Crucial to Eventual Success of Welfare Measure," *Congressional Quarterly Weekly Report*, Dec. 19, 1987, 3158-3159.

member opposed to the bill. Customarily, the Speaker recognizes a member of the minority party, usually the senior minority committee member, and specifically asks if that member opposes the bill. Recommittal is in order only in the House, not in the Committee of the Whole. The motion may be a simple, or "straight," motion to recommit, or it may contain instructions to the reporting committee.

A simple motion to recommit the bill to committee, if adopted, in effect kills the bill, although technically it may be returned to the House floor later in the session. No debate is permitted on the simple recommittal motion.

Instructions in recommittal motions often embody amendments that were defeated in the Committee of the Whole. This is the only way amendments rejected earlier in the debate can be brought before the full House. Until 1970 no debate was permitted on a recommittal motion. The Legislative Reorganization Act of that year authorized ten minutes of debate on recommittal motions with instructions. On occasion, a rule from the Rules Committee will authorize longer debate on recommittal motions with instructions. There are also occasions when the Rules Committee will prohibit a recommittal motion with instructions (but not the straight motion to recommit), which prevents the minority from offering its policy alternative when the Committee of the Whole rises.

Recommittal motions with instructions commonly provide that the committee report "forthwith." If the recommittal motion is adopted, the committee chairman immediately reports back to the House in conformity with the instructions, and the bill, as modified by the instructions, is automatically before the House again. The committee chairman states: "Mr. Speaker, pursuant to the instructions of the House on the motion to recommit, I report the bill, H.R. 1234, back to the House with an amendment." The House votes separately on this amendment, then again on the pro forma engrossment and third reading questions, and finally on passage of the bill.

Recommittal motions seldom are successful, but much depends on the size of the minority party in the House and political circumstances. Probably the most dramatic recommittal motion in recent Congresses occurred on September 25, 1984 (only a few weeks before national elections), when the Comprehensive Crime Control Act was enacted via the recommittal route. Rep. Dan Lungren, R-Calif., offered the recommittal motion with instructions, containing the recodification of the criminal code, debated it for five minutes, and urged members to pass a crime package that "has been languishing here in the House since March of this year." [31] A Democratic opponent of the recommittal motion then took the floor and urged rejection of the motion in his five minutes.

To the surprise of nearly everyone, the recommittal motion was agreed to by a 243-166 vote. Then the continuing resolution to which the crime bill was attached was agreed to by the House. Democratic leaders were chagrined that the crime package had passed in this manner. "I think it was the wrong way" to pass major crime legislation after only ten minutes of debate, declared Speaker O'Neill.[32] Interestingly, when the next Congress convened, the House changed its rules to permit the majority floor manager—but not the minority floor manager—to request up to an hour of debate, equally divided, on a motion to recommit with instructions.

If the recommittal motion is rejected, the Speaker moves to the third step, the final vote on the whole bill. "The question is on the passage of the bill," he says.[33] Normally, final passage is by a recorded vote. If the outcome is obvious, and the members are anxious to be done with it, the measure may be passed by voice vote. When the results of the final vote have been announced, a pro forma motion to reconsider is made and laid on the table (postponed indefinitely) to prevent the bill from being reconsidered later. House rules state that a final vote is conclusive only if there has been an opportunity to reconsider it on the same day or the succeeding day.

SUMMARY

Although the House decision-making process may appear to be quite complex, it accommodates varied institutional interests and members' needs. There are numerous restraints on what legislators can and cannot do. Success often depends on one side's gaining an advantage through use of the rules. Infinite variations are possible within the process, but basic House procedures are the same on almost all important bills:

1. A "rule" reported by the Rules Committee
2. Adoption of the rule by the House
3. Consideration of the bill in the Committee of the Whole
4. General debate
5. Consideration of amendments under the five-minute rule
6. Recorded votes on major amendments
7. Reporting the bill to the House once floor action is completed in the Committee of the Whole
8. Separate recorded votes, if requested, on any amendment adopted in the Committee of the Whole
9. A recommittal motion, with or without instructions
10. Final passage vote

The intensity of debate may vary, the complexity of the special "rule" may change, and a host of other factors may differ from issue to issue, but the pattern of decision making is the same regardless of the range or scope of the legislation.

After it is passed by the House, the bill moves to the Senate. There, the legislative process is quite different. If the House is characterized by devotion to rules and parliamentary procedures, the Senate is much more informal, often transacting its business by gentlemen's agreements, with the rules ignored or set aside. Chapter 4 covered the introduction of a bill, referral, and committee action in the Senate. The following chapter begins with a bill that has been reported by a Senate committee and discusses the scheduling procedure for moving a bill to the Senate floor.

NOTES

1. During the 95th Congress, the House developed a regular system of scheduling floor sessions. This was done in response to the desires of members, committees, and party leaders. Members complained about problems in arranging their personal schedules and their inability to make firm commitments for meetings in their districts; committees wanted more time early in the session to work on legislation without being interrupted by floor meetings; and party leaders wished to better synchronize committee and floor action and use the time in session more effectively. As a result, the House by standing order varies its starting time: noon on Mondays and Tuesdays, 3 p.m. on Wednesdays, 11 a.m. on Thursdays and the balance of the week until May 15, when the convening time for Wednesdays through the balance of the week, including Saturdays if the House is in session, is advanced to 10 a.m. for the remainder of the session.
2. Jeffrey H. Birnbaum and Alan S. Murray, *Showdown at Gucci Gulch* (New York: Random House, 1987), 163.
3. In the House sitting as the House, an hour is permitted for debate on amendments. "No member," the rule states, "shall occupy more than one hour in debate on any question in the House." Technically, then, all matters could be debated for 440 hours—1 hour each for the 435 representatives, 4 delegates (from the District of Columbia, the Virgin Islands, American Samoa, and Guam), and 1 resident commissioner (from Puerto Rico). In practice, measures are debated for only one hour in total and then are voted on.
4. For a description of the seventeenth-century English origins of the Committee of the Whole, see DeAlva Stanwood Alexander, *History and Procedure of the House of Representatives* (Boston: Houghton Mifflin, 1916), 257-258.
5. Technically, the first order of business in the Committee of the Whole is the reading of the bill. This usually is dispensed with either by unanimous consent or by the terms of the "rule," which is the ordinary practice today.
6. *U.S. News & World Report*, Aug. 20, 1984, 30.
7. *Washington Post*, Oct. 22, 1983, A19.
8. *Congressional Record*, daily ed., May 24, 1983, H3257.
9. *Congressional Record*, June 11, 1979, 14213-14215.
10. See the *Congressional Record* for Oct. 30, Oct. 31, and Nov. 2, 1987.
11. *Constitution, Jefferson's Manual and Rules of the House of Representatives*, 97th Cong., 2d sess., H. Doc. No. 97-271, 585-586.

12. Julie Rovner, "House Passes Labor-HHS Appropriations Bill," *Congressional Quarterly Weekly Report*, Aug. 8, 1987, 1790.
13. *Congressional Record*, daily ed., May 25, 1982, H2824. The amendment was not adopted.
14. *Procedure in the U.S. House of Representatives*, 97th Cong., 4th ed. (Washington, D.C.: Government Printing Office, 1982), 526.
15. Michael J. Malbin, "House Democrats Are Playing with a Strong Leadership Lineup," *National Journal*, June 18, 1977, 946. See also John F. Bibby, ed., *Congress off the Record* (Washington, D.C.: American Enterprise Institute for Public Policy Research, 1983), 23-24.
16. Richard F. Fenno, Jr., *The Power of the Purse* (Boston: Little, Brown, 1966), 74.
17. *Constitution, Jefferson's Manual and Rules of the House of Representatives*, H. Doc. No. 97-271, 212.
18. When amendments in the nature of substitutes are offered first, it is possible to have as many as eight amendments pending simultaneously on the House floor. Seldom does this situation occur because confusion is all too often the result.
19. Pat Towell, "After 42 Hours of Debate: Nuclear Freeze Resolution Finally Wins House Approval," *Congressional Quarterly Weekly Report*, May 7, 1983, 869.
20. Pat Towell, "House Approves Defense Authorization Bill," *Congressional Quarterly Weekly Report*, Aug. 16, 1986, 1870.
21. Customarily, the motion to strike also is used by members to obtain five more minutes of debate time.
22. See James M. Enelow and David H. Koehler, "The Amendment in Legislative Strategy: Sophisticated Voting in the U.S. Congress," *Journal of Politics* (May 1980): 396-413; and James M. Enelow, "Saving Amendments, Killer Amendments, and an Expected Utility Theory of Sophisticated Voting," *Journal of Politics* (November 1981): 1062-1089.
23. *Wall Street Journal*, April 30, 1987, 64.
24. *Congressional Quarterly Weekly Report*, Jan. 22, 1972, 153.
25. *Cannon's Procedure in the House of Representatives*, H. Doc. No. 86-122, 233. Cannon further notes: "It is obviously impossible for all Members to be present at every roll call, and in cases of unavoidable absence the privilege of pairing is invaluable in preserving the rights of Members and the representation of constituencies" (231).
26. *New York Times*, June 29, 1983, A14.
27. On factors influencing votes, see, for example, John W. Kingdon, *Congressmen's Voting Decisions* (New York: Harper & Row, 1973); and Donald P. Matthews and James A. Stimson, *Yeas and Nays* (New York: John Wiley & Sons, 1975).
28. *Congressional Record*, daily ed., July 16, 1986, H4558.
29. *New York Times*, May 13, 1986, A24.
30. See, for example, Martha Bridegam and Pat Towell, "'Goodwill Games' Spark Sharp Exchange," *Congressional Quarterly Weekly Report*, June 27, 1987, 1386.
31. *Congressional Record*, daily ed., Sept. 25, 1984, H10129.
32. *Christian Science Monitor*, Sept. 27, 1984, 32.
33. To summarize: There are several ways of voting in the House. These are: voice, standing (division), unrecorded teller, recorded vote by clerks, and electronic (recorded vote by electronic device). There are three ways to demand a recorded vote in the House that do not apply in the Committee of the Whole. First, a member may obtain a recorded vote if his request is

supported by one-fifth of a quorum (forty-four members). Second, there is the constitutional yeas and nays (required, for example, in Article I, Section 5). Finally, House rules permit "automatic" recorded votes. A member who both objects and makes a point of order that a quorum is not present is automatically entitled to a recorded vote if the chair indicates that a quorum in fact is not present.

CHAPTER 7

Scheduling Legislation in the Senate

The pace of activity on Capitol Hill places enormous demands on the time of legislators. Representatives and senators work long days, not only on the floor and in committee but also in meetings with executive branch officials, constituents, pressure groups, and the media. They also must stay in contact with the diplomatic community, party leaders, and state and local officials. It is not uncommon for a representative or senator to average eleven or more working hours a day while in Washington. To that must be added periodic trips home to attend important political functions, to "meet" with constituents, or to be present at campaign fund-raising events.

Of legislators in the two branches of Congress, senators lead the more harried existence. There are fewer senators (100 compared with 435 House members), and in most cases senators represent a larger number of constituents. Senators are more often in the public eye and are called upon more frequently to comment on national and international policy. The legislative and committee workload is as heavy in the Senate as in the House, but it must be carried out by fewer lawmakers. During the 99th Congress, the Senate was in session 2,531 hours; the House, 1,794 hours.

The workload is heaviest for senators from the larger states, not only because of the greater number of constituents that need assistance, but also because of the multiplicity of political and economic interests in those states. "I don't see how senators from big states like New York and California, Illinois and Pennsylvania do it [all]," Majority Leader Mike Mansfield, D-Mont. (1953-1977), once said.[1] A typical schedule for Sen. George J. Mitchell, a Democrat from Maine, a medium-sized state, shows the varied and often conflicting demands that arise on any given day (see box on p. 178). As is true of all his colleagues, Senator Mitchell frequently is expected to be in two or more places at the same time. In

Schedule for Sen. George J. Mitchell

(Thursday, March 17, 1988)

9:00 a.m.	Markup in Veterans' Affairs Committee of Fiscal 1988 Budget Russell Senate Office Bldg.
9:30 a.m.	Meeting of Finance Committee (Closed) with Secretary Baker and Ambassador Yuetter Dirksen Senate Office Bldg.
10:00 a.m.	Hearing of Finance Committee on U.S./Canadian free trade Dirksen Senate Office Bldg.
10:00 a.m.	Hearing of Water Resources Subcommittee on Water Resources Act of 1988 Russell Senate Office Bldg.
12:00 noon	Lunch with Rep. Pete Stark, other subcommittee members, Josh Weiner, and Alice Rivlin of the Brookings Institution Longworth Bldg.
1:00 p.m.	Photo with 60 students of Saco Middle School Capitol Steps
1:15 p.m.	Taping of radio show Recording Studio
1:25 p.m.	Satellite Feed on Honduras, Trade Swamp Site
1:30 p.m.	Photo session Russell Senate Office Bldg.
2:00 p.m.	Meeting with Anna Charney, daughter of a Soviet dissident Russell Senate Office Bldg.
2:30 p.m.	Meeting with Steve Lemenger of Princeton University Russell Senate Office Bldg.
3:00 p.m.	Meeting with Jay Nixon, Missouri Senate Candidate Russell Senate Office Bldg.
3:15 p.m.	Meeting with Laurie Cohen, attorney, on the presidential campaign Russell Senate Office Bldg.
4:45 p.m.	Photo with Stoney Dionne, a union official Russell Senate Office Bldg.
5:05 p.m.	Interview at Channel 6 with Senator Cohen 400 N. Capitol Street
7:00 p.m.	Speech as Boilermakers' Union Legislator of the Year Quality Inn

such a situation, a senator must select the top priority event to attend in person, and delegate staff members to cover the rest or, as a last resort, rely on a fellow senator to fill him in on what took place.

"It's absurd when you get a computer readout from your staff and it shows that you have four meetings at the same time," Senator Simpson once exclaimed. "And that happens more often than you would imagine."[2]

FLEXIBLE SCHEDULING SYSTEM

In response to the manifold pressures on members, the Senate has evolved a highly flexible legislative scheduling system that responds to the individual member's, as well as to institutional, needs. The system bears little resemblance to what the formal rules specify and rests largely on usage and informal practice. For example, senators' frustration with delays, uncertainty, and unpredictability in scheduling prompted a 1988 experiment. For every month, the Senate will be in session three weeks and off one week. The new approach "gives Senators some predictability, to schedule their trips back home to their constituencies, or to catch up on committee work here or other work here," said Democratic leader Byrd.[3]

The plan serves individual and institutional objectives. Senators can conduct their constituency-related business and other work during the Senate's week off without fear of missing senatorial votes. This feature is especially attractive to members who must campaign for reelection and to those from the western United States. The Senate now works five days a week during the three-week segment, including votes on Mondays and Fridays. The changes are meant to enhance the "quality of senatorial life" and the "quality of senatorial work."

Unlike House members, all senators have an opportunity to participate in scheduling legislation for floor action. This condition reflects both the comity that is prevalent in the hundred-member Senate and the power that every Senator has by virtue of senatorial rules. "One person can tie this place into a knot," emphasized Senator Simpson. "And two can do it even more beautifully."[4] Minor or noncontroversial bills are expedited to save time for major and controversial measures. Insofar as possible, action on important bills is scheduled to suit the convenience of members and to reduce to a minimum conflicts with legislative activity that takes place off the Senate floor. "The Senate operates largely on the basis of unanimous-consent agreements, comity, courtesy, and understanding," Democratic leader Byrd has noted.[5]

The Senate's system for classifying measures to be debated on the floor is simpler and more informal than the system used by the House. In contrast to the House, with its five calendars, the Senate has only two:

the *Calendar of General Orders* and the *Executive Calendar.* All legislation, major or minor, controversial or noncontroversial, is placed on the former; treaties and nominations under the Senate's "advice and consent" authority are placed on the latter.[6]

The Senate, by motion or unanimous consent, resolves into "executive session" to consider treaties or nominations. Within the course of a single day, the Senate may consider measures on both the Executive and General Orders calendars. It may go from executive session to legislative session before finishing the pending item on the Executive Calendar.

As discussed in Chapter 5, relatively noncontroversial legislation in the House comes up under the Consent Calendar, suspension of the rules, or the Private Calendar. Even specific days of the month are designated for consideration of such legislation. The Senate has no comparable procedure. Senate rules for calling up legislation—both major and minor—are cumbersome and consequently are generally ignored. One of these rules, for example, requires a daily calendar call, with the measures required to be brought up and debated in the order in which they appear on the calendar. (An example of a Senate calendar appears on p. 184.) Were the Senate to follow that rule, it would lose virtually all flexibility in processing its workload.

NONCONTROVERSIAL BILLS

Practically all noncontroversial measures are "called up by unanimous consent and enacted without debate," observes Democratic leader Byrd. "In this regard, I have reference to private bills, most nominations on the Executive Calendar—which run into the thousands—and bills that are not of general interest." [7] He estimated that "easily 98 percent of the business of the Senate is called up by unanimous consent." [8] The leaders and staff aides in both parties check with senators to clear minor or noncontroversial legislation before such measures reach the floor. A single dissent will hold up floor action until the roadblock is cleared away. But once cleared, minor and noncontroversial bills generally take from several seconds to a few minutes to pass. "Locomotive velocity may develop at this point, as bills come up and pass through with no objection," Byrd explains.[9] The box on page 181 illustrates how noncontroversial legislation typically is handled in the Senate.

The Senate's small size, flexibility, and tradition of cooperation means that the majority and minority leaders frequently can schedule noncontroversial legislation on a daily basis. Through informal floor discussions or colloquies, each examines the calendar to be sure the noncontroversial bills have been cleared by interested senators on their side. The measures then are passed quickly by voice vote.

Clearance of Noncontroversial Measures

MR. [WARREN] RUDMAN. Mr. President, I would inquire of the Democratic leader whether he is in a position to pass a number of calendar items. I will read which ones they are.

> Calendar Order No. 580, S. 2054; Calendar Order No. 589, Senate Resolution 332; Calendar Order No. 598, Senate Resolution 352; Calendar Order No. 599, Senate Joint Resolution 281; Calendar Order No. 600, Senate Joint Resolution 284; Calendar Order No. 601, Senate Joint Resolution 300; Calendar Order No. 602, Senate Joint Resolution 303; Calendar Order No. 603, Senate Joint Resolution 306; Calendar Order No. 604, Senate Joint Resolution 307; Calendar Order No. 605, Senate Joint Resolution 309; Calendar Order No. 606, Senate Joint Resolution 315; Calendar Order No. 607, Senate Joint Resolution 188, and Calendar Order No. 608, Senate Joint Resolution 199.

Mr. [ROBERT C.] BYRD. Mr. President, I am happy to respond to the distinguished acting majority leader. Those items that the Senator enumerated have been cleared on this side and we are ready to proceed.

Mr. RUDMAN. If that is so, Mr. President, I ask unanimous consent that the calendar items just identified be considered and passed en bloc and that all committee-reported amendments and preambles be considered and agreed to.

The PRESIDING OFFICER. Is there objection? Without objection, it is so ordered.

Source: Congressional Record, Daily ed., April 11, 1986, S4144.

Minor and noncontroversial measures also may reach the Senate floor on a motion of any senator. However, the majority and minority leaders normally try to reach agreement in advance on the floor schedule and are likely to oppose action that will bring bills to the floor without prior clearance from them. The leaders' prerogative of receiving preferential recognition from the presiding officer—first the majority leader, followed by the minority leader—enables them to control the agenda of activities on the floor. A senator who attempts to bring a measure or matter to the floor without consulting the majority leader in advance may find the proposal subject to a tabling motion. (The motion to table kills the action to which it is directed.)

MAJOR LEGISLATION

Once major Senate bills are reported from committee, there are two main avenues by which they may be brought to the floor: through unanimous consent or by motion. Before they get there, however, the legislation may be subject to the one-day rule, the two-day rule, or to "holds."

One-day and Two-day Rules

The one-day rule states that bills and reports must lie over on the calendar for one *legislative* day before they are eligible for floor consideration. This rule is seldom enforced and commonly is waived by unanimous consent. To speed up action, the majority leader states, "I ask unanimous consent that [these bills] be considered as having been on the calendar 1 legislative day for the purpose of the rules of the Senate." [10] There rarely is an objection to the request.

The two-day rule requires that printed committee reports accompanying measures or matters be available to members for at least two *calendar* days before those proposals are eligible for floor action. (The two-day rule was a three-day rule until the Senate changed it in February 1986; Chapter 8 explains the difference between legislative and calendar days.) This rule, too, may be waived by unanimous consent or by joint motion of the majority and minority leaders. However, it is common for the Senate to observe this rule, sometimes to the chagrin of the majority leader, who has primary responsibility for scheduling the Senate's business.

When the Senate considered the controversial nomination of Robert H. Bork to the Supreme Court, Democratic leader Byrd wanted to facilitate floor action on the nominee. He repeatedly asked GOP leader Robert Dole, Kan., to join him in waiving the two-day rule. "Would the distinguished Republican leader indicate whether or not he is willing to join with me in waiving the 2-day rule?" asked Senator Byrd. "I regret that I am not in a position now to waive the 2-day rule," answered Senator Dole.[11] The discussion surrounding the two-day rule involved jockeying by both parties as they tried to expedite or stretch out debate on the Bork judgeship.

"Holds"

"Holds" are an informal custom unique to the Senate. They permit any number of senators—individually or in clusters—to stop (sometimes permanently, sometimes temporarily) floor consideration of legislation or nominations simply by making requests of their party leaders not to take up such matters. For example, a Senate committee reports a measure by a 17-1 vote. The bill may even be slated for floor debate. Yet the dissenting senator can put a hold on the legislation and halt action on the measure. To be sure, party leaders can move ahead with the bill anyway, but then they face the daunting prospect of overcoming the probable filibuster. Unlike filibusters, which are ostensibly educational and occur in full view of everyone, holds require no public utterance and occur in shrouded circumstances.

Relatively little is known about holds even among insiders in Washington. There is no public record of who places holds, how it is done (often by letter to the party leader), how many holds are placed on any bill, or how long they will be honored by the leadership. Most holds, noted Democratic leader Byrd, are used so senators "might be assured that they will be informed or contacted so they can be present when the matter is called up, or have an opportunity to offer an amendment." [12] Yet secret holds can stymie action without anyone—press, constituents, interest groups, executive officials, or even other senators—knowing who is preventing consideration of a particular issue. "There is a hold on S. 1407," declared Sen. J. James Exon, D-Neb., and "this Senator cannot even find out which Senator or the staff of which Senator has placed a hold on that bill." [13]

Holds can stymie floor action because they are linked to the Senate's tradition of extended debate and unanimous consent agreements. Party leaders understand that to ignore holds can precipitate both objections to unanimous consent requests and filibusters. "As many as six senators had 'holds' on the [bridge repair] bill," wrote a journalist, "thereby blocking the unanimous consent that would be needed before the Senate could even consider it." [14]

Holds are a more prominent feature of today's Senate because assertive senators recognize the political and policy potential inherent in the concept. Holds "have come into a form of reverence which was never to be," declared Republican Whip Simpson.[15] Periodically, party leaders assert that senators cannot put indefinite or anonymous holds on matters. "I do not recognize [holds] as being legitimate reasons to delay indefinitely, ad infinitum, the action on a bill," declared Democratic leader Byrd.[16]

Holds are a potent blocking device on certain kinds of measures and during the hectic closing days of a session. For instance, it is on special purpose legislation that holds can be most effective. "Must" legislation, such as continuing resolutions, cannot be killed by holds. Where a hold "really works," observed Sen. William L. Armstrong, R-Colo., "is on a bill where nobody cares except two or three Senators." [17] If these few senators can resolve their differences, then the hold falls by the wayside.

Holds encourage bargaining not only among senators but between the Senate and the executive branch. Senator Helms sometimes places holds on diplomatic nominations to extract concessions from the State Department. Another senator blocked the confirmation of an undersecretary of the Commerce Department for three weeks because he wanted the "Commerce Department to award a $1 million grant for a marina development project in his home state." [18] The Reagan White House

SENATE OF THE UNITED STATES

ONE HUNDREDTH CONGRESS

FIRST SESSION { CONVENED JANUARY 6, 1987 } DAYS OF SESSION 129
SECOND SESSION { }

CALENDAR OF BUSINESS

Thursday, October 8, 1987

(LEGISLATIVE DAY, SEPTEMBER 25, 1987)

SENATE CONVENES AT 8:30 A.M.

(IN RECESS)

PENDING BUSINESS

S. 1394 (ORDER NO. 173)

A bill to authorize appropriations for fiscal year 1988 for the Department of State, the United States Information Agency, the Board for International Broadcasting, and for other purposes. *(Oct. 2, 1987.)*

(CONSENT AGREEMENTS ON P. 2)

PREPARED UNDER THE DIRECTION OF WALTER J. STEWART,
SECRETARY OF THE SENATE
By WILLIAM F. FARMER, JR., LEGISLATIVE CLERK

19-015 O

asked Senator Hatfield to place a hold on a measure that would limit the perquisites afforded former presidents.[19] Lobbying organizations, too, can ask sympathetic senators to place holds on legislation.

Unanimous Consent Requests

If the Senate strictly observed every rule, it would become mired in a bog of parliamentary complications. As a result, the Senate expedites its business by setting aside the rules with the unanimous consent of the members present. Any senator can object to a unanimous consent agreement, but this seldom occurs because all members may participate in formulating these agreements, and usually they concur in the need to keep legislation moving.

By longstanding tradition, the business of the Senate is "largely transacted through unanimous-consent agreements," Massachusetts Republican Henry Cabot Lodge said in 1913, and "not only the important unanimous-consent agreements which are reached often with much difficulty on large and generally contested measures, but constantly on all the small business of the Senate we depend on unanimous consent to enable us to transact the public business."[20] That statement holds true today. Once accepted, unanimous consent agreements are as binding on the Senate as any standing rule and may be set aside or modified only by unanimous consent. The trend in recent years, noted Senator Byrd, is "that there are not as many unanimous-consent agreements . . . as there were a year ago or 2 years ago or 3 or 4."[21] This general decline reflects in part the changed nature of decision making as Congress enacts fewer but bigger public laws.

There are two types of unanimous consent requests: simple and complex.

- Simple requests are made from the floor by any senator; these almost always deal with routine business or noncontroversial actions. They are made orally and normally are accepted without objection. For example, senators regularly ask permission for staff members to be present on the floor during a debate. Committees may not meet after the first two hours of a Senate session except by unanimous consent or unless special leave is obtained from the majority and minority leaders. Simple unanimous consent agreements also may rescind quorum calls, add senators as cosponsors of bills, insert material in the *Congressional Record,* or limit the length of time members have to be recorded on roll-call votes.
- Complex agreements usually set the guidelines for floor consideration of specific major bills. They are proposed orally—usually by

the leadership—often after protracted negotiations among party leaders and key senators.[22] Once agreed to, they are formally recorded. Such agreements may establish the sequential order in which measures will be taken up, pinpoint the time when measures are to reach the floor, and set rules for debate, including time limitations and, frequently, a requirement that all amendments be germane to the bill under consideration.

Before 1975 many unanimous consent agreements were worked out openly during the floor debate on the bill. They were offered to extricate the Senate from a difficult or confusing parliamentary situation. Today, such agreements are regularly worked out in advance of floor debate and then approved by the Senate and transmitted in printed form to all senators. To be sure, there are still plenty of piecemeal unanimous consent agreements—limiting debate on specific amendments or deciding when to call up a measure—hammered out on the floor. Party leaders and floor managers take what they can get when they can get it and work from there to more embracing unanimous consent agreements.

An example of a unanimous consent agreement (also called a "time-limitation agreement") is shown on page 210. In addition to identifying the bills involved, such agreements indicate each bill's position (Order No.) in relation to all other measures on the General Orders Calendar.

The fundamental objective of unanimous consent agreements is to limit the time it takes to dispose of controversial issues in an institution noted for unlimited debate. These agreements, therefore, expedite action on legislation and structure floor deliberation. Typically, agreements impose time limitations on every debatable—and thus delaying—motion, including amendments and final passage, points of order, or appeals from the rulings of the presiding officer. These agreements, however, usually allow an unlimited number of amendments to be offered, thus permitting what Sen. Ted Stevens, R-Alaska, once dubbed a "time agreement filibuster."

Other usual features of these agreements specify the senators who are to control the time for debate on the bill and all amendments, and provide that the time is to be controlled by senators on opposing sides of the issue. Common, too, is the requirement that amendments be germane. Senate rules do permit nongermane floor amendments, but unanimous consent agreements often prohibit them to prevent extraneous issues from being taken up. Some agreements also set the date and time for the vote on final passage of the measure. In brief, in an institution noted for procedural flexibility and sparseness (compared to the House), unanimous consent agreements underscore the Senate's recognition that it needs to voluntarily impose additional rules on itself to dispatch its business.

The Track System

Another device used to move legislation to the floor is of relatively recent origin. The track system was instituted in the early 1970s by Majority Leader Mansfield, with the concurrence of the minority leadership and other senators. It permits the Senate to have several pieces of legislation pending on the floor simultaneously by designating specific periods during the day when each proposal will be considered. The system is particularly beneficial when there are many important bills awaiting floor action or when there is protracted floor conflict on a particular bill.

Before the initiation of the track system, legislative business came to an abrupt halt during filibusters. The "two-track system enables the Senate to circumvent that barrier," noted Democratic Whip Alan Cranston. The Senate "can now continue to work on all other legislation on one 'track' while a filibuster against a particular piece of legislation is . . . in progress on the other 'track.'"[23]

Use of the track system on certain legislation is implemented by the majority leadership after obtaining the unanimous consent of the Senate. Or the different tracks can be put into place by agreement between the majority leader and the minority leader. On occasion, the Senate may operate on double, triple, or quadruple tracks. "This means there would be about . . . four tracks going here with the Verity nomination to be the first. . . . Following that the war powers has next priority," said Democratic leader Byrd. "Following that, catastrophic illness, and then, fourthly, the Labor-HHS appropriations bill."[24]

The use of unanimous consent agreements and the track system impose a measure of discipline on the Senate. Formerly, senators could arrive in the midst of a debate on a banking bill, for example, obtain recognition from the chair, and launch into a lengthy discussion of the wheat harvest prospects. Today, complex agreements and the track system prevent that from happening. Now, senators generally know what measure will be considered on a specific day and at what time, when they are scheduled to speak on that bill, and how long they will have the floor.

SCHEDULING PROCEDURES COMPARED

As is probably clear to the reader by now, the Senate has nothing that compares with the scheduling function of the House Rules Committee.[25] That panel, as described in Chapter 5, regulates the flow of major bills to the floor, specifies the time for general debate, stipulates whether amendments can be offered, and decides if points of order are to be waived. The legislative route in the House is clearly marked by firm rules and precedents, but that is not so in the Senate. "Rules are never observed in this body," a president pro tempore once observed, "they are only made to be broken. We are a law unto ourselves, and it is entirely immaterial in my judgment whether we have a code of rules or not." [26]

Nonetheless, unanimous consent agreements and the special rules drafted by the Rules Committee are similar in several respects. Each waives the rules of the respective chamber to permit timely consideration of important measures and amendments. Each must be approved by the members of the chamber—in the Senate by unanimous consent of senators present on the floor and in the House by majority vote of the representatives. Each effectively sets the conditions for debate on the legislation in question and on all proposed amendments. And rules and unanimous consent agreements are formulated with the involvement of party leaders, although such participation in the House is generally limited to the majority party leaders. And the House leadership generally plays a significant part only for rules on particularly crucial or controversial measures.

Among the more important differences between rules and unanimous consent agreements are that rules are drafted in public session by a standing committee, while unanimous consent agreements usually are negotiated privately by senators and staff aides. Measures given a rule in the House commonly are taken up almost immediately, but unanimous consent agreements generally involve prospective action on bills.

The amendment process in each house also makes for important differences. Rules from the Rules Committee may limit the number of permissible amendments or prohibit them altogether. Senate unanimous consent agreements, except those prohibiting nongermane amendments, do not usually limit or forbid floor amendments. Interestingly, Senate practices regard an amendment as germane if it is specifically enumerated in the unanimous consent agreement, even if it really is not germane at all. Of course, all senators must be willing to waive the germaneness requirement when the agreement is drawn up.

Finally, a special House rule specifies almost every significant floor procedure that will affect consideration of the bill. Complex agreements focus on two points in particular: (1) setting limits on the debate time to be allowed for amendments, motions, points of order, and appeals from the rulings of the chair; and (2) setting limits on debate on final passage of the bill. In general, procedural experimentation is easier to accomplish in the smaller Senate than in the 435-member House. Table 7-1 briefly summarizes the principal characteristics of rules drafted by the Rules Committee and Senate unanimous consent agreements.

TABLE 7-1 Comparison of House Rules and Senate Unanimous Consent Agreements

House Special Rule	*Senate Unanimous Consent Agreement*
Specifies time for general debate	Specifies time for debating the bill and amendments offered to the bill
Permits or prohibits amendments	Usually restricts the offering of nongermane amendments only
Formulated by Rules Committee in public session	Formulated by party leaders informally in private sessions; occasionally on the Senate floor
Approved by majority vote of the House	Agreed to by unanimous consent of senators present on the floor
Adoption generally results in immediate floor action on the bill	Adoption geared more to prospective floor action
Covers many aspects of floor procedure	Geared primarily to debate restrictions on amendments and final passsge
Does not specify date and exact time for vote on final passage	May set date and exact time for vote on final passage
Effect is to waive House rules	Effect is to waive Senate rules

SENATE LEADERSHIP AND UNANIMOUS CONSENT

Complex unanimous consent agreements are formulated through informal negotiations between party leaders and interested senators. Bargains or informal understandings sometimes are struck on the Senate floor to win approval of unanimous consent agreements. An example of the intricate negotiations that sometimes are necessary appears on page 190.

The job of the leadership is to ensure that the interests of all senators are protected, a difficult assignment given the heightened individualism and openness of the contemporary Senate. One scholar has written: "Because the system of unanimous consent would collapse if even one senator were habitually mistreated, Senate leaders strive to identify those senators interested in a given measure and to give them ample opportunity to express their interest." [27]

If members were ever to lose confidence in the unanimous consent procedure, the Senate would be in danger of reverting to hidebound observance of cumbersome rules. It would almost certainly lose the informality and flexibility that sets it apart from the more rules-

Winning a Unanimous Consent Agreement

STAGE 1: THE ATTEMPT

Mr. [ROBERT] DOLE. Mr. President, we are apparently stymied on S. 408, the Small Business Administration authorization bill. It was my understanding earlier that there would be no objection to a time agreement with reference to germane amendments to the SBA authorization proposal. Members on both sides had agreed to 2 hours on the bill and amendments offered by four or five Senators. With time agreements we thought we could dispose of that bill this afternoon.

It now appears that it is not possible, that there is objection to that agreement. There is a Senator who wants to offer a prayer amendment to the Small Business authorization bill.

STAGE 2: THE OBJECTION

A Congressional attempt to rescue the Small Business Administration from termination, as proposed by the White House, is being threatened by a resonant clash of Senate personalities, focused, at least ostensibly, on the issue of officially sanctioned prayer in the public schools.

Senator Lowell P. Weicker Jr., the chairman of the Senate Small Business Committee, had drafted a compromise bill that would reduce the cost of the small-business agency $2.5 billion over three years. The Connecticut Republican, who says the measure would continue the most important functions of the agency, had won support for it from Senate leaders and was prepared last week to bring it to the floor.

But then Senator Jesse Helms, Republican of North Carolina, introduced a proposal to legalize school prayer as an amendment to the Weicker bill, which had the effect of postponing floor action indefinitely. Under these circumstances, Senator Bob Dole, the majority leader, cannot bring up the business-agency legislation without risking tying up the Senate for weeks on school prayer any time Senator Helms chooses to call up his amendment.

Senator Weicker led the opposition to a school prayer amendment on its most recent appearance on the floor early in 1984, when it was defeated. Senator Helms, his opponents have discovered, never forgets.

STAGE 3: SUCCESS

Mr. DOLE. I am pleased to report that we have worked out an agreement with the distinguished Senator from North Carolina, Senator HELMS who has an amendment to the SBA bill which he now—I think he will indicate here in a minute—will not offer. In return, I have agreed to bring the amendment up as a freestanding resolution, a prayer resolution, sometime hopefully in September.

Sources: Congressional Record, daily ed., June 18, 1985, S8310; *New York Times,* July 1, 1985, B8; and *Congressional Record,* daily ed., July 16, 1985, S9538.

conscious House. Informal norms such as courtesy and fairness to all senators buttress trust in the wide use of unanimous consent agreements. The party leaders who negotiate complex unanimous consent agreements hold the key to the continued smooth operation of the Senate.

Two recent majority leaders—Democrats Mike Mansfield, who held the post longer than any other senator (1961-1977), and Robert C. Byrd (1977-1981; 1987-1989)—are largely responsible for refining and extending the use of unanimous consent agreements. Each had his own style. Mansfield was a mild-mannered leader who viewed himself as only "one among my peers." Byrd was an activist, who worked diligently to control all procedural phases of floor action. The two approached negotiations on consent agreements in differing fashion, but each was successful in achieving agreements even, at times, in the face of fierce opposition to particular bills. During their tenure unanimous consent agreements became more complicated and governed floor action on a larger number of measures.

During Howard Baker's tenure as majority leader (1981-1985), he, too, relied heavily on unanimous consent agreements to schedule legislation. Three considerations affecting their use during this period are worth noting, however. First, there were fewer major bills subject to such agreements, reflecting, in part, the public mood against the launching of new federal domestic programs. Further, the Republican-controlled committees generally opposed reporting new legislative initiatives.

Second, 1981 began the expanded use of the budget reconciliation procedure (see Chapter 3). Numerous pieces of legislation that previously would have been brought up independently under unanimous consent agreements were incorporated in an omnibus reconciliation bill. It is interesting to note that the Senate's procedure for considering reconciliation bills (incorporated in the 1974 budget act) is modeled after a standard unanimous consent agreement. A consent-like procedure, reconciliation was used to avoid the need to obtain agreements on a bill-by-bill basis.

Third, Senator Baker, especially during the early part of his leadership, brought measures to the floor without first obtaining comprehensive agreements. In many cases this was because he was unable to attract the unanimous approval of the Senate. With the Senate and White House in GOP hands, the Democrats were reluctant to enter into broad agreements restricting their floor options since they had no idea what amendments might surface. Thus, narrower agreements often were negotiated on the floor, typically regulating the consideration of a particular amendment or series of amendments.[28]

When Robert Dole became majority leader (1985-1987), he forcefully took charge of the Senate's agenda and orchestrated floor actions to accommodate GOP goals and policy preferences. A more partisan leader than Baker, Senator Dole used his power of recognition to sequence and control the consideration of issues on the floor. Senator Dole's assertive style coincided with a political situation different from Baker's. "Dole faces a situation with a lame-duck president and 22 Republicans up for re-election" and two fewer Republican members than Baker had, said Senator Rudman.[29] Senator Dole also wanted to use his post as a springboard to the presidency. (Like Baker before him, Dole was unsuccessful in his quest for the White House.)

Part of Dole's strategy for moving legislation was private meetings in his office. Here Dole and other senators and staff aides worked to find the compromises and accommodations that broke partisan, bicameral, or legislative-executive deadlocks on issues. "Much of the real work clearing legislative obstacles occurred in Mr. Dole's offices, where many problems were aired and resolved in private while out on the Senate floor quorum calls and recesses lasted hours." [30] Senator Dole did not simply call the meetings; he participated actively in working out agreements that produced legislative results.

When the Senate returned to Democratic control following the November 1986 elections, Senator Byrd again became majority leader. The Senate's most knowledgeable procedural strategist, Senator Byrd understood, as he phrased it, the "difficulties of contending first with differences of perspective and opinion on one's own side of the aisle before one can then contend with the differences of perspective and opinion between the two parties." [31]

Partisan disputes slowed senatorial decision making during parts of the 100th Congress. When Democrats wanted to move quickly on scores of initiatives to demonstrate their capacity to lead and govern, Republicans wanted to stymie some of their efforts and promote conditions that could lead to the GOP's recapturing control of the Senate. "We have two points of leverage," said GOP senator Richard Lugar, Ind. "The two magic numbers are 41 and 34." [32] With forty-one votes, Republicans can frustrate attempts to break filibusters (sixty votes are needed to invoke cloture; see Chapter 8). With thirty-four votes, Republicans can sustain presidential vetoes.

With the power to schedule, Democratic leader Byrd threatened to delay planned recesses and early adjournments, force repeated votes to focus public attention on stalling tactics, and postpone action wanted by the Republicans. In the end, the sheer neçessity of forging bipartisan compromises, along with outside events such as the October 19, 1987, stock market crash, combined to produce agreements on some important issues.

The majority leader generally has an important ally in the minority leader. In contrast to the House, where scheduling is the sole prerogative of the majority leadership, Senate scheduling traditionally has been a bipartisan effort. The Senate system involves not merely a question of equity, but of necessity, because Senate rules confer on each individual member formidable power to frustrate the legislative process, including the right to object to any unanimous consent request. The late James B. Allen, D-Ala. (1969-1978), once dubbed a "one-man wrecking crew" in the press, frequently employed his mastery of Senate rules to stymie the leadership's wishes.

The majority and minority leaders constantly consult with one another and with their top assistants, other senators, party colleagues, and key staff members on legislative scheduling. They also seek scheduling advice from committee leaders or receive it from committee leaders. "Every time I turned one corner, I would find the [Foreign Relations] Chairman meeting me and importuning me, adjuring me, beseeching me, urging me to get on to this State authorization bill," stated Senator Byrd.[33]

Outside groups also lobby party leaders to bring favored legislation to the floor. Executive branch and White House officials also importune party leaders to facilitate or delay action on certain legislation. Senators, too, might threaten to vote against so-called "must" legislation unless proposals of great interest to them are scheduled for Senate consideration.

In short, scheduling involves numerous considerations. Party leaders must balance their interest in planning the Senate's business on a daily, weekly, and annual basis with (1) the needs of committees, which require concentrated periods of time, particularly early in the session, to process legislation assigned to them, and (2) the needs of senators, who prefer some degree of predictability and certainty in the legislative agenda so they can schedule their time most efficiently. This often means that no matter how carefully Senate leaders plan the legislative agenda—the times and dates measures will be scheduled, and in what order they will be considered on the floor—they still must juggle bills to satisfy senators, take account of external events and political circumstances, and, where possible, influence policy outcomes in the interests of their own party.

BREAKDOWNS IN SCHEDULING

Party leaders work diligently to bring legislation to the floor by unanimous consent, and are understandably reluctant to call up measures without time-limitation agreements or unless their proponents can guarantee the necessary votes to cut off any filibusters. After all, the Senate's time is finite and its workload immense. Still, there are measures that are too important to be delayed by the intense divisions and strong feelings that make unanimous consent agreements impossible to reach. "When you cannot get an agreement through, there is . . . but one thing to do and that is just to put your head down and plow through," explained Majority Leader Baker.[34] When unanimous consent on scheduling cannot be reached, legislation is at the mercy of opponents, who have a vast array of obstructionist tactics—including the filibuster—at their disposal.

A failure to reach an agreement delays bringing the legislation at issue to the floor. A dramatic example occurred during the first session of the 100th Congress. Majority Leader Byrd tried to bring up the defense authorization bill by unanimous consent. Unable to proceed in that fashion, Byrd then tried to call up the legislation without triggering a filibuster on the motion to proceed. Republicans, however, immediately launched delaying actions that the Senate had seldom seen in decades (see "Parliamentary War Erupts over Defense Bill"). The GOP opposed a provision in the defense measure that required the White House to receive congressional approval before testing the antimissile Strategic Defense Initiative (SDI). Republicans vowed to prevent consideration of the Pentagon bill until Democrats deleted the offending provision.

For months the Senate was stymied in its effort to call up the defense measure. After a four-month filibuster, Republicans relented and voted with Democrats to take up the bill. They took this action because Democrats had finally won enough GOP votes to win a scheduled cloture vote on the motion to proceed. Another three weeks passed before the Senate passed the Pentagon bill with the SDI language still in the measure. An effort that began on May 13 to call up the bill ended October 2 with Senate passage of the legislation. (Then followed weeks of House-Senate and Congress-White House negotiations before acceptable compromises could be signed into law.)

Unlike the House, where failure to secure a rule from the Rules Committee usually spells certain defeat for important bills, the Senate, with its greater flexibility, has a variety of ways to secure action on legislation. Any senator can move to take measures off the General Orders Calendar. (Normally, however, such motions are made by the majority leader.) If such a move has the backing of party and committee leaders and a majority of the Senate, the proposal almost certainly will reach the floor. In situations in which a bill has been blocked by the leadership, a senator has the option of offering it in the form of a nongermane floor amendment to another bill. Finally, a senator can resort to the threat of a filibuster or object to all unanimous consent requests until the leadership yields and schedules his or her measure for floor action.

Keeping Senators Informed

At the start of each day, the majority leader often presents an overview of activities for the Senate, just as he announces the program for the next day or subsequent day at the conclusion of the daily session. Periodically, he indicates what the legislative agenda looks like for longer periods of time. Senators are kept informed of the legislative program through a variety of means, such as weekly "whip" notices (issued more frequently as needed by each party) listing the measures to be considered each day. Floor proceedings are telecast to senators' offices, where senators and staff aides may listen to floor debate while working on other matters. Both parties maintain a "hotline" (automatic telephone connection) to their members' offices to keep them abreast of impending floor developments. For example, during a typical session, a member of the GOP leadership announced that the hotline had "notified Senators on this side of the aisle [that] if we have not finished the bill by normal recess or adjournment hour . . . we will continue late into the evening."[35]

Senators and staff aides also monitor the *Congressional Record*, committee calendars, the daily Calendar of Business, newspapers, and other publications. Most Senate offices (like House offices) have computer terminals with access to an assortment of legislative information banks. These video terminals can call up summaries of bills describing key provisions and listing when the measures were introduced, their sponsors, the committees to which they were referred, and actions taken, such as hearings, markups, and floor action. Legislative support agencies, such as the Congressional Research Service, continually prepare reports for members, committees, and staff aides on current and prospective legislative activities.

SUMMARY

The informality of the unanimous consent process does not mean that Senate procedure is less complex than that of the House. On the contrary, unanimous consent requests are unique to each bill and are arrived at only after careful, patient, and often difficult negotiations. The differences between House and Senate scheduling procedures are summarized in Table 7-2. For example, the Senate, unlike the House, is filled with devices to stall action on legislation ("substantive delays"), and its party leaders frequently permit "personal delays" to accommo-

Parliamentary War . . .

The Senate May 13 exploded into an angry partisan shouting match, as Republicans rolled out heavy parliamentary artillery to block action on a bill limiting testing for President Reagan's strategic defense initiative (SDI).

Republicans employed little-known Senate rules to outflank Majority Leader Robert C. Byrd of West Virginia, who in turn was resorting to a procedural maneuver to circumvent a threatened GOP filibuster.

The dispute paralyzed the Senate for four hours, while Byrd and GOP leader Robert Dole of Kansas deployed competing parliamentarians in what another senator aptly described as a "dueling banjos routine."

Caught in the snarl was the fiscal 1988 defense authorization bill (S 1174), which ended up exactly where Republicans wanted it; mired in a filibuster that prevented Byrd from officially bringing the bill to the floor.

Republicans vehemently oppose provisions of the bill that would, in effect, give Congress veto power over any move to speed up testing and deployment of SDI.

It was the second time this year that Republicans have stalled the Senate in parliamentary gridlock, reminding Democrats that being in the majority does not guarantee control of the Senate. In February, a similar brawl broke out over a bill (S 83) setting energy efficiency standards for household appliances that was opposed by the White House.

"Morning Hour" Maneuver

The brouhaha over the defense bill erupted when Byrd tried to block Republican plans to filibuster his motion to bring the measure to the floor. He did so by arranging to call up the bill during the "morning hour"—a period within the first two hours of a legislative day during which, under Senate rules, any motion to proceed to a bill is non-debatable and therefore immune from filibusters.

To lay the groundwork for moving into morning hour, Byrd first called for a brief adjournment, so he could begin a new legislative day. He then called for the approval of the *Journal* of the previous day. Both moves were the subject of roll-call votes.

Republicans wanted to prevent Byrd from offering his motion to proceed to the defense bill for two hours—at which point morning hour would end and they would be able to filibuster.

With help from former Senate Parliamentarian Robert B. Dove, GOP leaders came up with an obscure rule that allows senators to ask to be excused from voting and to interrupt a roll call to explain why.

... *Erupts over Defense Bill*

Beginning with the vote on the *Journal,* Republicans took turns invoking that rule and calling for votes on their request not to vote—thus preventing one roll call after another from being completed. After three Republicans asked to be excused from consecutive votes, Byrd tried to call a halt to the tactic. He objected to the third GOP request, saying it was out of order because it was "dilatory," being made only for the purpose of delaying the vote on the *Journal.*

What followed was a procedural pileup of objections, roll calls, appeals and quorum calls, with Republicans and Democrats angrily accusing each other of parliamentary perfidy.

"Dictatorship!" cried Gordon J. Humphrey, R-N.H., after the presiding officer ruled in favor of the Democrats at one point.

"There is absolutely no precedent for this," Dole said at another point. "It is a strict flouting of the rules. Either we are going to play by the rules or not play by the rules."

Byrd charged that Republicans were trying to "drive me to the wall in my effort to carry out my responsibility to get a bill up."

He said his move to bring up the defense bill during "morning hour" would not have precluded Republicans from filibustering the bill itself.

"I often consider, in amusement, the explosion of interest in the arcane and esoteric rules and precedents of the Senate that occurs only when a situation such as we have seen occur today arises," Byrd said. "Suddenly there are many, many experts in the rules and precedents when a situation such as this arises."

An obviously baffled freshman, Timothy E. Wirth, D-Colo., was serving as the Senate's presiding officer during some of the most acrimonious exchanges. With the incumbent parliamentarian, Alan Frumin, whispering instructions to him, Wirth responded slowly and carefully to the repeated demands for rulings and clarification that were shouted at the chair.

As the situation deteriorated, Wirth was replaced by a savvy veteran, Wendell H. Ford, D-Ky., chairman of the Senate Rules and Administration Committee. He went so far as to declare Dole out of order with a blunt ruling: "You cannot go on forever stating your reasons for not voting."

Dole didn't, but by the time the parliamentary knots were untied, the Senate had long since wound its way through morning hour, and the motion to proceed to the defense bill was once again open to debate.

The Senate duly staggered from its flap to its filibuster.

Source: Janet Hook, "Parliamentary War Erupts over Defense Bill," *Congressional Quarterly Weekly Report,* May 16, 1987, 977.

TABLE 7-2 House and Senate Scheduling Compared

House	*Senate*
Important role for the Rules Committee	No equivalent body
Majority party leaders are the predominant force in scheduling, but on occasion they confront a Rules Committee that opposes their decisions	Majority party leaders control the flow of legislation to the floor in close consultation with minority party leaders
More formal process	Less formal process
Only key members are consulted in scheduling measures	Every reasonable effort is made to accommodate the scheduling requests of all senators
Elaborate system of calendars and special days for calling up measures	Heavy reliance on informal practice in scheduling
Party leaders can plan a rather firm schedule of daily and weekly business	Party leades regularly juggle several measures to suit events and senators

date individual senators. "I suppose at one time or another each Member of the Senate has asked to have his or her situation taken into account when votes are scheduled," stated Sen. David Pryor, D-Ark. The dilemma arises "when the efforts to accommodate Members reach the point" where the Senate is prevented from accomplishing its workload in reasonable fashion.[36] The need to balance institutional with individual prerogatives is a permanent feature of senatorial scheduling.

Similarities in scheduling between the two chambers also are worth noting. Scheduling is essentially a party function in both the House and Senate. As in the House, privileged legislation, such as conference reports, bills vetoed by the president, or Senate bills with House amendments, could be brought to the floor at almost any time on the motion of any member.[37] But in the Senate, to a greater degree than in the House, party leaders decide when such motions will be made.

Standing committees provide the legislation considered by both chambers. Although party leaders largely set the agenda, they are dependent on committees to process the legislation. There are occasions, too, when majority leaders ask the committee chairmen to stop reporting out controversial legislation because there is insufficient time remaining in a session to consider such measures.

As in the House, there are a number of ways in the Senate to bring up stalled bills, including measures never considered in committee. Senate rules provide for discharging committees, suspending rules, placing measures directly on the General Orders Calendar, and offering nongermane amendments on the floor. These are discussed in Chapter 8, "Senate Floor Procedure."

In the Senate, the extent of the support for or opposition to a bill is the critical factor in getting the bill to the floor. If a voting bloc is large enough, and intensely committed to a bill, it usually can overcome the resistance of even the most intransigent committee chairman. The process of gathering support is frequently done behind the scenes. As Senator Hollings put it: "The truth of the matter is all of us, 100 Members of this august body, understand that 95 percent of the activity and action, consideration, debate, decisions, and the formulation of legislation is done off the floor of the U.S. Senate and not on it." [38]

When there is a strong political consensus, bills may sail smoothly through the Senate. In the absence of such a consensus, the rules of that body can be applied to bring virtually any measure to a screeching halt. The art of legislating in the Senate requires an understanding of the procedural dynamics of floor action. The interplay of issues, rules, and personalities affect floor strategy and the eventual outcome of all bills.

NOTES

1. *U.S. News & World Report,* Aug. 16, 1976, 28.
2. *Christian Science Monitor,* Aug. 2, 1983, 13.
3. *Congressional Record,* daily ed., Dec. 9, 1987, S17474.
4. *New York Times,* May 21, 1987, B10.
5. *Congressional Record,* daily ed., March 21, 1980, S2789.
6. Each calendar is printed separately. There also are separate executive and legislative *Journals.* The General Orders Calendar is found in the Senate *Calendar of Business,* which is printed each day the Senate is in session. Measures on the calendar are assigned a calendar order number. The Senate *Executive Calendar* appears whenever there is executive business on it.
7. *Congressional Record,* Jan. 26, 1973, 2301. Byrd at the time was majority whip. It should be noted that according to Senate rules, "Any rule may be suspended without advance notice by unanimous consent of the Senate."
8. *Congressional Record,* daily ed., Aug. 5, 1987, S11293.
9. *Congressional Record,* daily ed., April 8, 1981, S3618.
10. *Congressional Record,* daily ed., Dec. 10, 1982, S14345.
11. *Congressional Record,* daily ed., Oct. 14, 1987, S14197.
12. *Congressional Record,* daily ed., Feb. 24, 1986, S1512.
13. *Congressional Record,* daily ed., Oct. 5, 1984, S13779.
14. *Washington Post,* Dec. 10, 1980, C6.
15. *Congressional Record,* daily ed., Dec. 5, 1985, S16916.
16. *Congressional Record,* daily ed., Sept. 10, 1987, S11953.
17. *Congressional Record,* daily ed., Feb. 24, 1986, S1511.
18. *Washington Post,* April 25, 1986, B9.
19. *Congressional Record,* daily ed., July 25, 1984, S9129.
20. *Congressional Record,* Jan. 11, 1913, 1388.
21. *Congressional Record,* daily ed., Feb. 20, 1986, S1452.

22. Unlike simple requests, which are formulated orally, complex unanimous consent agreements are formalized in writing and reported to senators by means of the *Congressional Record,* the front page of the daily *Calendar of Business,* and in party whip notices.
23. *Congressional Record,* Jan. 21, 1975, 928.
24. *Congressional Record,* daily ed., Oct. 13, 1987, S14112.
25. The Senate's Rules and Administration Committee has jurisdiction over internal Senate matters but is not involved in scheduling bills for floor debate.
26. *Congressional Record,* daily ed., Dec. 18, 1876, 266.
27. Robert Keith, "The Use of Unanimous Consent in the Senate," *Committees and Senate Procedures,* A Compilation of Papers Prepared for the Commission on the Operation of the Senate, 94th Cong., 2d sess., 161.
28. The information on Senate Majority Leader Baker's use of unanimous consent agreements was made available to the author by Martin Gold, counsel to the majority leader.
29. Andy Plattner, "Dole on the Job: Keeping the Senate Running," *Congressional Quarterly Weekly Report,* June 29, 1985, 1270.
30. *Washington Times,* Jan. 13, 1986, 8A.
31. *Congressional Record,* daily ed., Dec. 20, 1985, S18332.
32. Janet Hook, "Senate GOP Flexes Muscles of the Minority," *Congressional Quarterly Weekly Report,* May 23, 1987, 1061.
33. *Congressional Record,* daily ed., Oct. 2, 1987, S13441.
34. *Congressional Record,* daily ed., May 25, 1983, S7494.
35. *Congressional Record,* daily ed., Aug. 11, 1982, S10154.
36. *Congressional Record,* Oct. 31, 1985, 29990.
37. In general, privileged matter in the Senate means that such propositions are not subject to unlimited debate (the filibuster) on the motion to call them up for consideration; they are not referred to committee; they are in order at almost any time a senator can gain recognition from the presiding officer; they do not displace the pending business but rather suspend consideration of that measure temporarily; and they are not subject to the one-day layover rule.
38. *Congressional Record,* daily ed., July 25, 1986, S9666.

CHAPTER 8

Senate Floor Procedure

A visitor who moves from the House gallery to the Senate gallery is struck immediately by the contrast in atmosphere. The Senate chamber is more sedate, it is quieter, and business is conducted at a more relaxed pace. The chamber is smaller and more intimate. With fewer members milling about, senators are more easily recognizable than their House counterparts. Typically, only a handful of senators are present on the floor. The remainder are busy in committee meetings or occupied with constituent or other legislative business. All senators, however, generally arrive on the floor quickly in response to buzzers announcing roll-call votes or quorum calls.

There are four semicircular tiers of desks in the Senate. Each of the one hundred senators has an assigned desk, complete with snuffbox and open inkwell. There are no electronic voting machines in the Senate; each senator responds aloud as his or her name is reached during a roll call. Both the Senate and the House employ microphones on the floor, but, unlike representatives, each senator has a microphone.

The chamber is ringed by an upper level of galleries for the press, visitors, and dignitaries. On the floor, a broad aisle separates the Republicans, sitting on the right (facing the podium), from the Democrats, on the left. Depending on the makeup of the Senate, there may be more desks on one side than the other.

The senators face a raised platform. One of several persons may occupy the chair and preside over the session. When he is in attendance, the constitutional president of the Senate—the vice president of the United States—sits there. He may vote only to break a tie. Usually, of course, the vice president is not present. During the Reagan presidency, Vice President George Bush voted six times to break ties. By comparison, during his services as vice president, John Adams (1789-1797) "cast 29 tie-breaking votes, more than any of his 42 successors in that position," observed GOP leader Dole.[1]

The Constitution also provides for a Senate president pro tempore, elected by that body, to preside in the vice president's absence. The president pro tem usually is the most senior senator of the majority party. (The Senate has also established the post of deputy president pro tempore.) In practice, each day's session is chaired by several temporary presiding officers—majority-party senators chosen by the president pro tem to serve for a particular period of time.

On occasion, who sits in the presiding officer's chair is important politically and symbolically. When a group of thirteen Republicans came under intense White House pressure to change their votes and uphold the president's veto of a highway bill in 1987, Democrats made sure that first-year senator Brock Adams, Wash., was presiding during the crucial override vote. "It was no accident," said a Senate Democratic leadership aide.[2]

Brock Adams had defeated incumbent Republican Slade Gorton in 1986 in part because Gorton had flip-flopped on a controversial federal judgeship vote. Gorton first opposed the nominee and then supported him in exchange for White House backing for a judicial nominee from Washington supported by Gorton. Senator Gorton's switch handed the Adams campaign an important political issue. (On the highway measure, not one of the thirteen Republicans changed their vote, and the president's veto was overridden.)

Neither the president pro tem nor the presiding officer is analogous to the Speaker of the House, in part because neither possesses the political resources to exert such wide-ranging influence in the Senate. (One consequence is that rulings of the Senate presiding officer are often appealed and overturned by the Senate; the Speaker's parliamentary rulings in the House are rarely appealed and virtually never overturned.) For example, the president pro tempore "has never been able to establish his authority as a party leader to the extent of the Majority Leader," Democratic leader Byrd, has observed. "This is partly the result of the President pro tempore's irregular appointments and uncertain tenure over the years while serving in the absence of the Vice President."[3]

The principal elective leaders of the Senate are to be found at the front two desks on the center aisle, those assigned to the majority and minority leaders. To the left of the majority leader and to the right of the minority leader sit the party whips, second in command in the Senate party hierarchy. These party leaders, or their designees, remain on the floor at all times to protect their party's interests.

There is frequent contact between the leadership and individual senators. To a much greater extent than in the House, each member has the power to influence the course of the legislative process on a daily basis. Any senator can disrupt the Senate's consideration of a bill more easily and with more telling effect than any one representative in the House. That this does not occur on a regular basis is a tribute to the operation of the Senate's system of unanimous consent, the skill of party leaders, the long tradition of trust, accommodation, and reciprocal courtesy among members, which have survived periodic lapses into hard-line partisanship and confrontation.

Because it is smaller and can operate more flexibly, the Senate normally functions by setting aside many of its own time-consuming rules in order to process legislation efficiently. This chapter describes how the Senate processes legislation once it is readied for floor action. Four main topics are discussed: (1) the daily order of floor business, (2) consideration of major bills under a unanimous consent agreement, (3) consideration of bills without a unanimous consent agreement, and (4) special floor procedures that are used to bypass Senate committees.

Throughout this chapter various procedural devices used to delay or expedite legislation are examined, and comparisons with House procedure are highlighted. First, it is worthwhile to note what "day" means in the Senate.

"LEGISLATIVE" AND "CALENDAR" DAYS

The Senate, unlike the House,[4] regularly distinguishes between a "calendar" and a "legislative" day. The former is the commonly understood notion of what constitutes a day. The latter refers not to a day when the Senate is in session but to the period between a *recess* and an *adjournment* of the Senate. Recesses and adjournments, in short, determine the sequence of legislative days and calendar days. If the Senate adjourns at the end of a daily session, the legislative day ends with that calendar day. If, however, it chooses to recess, the legislative day is carried over to the next calendar day. Democratic leader Byrd once provided this illustration:

> The Senate has been recessing this year from day to day since January 3. There has not been an adjournment of the Senate since January 3. It has recessed over every day. So although today is calendar day Friday, March 28, 1980, we are still in the legislative day of January 3, 1980, because the Senate has never adjourned since it came in on January 3.
>
> If we should adjourn today until Tuesday . . . then, on Tuesday, the legislative day would have caught up with the calendar day, because we then would be in a new legislative day.[5]

In brief, once the Senate adjourns after a series of recesses, the legislative day and calendar day become the same.

The distinction between the types of days is important because many of the Senate's rules are tied to the legislative day. For instance, the "word 'day,' as used in the rules, unless it is specified as a calendar day, is construed to mean a legislative day," according to Senate precedents.[6]

The decision to adjourn or recess is made either by unanimous consent or by majority vote on a motion made by the majority leader. If a quorum cannot be obtained, the Senate must adjourn. Adjournment favors senators trying to delay business since it may trigger a series of time-consuming tactics when the Senate next convenes. The majority leader's decision to ask for a recess or an adjournment therefore can have a significant effect on controversial legislation before the Senate. Party leaders generally prefer recesses to adjournments. Recesses grant the leadership greater flexibility in shaping the Senate's daily business. Senate rules prescribe a daily order of business, but it can be followed only when the Senate begins a new legislative day.

DAILY ORDER OF BUSINESS

Under resolutions adopted at the start of each Congress, the Senate generally convenes each day at noon. The leadership, by a unanimous consent request or motion, may modify the time on a day-to-day basis to stay abreast of the Senate's workload.

The regular order of business in the Senate, as in the House, begins with a prayer and the approval of the *Journal* of the previous day's activities. "Mr. President, I ask unanimous consent that the Journal of the proceedings be approved to date," requests the majority leader at the start of a new legislative day. Invariably that request is granted by the Senate. (In 1986 the Senate amended its rules to permit a nondebatable motion for the *Journal*'s approval. Previously, reading the *Journal* was sometimes used as a filibustering device. Senators, however, can still propose amendments to correct the *Journal*.) Then there is a brief period reserved for remarks by the majority and minority leaders and, if it is the beginning of a new legislative day, the "morning hour" follows. This period technically runs for a maximum of two hours. "Morning business" is conducted during this time, including the receipt of messages, reports, and communications from the president, the House, and heads of executive branch departments. Bills and resolutions are introduced and referred to committee, committee reports filed, statements inserted in the *Congressional Record*, and brief speeches delivered. As Democratic leader Byrd summarized:

> "Morning business" and the "morning hour" do not mean the same. The morning hour is the first 2 hours after the Senate convenes

> following an adjournment. Morning business is that period within the morning hour during which Senators may introduce resolutions, bills, petitions, or memorials; committees may report matters, and certain matters come over from the previous day.[7]

Senators may speak during morning business only by unanimous consent. That is why the party leaders usually ask unanimous consent that there be a period for the transaction of routine morning business and that senators be allowed to speak therein for up to two minutes, or up to five minutes, and so on. Under the rules, bills and resolutions must be read twice—each reading on a different legislative day—before they can be referred to committee. But rarely is this rule invoked; unanimous consent is obtained to dispense with it. When morning business is concluded, the Senate considers "unobjected to measures" on the General Orders Calendar.

The leadership may restrict or change "morning business" by unanimous consent. Republican leader Dole once announced, "Mr. President, I ask unanimous consent there now be a period for the transaction of routine morning business not to extend beyond 7:15 p.m."[8] (Dole's request for morning business in the evening illustrates the importance of understanding congressional vocabulary.) A non-debatable motion to proceed to any item on the calendar also is in order during the morning hour. Seldom is such a motion made during this period, however (for an example, see p. 196).

Following morning hour, the leadership may schedule "special orders" for up to five minutes (formerly fifteen minutes, until the Senate in 1986 permitted television coverage of its floor sessions). Under special orders, members are given permission to speak for a limited time on any subject. The Senate then proceeds to "unfinished business"—legislation pending from a previous day.

If there is no unfinished business, the majority leader or another senator offers a motion to take up a new measure that the leadership, after consultation with the minority leader and other interested senators, has scheduled for floor action. This may be a critical juncture in the proceedings, for it is at this point that opponents of the bill in question might begin delaying tactics, such as a filibuster to prevent the bill from being considered.

This sequence of activities is subject to change by unanimous consent. It also may be affected by the method by which the previous daily session was ended—by recess or by adjournment. The distinction is important at this stage. If the Senate recessed, it can resume consideration of unfinished business, with no intervening activity, such as morning business. If it adjourned, it normally must begin its session with morning business, following the prayer and approval of the *Journal*.

DEBATE IN THE MODERN SENATE

In the early Congresses, the Senate was characterized by protracted debates and great orators: Daniel Webster, John Calhoun, and Stephen Douglas on slavery, and later by Henry Cabot Lodge and others on the League of Nations. Today, senators are so busy, and the legislative agenda so crowded, that extended give-and-take among numerous senators is the exception rather than the rule. "In this United States Senate it is rare indeed to have one-third of the members present to hear debate," observed Senator Simon. "There is dialogue and debate, but most of it does not take place on the floor under public scrutiny." [9] To be sure, debate still serves to publicize issues, address constituencies, identify areas of consensus, and influence Senate votes. After one spirited floor session, Sen. Spark M. Matsunaga, D-Hawaii, declared, "I was really undecided on the pending amendment, but [the] Senator so ably presented his case that I will join him" in opposing the amendment.[10]

On the other hand, the experiences of Sen. Daniel J. Evans, R-Wash., may hold true more often than members like. "There almost never is a mind changed by debate on the floor of the Senate because, for the most part, no one is ever listening." Or senators have already committed themselves before debate begins. "By the time formal debate . . . started [on the nomination of Robert Bork to the Supreme Court], 93 or 94 Senators had already declared themselves one way or the other," added Senator Evans. "So, it was virtually impossible at that point to change minds." [11]

There still are "great debates" that capture national attention and mobilize national sentiment on critical issues such as civil rights, arms control, or Social Security. But debate in the modern Senate consists primarily of prepared speeches perfunctorily read (or inserted in the *Congressional Record* without having been formally delivered before a largely empty chamber).[12] When intensive debate does occur, it is often among only a handful of senators with special interest in the legislation. To minimize personality clashes, the Senate (like the House) forbids first-person references during debate. "One of the reasons for the rule that a Senator must address another Senator through the Chair and not in the first person," stated Democratic leader Byrd, "is to avoid casting aspersions, and causing acridness in debate and hurt feelings." [13]

As in the House—even though only a scattering of members are on the floor—a quorum technically is present until a member suggests otherwise. Any senator may suggest the absence of a quorum. When this occurs the presiding officer is obligated to direct the clerk to call the roll of members. In contrast to House practice, the presiding officer may not first count the senators present to determine whether a quorum in fact exists, except during post-cloture proceedings. The calling of the roll is mandatory unless it is dispensed with by unanimous consent.

Quorum calls, however, are commonly employed to give senators time to work out procedural arrangements ("positive" delay, as opposed to "negative" delay), such as a unanimous consent agreement, or to give a member scheduled to speak time to reach the floor. "What I would like to do is suggest the absence of a quorum," said Senator Weicker, "so that the parties involved here might sit down in the quiet of some room to see exactly how we can get this particular [amendment] to a point where we can vote up or down." [14] Once this is done, further calling of the roll to establish a quorum is dispensed with by unanimous consent. When Lyndon Johnson was majority leader, he "would ask for a quorum call and wait, sometimes for close to an hour, while the reading clerk droned slowly through the names. Then, when Johnson was ready for the Senate to resume, he would suspend the calling of the roll." [15] Cumulatively, the Senate spends a lot of time on quorum calls. "In 1985 the Senate spent 247 hours on quorum calls," calculated Senator Pryor, or six weeks of its work year.[16]

Quorum calls to delay proceedings temporarily are to be distinguished from "live" quorums. Here a senator insists that at least a majority of the members come to the chamber and answer to their names. This can be a time-consuming process. Recalling that Sen. Strom Thurmond, R-S.C., once demanded a "live" quorum, a Senate colleague observed, "It took almost one hour to round up fifty-one Senators to respond to their names." [17] The two types of quorum calls are distinguished by the different number of bells that ring in members' offices and Senate committee rooms.

If the Senate officially discovers that it lacks a quorum, it has two options: (1) it must adjourn (recess if there is a previous order to that effect), or (2) it may instruct the sergeant-at-arms to request (compel) the attendance of senators.

Television and Debate

In 1986, after years of consideration, the Senate authorized gavel-to-gavel coverage of its floor proceedings over C-SPAN. On February 27, 1986, the Senate adopted a resolution that permitted television coverage on a trial basis (June 2 was the public debut); on July 29, 1986, the Senate voted to make the "electronic gallery" permanent.

An early review of television's impact reveals rather little change in floor debate or activity. Speeches are more numerous, but they are better organized and livelier than before. Senators "are making better speeches," said Senator Byrd. "They are using more gestures and rhetorical flourishes, and it seems to me that overall, the debate has improved from a substantive point of view." [18] Senators, too, are using more props, graphs, and charts to "illustrate" their points.

Doubtlessly, television heightens public awareness of issues, of members, and of the Senate as an institution. Senatorial staff alert local television networks about their bosses' floor speeches (so segments might be broadcast back home), and party leaders monitor floor actions to ensure that arguably partisan statements are answered by someone with another viewpoint. Some senators disapprove of television coverage, but television cameras have become a routine part of floor activity.[19]

Floor Manager's Role

Floor managers have the major responsibility for guiding legislation to final passage. "I lean on the manager of the bill and the ranking [committee] members to carry the load" on the floor, Democratic leader Byrd observed.[20] Usually, there are two floor managers (one from each party from the reporting committee) per measure. In the case of multiply referred legislation, there may be several majority and minority floor managers. To avoid having all the managers remain continuously on the floor, the Senate often works out a systematic schedule of senatorial action. As Democratic leader Byrd noted:

> Nine committees have reported components of the overall trade bill. . . . It is hoped that each chairman of each committee that has jurisdiction over a particular title, at a given moment when the Senate reaches that title, will be able to deal with that title so that we could proceed title by title and all nine chairmen [and ranking minority members] will not have to be over here all the time to protect all nine titles.[21]

Senate floor managers, like their House counterparts, have varied responsibilities. They identify favorable times to schedule their legislation; they negotiate time-limitation agreements; they may offer amendments to strengthen their bills or win more support as well as to counter proposed weakening amendments; they have to respond to any points of order raised against language in the legislation; and they must alert proponents when their support is needed on the floor.

Strategic calculations are a manager's stock in trade. For example, Sen. John C. Culver, D-Iowa (1975-1981), the floor manager, once was able to persuade Sen. William L. Scott, R-Va. (1973-1979), to offer a troublesome amendment at the most advantageous time from Culver's standpoint.

> The theory behind having Scott bring up the amendment now is that it is better to have such a proposal come up in the morning—a time when many senators are in committee meetings or in their offices and are more distracted than usual from the business that is taking place on the floor. Also, Culver figures that most of his colleagues will assume that

at this point, especially after a long day of taking up amendments—and major ones—yesterday, only routine "housekeeping" amendments are being considered, and that they will pay less attention to the issue, be less eager to join the fray, than they might be later on.[22]

By informal custom, floor managers are accorded priority of recognition by the presiding officer. Explained Senator Byrd: "The manager of a bill also is entitled to preferential recognition—not ahead of the [majority leader and minority leader], but following in line, and is accorded that recognition generally by the Chair."[23]

Staff aides often assist floor managers. Senators rely more heavily on staff assistance during floor debate than do House members. Aides draft amendments and arguments and negotiate with aides of other senators to marshal support for legislation being considered.

BILLS CONSIDERED BY UNANIMOUS CONSENT

The importance of unanimous consent agreements to the efficient operation of the legislative process in the Senate has already been cited. A typical example of a unanimous consent agreement is shown on page 210.

This complex agreement, like most others controlling major legislation, reflects standard operating procedure for the Senate: no day is specified for taking up the bill; nongermane amendments are prohibited with exceptions noted in the agreement; debate on each designated amendment is limited to one hour, with thirty minutes stipulated for any other amendments; thirty minutes' debate is permitted on any debatable motion, appeal, or point of order; and there are provisions regulating the division of time on amendments and other motions. There are two interesting features, however, which are seldom in most unanimous consent agreements. First, the agreement specifies the exact date and time when the Senate is to proceed to consideration of the measure. Second, it limits debate on the entire bill, including amendments, to thirteen hours.

As noted in the previous chapter, unanimous consent agreements are printed in the *Congressional Record,* the daily Senate *Calendar of Business* (illustrated on page 184), and party whip notices. Senators check with party leaders, committee members, and staff to learn when bills are to be considered. The next day's or the next week's legislative program also is announced by the majority leadership at the close of each daily session.

Measures governed by unanimous consent agreements may be called up by the majority leader at the conclusion of the period for five-minute special order speeches. Customarily, the presiding officer briefly

Unanimous Consent Agreement

S 66 (ORDER NO. 106)

Ordered. That at 1:00 p.m. on Monday, June 13, 1983, the Senate proceed to the consideration of S. 66 (Order No. 106), a bill to amend the Communication Act of 1934, and that there be 13 hours of consideration thereon, including debate on any amendments, debatable motion, appeals, or points of order which are submitted or on which the Chair entertains debate, with the time to be equally divided and controlled by the Senator from Oregon (Mr. Packwood) and the Senator from West Virginia (Mr. Byrd), or their designees.

Ordered further, That no amendment that is not germane to the provisions of the said bill shall be received, with the following exceptions: a Commerce Committee modification to the committee amendment; an amendment to be offered by the Senator from Oregon (Mr. Packwood) dealing with telecommunications; an amendment to be offered by the Senator from South Dakota (Mr. Abdnor) dealing with deleting the "two-way" grade communication; and an amendment to be offered by the Senator from South Dakota (Mr. Abdnor) dealing with insuring that all providers of telecommunications services share in the obligation of providing universal service: *Provided,* That there be 1 hour debate on each of the above amendments, with the time to be equally divided and controlled by the mover of such and the manager of the bill.

Ordered further, That there be 30 minutes debate on any other amendment, debatable motion, appeal, or point of order if submitted to the Senate, with the time to be equally divided and controlled by the mover of such and the manager of the bill.

Ordered further, That at the conclusion of the debate, the Senate proceed to vote on passage of S. 66. *(May 18, 1983)*

summarizes the terms of the agreement, then recognizes the bill's floor manager, usually the chairman of the committee or subcommittee that handled the bill, for a short description of the legislation and its intent. The floor manager is followed by the ranking minority committee or subcommittee member, who presents similarly brief opening remarks. The Senate then is ready to debate and consider amendments to the bill.

THE AMENDING PROCESS

Unlike the House, the Senate has no five-minute rule for debating amendments. There are no "closed" rules in the Senate. Any measure is open to virtually an unlimited number of amendments unless a unanimous consent agreement specifies otherwise. On occasion, a floor manager may ask that a measure pass without amendments. Opponents still are likely to offer amendments, but if the floor manager has sufficient support they are likely to be voted down or tabled (killed). For example, Agriculture Chairman Patrick J. Leahy, D-Vt., and ranking minority member Richard Lugar each put out the word on a farm relief bill they were managing that only technical amendments or amendments that did not add to the cost of the measure would receive their joint support. Otherwise, senators had better be prepared to debate their amendments in great detail, they said, and to answer pointed questions. The Leahy-Lugar strategy worked—the only amendment offered to the bill was rejected. "We really stared them down," said Senator Lugar.[24]

Senators, unlike House members in the Committee of the Whole, can modify their own amendments without the need for unanimous consent or the majority approval of the chamber. A senator, for example, might propose an amendment that the floor manager will support if the language is discretionary rather than mandatory. The senator can make the change on his or her own authority and facilitate the amendment's chances of being adopted by the Senate. These modifications are permissible until the Senate takes some action on the amendment, such as agreeing to take a vote on it or arranging a unanimous consent agreement limiting debate time. Senators sometimes quickly ask for action on their amendments because even though they lose the right to modify them they gain the right to offer amendments to their own amendments, should the need arise.

Senators must be recognized by the presiding officer before they can offer amendments. Officially reported committee amendments automatically take precedence over those offered by other members from the floor. Committee amendments, however, are subject to further amendment from the floor.

Senators can propose amendments at any time to any section of a bill. This approach differs from the more orderly routine followed by the House, where the rules specify that each part of a measure be considered in sequential order, usually section-by-section. Senate custom gives individual senators greater flexibility in amending legislation. Amendments must be read by the Senate clerk, but this usually is dispensed with by unanimous consent unless an attempt is being made to delay the bill.

Principle of "Precedence"

An important concept that shapes the amending process in the Senate is "precedence." While both the House and Senate have a rule specifying that only amendments in the first and second degree are permitted, there are basic differences in how each chamber interprets first and second degree amendments. This, in turn, affects the number of amendments that can be pending to a bill at the same time. In the Senate, even third degree amendments occasionally are made in order by unanimous consent.

The principle of precedence determines which amendments (perfecting or substitute) may be offered when others are pending and the order in which those amendments are voted on. A perfecting amendment is one that simply alters language, either to the bill or to a pending amendment, but does not seek to substitute new text for the pending proposal. Perfecting amendments have precedence over substitutes. Thus, if Senator A offers a perfecting amendment to a bill (a first degree amendment), and Senator B then proposes a second degree perfecting amendment to it, no other amendments are in order until the second degree proposal is disposed of. And if the latter is adopted, other second degree amendments—perfecting or substitute—may be offered until the entire text of the first degree amendment has been disposed of.

Alternatively, Senator B may offer a second degree substitute for Senator A's amendment to the bill. Then Senator C, under the Senate's principle of precedence, can introduce a second degree perfecting amendment to Senator A's amendment, which would be voted upon before the substitute. These steps in the Senate amendment process differ from those followed by the House.

To recapitulate, policy decisions often are affected by the Senate's precedence principle, which determines (1) the number of amendments that may be pending simultaneously to a bill, and (2) the order of voting on them. For example, Majority Leader Byrd used his privilege of being recognized ahead of other senators to offer a nongermane strip mining amendment (first degree, perfecting) to a maritime cargo bill. The GOP leader, who supported Byrd's move, asked for the yeas and nays (a roll-call vote) on Byrd's amendment. Then Byrd offered a second degree perfecting proposal to his own amendment.

This parliamentary maneuver (filling the amendment tree), which shut off further floor amendments to Byrd's original amendment, angered Sen. Howard M. Metzenbaum, D-Ohio, who opposed the effort to modify the strip mining reclamation law. When you "have access to the floor," he said to Byrd, "and offer a perfecting amendment and then an amendment to that perfecting amendment, you are in a position to foreclose the right of other Members of the Senate to offer their amendments."[25] Senators Metzenbaum and John Melcher, D-Mont., "were ready to introduce 272 amendments to delay debate on the Byrd proposals."[26] Senator Byrd's tactic prevented them from offering their amendments. In the end, the Senate approved the Byrd amendments.

The Senate, unlike the House, commonly employs the motion to recommit with instructions for broad amendment purposes. If troublesome amendments have been agreed to, the majority leader can "move to recommit with instructions to report back with all amendments that have been adopted thus far with the exception" of the troublesome amendments.[27] Because the motion to recommit has precedence under Senate rules over pending amendments, the majority leader can offer this motion and construct an amendment tree (amending the instructions) that forecloses others from offering amendments and produces the first votes on policy alternatives favored by the majority leader.

For instance, Democratic leader Byrd offered the motion to recommit with instructions on a bill limiting campaign expenditures for Senate elections. At the time the recommittal motion was offered, two nongermane amendments dealing with Contra aid were pending to the campaign bill. Senator Byrd moved "to amend the instructions in such a way that the Senate [had] before it" only issues dealing with campaign finance. "So we have a line of amendments here," said Senator Byrd, "which cannot be amended at the moment until action is taken on the second-degree amendment" that addresses campaign expenditures.[28]

The order of voting on amendments can be of strategic importance, too. Senators may introduce amendments following the precedence principle in order to obtain an early test vote on their policy alternatives. One purpose would be to identify defecting senators who might be kept in line through personal persuasion. Or members might want their amendment to be voted on last, on the assumption that they have enough support to defeat all damaging amendments and thus can demonstrate to opponents that the choice is between the pending amendment or nothing at all.

Strategic Uses of Amendments

Timing, strategy, lobbying, patience, and skillful drafting are important parts of the amending process. Party leaders and floor managers often try to get unanimous consent to arrange the order in which senators call up their amendments. On important measures, senators regularly jockey for position in offering amendments. When the 1986 tax overhaul measure reached the floor, senators realized that amendments to the popular package stood a better chance of adoption if proposed early in the debate. Because of the revenue neutral requirement of Gramm-Rudman-Hollings, members who offered amendments to restore tax breaks needed to propose a source of offsetting revenues. "There's only so many ways to raise . . . money," said the Finance chairman at the time, Robert Packwood. "And if somebody gets an amendment in first and uses up the most attractive way to [raise] the money, that is not available for the next amendment."[29] Whether an amendment is accepted or rejected sometimes depends on its purpose, and its purpose may not always be to amend the bill under consideration. Two examples will illustrate the point.

DEFEATING LEGISLATION. One strategy of opponents of a bill is to load the legislation down with controversial amendments, possibly sparking a filibuster and jeopardizing Senate passage. "Overweight the plan, sabotage it with an unrealistic amendment," and that will ensure defeat of the legislation, noted Senator Hollings.[30]

Floor managers are on the alert for "killer amendments" that can torpedo their measures or treaties. During consideration of legislation imposing economic sanctions against South Africa because of its officially approved apartheid (racial separation) policy, an amendment was proposed to permit the president to waive the sanctions if enough South African blacks became unemployed as a direct or indirect result of the act. Asked if this was a killer amendment, the floor manager said: "It would be a killer amendment. I indicated it seems to me it would terminate the rest of the legislation."[31] The floor manager successfully moved to table the amendment.

"MAKE-A-POINT" AMENDMENTS. Senators sometimes offer amendments to make a point or to obtain something they want. For example, the chairman and ranking minority member of the Budget Committee offered an amendment that provided for the termination or substantial reduction of forty-three domestic programs. The Budget chairman said he offered the amendment "to demonstrate that wholesale program terminations sought by the White House lack congressional support."[32] The Senate rejected the termination amendment by a 14-83 vote. Even the amendment's sponsors voted against it.

Amendments are also proposed to extract commitments from committees that fail to take action on legislation. For instance, Senator Byrd introduced legislation to require reconfirmation of the president's top officials if they continued in office during the president's second term. The committee of jurisdiction took no action on the measure. "Never do I remember" a situation where a committee refused a colleague's request to hold a hearing on his or her legislation, remarked the Democratic leader. The only recourse I have, said Senator Byrd, "is to offer the subject matter as an amendment to a vehicle which comes up on the floor." If the committee will not hold a hearing, "then I will let the Senate be the judge, and I will get my hearing on the floor."[33] Needless to say, Senator Byrd received quick assurances from the committee chairman that hearings would be held on the reconfirmation proposal. "So the matter of amendment not only involves its value in terms of what can be passed and goes into law," explained Senator Weicker, "but also in terms of raising issues which later on could very well become law." [34]

Voting on Amendments

The Senate has three types of voting: voice, division (standing), and roll call. Voice and division voting are similar to House procedures, but there is nothing comparable to the recorded teller vote or the electronic voting procedures of the House. The system of buzzers that summons senators to the floor is much like that of the House. During a roll call members respond "yea" or "nay" as their names are called alphabetically.

The Senate establishes the length of time for roll-call votes at the start of each Congress. When the 100th Congress convened on January 6, 1987, the Senate agreed by unanimous consent:

> That for the duration of the 100th Congress, there be a limitation of 15 minutes each upon any roll call vote, with [a] warning signal to be sounded at the midway point, beginning at the last 7½ minutes, and when rollcall votes are of 10 minutes duration, the warning signal [is to] be sounded at the beginning of the last 7½ minutes.

For the second session of the 100th Congress, Democratic leader Byrd informed members that to improve senatorial efficiency every effort would be made to enforce strictly the fifteen-minute limit on votes (the average had been thirty minutes per vote). To be sure, there were still occasions when votes were extended to accommodate senators. When votes are grouped back to back, referred to as "stacking," the second and succeeding votes often occur, by unanimous consent, at ten-minute intervals.

Party leaders and floor managers make every effort to assure that their supporters are on the floor when needed for a vote. "My experience convinces me," commented Senator Byrd, that voting "is the most critical step in the legislative process. . . . [The leaders and the floor managers must] "have the right members at the right place and at the right time." [35]

Party leaders give advance notice of impending votes in whip notices and announcements from the floor. Occasionally, complex unanimous consent agreements specify the exact date and time for votes on final passage of a bill. On the other hand, the times for votes on amendments sometimes are agreed to by unanimous consent without elaborate negotiations during the debate on the bill.

Recorded votes in the Senate usually can be obtained quite easily; only a "sufficient second"—one-fifth of the senators present—is needed, with a minimum of eleven required by the Constitution. If the minimum number is not on the floor at the time the request is made, a senator can summon other colleagues through a quorum call, try to get their support, and then renew the request for a roll-call vote. As Senator Byrd explained: "If any Senator wants a rollcall vote around here, he will ultimately get it. If he does not get it at first, he will put in a quorum and he will not let us call off the quorum. So we have to have a live quorum or give him the yeas and nays." [36] Most roll calls occur on amendments.

VOTING TRENDS. There was a significant increase in the number of roll-call votes during the 1970s, with some drop-off in later years. The increase may have occurred for several reasons: pride of authorship, evidence of having taken a position on critical and controversial issues, demonstration of Senate support for a measure that may end up in a conference committee to resolve differences with the House, and the diffusion of power within the institution. The general decline in votes during the 1980s reflects such factors as reliance on megabills to process much of the Senate's workload, difficulty in passing measures because of split party control of Congress and sharp legislative-executive conflicts, and lowered public expectations about the federal government's role. Table 8-1 shows the trend in voting since 1971.

"CUE-GIVERS." Senators, like representatives, rely on numerous "cue-givers" for guidance on voting because of the range and complexity of legislation. "When it comes to voting," Sen. James L. Buckley, C/R-N.Y. (1971-1977), once wrote, "an individual senator will rely heavily not only on the judgment of staff, his own and his committee's, but also on a select number of senators whose knowledge he has come to respect and whose general perspectives he shares." [37] The position of the reporting committee is an important factor to many senators. "A lot of members of the Senate," commented Sen. Edmund S. Muskie, D-Maine (1959-1980), "will arrive on the floor, and there's an amendment up that they really haven't had a chance to look at, and they'll just come up and ask, 'What's the committee position?' " [38]

CASTING PROCEDURAL VOTES. On controversial amendments, members often maneuver for procedural, rather than substantive, votes. A vote to table (kill) amendments or other motions is a classic procedural ploy to avoid being recorded directly on politically sensitive policy issues. Senator Byrd has explained the difference:

> A motion to table is a procedural motion. It obfuscates the issue, and it makes possible an explanation by a Senator to his constituents, if he wishes to do so, that his vote was not on the merits of the issue. He can claim that he might have voted this way or he might have voted that

TABLE 8-1 Roll-call Votes in the Senate, 1971-1987

Year	*Number of Roll Calls*	*Year*	*Number of Roll Calls*
1971	423	1980	531
1972	532	1981	483
1973	594	1982	469
1974	544	1983	381
1975	611	1984	292
1976	700	1985	381
1977	636	1986	359
1978	516	1987	420
1979	497		

> way, if the Senate had voted up or down on the issue itself. But on a procedural motion, he can state he voted to table the amendment, and he can assign any number of reasons therefore, one of which would be that he did so in order that the Senate would get on with its work or about its business.[39]

Therefore, if a procedural vote can be arranged to kill or delay a bill, it is more likely to win the support of senators, who may prefer to duck the substantive issue. Moreover, senators generally support the party leadership on procedural votes. "[B]ecause this is a procedural vote . . . [senators] traditionally stick with the leadership on such votes," declared Senator Packwood.[40]

Part of members' consideration in casting procedural or substantive votes involves their role in political campaigns. Votes are not simply used to make decisions or as trading material; they are used by interest group organizations, who select issues of concern to them, to characterize legislators as "heroes or zeroes," conservatives or liberals, depending on how members voted on the groups' chosen topics. As Minority Whip Simpson told the Democrats when they recaptured control of the Senate following the November 1986 elections, "We'll be standing there with our little score cards, waiting for them to jump over the cliff" on the tough political votes.[41]

Like the House, the Senate permits vote "pairing," either "live" or "dead" pairs. In a live pair, one senator is present on the floor during the vote. The practice is for the senator to cast his vote, yea or nay, then withdraw it and announce, "I have a pair with the senator from [naming the state]. If he were present and voting, he would vote [yea or nay]. If I were at liberty to vote, I would vote [yea or nay]." In a dead pair, both senators are absent from the floor. Their positions are printed after each roll call in the *Congressional Record*. Live and dead pairs are not tabulated on roll-call votes, but a live pair can affect the outcome of a vote. Explained Senator Byrd:

> The arranging of pairs has been decisive from time to time on very close votes, because it is possible to pair off enough present Senators to affect the outcome of the vote and perhaps make a difference of 1 or 2 votes which, had the Senators present not been paired, would have decided the issue opposite to the outcome that resulted.
>
> However, Senators generally will not agree to give a "live" pair except on the condition that the outcome is not changed by virtue of the pair given.[42]

In 1986, a "live" pair influenced the outcome of a controversial judicial nomination.[43]

Final Action on a Bill

"When no Senator seeks recognition," Senator Byrd explained, "the Chair automatically puts the question of adoption of amendments and passage of bills."[44] Thus, once the amending process is completed the Senate proceeds to a vote on final passage, unless a unanimous consent agreement has been made setting a later date and time for the final vote. The floor manager announces that there are no further amendments. He then requests a third, and final, reading of the bill. The presiding officer orders the bill engrossed—put in the precise form in which it emerged from the Senate's amending process—and "read" a third time (the title of the bill only), a procedure that takes only a few seconds.

The final vote is not over until the chair announces the outcome. Senate rules prohibit "any Senator from voting after the Chair has announced the decision," Senator Byrd pointed out. Senate rules provide "that the Chair cannot even entertain a unanimous consent request to suspend this rule."[45] Senators, like House members, may change their vote during the regular fifteen-minute voting period, which in the Senate may be a minimum and not the maximum time allowed. For example, during an unusually lengthy Senate roll call dozens of senators switched their votes and defeated a proposal offered by Sen. Dale Bumpers, D-Ark. "I just want to announce that Dr. Cary's in his office for everyone whose arm is out of socket," exclaimed the senator from Arkansas.[46] (Dr. Freeman Cary was the Senate physician.)

After the result of the final vote on the bill has been announced, there is still one more parliamentary step required before Senate action is complete. This step is available only to the side that prevailed on the final vote. If the bill has been passed, a senator who voted for the bill, or who did not vote, makes a motion to reconsider the vote. (On a voice or standing vote, any senator can offer the motion.) Immediately thereafter, another proponent of the bill moves to table the motion to reconsider.

By this procedural device Senate rules protect the bill from further consideration. Rarely does the motion to table fail. This procedure also is used after votes on amendments. The House procedure, described in Chapter 6, is identical.

To summarize, the usual Senate floor procedure for major legislation is as follows: first, a unanimous consent agreement is negotiated; second, the bill is called up by the floor manager after being scheduled by the joint majority and minority leadership; third, the bill is considered for amendment, with the debate time regulated by the unanimous consent agreement; fourth, there is a final vote (voice vote or roll call) on final passage.

But what happens when a major bill reaches the floor in the absence of a unanimous consent agreement? By and large, the procedural sequence is much the same, but the legislation is much more vulnerable to obstructionist tactics, particularly the filibuster.

BILLS WITHOUT UNANIMOUS CONSENT

Sometimes party leaders are unable to achieve unanimous consent agreements. This may happen for a variety of reasons: intense opposition to the bill by certain senators, a general desire for unrestricted debate and amendment, commitments by some senators to protect the interests of absent colleagues, or simply personal pique of some senators against party leaders. Passage of legislation then becomes a much more difficult task. At the very least, debate will be extensive and amendments will be numerous. Operating under the Senate's rules, this can be extremely time-consuming. Moreover, if there is intense opposition to a bill on the part of one or more senators, the well-known device of the filibuster may be threatened (the "silent filibuster") or actually used.[47] Particularly near scheduled recesses or the end of legislative sessions the threat or use of filibusters is especially effective. "It's late in the session and there's a lot to do," remarked Senator Cranston. "That's the time a filibuster could be most effective."[48]

It is sometimes difficult to tell when "extended debate" becomes a filibuster; a senator does not make a motion to filibuster a bill. Senator Byrd once said, "I will be able to perceive one, because I know one when I see it."[49]

Typically, the filibuster is viewed as the last recourse, forcing an almost complete stoppage of normal floor business—a situation most senators try to avoid if at all possible. Nevertheless, it is the most distinctive feature of Senate floor procedures and deserves thorough discussion.

THE FILIBUSTER

Generally characterized in the public mind as a nonstop speech, a filibuster in the fullest sense employs every parliamentary maneuver and dilatory motion to delay, modify, or defeat legislation. Asked for filibustering pointers by a colleague, Senator Metzenbaum, said: "If it takes unanimous consent, object. If not, you make a little speech, suggest the absence of a quorum, then ... use parliamentary procedures ... motions to adjourn, motions to recess." He added: "You have to have the floor protected 100 percent of the time." [50]

More has been written about "extended debate" in the Senate than any other congressional procedure. Hollywood even glamorized the filibuster in a 1930s movie, "Mr. Smith Goes to Washington," starring Jimmy Stewart.

The filibuster has been part of the Senate from its earliest days. It is a formidable weapon—particularly late in a session when time is running out—that can be used by any senator or group of senators. Defenders of the filibuster say it is needed to prevent bad bills from becoming law, protect minority rights against majority steamrollers, ensure thorough analysis of legislation, and dramatize issues for the public. Opponents argue that the filibuster thwarts majority rule, brings the Senate into disrepute, and permits small minorities to extort unwarranted concessions in bills supported by Senate majorities.

These pro and con arguments highlight a dilemma: how to strike a balance between the right to debate and the need to decide. There is no easy answer. What is apparent is that the filibuster is a powerful bargaining device. Even the possibility of its use can force compromises in committee or on the floor. Senators of widely diverse viewpoints have resorted to it from time to time or have threatened to use it in order to influence legislation. There are numerous examples that can be used to illustrate the impact of the filibuster.

CIVIL RIGHTS FILIBUSTERS. Before the 1970s, filibusters were most often identified with southern Democrats, who used them to defeat or delay civil rights measures. The 1957, 1960, and 1964 Civil Rights Acts were the objects of systematic filibusters by southern senators, each of whom held the floor for several hours, yielding to colleagues for long questions, while others remained in their offices or left Capitol Hill until it was their turn to talk. (Senator Strom Thurmond of South Carolina holds the individual record by talking for over 24 hours against the 1957 civil rights bill.) The southerners demanded periodic quorum calls, keeping the pressure on supporters of civil rights legislation, who had to stay near the chamber to prevent the Senate from adjourning rather than recessing.

Adjournment would have played into the hands of the senators conducting the filibusters by requiring a series of routine, but time-consuming, procedures every time the Senate was forced to convene anew. Senators supporting a filibuster certainly would refuse unanimous consent requests to dispense with any of the elements of daily procedure, thereby further delaying action on the bills being filibustered. During an extended filibuster, the Senate sometimes remains in session throughout the night, with filibuster opponents forced to remain near the Senate floor—sometimes sleeping on couches and cots—to be ever ready in the event of quorum calls.

Every bill faces two potential filibusters: the first on the motion to take up the legislation (to expedite the Senate's business, there have been proposals to limit debate on the motion to proceed) and the second on consideration of the bill itself. The 1964 civil rights filibuster consumed sixteen days on the motion to take up the measure and fifty-seven days on the legislation itself. Those filibusters were unique in that they marked the first time the Senate had ever voted to end an extended debate on a civil rights bill.

WIDER USE OF FILIBUSTERS. Moderate and liberal senators traditionally had opposed use of the filibuster, but times changed. During the 1970s and 1980s, Senators Cranston, Frank Church, D-Idaho (1957-1981), Charles McC. Mathias, R-Md. (1969-1987), Weicker, Packwood, Birch Bayh, D-Ind. (1963-1981), and others conducted filibusters against the Vietnam War; President Richard Nixon's nominations of Clement Haynsworth, G. Harrold Carswell, and William H. Rehnquist to the Supreme Court; a 1981 anti-busing amendment; a 1982 anti-abortion bill; and a 1987-1988 campaign spending measure.

While liberal and moderate senators had employed the filibuster in the past (on the 1948 Taft-Hartley Act, for example), the "recent obstructionism represents, in frequency alone, a significant departure from past liberal practice." [51] Conversely, senators who had unswervingly supported the filibuster, often as a matter of principle, became more flexible. In 1971 Sen. John C. Stennis, D-Miss., a traditional defender of the practice, urged his colleagues to terminate an extended debate on a draft extension bill in the name of national security.

In sum, the filibuster is a "parliamentary tool available to liberals and conservatives who wish to dramatize issues in the only forum of our national government that provides for thorough analysis and unhurried consideration of proposed public laws." [52] In today's Senate, the filibuster (and its threatened use) is employed routinely by senators of every ideological stripe. Sen. Tom Eagleton, D-Mo., who voluntarily retired from the Senate in 1986, observed that "we've had many more filibusters in the 17 years I have served in the Senate than in the 120 years before I got here."[53] Filibusters occur not simply on issues of great national importance and visibility but on a wide range of less momentous topics. Moreover, there is a new-style filibuster that relies less on talking than the exploitation of Senate rules—appealing the presiding officer's parliamentary rulings and demanding roll-call votes on them, for instance—to frustrate action on measures.

ENDING A FILIBUSTER. There are two interrelated methods of ending a filibuster: by informal compromise or by cloture—a formal Senate procedure used to terminate debate. Frequently, cloture cannot be obtained unless compromises are made. Party leaders sometimes try "shuttle diplomacy" between the two sides, noted Senator Stevens, to avoid full-scale filibusters.[54]

Informal Compromise—In 1986, the Senate was engaged in a strongly contested battle over two measures: economic sanctions against South Africa and military aid to the Nicaraguan Contras. Opponents of each measure threatened a filibuster. For weeks, Senate leaders struggled to fashion an agreement that produced action on both measures without a time-consuming talkathon. Finally, a complex agreement was reached that forestalled the threatened filibusters and facilitated enactment of both bills (see box on pp. 224-225).

During a filibuster, senators may meet in the cloakroom—off the Senate floor—or in the offices of the party leaders to conduct negotiations, which can go on day and night. The process may take several days or even weeks, depending on how controversial the bill may be. If compromise fails, the odds increase that opponents of the legislation may win the battle and thus sidetrack the bill indefinitely. Alternatively, proponents may manage to invoke cloture.

Cloture—After decades of determined resistance by many senators, the Senate in 1917 adopted Rule XXII, which for the first time gave the Senate the formal means (cloture) to end extended debate. Until that time, debate could be terminated only by unanimous consent, an impossibility in the face of a filibuster.

What finally prompted the Senate to adopt Rule XXII was a filibuster that had killed a bill to arm U.S. merchant ships against attacks by German submarines. President Woodrow Wilson strongly criticized the filibuster and called a special session of the Senate, which adopted the cloture rule on March 8, 1917, five weeks before war was declared.

Under Rule XXII a cloture petition signed by sixteen senators first must be filed with the presiding officer. Two days later, and one hour after the Senate convenes, the presiding officer must ascertain whether a quorum is present. That having been established, the presiding officer is obliged to ask, "Is it the sense of the Senate that the debate shall be brought to a close?" A vote immediately is held. If three-fifths of the entire Senate membership (60 of 100 members) vote in favor, cloture is invoked. Thereafter, no senator may speak for more than one hour. Before 1975, when the current three-fifths rule was adopted, a two-thirds majority of those senators present and voting was required to invoke cloture. (The two-thirds requirement still applies to proposals to amend the Senate's rules.)

Once cloture is invoked, only germane amendments may be offered, and the presiding officer may rule out of order dilatory motions. The cloture rule has helped ease some types of delaying tactics but has not effectively ended all of them, as pointed out in the discussion of the so-called postcloture filibusters that follows.

There is no limit to the number of times cloture can be sought on a single piece of legislation. The record for cloture votes is eight, which occurred during the 100th Congress on a bill (S 2) to limit campaign expenditures for Senate general election races. Majority Leader Byrd had made the spending-limit measure a priority, but Senate action was stymied by a three-month GOP-led filibuster.

Cloture may be tried immediately after a bill is brought to the floor, but usually senators respect and value the tradition of extended debate. Sen. George D. Aiken, R-Vt. (1941-1975), once said he would refuse "to vote for cloture until discussion and debate on an important measure has been carried on for at least two weeks." [55] Occasionally, cloture is sought soon after a bill is called up in order to block a threatened filibuster, test sentiment for or against a measure, or expedite action on the legislation. Cloture helps to speed up floor action on a bill because once cloture is achieved all further amendments must be germane.

For example, Sen. Gordon J. Humphrey, R-N.H., offered a nongermane amendment (repealing a legislative pay hike) to a homeless aid measure. "This can very well be a killer amendment," declared Democratic leader Byrd.[56] To prevent a vote on Humphrey's amendment, Senator Byrd filed a cloture petition. Subsequently, the Senate invoked cloture by a 68-29 vote. "Under the precedents of the Senate," said the presiding officer in ruling Humphrey's amendment out of order, "once cloture is invoked, the Chair is required to rule out of order each nongermane amendment that is pending [or] subsequently called up." [57]

On the theory that even a weak bill is better than no bill, supporters of a certain measure frequently are willing to compromise with filibustering senators. Yet there are measures on which both sides are deeply divided. In these situations there is very little room for bargaining. When possible, cloture is the preferred tactic of the majority in such cases. But the relative ease of invoking cloture under the three-fifths rule has brought forth increasing reliance on yet another dilatory tactic—the postcloture filibuster (which, in turn, has led to several changes in the cloture rule).

Senate's Climate of Partisanship Yields . . .

It took more than two weeks to negotiate, sometimes in closed-door meetings among senators and staff, other times on the floor of the Senate, with tempers flaring and the traditional senatorial courtesy frayed almost to the breaking point. When completed, it took nearly an hour for the majority leader to read aloud to his colleagues, and when printed in the *Congressional Record* it consumed three pages. It was so complicated that many senators admitted they could not understand it even after two or three readings. It was not a piece of legislation. It was merely a "unanimous consent agreement," in most cases a routine procedure by which the Senate agrees without objection on a schedule for conducting its business.

But when the Senate prepared to take up the issues of sanctions against South Africa and military aid to the "contra" guerrillas in Nicaragua, there was no unanimous consent for anything. The two questions, tinged with partisanship, were among the most emotional and vexing facing Congress The root of the Senate's problem: An overwhelming majority of senators in both parties, certainly more than the 60 needed to shut off a filibuster, wanted to pass legislation imposing sanctions against the white minority government of South Africa. However, only a bare majority, nearly all of them Republicans, wanted to give President Reagan $100 million for contra aid.

Enter Majority Leader Robert Dole, R-Kan., acting on behalf of the contra assistance, and Minority Leader Robert C. Byrd, D-W.Va., acting against the contra aid and on behalf of South Africa sanctions. Never on the best of terms, the two men on July 24 began a series of direct and indirect negotiations that were aimed at producing an agreement for the Senate to consider both issues.

Each leader had leverage. Dole's advantages were his prerogative as majority leader to schedule legislation and his willingness to threaten the cherished mid-August recess if the Senate did not complete action on contras. Byrd's bargaining chip was the knowledge that he had the votes to shut off a filibuster against the South Africa bill and that Dole was uncertain whether he had the votes to stop one on the contras.

In the middle of negotiations, a third actor and issue entered the scene: David L. Boren, D-Okla., who reminded Dole that he had promised action this year on a proposal to curtail contributions to congressional campaigns by political action committees.

Meanwhile, the Senate debated two major pieces of legislation—an extension of the federal debt limit and a 1987 defense authorization bill—both of which were candidates for amendments on the South Africa and contra issues.

The negotiations among Dole, Byrd and other senators proceeded slowly during the week of July 28, as the Senate worked on the debt bill. By Aug. 1, Dole and Byrd had reached a partial agreement to finish work on the debt bill but to stop short of final passage so it could be held in reserve for amendments on contras and South Africa.

The next week, the Senate turned to the defense bill. On Aug. 4, Dole surprised Democrats by introducing a petition to invoke cloture (shut off debate) on that measure. If successful, it would have precluded senators from offering other amendments, such as South Africa and contras, to that bill.

...An Agreement of Unusual Complexity

In response, Byrd on Aug. 5 offered a South Africa amendment to the defense bill, including with it a cloture petition that, if passed, would have blocked a contra amendment. Furious, Dole countered with his own amendment coupling South Africa and contra aid, also along with a cloture petition. The two leaders then engaged in an acrimonious finger-pointing contest over who had violated the spirit of the negotiations. Others said they feared that the dispute damaged the possibility of getting an agreement.

Byrd took an unusual step on Aug. 6, releasing to reporters a description of his latest proposal for an agreement; that prompted a flurry of leaks, with each side attempting to portray its position in the best light.

As negotiations proceeded, the Senate repeatedly established times for, then postponed, votes on cloture. The Senate took only one such vote, on Aug. 6, with Dole's original cloture petition falling seven votes short of the 60 needed to end debate.

The Senate was facing an "invisible filibuster," said Alan Cranston, D-Calif. Nobody was actually filibustering either South Africa or contra aid, but opponents on each side stood ready to do so, jeopardizing the recess.

By Saturday, Aug. 9, Dole, Byrd, and a half-dozen other senators directly involved reached an agreement. Dole read it to the Senate shortly after 1 p.m., admitting at the end that it "may be somewhat confusing." Senators laughed, but some also had last-minute qualms, and so Dole and Byrd again tinkered with the text in hopes of satisfying everyone.

The agreement provided that the Senate would: debate the Boren campaign finance proposal and the contra aid on Aug. 11; vote on the Boren proposal and amendments to contra aid on Aug. 12; vote on cloture petitions on both South Africa and contras on Aug. 13; and finish both issues during the week if cloture was invoked on both, or use as much of the recess as necessary if cloture was not invoked on both. Somehow along with those votes, the Senate was to consider up to 93 amendments on South Africa (most offered by Republicans) and 31 amendments on contra aid (most offered by Democrats).

Senators on all sides said the agreement was fair, and praised both Dole and Byrd for leading the negotiations producing it. Ted Stevens, R-Alaska, who had fought Dole for the majority leadership, called it "a monumental agreement, the best one I have ever seen in my 18 years here."

Both Dole and Byrd got what they wanted. But Dole, by virtue of his leadership clout, may have gotten the most. The key clause of the agreement—inserted at Dole's insistence—provided that the Senate had to invoke cloture on both South Africa and the contras before it could pass either bill. That meant Democrats who opposed contra aid would have to give up a filibuster against it if they wanted to pass the South Africa sanctions.

The strategy worked, and on Aug. 13 the Senate invoked cloture on both bills. But while a substantial accomplishment, the unanimous consent agreement was not the finished product. The product was to be the legislation that, for a while, had become secondary to the Senate's need to straitjacket itself.

Source: John Felton, "Senate's Climate of Partisanship Yields an Agreement of Unusual Complexity," *Congressional Quarterly Weekly Report*, Aug. 16, 1986, 1878-1879.

Postcloture Filibuster

Filibusters are used to defeat or weaken bills by talking them to death. The postcloture filibuster attempts to do the same thing by employing an array of parliamentary tactics to delay final action. The technique involves extensive use of roll calls, quorum calls, and other delaying tactics, none of which counts against the one hour of floor time allotted to each member after cloture is invoked. Before several senators' hour has been used up, weeks may elapse. The postcloture filibuster is particularly effective if opponents of a bill have had the foresight to offer a large number of germane amendments before cloture is achieved. These amendments remain pending after cloture. However, no new amendments are in order after the cloture vote, except by unanimous consent.

For the most part, the postcloture filibuster is a contemporary and innovative dilatory tactic. Senators were long aware of its availability, but they seldom employed it. Members apparently believed that it violated the spirit of fair play. Once the battle had been fought and cloture invoked by a large majority, the informal rules of the game dictated that further delaying actions be ended. The postcloture filibuster, however, was used three times in 1976 and once in 1977. Sen. James B. Allen, D-Ala. (1969-1978), is often credited with discovering this tactic.

In 1977 Senators James G. Abourezk, D-S.D. (1973-1979), and Howard Metzenbaum, prolonged consideration of an intensely controversial natural gas deregulation bill for two weeks after cloture had been invoked. The Senate leadership even held an all-night Senate session, the first in thirteen years, in an attempt to break their postcloture filibuster. The story of the efforts of the two senators and the extraordinary countertactics employed to combat them is a classic example of the use of this form of filibuster.

CLOTURE RULE LOOPHOLES. Under Senate rules, any senator who offers a germane amendment before the vote to invoke cloture occurs is eligible to call it up after cloture is agreed to. Senator Metzenbaum had introduced 212 printed amendments in one day alone. They were a mixture of substance and technicalities. He proposed numerous alternative dates for the various deadlines in the bill, alternative sums of money, redefinitions of terms, and various deletions and additions to the bill. Altogether, 508 amendments were pending when cloture was invoked.

With so many amendments pending, the two senators had plenty of ammunition with which to delay Senate proceedings. Here is how their strategy was carried out:

- Senators Abourezk and Metzenbaum called up numerous amendments and objected to unanimous consent requests to suspend the required reading. In one case, the clerk took fifty-five minutes to read an amendment.
- Occasionally the senators would demand two roll-call votes on a single amendment, one on the proposal itself and another on the routine motion to reconsider. In such instances, the two senators shrewdly voted with the majority to reject the amendments so that they would be eligible to offer the motions to reconsider.
- Although debate on the amendments was minimal under cloture, the two senators demanded roll-call votes on each amendment, a process requiring fifteen minutes. They made repeated quorum calls to ensure that fifty-one senators were present on the floor. Each "live" quorum call could take an hour or more.

These relatively simple steps enabled Abourezk and Metzenbaum to tie the Senate in knots. None of the time consumed for their procedural motions counted against the hour each controlled once cloture was invoked. Frustration and bitterness grew as the postcloture filibuster rolled on. "In the course of the last few days," commented Senator Baker, "we have gone through a torture that the Senate has seldom encountered, including not just an all-night session, but an all-night session that was unique and different from others, as we painfully knew, because the roll calls and quorum calls came at 15-, 30-, and 45-minute intervals."[58]

Finally, Sen. Byrd and several members and staff aides devised a counterstrategy. The aim was to rule out of order the bulk of the Abourezk-Metzenbaum amendments pending at the desk. Byrd enlisted the cooperation of Vice President Walter F. Mondale, the presiding officer of the Senate under the Constitution.

When the Senate convened on October 3, 1977, Mondale recognized Majority Leader Byrd, who made the point of order "that when the Senate is operating under cloture, the Chair is required to rule out of order all amendments which are dilatory or which on their face are out of order." Under previous Senate precedents, the chair had to wait for a point of order to be raised against each amendment before ruling whether it was dilatory.

Mondale sustained Byrd's point of order. Abourezk appealed the decision but lost on a 79-14 vote. The stage then was set for a prearranged plan. Reading from a typed script given him by Byrd, Mondale recognized only the majority leader (recall his priority of recognition), who called up thirty-three of Metzenbaum's amendments.

(Technically, a senator can call up any amendment pending at the desk, even if it is not his own.) Each of the senator's amendments was quickly ruled out of order by the presiding officer, who ignored the senators who wanted to appeal the chair's ruling, a customary right of members.

Bedlam broke out on the floor. Cries of "dictatorship" and "steamroller" were heard. "The Senate of the United States has just seen an outrageous act," declared Sen. Gary Hart, D-Colo. Abourezk and Metzenbaum, feeling betrayed by the administration, ended their filibuster. With nine days of debate and 129 roll-call votes behind it, the Senate enacted the natural gas deregulation measure.

1979 REVISION OF RULE XXII. On February 22, 1979, the Senate amended Rule XXII to restrict opportunities for the postcloture filibuster. Once cloture is invoked, under the change, a hundred-hour cap is imposed on all postcloture action, including the time spent reading and voting on amendments, quorum calls, and any other procedural motion. No measure, then, is to be debated beyond a total of one hundred hours following a successful cloture vote. The change also provided "that no Senator shall call up more than two amendments until every other Senator has had the opportunity to call up two amendments." [59] The presiding officer is directed to give priority of recognition to another senator rather than to a member seeking to call up a third amendment. All first and second degree amendments also must be submitted prior to the cloture vote.

Collectively, these changes were designed to reduce the ability of senators to carry on postcloture filibusters. They have had limited impact, however. Senators continue to conduct effective postcloture filibusters. Senators sometimes even vote against cloture to avoid the frustrations of the postcloture filibuster. "I am voting against cloture," said Senator Byrd in 1982, "because I want to avoid a post-cloture filibuster." This dilatory technique, he added, "is an abomination to the Senate and to the legislative process." Senator Baker expressed similar sentiments. The Senate must address the postcloture filibuster because I think now we have made Rule XXII "a nullity." [60]

1986 Revision

When the Senate took up the proposal to televise floor sessions gavel-to-gavel, party leaders supported changes to improve senatorial operations and inhibit the spectacle of lengthy filibusters. One of these changes reduced the "time for debate once cloture is invoked from 100 hours to 30 hours." [61] This reduction means that senators during the postcloture period would still be recognized for one hour, but the thirty hours would be allocated on a first come, first served basis.

This revision along with other postcloture rules and precedents, such as dispensing with the reading of amendments and enabling the chair to rule dilatory amendments and motions out of order, have reduced the inordinate delaying potential of this type of filibuster. "The threat of a [postcloture] filibuster loses some of its sting if only [thirty] postcloture hours are allowed," remarked Senator Bumpers.[62] Another factor dampening use of postcloture filibusters is the senatorial consensus that this type of dilatory tactic is an abuse of the lawmaking process.

Summary Observations

There has been a contemporary surge in filibusters and, relatedly, cloture attempts. "The Senate has cloturitis," stated Senator Quayle.[63] Just the threat of a filibuster sometimes prompts senators to file cloture petitions on the legislation even before it reaches the floor. From sparing use of cloture (it was invoked only four times from 1917 until 1962), the 1970s and 1980s have witnessed routine use of the cloture procedure. Where one cloture vote per measure was once the norm, the modern Senate reached a record eight cloture votes on one measure.

Several factors account for the increase in filibusters and cloture attempts. One is the influx of new senators who prefer to push their own agendas even if the Senate's institutional activities grind to a halt. There are occasions, noted Senator Hatfield, when senators are "determined to follow [their] own perspective even to the perversion, the distortion, and the destruction of the [legislative] process."[64] Senate rules permit this behavior, for they provide aggressive senators with an arsenal of devices to advance their objectives. (The 1975 amendment to Rule XXII, permitting cloture by a three-fifths vote, also made it easier to invoke this procedure and encouraged the use of postcloture filibusters.)

Among other reasons for wider use of filibusters is their enhanced potency in an institution that is workload-packed and deadline-driven. There is insufficient time to accommodate the manifold claims on the Senate's agenda. In such an environment, senators who even indicate their intention to filibuster can exercise significant policy leverage.

Gone, too, are internal incentives ("to get along, go along," for instance) that fostered deference to seniority and party leaders, such as Majority Leader Lyndon Johnson. Johnson exercised tight control over floor proceedings, including use of the filibuster.

> While Johnson went to great lengths to avoid filibusters, once they had begun . . . he tended to regard filibusters as a personal challenge to his stewardship. Instead of making an end run around the combatants . . . he often preferred to break the filibuster by keeping the Senate in session for long hours, even around the clock, and forcing the minority ultimately to give up in exhaustion.[65]

By contrast, contemporary party leaders often accommodate filibustering senators who have meetings to attend back home. To be sure, there can be exceptions to this general practice.

For example, Democratic leader Byrd forced an old-fashioned, around-the-clock, talk-all-night filibuster on the measure to limit campaign expenditures. The Senate even directed the Sergeant-at-Arms (a Senate official) to arrest absent senators, so the body could obtain a quorum to function. Without a quorum, the Senate would be forced to adjourn. GOP strategists had told their partisan colleagues to stay away from the floor, so Democratic proponents of the bill would have the burden of finding and maintaining quorums throughout the all-night sessions. (To make a quorum Senator Packwood was even arrested in his Capitol office and carried feet first into the chamber by three police officers.) In the end, the Senate failed to invoke cloture on the GOP-led filibuster for a record-setting eighth time. Democratic leader Byrd then pulled the measure from the schedule.[66]

In brief, filibusters may be terminated through such means as the invocation of cloture, expiration of the thirty-hour cap, compromises between the contending sides, or mistakes that cause filibustering senators to lose the floor, such as violation of the two-speech rule. That rule forbids members from making a third speech on the same question in the same legislative day.[67]

Final Vote on a Bill

Once cloture is invoked, filibusters by amendment broken, and other delaying tactics ended, the Senate proceeds to a final vote on the bill under consideration. If obstructionist tactics cannot be ended, the leadership may withdraw the bill and proceed to other business.

On legislation not regulated by complex agreements and not the target of deliberate obstructionist tactics, the floor managers and party leaders try to fashion ad hoc agreements under which amendments can be disposed of. But because of the strong commitment in the Senate to giving every member ample opportunity to be heard, this can be a lengthy process. For example, one tax measure, which was not filibustered, consumed twenty-five days of debate. There were 209 amendments and motions on the bill and 129 roll-call votes. The length of debate on this legislation reflected its importance to senators and the country as well as the complexity of its provisions.

Paradoxically, while it is relatively easy to frustrate floor action, Senate rules make it difficult for committees to bottle up legislation and prevent it from reaching the floor. The means by which senators can force bills to be considered by the Senate are discussed in the following section.

PROCEDURES TO CIRCUMVENT COMMITTEES

In an earlier chapter, it was seen that the House has a number of procedures for bringing bills to the floor that are blocked in committee. These include Calendar Wednesday, the discharge petition, the power of extraction by the Rules Committee, and the suspension of the rules procedure. Except for suspension, which generally is used for relatively noncontroversial bills, these alternative House procedures are seldom employed and rarely successful.

Bypassing committees, while not an everyday occurrence in the Senate, is easier to accomplish than in the House. At least four techniques are available to senators: (1) use of nongermane amendments, also known as riders; (2) placing House-passed and Senate-introduced bills immediately on the Calendar of General Orders; (3) suspending Senate rules; and (4) implementing the discharge procedure. The first two are the most effective.

NONGERMANE AMENDMENTS

Unlike the House, the Senate has never had a rule requiring amendments to be germane to pending legislation. This feature probably ranks just below the filibuster as one of the Senate's most distinctive characteristics. "Amendments may be made," Jefferson wrote in the parliamentary manual he prepared during his service as president of the Senate (1797-1801), "so as totally to alter the nature of the proposition." [68] A classic case occurred in 1965 when Sen. Everett McKinley Dirksen, R-Ill. (1951-1969), tried to add a proposal for a constitutional amendment on legislative reapportionment to a joint resolution designating August 6 to September 6 as "National American Legion Baseball Month." Dirksen's amendment had been blocked by the Judiciary Committee. An opponent of the proposal called the senator's attempt a "foul ball."

Periodically, the Senate has considered rules changes that would permit it to impose a germaneness requirement on floor amendments. Proponents argue that such a requirement would improve senatorial efficiency, expedite the workload, enhance relations with the House (which has a strict germaneness requirement), strengthen committees as centers of policy making, and promote predictability in scheduling. Opponents contend that the right of senators to offer nongermane amendments serves as a safeguard against capricious committee actions, permits any senator to raise important issues, and enables the Senate to respond quickly to new developments. "What is at stake [in the ability of senators to offer nongermane amendments] is the right of a minority—even a tiny minority, even one Senator—to raise an issue," declared Senator Armstrong.[69]

SENATE PROHIBITIONS. Although the Senate does not have a general germaneness rule, there are four situations where the Senate requires germane amendments to pending legislation:

1. Unanimous consent agreements as usually drawn up contain a requirement that amendments are to be germane.
2. Amendments to general appropriations bills.
3. When cloture has been invoked.
4. During consideration of concurrent budget resolutions and reconciliation bills.

"The intent of the 'germaneness' restriction" in the 1974 budget act, remarked Sen. Lawton Chiles, D-Fla., "was to prevent extraneous nonbudgetary amendments from being added to budget resolutions." [70] (A few laws that contain expedited procedures for Senate action also require germane amendments.)

Interestingly, when the Senate operates under a germaneness requirement, its tests for determining the relevancy of amendments is stricter than those in the House. Only four types of amendments are in order in this situation: amendments that strike something from the pending bill; amendments that express the sense of the Senate with respect to something within the reporting committee's jurisdiction; amendments to change a number up or down; or amendments that narrow the scope of a bill. For example, a presiding officer once noted, if an "amendment expands the effect of the bill or introduces new subject matter it is not germane." [71] Thus, if a farm bill dealt with five items, barley, wheat, rice, cotton, and soybeans, and a senator sought to amend the measure by adding corn to the list, a germaneness point of order could be made against the amendment.

USES OF RIDERS. There is little doubt that the Senate's deliberative role is strengthened because it permits senators to raise new issues on the floor through nongermane amendments. Proposals bottled up in committee that a majority favors can be offered as riders to pending measures. "Must" bills, such as debt ceiling and appropriations legislation, often are handy vehicles for this purpose.

The practice also enables members to air important issues, and respond with dispatch to changing circumstances. For example, Senator Metzenbaum offered an extraneous amendment to a veterans bill to ban the sale, manufacture, or importation of plastic guns, which are not detectable at airport screening points. "This is an amendment that would actually have some impact upon terrorists who . . . could go on planes with plastic guns," stated Senator Metzenbaum.[72] The Senate tabled Metzenbaum's amendment in part because it threatened prompt passage of the veterans legislation. Still, the issue was raised and encouraged the committee of jurisdiction to explore the ramifications of the Metzenbaum proposal.

In brief, germaneness sometimes has been a vexing issue for the Senate. On the one hand, the lack of a general prohibition on riders permits senators to raise and debate popular and unpopular issues and lessens the opportunity for arbitrary committee action. On the other hand, some senators complain that the practice wastes the Senate's time by permitting contentious debate on matters unrelated to the fundamental purpose of a pending bill.

Placing Measures on the Calendar

When measures are passed by the House and sent to the Senate, they customarily are referred to a committee. As noted earlier, all measures, including House-passed bills, must be read twice on different legislative days before they can be referred to committee. Under Senate Rule XIV, if any senator objects to the second reading the committee stage is bypassed and the House-passed bill, or Senate-introduced bill, is placed directly on the calendar.

This procedure was used by supporters of the 1957 and 1964 Civil Rights Acts (the 1960 Civil Rights Act was introduced as a nongermane amendment). Backers of those measures wanted to avoid sending the bills to the Judiciary Committee, which had an unbroken record of never reporting a civil rights bill. Placing a bill on the calendar also gives the leadership the option of calling up either the House-passed measure or, should there be one, the version reported by the Senate committee.

Although effective, Rule XIV is used sparingly because of the general deference to committee prerogatives. It is sometimes used when the proponent of a bill feels intensely enough about it to flout the jurisdiction of a committee that is known to oppose it.[73] In some instances, committee chairmen may even employ the rule. Tired of partisan delays in getting anticrime legislation reported from his committee during the GOP-controlled 99th Congress, Judiciary Chairman Strom Thurmond used Rule XIV to get the bill on the calendar. "I think Senator Thurmond just reached the end of his patience with what he considers to be dilatory tactics," said a Judiciary Committee aide.[74]

More commonly, House-passed measures are held at the clerk's desk by unanimous consent. When the House passed President Carter's 1977 energy package, it was held at the desk until Senate leaders decided how the package was to be handled by various committees. House-passed measures are also held at the desk when similar Senate bills are already pending on the calendar or are expected shortly to be reported out of committee.

Suspension of the Rules

Senate rules can be suspended, provided there is one day's notice in writing and the terms of the suspension motion are printed in the *Congressional Record*. The rules are silent on the number of votes needed to suspend Senate rules. Precedents have required two-thirds of those present and voting to approve suspensions. The procedure is rarely used because it represents a challenge to the committee system and is open to dilatory tactics. In effect, three filibusters are possible on suspension motions: first, on the motion to suspend the rules; second, on the motion to take up the bill; and third, on the bill itself.

Suspension motions occasionally are made by senators who want to offer policy amendments to general appropriations measures. Policy amendments (legislative language) to appropriations measures are forbidden by Senate rules but can be made in order in various ways, including the suspension route.

The Discharge Procedure

Discharging a bill from a committee has taken place only fourteen times in the history of the Senate. It was last employed successfully in 1964. The prevailing sentiment is that the procedure undercuts the committee system and also that the rules governing its use are cumbersome. The discharge motion can be made only during the "morning hour" and must remain at the clerk's desk for one legislative day. Party leaders can forestall discharge motions for days or weeks simply by recessing, thus keeping the Senate in the same legislative day. If debate on the motion is not concluded within the morning hour, the motion is placed on the Calendar where it faces the threat of a series of filibusters. A vote to discharge a committee of a bill requires a simple majority vote unless it is necessary to invoke cloture to stop a filibuster.

There is technically yet another way to bypass a Senate committee: by unanimous consent. The Senate, as has been seen in this chapter, can do almost anything it wants by unanimous consent. However, unanimous consent will not be obtained if a single member—presumably a member of the committee that would be bypassed—objects.

SUMMARY

There are more differences than similarities between Senate and House floor procedures, the result primarily of the smaller size and greater opportunity for informal arrangements in the Senate. Procedures such as unanimous consent agreements, the track system, the filibuster and the cloture rule, nongermane amendments, morning business, legislative days, and executive sessions have no real counterpart in the House. Conversely, the five-minute rule, rules from the Rules Committee, recorded teller votes, and electronic voting cannot be found in the Senate.

The larger, more complex House emphasizes formal rules and precedents. The Senate functions in a largely ad hoc fashion, emphasizing reciprocity and courtesy among senators. House procedure is relatively straightforward, with few detours. The Senate changes its procedures to meet new contingencies, accommodate members, and resolve unforeseen problems. The Senate occasionally observes its formal rules, but more commonly waives them by unanimous consent and modifies its debate arrangements to suit each bill.

Senate rules emphasize the influence of individual members. As Senator Byrd has observed: "The rules of the Senate are made for the convenience of those who wish to delay." [75] As a result, it is often more difficult to create winning coalitions in the Senate than in the House. The discipline imposed by House rules generally aids party leaders in forming and sustaining majorities. These House-Senate procedural differences occasionally produce bicameral dissension even when the same party controls both bodies. "Obviously the Senate was set up to be a slow, deliberative body, but they weren't supposed to come to a standstill" because of their procedures, said Rep. Marty Russo, D-Ill.[76]

There also are more opportunities to revise legislation on the Senate floor than in the House. Senators feel freer to offer amendments to legislation coming from committees, other than their own, than do members of the House, who are somewhat more likely to defer to the committees' decisions. And to a far greater degree in the Senate than in the House, members are assured that their party leaders will make every effort to accommodate their scheduling needs.

A crucial legislative arbiter on virtually all important legislation is the conference committee. Composed of groups of legislators from each chamber, this "third house of Congress" reconciles differences between House- and Senate-passed versions of bills. The next chapter examines this important congressional institution and other ways of resolving differences in bills passed by the two houses of Congress.

NOTES

1. *Congressional Record,* daily ed., April 21, 1987, S5204.
2. *Washington Post,* April 7, 1987, A4.

3. *Congressional Record,* daily ed., May 21, 1980, S5674.
4. On November 17, 1982, for the first time since 1793, the House operated on two legislative days in the same day. It adjourned at 1:19 p.m. (the first legislative day) and then reconvened at 4 p.m. that day (the second legislative day). Sharp partisanship stimulated the Democratic leadership to employ this rare scheduling device. On October 29, 1987, the House again adjourned and reconvened.
5. *Congressional Record,* daily ed., March 28, 1980, S3234.
6. *Senate Procedure, Precedents and Practices,* 97th Cong., 1st sess., S. Doc. No. 97-2, 565.
7. *Congressional Record,* daily ed., March 26, 1987, S3927.
8. *Congressional Record,* daily ed., Sept. 24, 1986, S13597.
9. *Congressional Record,* daily ed., April 16, 1985, S4256.
10. *Congressional Record,* June 9, 1977, 18179.
11. *New York Times,* Dec. 1, 1987, A22.
12. A Senate rule requires three hours of germane discussion at the beginning of each day's debate on a measure. Called the Pastore Rule after its sponsor, Sen. John O. Pastore, D-R.I. (1950-1976), its purpose is to confine debate to pending business.
13. *Congressional Record,* daily ed., Jan. 21, 1986, S8.
14. *Congressional Record,* daily ed., May 21, 1987, S6979.
15. Rowland Evans and Robert Novak, *Lyndon B. Johnson: The Exercise of Power* (New York: New American Library, 1966), 115.
16. *Congressional Record,* Oct. 31, 1985, 29990.
17. Joseph S. Clark, *Congress: The Sapless Branch* (New York: Harper & Row, 1964), 247-248.
18. *New York Times,* June 8, 1986, E5.
19. For a one-year review of television coverage in the Senate, see *Congressional Record,* daily ed., June 2, 1987, S7394-S7401. For adverse commentary on the Senate's television coverage, see the remarks of Sen. William Proxmire, D-Wis., in *Congressional Record,* daily ed., April 28, 1987, S5549.
20. *Congressional Record,* Oct. 28, 1977, 5857.
21. *Congressional Record,* daily ed., June 24, 1987, S8583.
22. Elizabeth Drew, *Senator* (New York: Simon & Schuster, 1979), 173-174.
23. *Congressional Record,* daily ed., April 18, 1980, S3923. See also Stanley Bach, "Parliamentary Strategy and the Amendment Process: Rules and Case Studies of Congressional Action," *Polity* (Summer 1983): 573-592.
24. *New York Times,* May 6, 1987, B10.
25. *Congressional Record,* daily ed., Aug. 19, 1980, S11212.
26. Kathy Koch, "Senate Votes to Weaken Strip Mining Law," *Congressional Quarterly Weekly Report,* Aug. 23, 1980, 2453.
27. *Congressional Record,* daily ed., June 30, 1987, S8975.
28. *Congressional Record,* daily ed., Feb. 17, 1988, S795.
29. *USA Today,* May 19, 1986, 13A.
30. *Congressional Record,* daily ed., Nov. 5, 1985, S14793.
31. *Congressional Record,* daily ed., Aug. 15, 1986, S11840-S11841.
32. *Washington Times,* April 24, 1986, 10A; *Congressional Record,* daily ed., April 23, 1986, S4736.
33. *Congressional Record,* daily ed., June 20, 1985, S8500.
34. *Congressional Record,* daily ed., Feb. 26, 1986, S1664.
35. *Congressional Record,* Jan. 26, 1973, 2301.

36. *Congressional Record,* daily ed., Dec. 9, 1987, S17476.
37. James L. Buckley, *If Men Were Angels* (New York: G. P. Putnam's Sons, 1975), 129.
38. Bernard Asbell, *The Senate Nobody Knows* (Garden City, New York: Doubleday, 1978), 267.
39. *Congressional Record,* Sept. 23, 1975, 29814.
40. *Congressional Record,* daily ed., June 23, 1987, S8442.
41. *New York Times,* Nov. 25, 1986, A22.
42. *Congressional Record,* daily ed., April 8, 1981, S3618.
43. Nadine Cohodas, "Decision on Manion Put off after 'Roll of Dice' in Senate," *Congressional Quarterly Weekly Report,* June 28, 1986, 1508-1509.
44. *Congressional Record,* daily ed., July 22, 1983, S10701.
45. *Congressional Record,* daily ed., Oct. 10, 1985, S13114.
46. *New York Times,* Dec. 21, 1982, D29.
47. The word derives from the Dutch word *Vrijbuiter,* meaning freebooter. Passing into Spanish as *filibustero,* it was used to describe military adventurers from the United States who in the mid-1800s fomented insurrections against various Latin American governments. For an account of William Walker, filibusterer of the 1850s, see *Smithsonian,* June 1981, 117-128. The first legislative use of the word is said to have occurred in the House in 1853, when a representative accused his opponents of "filibustering against the United States." By 1863 the word filibuster had come to mean delaying action on the floor, but the term did not gain wide currency until the 1880s.
48. *New York Times,* July 17, 1986, A3.
49. *Congressional Record,* daily ed., July 18, 1983, S10216.
50. *New York Times,* Dec. 12, 1982, 4E.
51. Allan L. Damon, "Filibuster," *American Heritage,* December 1975, 97.
52. *Congressional Record,* Feb. 26, 1979, 3232.
53. *Congressional Record,* daily ed., Nov. 23, 1985, S16476.
54. *Washington Post,* June 11, 1982, A11.
55. George D. Aiken, *Aiken: Senate Diary* (Brattleboro, Vt.: Stephen Greene Press, 1975), 325.
56. *Congressional Record,* daily ed., April 9, 1987, S4825.
57. Ibid., S4944.
58. *Congressional Quarterly Weekly Report,* Oct. 1, 1977, 2070.
59. *Congressional Record,* daily ed., March 10, 1981, S1934.
60. *Congressional Record,* daily ed., Sept. 22, 1982, S11939-S11940.
61. *Congressional Record,* daily ed., Feb. 27, 1986, S1752.
62. *Congressional Record,* daily ed., Feb. 6, 1986, S1113.
63. *Congressional Record,* daily ed., Sept. 28, 1984, S12271.
64. *Congressional Record,* daily ed., Sept. 27, 1984, S12137.
65. *Congressional Record,* daily ed., March 3, 1986, S1915.
66. See for example, *Congressional Record,* daily ed., Feb. 23, 1988, S1152-S1153; *New York Times,* Feb. 25, 1988, A26.
67. For a contentious debate on the two-speech rule, see *Congressional Record,* daily ed., Sept. 25, 1986, S13687-S13710; *Washington Post,* Oct. 1, 1986, A17.
68. *Constitution, Jefferson's Manual and Rules of the House of Representatives,* 97th Cong., 2d sess., H. Doc. No. 97-271, 235.
69. *Congressional Record,* daily ed., Feb. 26, 1986, S1663.
70. *Washington Post,* May 18, 1982, A23. For the prohibition against extraneous material in reconciliation bills, see *Congressional Record,* daily ed. Oct. 16, 1986, S16415.

71. *Congressional Record,* daily ed., Feb. 9, 1982, S599.
72. *Congressional Record,* daily ed., Dec. 4, 1987, S17305.
73. For a discussion of the leadership's concern about overuse of Rule XIV, see *Congressional Record,* daily ed., Sept. 27, 1983, S12971.
74. *Washington Post,* April 18, 1986, A5; *Congressional Record,* daily ed., April 14, 1986, S4211.
75. *Congressional Record,* Aug. 31, 1976, 28607.
76. Janet Hook, "House-Senate Acrimony Bedevils Democrats," *Congressional Quarterly Weekly Report,* Feb. 13, 1988, 298.

CHAPTER 9

Resolving House-Senate Differences

Before legislation can be sent to the president for his consideration, it must be passed by both houses in identical form. House- and Senate-passed versions of the same bill frequently differ, sometimes only slightly but often on critical points. The two versions must be reconciled by mutual agreement. Whenever possible, this is done informally. However, a fair percentage of all bills passed by both chambers require action by a House-Senate conference committee—an ad hoc joint committee composed of members selected by each chamber to resolve differences on a particular bill in disagreement.[1] Of the 663 public laws enacted by the 99th Congress, 12.5 percent (or 53) went through conference.[2] It is usually major and controversial legislation that requires conference committee action.

Obscurity of the Process

The conference committee process is older than Congress itself. State legislatures used conference committees before 1789 to reconcile differences between the chambers of their bicameral legislatures. The conference committee system was taken for granted when the first Congress convened, and it has been in use ever since.[3] Nevertheless, for many citizens the conference committee is little known or understood, compared with the other aspects of the legislative process.

The relative obscurity of the conference process is explained by the fact that until the mid-1970s, conference committees almost always met in secret sessions with no published record of their proceedings. The conference committees produced a conference committee report that showed the results of the secret negotiations, but the bargaining and deliberations that led to these results were not formally disclosed.

In one of the most significant reforms of congressional procedure, both chambers in 1975 adopted rules requiring open conference committee meetings unless a majority of the conference members (called conferees or managers) from either chamber voted in public to hold secret sessions. In 1977 the House went a step further, adopting a rule requiring the full House to vote to close a conference. This occurs usually on legislation dealing with national security.

To be sure, conferees still conduct much of their important business in secret. As thirty-eight-year veteran Senator Russell B. Long, D-La. (who voluntarily retired at the end of the 99th Congress), once noted:

> The Senator knows when we started the openness thing we found it more and more difficult to get something agreed to in the conferences, it seemed to take forever. So what did we do? The Senator knows what we did. We would break up into smaller groups and then we would ask our chairman . . . to see if he could not find his opposite number on the House side and discuss this matter and come back and tell us what the chances would be of working out various and sundry possibilities.[4]

There are relatively few complaints about closed sessions. No doubt political commentators and others recognize the value of candid exchanges (away from the glare of special interest groups) in closed meetings. Further, reporters are usually kept well informed of the results of closed conferences.

A Critical Juncture

The conference committee, sometimes called "the third house of Congress," is one of the most critical points in the legislative process. For several reasons, however, members of Congress may try to avoid this stage and resolve House-Senate differences on legislation without recourse to the conference committee process. For one thing, there is pressure to approve the legislation quickly. For another, there may be concern in one house that conferees of the other chamber will try to weaken (or filibuster) the legislation. And third, there always is the possibility that a conference committee will become deadlocked—particularly in the weeks and days before the final adjournment of Congress. Failure of the conferees to reach agreement before the end of a Congress means that the bill dies.

This chapter first discusses how House-Senate differences on a bill are resolved without a conference. It then explores the complexities of the conference committee process. Finally, the chapter examines the last steps of the legislative process—final House and Senate approval of legislation (of the conference compromise for bills sent to conference committees) and presidential approval or veto, with subsequent action by Congress on vetoed bills.

AGREEMENT WITHOUT A CONFERENCE

There are two principal methods of resolving House-Senate differences without a conference. First, there is verbatim adoption of one chamber's version of a bill by the other. This is a common occurrence and may involve informal consultation before or after passage of the bill by one chamber. Second, the two houses may send measures back and forth several times, amending each other's amendments, before they agree to identical language on all provisions of the legislation. Table 9-1 shows how often different procedures for reaching bicameral agreement were used in the 99th Congress.

It is usual for House and Senate committee staff to communicate regularly on legislation of mutual interest. Drafts of measures are exchanged for comment and consistency, companion bills are studied, and strategies are devised to facilitate passage in each chamber. Executive branch officials and pressure groups often participate in these informal strategy sessions. This kind of prior consultation frequently helps clear away obstacles to passage—allowing legislation to be approved by both houses in identical form, thus avoiding the need for a conference.

Consultation also may take place after one or both chambers have passed a bill. For example, the House originally passed a health training measure (HR 2410) and sent it to the Senate. That chamber amended HR 2410 and returned the amended measure to the House. Then, to facilitate the measure's enactment without the necessity of convening a conference committee, the House and Senate committees of jurisdiction met informally and agreed to a compromise. As Rep. Henry A. Waxman, D-Calif., explained:

> This compromise was the result of lengthy negotiations between the [House] Subcommittee on Health and the Environment and the Senate Committee on Labor and Human Resources. It has broad bipartisan support. Approval of this [compromise] amendment [by the House] will permit immediate consideration in the Senate.[5]

The House and Senate approved the compromise—a House amendment (jointly crafted by both panels) to the Senate amendment to HR 2410—and the measure was signed into law.

Limits to Non-conference Tactics

Under the "back-and-forth" approach, two points are worth noting:

- There is a limit to the number of times measures may be shuffled between the chambers. In brief, the third-degree amendment prohibition, discussed in Chapters 6 and 8, also applies to amendments between the House and Senate. Each chamber gets two shots

TABLE 9-1 Bicameral Reconciliation of Legislation, 99th Congress

Method of Reconciliation	*Number of Laws*
Simple adoption by one chamber of the version sent to it by the other	477
Amendments between the houses	133
Conference reports	39
Both conference reports and amendments between the houses	14
Public laws (total)	663

Source: Ilona Nickels, Government Division, Congressional Research Service, Library of Congress.

at amending the amendments of the other body. Like many legislative procedures, the "two-shot" principle can be waived, ignored, or overturned. The Consolidated Omnibus Reconciliation Act of 1985, for example, was a record breaker. It was bounced between the chambers a record-setting nine times (see box on p. 243).

- The back-and-forth alternative procedure is employed intentionally to avoid conferences and is feasible only when circumstances warrant its use. For instance, a House chairman may ask the chamber to concur in the Senate amendment to the House amendment to the Senate-passed bill. House approval is "appropriate parliamentary procedure, which allows us to avoid the trouble of a conference when faced with such small [bicameral] differences." [6] The House in this case agreed to the Senate amendment, which cleared the bill for the president.

WHY CONFERENCE COMMITTEES?

It is often clear from the outset that controversial measures will end up in conference. Members plan their floor strategy accordingly. They make floor statements that emphasize their unyielding commitment to their own chamber's positions. In advance of a "House-Senate conference," noted one senator, "it is not unusual for the respective [chambers] to stake out positions for themselves and even to utter statements about their absolute intransigence, that sometimes does not always prevail when the conference convenes." [7]

100TH CONGRESS
1st Session } HOUSE OF REPRESENTATIVES { REPORT
100–452

INDEPENDENT COUNSEL REAUTHORIZATION ACT OF 1987

NOVEMBER 20, 1987.—Ordered to be printed

Mr. RODINO, from the Committee of conference,
submitted the following

CONFERENCE REPORT

[To accompany H.R. 2939]

The committee of conference on the disagreeing votes of the two Houses on the amendment of the Senate to the bill (H.R. 2939) to amend title 28, United States Code, with respect to the appointment of independent counsel, having met, after full and free conference, have agreed to recommend and do recommend to their respective Houses as follows:

That the House recede from its disagreement to the amendment of the Senate and agree to the same with an amendment as follows:

In lieu of the matter proposed to be inserted by the Senate amendment insert the following:

SECTION 1. SHORT TITLE.

This Act may be cited as the "Independent Counsel Reauthorization Act of 1987".

SEC. 2. AMENDMENTS RELATING TO INDEPENDENT COUNSEL.

Chapter 40 of title 28, United States Code, is amended to read as follows:

"CHAPTER 40—INDEPENDENT COUNSEL

19–006

Members frequently add expendable amendments to use as bargaining chips in conference. Such amendments can be traded away for other provisions considered more important. Use of such tactics has been refined to an art form by some senators. When Senator Long was Finance Chairman (1966-1980), he usually came "to conference with a bill loaded up with amendments added on the Senate floor. . . . Long has plenty of things he is willing to jettison to save the goodies." [8] Members who sponsor floor amendments are mindful of the "bargaining chip" ploy. As one senator remarked:

> I have been in this body long enough to beware of the chairman of a committee who says in an enticing voice, "Let me take the amendment to conference," because I think that is frequently the parliamentary equivalent of saying, "Let me take the child into the tower and I will strangle him to death." [9]

With conference committees open, or at least subject to public review, it sometimes is necessary for conferees to put up a fight for such amendments before dropping them. Conferees understand, too, that some bargaining chips are more influential than others. Before these amendments are dropped, conferees will consider the implications of offending powerful members.

Another preconference tactic is for one chamber to deliberately keep out of its bill something it knows the other chamber really wants. During a conference, the House conferees, for instance, may give in to the Senate, but only in return for Senate acceptance of something favored by the House. For these reasons it is difficult to identify the winners or losers in conference simply by counting the number of times one house appeared to give in to the other.[10]

House and Senate floor managers also consider whether they want recorded votes on certain amendments when they are debated in their chamber. For example, Sen. John C. Culver's, D-Iowa (1975-1981), strategy on an amendment he opposed was to seek a recorded vote on it in order "to beat the amendment, and beat it good, burying the issue in the Senate once and for all, and also putting him in a position to tell a Senate-House conference on the bill that the proposal was resoundingly defeated in the Senate." [11] Alternatively, floor managers sometimes prefer not to draw attention to amendments they oppose—and thus hope to avoid taking roll-call votes—on the assumption that it then will be easier to drop them in conference.

Finally, floor managers are sensitive to the overall contours of their bill and the margin of support for its passage on the floor. On the massive trade bill considered by the 100th Congress, Senate Finance Chairman Lloyd Bentsen, D-Texas, "consciously kept the Senate bill sufficiently different from the House bill in key provisions . . . so that he will have room to bargain" in conference.[12] And on the landmark 1986 overhaul of the internal revenue code, Senator Packwood (then Finance chairman) wanted a big Senate vote on final passage for "momentum" purposes. "If it passes here 100 to nothing or even if it passes 75 to 25," he said, "I think the chances are pretty good for the bulk of the substance of this bill being adopted in conference." [13]

CONFERENCE COMMITTEE PROCESS

There are five major steps in the conference committee process: (1) requesting a conference, (2) selecting conferees, (3) conference committee bargaining, (4) the conference committee report, and, (5) final House and Senate action on the conference committee version of the bill.

Requesting a Conference

When the House passes a bill, and it then is amended by the Senate and returned, the House has several options. It may (1) refuse to take further action, in which case the measure dies; (2) approve an entirely new version of the bill and send it to the Senate, (3) agree to the Senate's amendments, negating the need for a conference; or (4) amend the Senate's amendments and return the measure once again to the Senate; or (5) request a conference.

Occasionally, the Speaker may refer the Senate amendments, especially if they are nongermane to the House-passed measure, to the standing committee having jurisdiction over the subject matter of the amendments. More commonly, though, on major legislation a member will ask and receive unanimous consent for the House to disagree to the Senate's amendments and request a conference with the Senate. The Speaker usually recognizes an appropriate committee member to offer the motion—which requires majority approval—to go to conference on the bill.

When the situation is reversed, and a Senate-passed bill is amended by the House and returned to the Senate, it is "held at the desk and almost always subsequently laid before the Senate by the Presiding Officer upon request or motion of a Senator [usually the manager of the bill.]" [14]

The House amendment or amendments may be dealt with in four ways by the Senate: (1) by adopting a motion to refer the amendment(s) to the appropriate standing committee, (2) by further amending the House amendments, (3) by agreeing to the House amendments (thus clearing the bill), or (4) by disagreeing to the House amendments, in which case a conference is requested by motion or unanimous consent.

In short, both chambers vote themselves into a state of disagreement before going to conference. Technically, each chamber goes to conference on one bill—an S- or HR-numbered measure. One house will often take the other's bill, HR 1234, for instance, strike everything after the enacting clause, and then insert its own alternative. The conference meets to resolve differences on one bill, but there are House and Senate versions of the measure.

Selecting Conferees

The selection of conferees is governed in both chambers by rules and precedent. For each occasion on which a bill is sent to conference, the House Speaker and the presiding officer of the Senate formally appoint the respective conferees. In fact, both chambers usually rely on the chairman and ranking minority member of the committee that originally considered and reported the bill to make the selection. (Sometimes chairmen will delay in naming conferees to signal displeasure with the other body and to apply "leverage on the other body [and encourage it to] cave in on ... key issues" even before a conference is formally convened.[15]

The Speaker and the presiding officer appoint conferees from the list given them in advance by the committee leaders, who generally select members of their own committees. A member of another committee may be appointed when he or she has special knowledge of the subject matter or if the bill is of particular interest to the member's state or district. (Or members may be invited to attend the bicameral meetings without formally being named conferees, because of their specialized knowledge.) When a bill has been referred to several committees (multiple referral), it is common to have conferees from all the committees that handled it. Senator Bentsen described arrangements for the twenty-three House and Senate committees represented on an oversized trade conference.

> Today the chairmen and ranking members of the 23 committees conferring on the trade bill ... met and established a conference structure designed to finish this massive conference [nearly 200 conferees from both chambers]. We established 17 subconferences and a procedure for coordinating the activities of the subconferences.[16]

Seniority used to be a dominant criterion in the appointment of conferees. But in the wake of contemporary procedural reforms, junior members, especially those with particular expertise or interest in the legislation going to conference, are now often selected. Seniority was set aside by the chairmen of Congress's tax-writing committees when the 1986 tax reform bill went to conference. House Ways and Means Chairman Rostenkowski bypassed seniority both to get conferees supportive of his views (thus maximizing the chairman's bargaining leverage) and also for partisan purposes. Speaker O'Neill informed Rostenkowski that he wanted Ways and Means Democrat Richard Gephardt named a conferee even though he had little seniority on the panel.

> "I want Gephardt on there," O'Neill said. Rep. Gephardt had little seniority on the Ways and Means panel and had not been a major player in drafting the tax bill. But O'Neill knew that having Gephardt on the [conference] would highlight the Bradley-Gephardt [tax overhaul] bill and help focus attention on the Democrats' role in reform.[17]

Similarly, ranking Finance member Long set aside seniority to name Senator Bradley (near the bottom in committee seniority on Finance but known as the godfather of tax reform) to the conference.

Increasingly, members of the subcommittee that reported the bill are being appointed conferees, as they often are the most knowledgeable about the legislation. Rules of several House committees, in fact, require conferees to be named from the appropriate subcommittees. Party ratios on conference committees generally reflect the party membership in the House and Senate.

The trend in recent years has been to increase the size of conference delegations. The largest conference in congressional history involved the 1981 omnibus budget reconciliation bill. "Over 250 Senators and Congressmen met in 58 [subconferences] to consider nearly 300 issues" in disagreement, noted Senator Baker.[18] The use of subconferences enables bicameral negotiators to proceed on several fronts simultaneously and to expedite what is inherently (because of numbers) a more complex process. To be sure, the nature of the issues in disagreement may account most for the length of conferences on megabills.

The conferees from each house vote as a unit, with a majority vote deciding each issue. The House and Senate have, in effect, one vote each. Bargaining and compromises are enhanced by this feature of the conference process.

Rules and precedents require that a majority of conferees must have "generally supported" the bill. In 1960 Sen. Richard B. Russell, D-Ga. (1933-1971), expressed a view that is still strongly held by most members:

> When I go to a conference as a representative of the Senate, I represent the Senate viewpoint as vigorously as possible, even though it may not be in accord with the vote or votes I cast on the floor of the Senate. I conceive that to be the duty of the conferee.[19]

Selecting conferees according to this criterion is not always easy, particularly in the case of highly controversial bills that have passed one or the other chamber by narrow margins.

Usually, a member's vote on final passage is taken as evidence of an overall position on a measure for purposes of selection to a conference committee. Yet a member who votes for the final version may have voted against critical amendments that were adopted during floor debate or for amendments intended to cripple the bill. House rules address this knotty issue by directing the Speaker to name no less than a majority of conferees who generally supported the House position "as determined by the Speaker."

In case of a conflict of interest or views, conferees are permitted to resign from conference committees. That step once was taken by Senate Democratic leader Byrd. He explained:

> I was named as a Senate conferee. I do not feel—after thinking overnight about the matter—that I can conscientiously serve as a conferee on that amendment. Although there is no rule that would bind me to support the Senate position on the amendment, I would not wish to go to the conference and oppose the Senate position, because in so doing I would be putting myself and my will above the Senate and the majority will of the Senate.[20]

Senator Byrd's remarks illustrate another important point about conferees: the House or Senate may adopt motions instructing their conferees to sustain the majority position of the chamber on a particular amendment or provision of a bill. This places additional political and moral pressure on the conferees and normally hardens their position in conference committee bargaining. "We need to give the House conferees some backbone to stand up to the Senate on this issue," declared a House member in support of a motion to instruct conferees.[21] However, instructions adopted by either chamber are not binding. Conferees may disregard them, particularly when they feel the need for room to maneuver or compromise. Of course, the full House and Senate still have an opportunity to accept or reject the conference committee report on the bill, and a new conference may be requested if either house feels that its conferees have grossly violated their instructions.

The House and Senate seldom reject the list of conferees designated by the Speaker or the presiding officer. The House requires unanimous consent to change the Speaker's choices. The Senate's rules provide several ways to overrule the presiding officer. Senators may offer substitute motions naming conferees other than those appointed by the presiding officer. Senators also are free to filibuster or threaten to filibuster the motion to appoint conferees in an effort to change the list. Finally, a senator may challenge the conferees at the time they actually are appointed. These procedures are rarely invoked, however. Challenging the presiding officer's decision is tantamount to questioning the basic prerogative of committee leaders (often in consultation with party leaders) to select the conferees since the presiding officer only *formally* appoints the conference delegation.

Challenging conferees is even more difficult in the House, where the Speaker not only endorses the nominees of the committee chairmen but also is the leader of the majority party.

Who gets named a conferee (or who is passed over) sometimes can be critical to conference outcomes. In 1983, for instance, freshman representative Bob Wise, D-W.Va., persuaded the House to delete funding for a dam in his district. The Senate restored the funding for the project, and the matter went to conference. Wise was not selected as a conferee. West Virginia's Senator Byrd, a strong proponent of the dam, was a member of the conference. "I'll be a conferee," he said. "I'm not going to take anything lying down." [22] Byrd personally telephoned over 120 House members to praise the dam. In the end, the two chambers voted to support Byrd's position rather than Representative Wise's. (Of course, there was no guarantee that a majority of the House conferees would have accepted Wise's position on the dam even if he had been named a conferee.)

Bargaining in Conference

Conferees usually convene in the Capitol building itself rather than in one of the Senate or House office buildings. A conference chairman is selected in ad hoc fashion, as there are no congressional rules governing the procedure. On recurring measures that go to conference annually, such as appropriations and revenue bills, the chairmanship often rotates between the two houses. Despite the informal nature of the selection process, the chairman plays an important role in the conference process, arranging the time and place of meetings, the agenda of each session, and the order in which the disagreements are negotiated. The chairman sets the pace of conference bargaining, proposes compromises, and recommends tentative agreements.

Staff members, too, play an important role in conference deliberations. They draft compromise amendments, negotiate agreements, provide advice to members, and prepare the conference reports. Aides played a particularly important role during the complex conference on the 1981 omnibus reconciliation bill. According to the executive director of the House Budget Committee:

> The role of the staff has been not only to explore where there may be areas of agreement, but also to make the deal. How else are you going to get hundreds of issues resolved in a couple of weeks unless you give the staff some kind of license?[23]

Conference committee bargaining, like bargaining throughout the legislative process, is subject to outside pressure. Even before the 1975 "sunshine" rules required open conference meetings, conferees were lobbied heavily by special interest groups, executive agency officials, and even the president on occasion. On important measures, the president or presidential aides "write letters to conferees; . . . administration personnel show up at conference meetings; and the president freely threatens to use his veto unless conferees compromise." [24] The party leaders of Congress also get directly involved on some occasions—brokering compromises or urging on bicameral negotiations to meet a certain timetable.

BARGAINING OBJECTIVES Two key objectives underlie the bargaining at conference sessions: first, conferees want to sustain the position of their respective chambers on the bill; second, they want to achieve a result acceptable both to a majority of each chamber's conferees and to a majority of the membership of both chambers. Normally, bargaining and compromise are necessary. The conferees may be able to reach compromises quickly on their differences. For example, it often is relatively painless to split the difference on bills appropriating funds for federal programs. Or logrolling may occur, with House conferees agreeing to certain Senate-passed provisions in order to gain leverage to win acceptance of House-passed provisions that are strongly supported by members of their own chamber. Offers and counteroffers are part of the often exhausting conference process.

One tactic sometimes used to break a deadlock is for the conferees of one chamber to threaten to break off negotiations and return to their chamber for instructions—thereby reinforcing their position when negotiations resume. A House member once described this ploy as follows:

> Last year there was a difference of about $400 million between the House and Senate versions of the foreign aid appropriations [bill]. The chairman of the House delegation in the conference took a very firm position that we had to end up with slightly less than 50 percent of the difference as a matter of prestige. It was the day we [Congress] were to adjourn. We were in conference until about 10:30 p.m., and the Senate [conferees] wouldn't give in. I think the difference between conferees was only five or ten million dollars. The Senate was fighting for its prestige, and our chairman for his. At 10:30 he started to close his book [staff papers prepared for the conference] and he got up saying he would get instructions from the House. All the rest of our [House] conferees did the same. That prospect was too much for the senators. They capitulated.[25]

This example illustrates a number of factors in conference bargaining: the importance of timing and leadership; the influence of certain members on the negotiations; the impact of threats to convene another series of protracted meetings after one side receives instructions; the role that fatigue can play in resolving hotly contested issues; and the political and professional investment that senators and representatives have in upholding the prestige of their respective chamber and committees.

PROCEDURAL LIMITS ON BARGAINING. During the bargaining process conferees are aware that their completed product may be subject to points of order in the House and Senate if it violates certain rules and precedents. Conferees may not go beyond the scope of the bills agreed to by the House and Senate. If, for example, the House authorizes $5 million for a program and the Senate authorizes $10 million, precedents state that an agreement must be sought within these high and low figures. In these cases, splitting the difference ($7.5 million in the example) is a common compromise device. (Conferees may exceed the fiscal recommendations in each house's bill if neither version contains an overall total amount.)

Equally important, conferees can consider only the points of disagreement between the two Houses; they may not reconsider provisions agreed to in identical form by both houses.

Another result of the rule requiring conferees to stick to the specific matters committed to them is that they may not insert in the conference version of the bill provisions on new subjects—such as new programs or amendments to laws not already amended by the bill. This precedent was formalized in the Legislative Reorganization Act of 1970. This restriction, like many other rules and precedents, sometimes is waived or ignored and new material is in fact incorporated in the conference version.

The new congressional budget process places further constraints on conferees. Discipline and coordination have replaced the piecemeal, uncoordinated approach of the past. The House and Senate budget committees monitor the recommendations of all committees, including those of conference committees, to see that they conform to overall budget guidelines.

"AMENDMENT IN THE NATURE OF A SUBSTITUTE." A conference committee has maximum flexibility when, during initial floor action, one of the houses takes a bill from the other and instead of passing it with amendments strikes out everything after the enacting clause and inserts a completely new version of the bill. This is an "amendment in the nature of a substitute." In such cases, the conference committee can consider the versions of both houses (in effect, two entirely separate bills) and actually draft a third version of the legislation, provided, of course, that it is a reasonable (that is, germane) modification of either the House or Senate version.

NONGERMANE SENATE AMENDMENTS. As discussed in Chapter 8, the Senate's practices and flexibility enable it to add amendments that are considered nongermane under House rules. House conferees traditionally opposed amendments of this kind, contending that they undercut the role of House committees and enabled important and controversial issues to be adopted with minimum consideration. House rules permit only one hour of debate on conference reports.

Frequently, the House was faced with a "take it or leave it" proposition—accept the nongermane Senate amendments or lose the bill in its entirety, including the House-passed provisions, since conference reports are not open to amendment. Members of the House expressed frustration over this recurring dilemma. "I have chafed for years," declared Rules Committee Chairman Colmer, in 1970, "about the other body violating the rules of this House by placing entirely foreign, extraneous, and nongermane matters in House-passed bills." [26] As a result, the House finally acted against the Senate practice in the 1970s by taking several procedural steps including a 1972 rules change permitting separate votes on the nongermane portions of conference reports. The changes were designed to accommodate the Senate's right to offer nongermane amendments while protecting the procedural prerogatives of the House.

Any House member may make a point of order against a conference report when it is called up for final approval on the ground that it contains nongermane material. The member simply says, "Mr. Speaker, I make a point of order under House rule XXVIII that the last section of the conference report contains nongermane material." There are occasions, to be sure, when special rules are obtained from the Rules Committee to protect the conference report against such points of order. Assuming there is no rule, the Speaker sustains the point of order; the representative who raised the objection on the floor then moves to reject the nongermane conference matter. Forty minutes of debate, equally divided between those who support and those who oppose the motion, are permitted under this procedure, after which the House votes on the motion to reject. If it is adopted, the nongermane material is deleted, and the question before the House is disposition of the remaining conference material minus the nongermane portion. Defeat of the motion permits the House to keep the nongermane matter in the conference report.

The effect of these House procedural changes was to cut back somewhat the addition of nongermane Senate amendments to conference reports. House conferees now are able to request that certain Senate nongermane amendments be dropped in conference, as they would otherwise be subject to points of order in the House. And during Senate floor debate, senators sometimes urge their colleagues not to offer nongermane amendments because their adoption might jeopardize enactment of the legislation itself. As Senator Long emphasized, "We should not add [nongermane] amendments that might prevent . . . bills from getting through the House." [27]

THE CONFERENCE REPORT

When at least a majority of the conferees from each chamber have reached agreement, they instruct committee staff aides to prepare a report explaining their conference decisions. A majority of the conferees from each house must sign the report in order for it to be sent back to the House and Senate. When that is done, the conference committee has concluded its work. (An example of a conference report is on p. 254.)

Conferees who oppose the final conference compromise may refuse to sign the report (unlike reports of standing committees of each chamber, conference committee reports are prohibited by precedent from including minority or additional viewpoints).

Conference reports must be printed in the *Congressional Record* before they are brought before the House or Senate for final action. House rules require a three-day layover for conference reports; Senate rules state that conference reports must be available on each senator's desk before they can be taken up on the floor. In each chamber, these rules can be set aside, usually by a "rule" from the House Rules Committee and by unanimous consent in the Senate.

In addition, the 1970 Legislative Reorganization Act requires conference reports to be accompanied by a joint explanatory statement that discusses specific changes made by conferees. This statement is prepared jointly by the conferees (and appropriate staff) of both houses so that the explanation of what was decided upon will not be different in the two houses and thus subject to differing interpretations.

FLOOR ACTION ON CONFERENCE REPORTS

Once the conference report is agreed to and filed with the House and Senate, it must be acted upon by both chambers before it is cleared for the president.

Customarily, the chamber that requests a conference acts last on the conference report, but only if the "papers" are in its possession. The papers are the official documents, such as the bill as originally passed by one chamber and the amendments added to it by the other chamber. Normally, the papers are held by the chamber that agreed to go to conference; that house then would be the first to consider the conference report. However, the papers may be transferred to the other chamber by agreement of the conference committee.

There are occasions when policy outcomes are influenced by which chamber acts first or last on the conference report. In 1979, for example, House Government Operations Committee Chairman Jack Brooks, D-Texas, got the House to ask for a conference with the Senate on a measure creating the Department of Education. He wanted the House to

Public Law 100-231
100th Congress

An Act

To extend the authorization of the Renewable Resources Extension Act of 1978, and for other purposes.

Jan. 5, 1988
[H.R. 2401]

Be it enacted by the Senate and House of Representatives of the United States of America in Congress assembled,

Renewable Resources Extension Act Amendments of 1987.
16 USC 1600 note.

SECTION 1. SHORT TITLE.

This Act may be cited as the "Renewable Resources Extension Act Amendments of 1987".

SEC. 2. EXTENSION.

The Renewable Resources Extension Act of 1978 (16 U.S.C. 1600 note) is amended—

(1) in section 6 (16 U.S.C. 1675) by striking out the first sentence and inserting in lieu thereof the following: "There are authorized to be appropriated to implement this Act $15,000,000 for the fiscal year ending September 30, 1988, and $15,000,000 for each of the next twelve fiscal years."; and

(2) in section 8 (16 U.S.C. 1671 note) by striking out "1988" and inserting in lieu thereof "2000".

SEC. 3. PROGRAM DEVELOPMENT AND EVALUATION.

Section 5 of the Renewable Resources Extension Act of 1978 (16 U.S.C. 1674) is amended—

(1) in subsection (a) by striking out "Congress" and inserting in lieu thereof the following: "the Committee on Agriculture of the House of Representatives and the Committee on Agriculture, Nutrition, and Forestry of the Senate"; and

(2) by adding at the end thereof the following new subsection:

"(d) To assist Congress and the public in evaluating the Renewable Resources Extension Program, the program shall include a review of activities undertaken in response to the preceding five-year plan and an evaluation of the progress made toward accomplishing the goals and objectives set forth in such preceding plan. Such review and evaluation shall be displayed in the program, for the Nation as a whole, and for each State.".

Approved January 5, 1988.

LEGISLATIVE HISTORY—H.R. 2401:

HOUSE REPORTS: No. 100-239 (Comm. on Agriculture).
CONGRESSIONAL RECORD, Vol. 133 (1987):
July 27, considered and passed House.
Dec. 19, considered and passed Senate, amended.
Dec. 21, House concurred in Senate amendments.

O

19-139 O - 88 (231)

act last on the conference report so that the parliamentary options available to the bill's opponents—who were more numerous in the House—would be limited.

The first chamber to act on a conference report has three options: adopt, reject, or recommit the conference report—return it to the conferees for further deliberation. When the first chamber to act adopts the conference report, however, this automatically dissolves the conference committee, and the other chamber is faced with a yes or no vote on the conference report. Chairman Brooks's strategy worked. Through intense lobbying by the White House and various education groups, the House agreed to the conference report establishing the new department.

Conference reports are privileged and may be brought up at almost any time the House and Senate are in session. Usually, this is with the prior approval of the leadership. The senior majority and minority conferees from each house's delegation normally act as the floor managers of the conference version.

Conference reports can be filibustered in the Senate, but usually they are debated under a time-limitation agreement. In the House, conference reports are considered under the one-hour rule. However, House rules provide that in the event both floor managers support the conference report, one-third of the hour is available to a member who requests opposition time from the Speaker.

Both chambers require conference reports to be accepted or rejected in their entirety. In some instances (where conferees are dealing with a number of amendments in disagreement rather than one), if conferees cannot agree on certain amendments, these are submitted to each chamber individually and acted upon separately. These are called "amendments in disagreement." In such cases, the conference report is debated and agreed to first; then any amendments in disagreement are considered. Every amendment must be agreed to in identical form before congressional action on the bill is complete.

Conference reports are seldom rejected. Outright rejection of a report kills the bill and may require a repetition of the entire legislative process. This becomes particularly significant in the weeks immediately before the final adjournment of a Congress, when members face the choice of (1) accepting the bill as is, (2) recommitting it to a conference committee, in all probability jeopardizing final approval, or (3) killing the bill, knowing there is no time to move a revised bill through Congress.

Once the conference report is approved by both houses, the papers are delivered to the house that originated the measure. A copy of the bill as finally agreed to by Congress is prepared by an enrolling clerk. The "enrolled bill" is signed by the Speaker and presiding officer of the Senate, or by other authorized officers, and sent to the president.

PRESIDENTIAL APPROVAL OR VETO

Under the Constitution (Article I, section 7), the president has a qualified veto power. The president can disapprove of legislative acts, subject to the ability of Congress during its two-year life to override the vetoes by a two-thirds vote of the members present and voting in each house. Once an enrolled bill is sent to the White House, the president has ten days, excluding Sundays, to sign or veto it. If no action is taken within the ten-day period, and Congress is in session, the bill automatically becomes law without the president's signature. If the final adjournment (called *sine die)* of a session of Congress takes place before the ten-day period ends, and the president does not sign the measure, the legislation dies as a "pocket veto" (see box on p. 257).

Woodrow Wilson wrote that the president, in using the veto power, "acts not as the executive but as a third branch of the legislature." [28] The president can use the veto, or the threat of a veto, to advance legislative and political goals. Often, the threat of a veto is itself enough to persuade Congress to change its legislative course.

Senator Proxmire put the matter vividly when he told the Senate why a specific compromise on another measure was agreed to by a conference committee. "There is another fundamental reason we did it—that is because we faced the veto, that great, big monster of a veto." [29]

The veto is one of the president's most effective legislative weapons. Congress, particularly during periods of divided party control of the chambers, finds it very difficult to attract the two-thirds vote in each house that is required to override presidential vetoes.

The frustration is not entirely one-sided. Presidents can be tied up by adroit congressional maneuvering. Congress virtually can force the president to approve measures by attaching them as "riders" to legislation regarded as essential by the president. Recall the discussion of continuing resolutions in Chapter 3 and how they can eviscerate the president's veto power. Interestingly, President Reagan, in his 1988 State of the Union message, promised to veto any massive continuing resolution Congress sends him. Moreover, members of both chambers who are dissatisfied with lawmaking by continuing resolution have stated that they will work to sustain the president's veto.

Presidents veto measures for a variety of reasons: they are considered unconstitutional; they believe they encroach on the chief executive's powers and duties; or they hold them to represent ill-advised policies. When President Richard Nixon vetoed the 1973 War Powers Resolution (which Congress subsequently enacted by overriding his veto), he cited all three factors as the basis of his action. Vetoing bills because they cost too much is another favorite rationale of presidents.

The Pocket Veto Controversy

As the 100th Congress approaches its midterm recess, lawmakers are working amid legal uncertainty about the extent of the president's power to kill legislation while they are gone.

Congress has long been at odds with Reagan administration officials over their view that the president can "pocket veto" bills any time the House and Senate recess for more than three days, as is expected beginning sometime in mid-December. Congressional leaders contend that his pocket-veto power is more limited.

A pocket veto allows the president to kill a bill by not signing it when Congress is not in session. Unlike a regular veto, it cannot be overridden.

Open conflict may be avoided if contested bills are cleared early enough to ensure that Congress is still in session if and when Reagan vetoes them.

"If there are people who want to be sure [bills are] not pocket-vetoed, they're probably working very hard to get those measures up now," said Michael Davidson, Senate legal counsel.

Concern about the pocket veto has been raised about a housing bill (S 825) stalled by budget objections in the Senate.

While Congress is in session, the president has 10 days (not counting Sundays) to sign a bill or veto it by returning it to Congress unsigned.

No one questions the validity of the pocket veto when a two-year Congress has adjourned and the next has not yet taken office. At issue is whether a pocket veto is valid in recesses during a session of Congress. A case that had been expected to clarify the issue, *Burke v. Barnes,* was declared moot by the Supreme Court in January.

Sen. Edward M. Kennedy, D-Mass., who was involved in pre-Reagan lawsuits over the issue, wrote to House and Senate leaders in November to warn of the danger of pocket vetoes during the forthcoming recess. A White House spokesman said the administration regards the pocket veto as one option available to it during the recess, but declined to comment further.

While the *Burke* case was pending, Reagan had avoided pocket vetoes in disputed recesses, sending such bills back to Congress with a disclaimer that he believed he had the pocket-veto authority. All of Reagan's vetoes this year came while Congress was in session.

Based on correspondence with the Justice Department after the *Burke* decision, Kennedy said he believed the administration would continue to send vetoed bills back to Congress during a recess. But he warned that the administration seemed to be "reserving the right to assert that the bill has been pocket-vetoed and has not become law" if Congress overrode the veto. That likely would provoke a new legal battle.

Source: Janet Hook, "End of Session Resurrects Pocket-Veto Issues," *Congressional Quarterly Weekly Report,* Dec. 5, 1987, 3002.

Presidents may use vetoes as a political technique to gain public support for administration policies. "I'll veto a [tax hike] in less time than it takes Vanna White to turn the letters V-E-T-O," said President Reagan in his continuing battle with Congress over how to reduce fiscal deficits.[30] President Franklin D. Roosevelt dramatized his disapproval of a 1935 measure by personally delivering his veto message to a joint session of Congress. Presidents Nixon and Reagan each vetoed bills on nationwide television.

The president, to be sure, receives recommendations from many quarters during the ten-day period allowed under the Constitution to decide whether to sign or veto legislation. He receives advice from the Office of Management and Budget (OMB), appropriate Cabinet officers, White House aides, members of Congress, and scores of groups and officials. The OMB, for instance, once prepared a "menu" that contained an "A list" and a "B list." On the A list were provisions that merited a veto; on the B list were items that in some combination could trigger a veto.[31]

Veto Override Procedures

When the president vetoes a measure, the Constitution provides that "he shall return it with his objections to that House in which it shall have originated." Neither chamber is under any obligation to schedule an override attempt. And neither the Constitution nor Congress sets a deadline for overriding a veto. Party leaders may realize they have no chance to override and may not even attempt it. Because of popular support for the president's action, or for other reasons, the political environment may not be conducive to a successful override.

If an override attempt fails in one chamber, the process ends and the bill dies. If it succeeds, the measure is sent to the other chamber, where a second successful override vote makes it law. The Constitution requires roll-call votes on override attempts.

Whether signed by the president or passed over a veto, the bill now becomes a public law and is sent to the General Services Administration, the government's housekeeping department, for deposit in the National Archives and publication in the *Statutes at Large*, an annual volume that compiles all bills that have been passed by Congress and signed into law, or have become law through a veto override. (An example of a public law is on p. 259.)

SUMMARY

Both chambers must approve identical versions of a bill before it can be sent to the White House. Usually, House-Senate differences are resolved

How a Bill Becomes a Law (Revised)

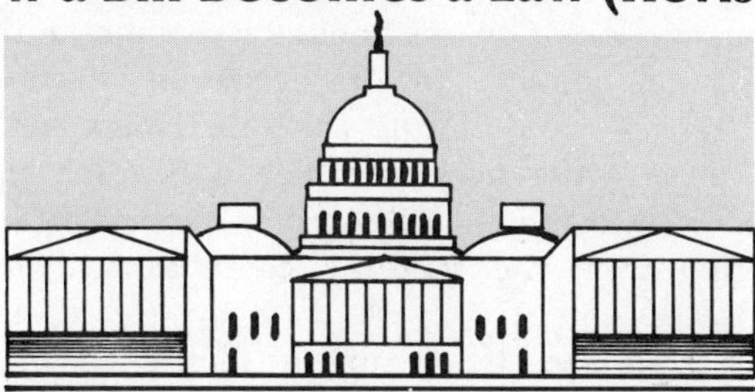

Robert B. Dove, then Senate parliamentarian, said he knew of no bill that bounced between the Senate and House as many times as did HR 3128, the fiscal 1986 reconciliation (or deficit-reduction) bill. HR 3128 went back and forth nine times in late 1985 and early 1986 after the conference report was filed.

HOUSE

OCT. 24
House passed HR 3500, containing deficit-reduction proposals from most House committees.

OCT. 31
House passed HR 3128, containing deficit-reduction proposals from the Ways and Means Committee. (HR 3500 was later combined with HR 3128 for conference.)

SENATE

NOV. 14
Senate passed S 1730, containing deficit-reduction proposals from all Senate committees. The bill was renumbered HR 3128.

DEC. 19
More than 240 conferees, meeting in 31 groups over two weeks, reached agreement on HR 3128.

DEC. 19
Senate adopted the conference report.

DEC. 19
House rejected the conference report, voting to strip off a conference provision establishing a new manufacturers' tax to pay for the "superfund" hazardous-waste cleanup program.

DEC. 19
Senate voted to reinstate the superfund tax.

DEC. 19
House rejected the Senate proposal.

DEC. 20
Senate voted again to keep the superfund tax.

MARCH 6
House voted to strip off the superfund tax, but also offered compromises on health care and offshore oil revenues.

MARCH 14
Senate agreed to delete the superfund tax, but at White House insistence also demanded elimination of welfare and offshore drilling provisions and further cuts in offshore oil revenues for states.

MARCH 18
House rejected the latest Senate proposal.

MARCH 18
Senate insisted on its March 14 proposal.

MARCH 20
House accepted March 14 Senate proposal, clearing the bill for the president.

Source: Congressional Quarterly Weekly Report, April 5, 1986, 753.

by informal consultation or by one house's acceptance of the other's bill, without further amendment. Major legislation, however, generally contains controversial provisions on which the House and Senate differ. Resolution of these differences is achieved through the conference committee process. A conference committee is appointed, composed of members selected from the standing committees that handled the legislation.

The conferees are expected to support their chamber's positions on the major issues in the bill regardless of their committees' or their personal views. Sometimes, their bargaining positions are reinforced by instructions from their parent chamber. Conference committee bargaining resembles bargaining elsewhere in the legislative process. It includes the traditional techniques of compromise and logrolling. Important, too, is knowledge by each chamber of what it wants and what the other body wants. There are, however, some restrictions that are unique to the conference process. Conferees are not allowed, for example, to go beyond the scope of the bills agreed to by their respective chambers.

Until the 1970s, the Senate's more flexible floor procedure permitting nongermane amendments to House-passed bills enabled the Senate to force the House to accept many provisions unrelated to the legislation at hand. House floor procedure on conference reports did not permit members to consider and vote separately on Senate nongermane amendments added to conference reports. The House responded several times in the 1970s by amending its own procedures, with the result that the nongermane Senate amendment now is a somewhat less effective device for winning congressional approval of provisions that were never considered by the House.

Conference reports generally are accepted by both chambers for two important reasons: (1) members' disinclination to repeat the entire legislative process, and (2) their deference to the expertise of the conferees.

The final step of the legislative process is presidential action, but the president's veto power influences the entire legislative process. The extraordinary majority (two-thirds) required to override a veto forces Congress to consider the White House's position from the moment a bill is introduced until it is finally passed in identical form by both houses. Congress occasionally tries to achieve certain objectives by attaching riders opposed by the president to legislation that the administration regards as essential.

Enactment of legislation does not bring the legislative process to a close. Once a bill becomes law, it may set in motion a new federal program, redefine the role of executive branch agencies, or change the responsibilities of federal, state, and local governments in numerous program areas. All these new activities generated by a law become, in time, the subject of renewed congressional scrutiny as Congress endeavors to monitor the implementation and effects of the laws it passes. The next chapter turns to this broad area of congressional activity, usually termed "legislative oversight."

NOTES

1. Ada G. McCown, *The Congressional Conference Committee* (New York: Columbia University Press, 1927), 12. Also see Gilbert Steiner, *The Congressional Conference Committee, Seventieth to Eightieth Congresses* (Urbana: University of Illinois Press, 1951); and David J. Vogler, *The Third House, Conference Committees in the United States Congress* (Evanston, Ill.: Northwestern University Press, 1971).
2. Information compiled by Ilona Nickels, Government Division, Congressional Research Service, Library of Congress.
3. Roy Swanstrom, *The United States Senate, 1787-1801*, 87th Cong., 1st sess., S. Doc. No. 64 (Washington, D.C.: Government Printing Office, 1962), 232.
4. *Congressional Record,* daily ed., Feb. 20, 1986, S1463.
5. *Congressional Record,* daily ed., Oct. 3, 1985, H8112.
6. *Congressional Record,* March 21, 1974, 7589. See also the *Record* for April 10, 1974, 10569. When either chamber acts for the first time to amend the other's legislation, that change is considered to be part of the original text. In short, it is a "free" amendment. For instance, if the House passes a measure and the Senate amends it, the Senate amendment is viewed as part of the original text. If the House then amends the Senate's change, that is a first degree amendment. A subsequent Senate amendment to the House amendment is a second degree amendment. No other interchamber amendments are in order because they would be in the third degree. Absent bicameral agreement at this juncture, (1) the two chambers may decide to go to conference, (2) the House may concur in the Senate's amendment, or (3) the Senate may recede from its amendment to the House amendment.
7. *Congressional Record,* daily ed., Dec. 20, 1982, S15757.
8. *National Journal,* May 22, 1976, 694.
9. Richard F. Fenno, Jr., *The Power of the Purse* (Boston: Little, Brown, 1966), 610.
10. John Ferejohn, "Who Wins in Conference Committee?" *Journal of Politics* (November 1975): 1033-1046; Walter J. Oleszek, "House-Senate Relationships: Comity and Conflict," *The Annals* (January 1974): 80-81.
11. Elizabeth Drew, *Senator* (New York: Simon & Schuster, 1979), 174.
12. Bruce Stokes, "Bentsen's Benchmark," *National Journal,* July 25, 1987, 1902.
13. *Congressional Record,* daily ed., June 10, 1986, S7157.
14. *Enactment of a Law,* 97th Cong., 2d sess., S. Doc. No. 97-20, 24.
15. *Congressional Record,* daily ed., July 18, 1985, H5937.
16. *Congressional Record,* daily ed., Sept. 29, 1987, S13055.
17. Jeffrey H. Birnbaum and Alan S. Murray, *Showdown at Gucci Gulch* (New York: Random House, 1987), 257.
18. *Congressional Record,* daily ed., July 29, 1981, S8711.
19. *Congressional Record,* Aug. 26, 1960, 17831.
20. *Congressional Record,* Dec. 11, 1975, 39864.
21. *Congressional Record,* daily ed., June 23, 1983, H4435.
22. *Washington Post,* June 22, 1983, A2, and July 16, 1983, A23.

23. *New York Times,* July 23, 1981, A19. Also see Michael J. Malbin, *Unelected Representatives: Congressional Staff and the Future of Representative Government* (New York: Basic Books, 1980), chap. 5.
24. Ted Siff and Alan Weil, *Ruling Congress* (New York: Grossman, 1975), 184.
25. Quoted in Charles L. Clapp, *The Congressman* (Washington, D.C.: Brookings Institution, 1962), 249.
26. *Congressional Record,* Sept. 15, 1970, 31842.
27. *Congressional Record,* Oct. 1, 1976, 34518.
28. Woodrow Wilson, *Congressional Government* (Boston: Houghton Mifflin, 1885), 52. Later in his book, Wilson wrote that the "president is no greater than his prerogative of veto makes him; he is, in other words, powerful rather as a branch of the legislature than as the titular head of the Executive." 260.
29. *Congressional Record,* daily ed., Dec. 20, 1982, S15678.
30. *Wall Street Journal,* July 13, 1987, 1.
31. *Washington Post,* Oct. 15, 1986, A7.

CHAPTER 10

Legislative Oversight

Congress "sometimes gets in the habit of 'pass it and forget it' lawmaking," Sen. Hubert H. Humphrey, Jr., D-Minn. (1949-1964, 1971-1978), once lamented.[1] Efficient government, he realized, requires careful attention by Congress to the administration of laws. A thoughtful, well drafted law offers no guarantee that the policy intentions of legislators will be carried out. In short, there is a difference between making policy and conducting policy.

The laws passed by Congress are often general guidelines, and sometimes their wording is deliberately vague. The implementation of legislation involves the drafting of administrative regulations by the executive agencies and day-to-day program management by agency officials. Agency regulations and rules are the subject of "legislative oversight"—the continuing review by Congress of how effectively the executive branch is carrying out congressional mandates. As Senator Leahy, has put it:

> I believe that oversight is one of the Congress's most important constitutional responsibilities. We must do more than write laws and decide policies. It is also our responsibility to perform the oversight necessary to insure that the administration enforces those laws as Congress intended.[2]

Congress formalized its legislative oversight function in the Legislative Reorganization Act of 1946. That act required congressional committees to exercise "continuous watchfulness" of the agencies under their jurisdictions and implicitly divided oversight functions into three areas:

1. Authorizing committees (such as Agriculture, Education and Labor, and Commerce) were required to review federal programs and agencies under their jurisdictions and propose legislation to remedy deficiencies they uncovered.

2. Fiscal oversight was assigned to the Appropriations committees of each chamber, which were to scrutinize agency spending.
3. Wide-ranging investigative responsibility was assigned to the House Government Operations Committee and the Senate Governmental Affairs Committee to probe for inefficiency, waste, and corruption in the federal government. To some degree, all committees perform each type of oversight.

Formalizing Oversight

The House and Senate have always had authority to investigate programs and agencies of the executive branch. The first congressional investigation in American history, in 1792, delved into the conduct of the government in the wars against the Indians. One of the broadest investigations was an 1861 inquiry into the conduct of the Civil War. Other notable probes have included investigations into the Credit Mobilier in 1872-1873, the Money Trust in 1912, the Teapot Dome scandal in 1923, Stock Exchange operations in 1932-1934, and defense spending during World War II. Recently a congressional joint committee investigated, with nationally televised hearings, the Iran-Contra affair, which involved covert and deceptive operations by the National Security Council and others.

The 1946 reorganization act stated Congress's intention to exercise its investigative authority primarily through standing committees rather than by means of specially created investigating committees. The act provided for continuous review of programs instead of sporadic hearings whenever errors, malfeasance, or injustices surfaced. The "continuous watchfulness" precept of the act implied that Congress henceforth would participate actively in administrative decision making, in line with the observation that "administration of a statute is, properly speaking, an extension of the legislative process." [3]

During the 1970s, both houses amended their rules to grant additional oversight authority to the standing committees. The Legislative Reorganization Act of 1970 rephrased in more explicit language the oversight duties of the committees and required most House and Senate panels to issue biennial reports on their oversight activities. The House Committee Reform Amendments of 1974 assigned "special oversight" responsibilities to several standing committees; the Senate adopted the same approach, called "comprehensive policy oversight," when it adopted the Committee System Reorganization Amendments of 1977. Both special oversight and comprehensive policy oversight are akin to the broad review authority granted the House Government Operations Committee and the Senate Governmental Affairs Committee.

Explained Sen. Adlai E. Stevenson III, D-Ill. (1970-1981), floor manager during Senate debate on the 1977 change:

> Standing committees are directed and permitted to undertake investigations and make recommendations in broad policy areas—for example, nutrition, aging, environmental protection, or consumer affairs—even though they lack legislative jurisdiction over some aspects of the subject. Such oversight authority involves subjects that generally cut across the jurisdictions of several committees. Presently, no single committee has a comprehensive overview of these policy areas. [This rule change] corrects that. It assigns certain committees the right to undertake comprehensive review of broad policy issues.[4]

Rules Governing Oversight

Several other changes in House and Senate rules are worth noting.

- The House directed its committees to create oversight subcommittees, undertake futures research and forecasting, prepare oversight plans, and review the impact of tax expenditures (credits, incentives, and the like) on matters that fall within their respective jurisdictions.[5]
- The Senate required each standing committee to include "regulatory impact statements" in committee reports accompanying the legislation it sends to the floor. One of these statements, for instance, might evaluate the amount of additional paperwork that would result from enactment of a proposed bill.
- Passage of the 1974 Congressional Budget and Impoundment Control Act strengthened Congress's review capabilities by directing the General Accounting Office (GAO)—a legislative support agency of Congress—to assist House and Senate committees in program evaluation and in the development of "methods for assessing and reporting actual program performance."

Congress requires these additional oversight devices because it faces an executive establishment of massive size and diffuse direction. Even with the "increasing demand for balanced Federal budgets," wrote a scholar, "we should not deceive ourselves into thinking that the Federal Government of the future will be a shrinking violet, retreating to the modest proportions it had in George Washington's or Grover Cleveland's time."[6] For example, even though the Reagan administration stressed limited national government, the federal government became larger during the president's tenure in terms of civilian employees and fiscal expenditures. (The growth in both areas occurred in the defense area while domestic discretionary programs shrank.)

Congress, in short, needs a variety of oversight techniques to hold agencies accountable so that if one technique proves to be ineffective, committees and members can employ others singly or in combination.

TECHNIQUES OF OVERSIGHT

Congress's decentralized committee system means that oversight generally is initiated on an ad hoc, unsystematic basis. No single legislative agency or leadership group coordinates the numerous oversight activities of the House and Senate.

The objectives of oversight often vary from committee to committee. The focus may be on promoting administrative efficiency and economy in government, protecting and supporting favored policies and programs, airing an administration's failures or wrongdoing, or its achievements, publicizing a particular member's or a committee's goals, reasserting congressional authority vis-à-vis the executive branch, or assuaging the interests of pressure groups.

The following sections describe the most common methods by which Congress exercises its oversight responsibility.

Hearings and Investigations

The traditional method of exercising congressional oversight is through committee hearings and investigations into executive branch operations. Legislators need to know how effectively federal programs are working and how well agency officials are responding to committee directives. And they want to know the scope and intensity of public support for government programs in order to assess the need for legislative changes.

Although excessive use of hearings and investigations can bog down governmental processes, judicious use of such tools helps to maintain a more responsive bureaucracy while supplying Congress with information needed to formulate new legislation.[7] Committee members and committee staffs may conduct oversight hearings around the country (field hearings) to watch public programs in operation and to take testimony from citizens and local officials.

Legislative Veto

Numerous statutes contain provisions that, while delegating authority to the executive branch, reserve to Congress the right to approve or disapprove executive actions based on that authority within a specified time period. This power generally is referred to as the "legislative veto." This procedure allows one or both houses, by majority vote, to veto certain executive branch initiatives, decisions, and regulations. (Sometimes Congress authorizes committees or subcommittees—the "committee veto"—to approve, or disapprove, executive actions.) As the Senate Committee on Judiciary explained:

> All too often Congress finds that what it thought was a clear message of legislative purpose has been skewed by the implementing agency in the regulatory process so that it no longer reflects the legislative intent. In those situations, Congress conducts oversight hearings, threatens the agency's appropriations, or revisits the authorizing language. But these acts by Congress most often occur after the rule has taken effect and after the public has had to live with the adverse effects of the rule and in so doing, decided to protest it. The legislative veto reverses this order of events and allows Congressional involvement before the rule actually becomes operational.[8]

Since 1932, when a legislative veto provision was first used by Congress in an executive reorganization law, "more than 200 statutes, containing well in excess of 300 separate veto provisions, have subjected the implementation of executive decisions to some further form of congressional review."[9]

The legislative veto was an attractive oversight technique because, even though Congress seldom exercised its veto prerogative to overturn agency decisions, committees and members felt the practice kept federal administrators sensitive and responsive to congressional interests. It was employed in legislation dealing with both domestic and international issues. The legislative veto also served executive branch purposes by permitting agencies to make binding decisions without going through the lengthy lawmaking process. In short, this device served the interests of both the legislative and executive branches.

On June 23, 1983, however, the Supreme Court declared in a historic decision, *Immigration and Naturalization Service v. Chada*, that the legislative veto was unconstitutional. In a 7-2 vote, the court majority said the device violated the separation of powers, the principle of bicameralism, and the presentation clause of the Constitution (legislation passed by both chambers must be presented to the president for his signature or veto). The decision, wrote Justice Byron R. White in a dissent, "strikes down in one fell swoop provisions in more laws enacted by Congress than the court has cumulatively invalidated in its entire history."

Despite the *Chadha* ruling, Congress still employs legislative and committee vetoes. As scholar Louis Fisher pointed out:

> In response to the Court's ruling, Congress repealed some legislative vetoes and replaced them with joint resolutions, which satisfy the [Supreme Court's] ruling because joint resolutions must pass both Houses and be presented to the President. However, Congress has also continued to enact legislative vetoes to handle certain situations. From June 23, 1983 to the end of the 99th Congress, 102 legislative vetoes

> (generally the committee-veto variety) have been enacted into law in 24 different statutes. Some of these legislative vetoes were about to be enacted at the time of the Court's decision. Others have been introduced, reported, and enacted long after Congress became aware of the Court's ruling.[10]

In brief, both Congress and the executive branch have adapted to the post-*Chadha* era largely through informal accommodations and statutory adjustments. On the one hand, executive agencies want discretion and flexibility in running their programs; on the other hand, Congress is generally unwilling to grant open-ended authority to executive entities without strings attached. The legislative and committee vetoes remain important review devices, because both branches recognize their value.

Authorization Process as Oversight

Congress not only has the authority to create or abolish executive agencies and transfer functions between or among them; it also can enact "statutes authorizing the activities of the departments, prescribing their internal organization and regulating their procedures and work methods."[11] The authorization process, as noted in Chapter 3, is an important oversight tool. As a House member observed during debate on a bill to require annual congressional authorization of the Federal Communications Commission (FCC):

> Our subcommittee hearings disclosed that the FCC needs direction, needs guidance, needs legislation, and needs leadership from us in helping to establish program priorities. Regular oversight through the reauthorization process, as all of us know in Congress, is necessary, and nothing brings everybody's attention to spending more forthrightly than when we go through the reauthorization process.[12]

Congress, too, may pass laws that "deauthorize" previously approved projects, such as the construction of dams.

Appropriations Process as Oversight

Congress probably exercises its most effective oversight of agencies and programs through the appropriations process. By cutting off or reducing funds, Congress can abolish agencies or curtail programs. By increasing funds, it can build up neglected program areas. In either case, it has formidable power to shape ongoing public policies. The power is exercised mainly by the House and Senate Appropriations committees, particularly through their powerful subcommittees, whose budgetary recommendations are only infrequently changed by the full committee or by the House and Senate.

For instance, House Appropriations Chairman Jamie Whitten, who has headed the panel's agriculture subcommittee for forty years, exercises wide-ranging supervision of the Agriculture Department. During the 100th Congress, Chairman Whitten succeeded in getting an assistant secretaryship abolished because of disagreements over funding for soil conservation. The Agriculture Department kept submitting budgets that curtailed soil conservation spending. Chairman Whitten favored additional spending. To highlight his displeasure with the department, Chairman Whitten persuaded Congress to eliminate the job of the assistant secretary who oversaw the conservation program.[13]

The Appropriations committees define the precise purpose for which money may be spent, they adjust funding levels, and often they attach provisos prohibiting expenditures for certain purposes. In sum, the appropriations process as an oversight technique, notes congressional budget expert Allen Schick, is comparable to a Janus-like weapon: "The stick of spending reductions in case agencies cannot satisfactorily defend their budget requests and past performance, and the carrot of more money if agencies produce convincing success stories or the promise of future results."[14]

Inspectors General

Congress, too, has created statutory offices of inspectors general (IGs) in nearly twenty major federal agencies and departments. Granted wide latitude and independence by the Inspectors General Act of 1978, these officials conduct investigations and audits of their agencies to improve efficiency, end waste and fraud, and discourage mismanagement. IGs keep Congress informed about federal activities and problems through the issuance of periodic reports (see box on p. 270).

Nonstatutory, Informal Controls

There are various informal ways in which Congress can influence federal administrators. Executive officials, conscious of Congress's power over the purse strings, are attuned to the nuances of congressional language in hearings, floor debate, committee reports, and conference reports. For example, in committee reports the verbs "expects," "urges," "recommends," "desires," and "feels" display in roughly descending order how obligatory a committee comment or viewpoint is intended to be.[15] If federal administrators believe congressional directives to be unwise, they are more likely to ask for informal consultation with members and committee staff than to seek new laws or resolutions. In fact, executive officials are in frequent contact with committee members

Inspectors General

In 1978, the Committee on Governmental Affairs, which I now chair, secured the enactment of the Inspectors General Act. This legislation established offices of inspector general in most of the Federal Cabinet-level departments and some of the larger agencies. The purpose of this act was to create a more independent atmosphere for audit and investigative activities and to achieve more efficient and effective management operation in key Federal establishments. The act required consolidation of the various audit and investigative units in affected agencies under the leadership of an inspector general. This person reports to the agency head and Congress concerning significant abuses or deficiencies and makes recommendations for corrective action. At the time the original law was enacted, we in Congress believed that the inspector general concept was sound, but we were not sure how well the program would work. Indeed, Congress passed the original legislation in the face of opposition from every department and agency affected.

Today, it is widely recognized that the statutory inspectors general—who now number 19—have had outstanding success in improving the operations of their respective Federal establishments. According to a recent report from the council that coordinates IG activities, these offices have saved more than $71 billion of the taxpayers' money over the past 5 years alone. During the same period, they have been responsible for obtaining over 16,000 successful prosecutions and 15,000 administrative actions. GAO recently reported that the inspectors general have been "a key factor in correcting deficiencies and strengthening Federal internal audit and investigative activities."

Source: Remarks of Sen. John Glenn, D-Ohio, chairman of the Senate Committee on Governmental Affairs, *Congressional Record,* daily ed., April 3, 1987, S4563.

and staff. Analyzing the House Appropriations Committee's relationship with the federal bureaucracy, one scholar wrote:

> [There] is a continuing and sometimes almost daily pattern of contacts between the Committee on Appropriations and the executive branch. When Congress is not in session, communication continues by telephone or even, on occasion, by visits to the homes of members of the committee. If the full story were ever known, the record probably would disclose a complex network of relationships between members of the Committee on Appropriations and its staff and officials, particularly budget officers, in the executive branch.[16]

Such informal contacts enable the committees to exercise policy influence in areas where statutory methods might be inappropriate or ineffective.

Members sometimes urge their colleagues, administrative agencies, and the courts to exercise caution in interpreting committee reports, floor debate, and other nonstatutory devices as expressions of the intent of Congress. Federal Judge Abner J. Mikva, a former House member, recounted a story about the pitfalls of interpreting the legislative history of a bill.

> I remember when Mo Udall was managing the strip-mining bill, and there had been all sorts of problems getting it through. They'd put together a very delicate coalition of support. One problem was whether the states or the feds would run the program. One member got up and asked, "Isn't it a fact that under this bill the states will continue to exercise sovereignty over strip mining?" And Mo replied, "You're absolutely right." A little later someone else got up and asked, "Now is it clear that the Federal Government will have the final say on strip mining?" And Mo replied, "You're absolutely right." Later, in the cloakroom, I said, "Mo, they can't both be right." And Mo said, "You're absolutely right." [17]

General Accounting Office Audits

The General Accounting Office (GAO) was created by the Budget and Accounting Act of 1921. Under the direction of the comptroller general, the GAO conducts audits of executive agencies and programs at the request of committees and members of Congress to make sure that public funds are properly spent. The Legislative Reorganization Act of 1970 and the Congressional Budget and Impoundment Control Act of 1974 expanded the GAO's investigative authority.[18]

The GAO is Congress's premier field investigator. The agency sends Congress about 1,000 reports annually addressing ways to root out waste and fraud in government programs and promote program performance. GAO studies frequently lead to the introduction of legislation, congressional hearings, or cost-saving administrative changes. The head of the GAO, the comptroller general, is appointed for a single fifteen-year term by the president, subject to the advice and consent of the Senate. The GAO works only for Congress.

Reporting Requirements

Numerous laws require executive agencies to submit periodic reports to Congress and its committees. As one scholar explained:

> Reporting requirements are provisions in law requiring the executive branch to submit specified information to Congress or committees of Congress. Their basic purpose is to provide data and analysis Congress needs to oversee the implementation of legislation and foreign policy by the executive branch.[19]

Some reports are of minimal value because they are couched in broad language that reveals little about program implementation; others may be more specific. Generally, however, the report requirement encourages self-evaluation by the executive branch and promotes agency accountability to Congress. For example, when Congress became exasperated with Pentagon delays in implementing a major reorganization of defense offices, it directed the secretary of the army "to report every 30 days to Congress on what he is doing to put the legislation into place." [20]

Periodically, Congress and the executive branch recommend the elimination of certain reports (currently, there are more than 3,000 reports submitted to Congress). Sometimes the impulse to eliminate reports reflects legislative and executive concern about "micromanagement" of executive affairs by legislative committees. Senate Armed Services Chairman Nunn, for example, expressed dismay that over a fifteen-year span (1970-1985) the number of reports required of the Defense Department increased twelvefold (from 36 to 458).[21] This kind of concern about reporting requirements involves seeking an appropriate weighing of Congress's need for information to conduct evaluations of agencies and programs against the imposition of burdensome, costly, or irrelevant obligations on executive entities.

Ad Hoc Groups

There are numerous informal groups and caucuses of Senate and House members that focus on specific issues and programs. For example, the bipartisan House and Senate Arms Control and Foreign Policy Caucus published a report about the misuse of U.S. aid in El Salvador.[22] The Military Reform Caucus, another bipartisan and bicameral organization, is concerned about a variety of defense issues. This group, for instance, supports enactment of legislation that establishes a "solid procedure whereby military whistleblowers who feel they have been harassed as a result of reporting waste or fraud to the Congress or Inspector General could obtain review of their cases." [23]

Outside organizations also provide Congress with information on inadequacies in federal programs and other problems with the bureaucracy and exert pressure for more ambitious oversight. Many of these groups also employ computers "to assist them in research on such subjects as the performance of Governmental agencies." [24] "Think tanks" such as the Brookings Institution and the American Enterprise Institute periodically conduct studies of public policy issues and advise members of Congress and others on how well federal agencies and programs are working. For example, the Washington, D.C.-based Center for Excellence in Government has prepared a "Prune Book"—"descriptions of

The Advice and Consent Role of the Senate

The Senate often finds itself in positions where it will draw criticism no matter what it does. If the Senate probes too long or too deeply into a nominee's past, it is accused of denying the president the assistance he needs when he needs it. If the Senate rushes through a nomination without adequate investigation, it is accused of "consent without advice" or "half rubber, half stamp." From years of experience, I would say that we do a president a disservice by rushing any nomination, unless there is a vacancy and a clear record as to the nominee's integrity, his capability, his honesty, his qualifications, and a clear need for speedy action.

If damaging information about a nominee's past is to be found, or serious character flaws are to be uncovered, better that it become public knowledge before the individual is confirmed rather than afterwards. That is a hard message to deliver to any president of any party, but it is a lesson that has been learned too frequently to be forgotten. In sum, the Senate must continue to seriously and painstakingly perform its Constitutional responsibility of advising and consent on presidential nominations if we are to maintain the unique system of checks and balances that has brought our democratic form of government to its bicentennial.

Source: Remarks of Sen. Robert C. Byrd, D-W.Va., *Congressional Record,* daily ed., July 29, 1987, S10835.

the government's top 130 jobs and the qualifications necessary to hold them"—for President Reagan's successor. (The Prune Book is a take-off on the "Plum Book," a list of the top political appointive positions in the executive branch.)[25] The center's publication is designed in part to improve the quality of administrative performance by executive officials.

Senate Confirmation Process

High-ranking public officials are chosen by the president "by and with the Advice and Consent of the Senate," in accord with the Constitution. In general, the Senate gives presidents wide latitude in selecting Cabinet members but closely scrutinizes judicial and diplomatic appointments as well as nominees to regulatory boards and commissions. Increasingly in recent years, Senate committees are probing the qualifications, independence, and policy predilections of presidential nominees, seeking information on everything from physical health to financial assets (see box on p. 273).

Nomination hearings establish a public record of the policy views of nominees, on which appointed officials can be called to account at a later time. "We all ask questions at confirmation hearings, hoping to obtain answers that affect actions," observed Sen. Carl Levin, D-Mich.[26] For example, committees try to extract pledges from nominees that they will testify at hearings when requested to do so, with the not so subtle threat that otherwise the appointee's name will not be sent to the full Senate for action.

Program Evaluation

Program evaluation is an approach to oversight that uses social science and management methodology, such as surveys, cost-benefit analyses, and efficiency studies, to assess the effectiveness of ongoing programs. It is a special type of oversight that has been specifically provided for in many agency appropriations bills since the late 1960s and in the 1974 Congressional Budget and Impoundment Control Act. The studies often are carried out by the GAO and by the executive agencies themselves.[27]

Despite the multiplicity of methods to evaluate programs, members sometimes disagree about how to measure performance. Several factors frequently account for their divergent perspectives. People may not agree on the objectives of certain programs. Public laws often are the products of conflicts and compromises, and when those compromises are translated into legislative language ambiguity about program goals may be the result. Many policies have competing objectives or produce unintended results. In addition, there may be no agreement about criteria—quantitative or qualitative—for determining program success or failure. Finally, even if decision makers agree on objectives and criteria, they may interpret the assessments differently. Members and committees who support particular programs are unlikely to view with favor evaluations that recommend repeal or revision of those programs.

Casework

Each senator's and representative's office handles thousands of requests each year from constituents seeking help in dealing with executive agencies. The requests range from inquiries about lost Social Security checks or delayed pension payments to disaster relief assistance and complicated tax appeals to the Internal Revenue Service. "Constituents perceive casework in nonpolitical terms," wrote two scholars. "They *expect* their representatives to provide" this service.[28]

Most congressional offices employ specialists, called "case workers," to process these petitions. Depending on the importance or complexity of a case, a member himself may contact federal officials, bring up the matter in committee or even discuss the case on the floor. Casework has the positive effect of bringing quirks in the administrative machinery to members' attention. And solutions to an individual constituent's problems can suggest legislative remedies on a broader scale.

Support Agency Studies

There are three other support agencies of Congress in addition to the GAO: the Congressional Research Service (CRS), the Office of Technology Assessment (OTA), and the Congressional Budget Office (CBO). Each prepares, or contracts for, reports or studies to assist committees and members in reviewing federal agency activities, expenditures, and performance. Their analyses frequently spark legislation to correct administrative shortcomings.

Oversight by Individual Members

Some members conduct their own personal reviews of agency activities and develop ways to publicize what they believe to be examples of governmental waste and inefficiency. Senator Proxmire, for instance, since 1975 has periodically bestowed a "Golden Fleece Award" on agencies that, in his estimation, wastefully spend tax dollars.[29] Senator Terry Sanford, D-N.C., emulated the Proxmire idea by creating the "Great Turkey Award" for "noteworthy acts by ill-informed, intellectually clumsy, or generally inadequate political appointees." [30] Former representative Berkley Bedell, D-Iowa (1975-1987), utilized another technique.

> One of the practices I have is to make unannounced visits to the executive branch of the Government. I simply select an agency at random, open a door, walk in, and start asking questions of the people who work in that office.[31]

On occasion, individual members will conduct ad hoc field oversight hearings of their own. These sessions usually permit constituents to testify about their problems with federal agencies. They usually garner favorable publicity for the legislator, too.

OVERSIGHT TRENDS

While some legislators and scholars complain that congressional oversight is irregular and shallow, the period after the mid-1970s saw a surge of legislative interest in the process. The bipartisan House leadership even dubbed the 96th Congress (1979-1981) the "Oversight Congress."

Speaker O'Neill concluded that "members appear to be more committed to tightening up controls on the executive branch."

Among the many factors that contributed to this surge of oversight activity, several are worth noting. They included:

1. Heightened public dissatisfaction and concern about governmental waste, fraud, program mismanagement, and escalating expenditures (Two recent presidents—Carter and Reagan—even campaigned against the federal "establishment.")
2. Congressional assertiveness and distrust of the executive branch in the wake of the Vietnam War; Watergate, and revelations of abuses by such agencies as the CIA, FBI, and IRS; and the Iran-contra affair
3. The election of representatives and senators who were skeptical about the national government's ability to resolve public problems
4. The proliferation of federal programs and regulations that touched the lives of practically every citizen; citizens in turn told their elected officials about problems they encountered with federal agencies
5. A rapid increase in the number of groups and trade associations that moved to Washington and pressured Congress to examine governmental actions that affected these special interests
6. The expansion of autonomous subcommittees and staff resources on Capitol Hill, which permitted the new breed of aggressive legislators to scrutinize federal activities.
7. Aggressive investigative reporting into executive activities by the print and broadcast media

To be sure, the switch from the "politics of fiscal abundance" to the "politics of fiscal austerity" has compelled members and committees to scrutinize program activities and expenditures. No longer is the debate in the Capitol centered on program initiatives or increases; rather the debate increasingly addresses whether the national government has the resources to meet new problems, which programs should be cut or kept at the same level, and what can be done to protect valuable programs in the face of competing priorities and limited resources. This is why "management" will be an important catchword during the 1990s. Congress is "going to have to examine every function of government and say, Can we do this more efficiently?" declared Rep. Ralph Regula, R-Ohio.[32] Or as Rep. William H. Gray, III, D-Pa. (chairman of the House Budget Committee during the 100th Congress), put it, Congress will have to categorize federal spending into "essential vs. desirable" functions. "Those things that are not an absolute may have to be reduced significantly," he said.[33]

LACK OF CONSENSUS ON OVERSIGHT

Despite the demonstrable increase in legislative review activities and Congress's augmentation of its staff, budget, and authority for oversight, many members and commentators still fault congressional efforts in this area. Several factors help to explain why doing more in oversight is often perceived as doing less.

First, there is no clear consensus on how to measure oversight, quantitatively or qualitatively. As a result, members' anxiety about Congress's ability to review the massive federal establishment remains high. Quantitatively, no one really knows how much oversight Congress is doing. It is clear, however, that undercounting characterizes statistical analyses of oversight no matter what definition of that activity is employed. Part of the problem is that legislative review is a ubiquitous activity carried out by many entities: committees, members' offices, legislative support agencies, and committee and personal staff aides. Almost any committee hearing, for example, even ones ostensibly devoted to formulating new legislation, might devote considerable attention to reviewing past policy implementation. Qualitatively, there is little agreement among members on the criteria that can be used to evaluate effective oversight.

Second, some legislators hold oversight objectives that appear impossible to meet. They would like to see Congress conduct comprehensive reviews of the entire executive establishment. In brief, they find Congress's selective and unsystematic oversight approach generally unsatisfactory even when there is more of it. Oversight is too often a "guerrilla foray" rather than the continuous watchfulness contemplated by the 1946 Legislative Reorganization Act. Congress performs, two scholars noted, "fire-alarm" oversight instead of "police-patrol" oversight. The former occurs when outside events or public interest trigger agency reviews; it is episodic and reactive in character. The latter is proactive and involves deliberate House and Senate decisions to oversee certain federal activities.[34]

Third, many committees and individual members feel they have minimal impact on the bureaucracy. Exclaimed Speaker Wright:

> Fighting the redtape and the overregulation of bureaucratic rulemaking and guideline writing are among the most frustrating things any of us have had to do in Congress—it is almost like trying to fight a pillow. You can hit it—knock it over in the corner—and it just lies there and regroups. You feel sometimes as though you are trying to wrestle an

> octopus. No sooner do you get a hammerlock on one of his tentacles than the other seven are strangling you.[35]

To many members of Congress, as to the rest of us, federal agencies often seem impenetrable mazes.

Fourth, oversight may produce more questions than answers. Congress finds it easier "to highlight what's going wrong and to blame it on someone," declared Senator Chiles, "than to try to determine what to do about it." [36] In short, more oversight still can mean that agency problems remain uncorrected.

Fifth, Congress seeks to shape executive actions to its own objectives, not simply to conduct or commission neutral evaluation studies of departmental activities. Oversight is part of the legislative-executive tug-of-war that characterizes our separation of powers system. According to one commentator:

> The key issue for Congress is not administrative performance but its ability to influence agency actions. Congress is interested in performance, but it expresses this interest by seeking dominion over agencies. The distribution of political power between the legislative and executive branches, not simply [or even mainly] the quality of programs, is at stake.[37]

In brief, a fragmented and assertive Congress is often frustrated by its inability to control and coordinate a fragmented and sophisticated bureaucracy.

Despite Congress's general interest in oversight, there are other considerations that limit effective performance. Legislators still have too little time to devote to their myriad tasks, including oversight. Huge investments of time, energy, and staff assistance are required to ferret out administrative inadequacies. Some members are reluctant to support massive investigations that may only reveal that a program is working fairly well, not a determination that attracts much constituent attention or media coverage. "Effective oversight is, of necessity, time-consuming and tedious," said a Republican senator. "To do it right, you have to hear an endless stream of witnesses, review numerous records, and at the end of it you may find an agency was doing everything right. It is much more fun to create a new program." [38] However, many members accept the fact that much of their effort in this area is unglamorous.

The review process sometimes is inhibited by the alliances that develop between committees, agencies, and clientele groups. Examples of these "subgovernments" or "iron triangles," as the alliances often are called, are the House and Senate Merchant Marine committees-Federal Maritime Commission-Maritime unions axis and the Education committees-Department of Education-National Education Association combine.[39] Each component of the alliance usually is supportive of the other.

TABLE 10-1 Members and Committee Aides of the 100th Congress Assess Oversight

Members and Committee Staff	*Members* House *(N=87)*	Senate *(N=27)*	Total *(N=114)*	*Committee Staff* House *(N=28)*	Senate *(N=25)*	Total *(N=53)*
There is not enough time in the session to do oversight.	19.5%	44.4%	25.4%	25.0%	12.0%	18.9%
Congressional oversight is not declining.	28.7	7.4	23.7	17.9	36.0	26.4
No incentives to do oversight.	11.5	14.8	12.3	17.9	12.0	15.1
Most oversight is politically motivated.	8.0	14.8	9.6	3.6	32.0	17.0
The budget process leaves members with no time to do oversight.	5.7	14.8	7.9	17.9	24.0	20.8
Not enough resources are available to do oversight properly.	2.3	3.7	2.6	7.1	4.0	5.7
Other.	6.9	11.1	7.9	3.6	4.0	3.8

Source: Congress Speaks—A Survey of the 100th Congress, Washington, D.C.: Center for Responsive Politics, 1988, 165.

In such cases, committees are less likely to review agency programs critically.

Finally, there are members and scholars who say that Congress lacks electoral, political, and institutional incentives for oversight. As a result, legislators are "insufficiently dissatisfied with their oversight behavior to feel a strong enough stimulus to alter existing patterns." [40] Or, as Table 10-1 reveals, member and committee aides emphasize insufficient time as a deterrent to thorough reviews of executive agencies and programs. "By the time [my committees] have finished with all our budget work," said a Republican senator, "there is no time left to do some real oversight." [41]

SUMMARY

To some extent, Congress's interest in oversight has been a cyclical phenomenon. Historically, oversight often has been more intense when the executive and legislative branches of government have been controlled by different parties. Recent changes in rules and procedures, which have strengthened the tools of oversight, may have evened out the cyclical curve somewhat by encouraging regular monitoring of federal programs. In the current climate, these changes, combined with the influx of activist legislators, probably mean that for the next few years at least the legislative branch will actively assert policy and oversight initiatives, regardless of which party occupies the White House.

The important issue is how to balance Congress's oversight responsibilities with the executive's need for reasonable discretion in program administration. Too much congressional interference can wreak havoc with agency routines. On the other hand, for Congress to ignore its oversight role is tantamount to abandoning the implementation of the law—and its interpretation—to the whims of nonelected officials.

NOTES

1. *Congressional Record,* March 28, 1974, 4611.
2. *Congressional Record,* daily ed., June 21, 1983, S8822. For several studies on oversight, see Morris S. Ogul, *Congress Oversees the Bureaucracy* (Pittsburgh: University of Pittsburgh Press, 1976). Professor Ogul's book contains a lengthy bibliography on oversight. Joseph P. Harris, *Congressional Control of Administration* (Washington: Brookings Institution, 1964); Seymour Scher, "Congressional Committee Members as Independent Agency Overseers: A Case Study," *American Political Science Review* (December 1960): 911-920.
3. David B. Truman, *The Governmental Process* (New York: Alfred Knopf, 1953), 439. The continuous watchfulness provision was retitled legislative "review" in the Legislation Reorganization Act of 1970. That act also directed House and Senate committees to submit biennial reports on their oversight activities.
4. *Congressional Record,* Feb. 1, 1977, 2897.
5. Michael J. Malbin, *Unelected Representatives* (New York: Basic Books, 1979). See Chapter 6 for an analysis of a House oversight subcommittee in action.
6. *Workshop on Congressional Oversight and Investigations,* 96th Cong., 1st sess., H. Doc. No. 96-217, 198. See also Louis Fisher, "Congress and the President in the Administrative Process: The Uneasy Alliance," in *The Illusion of Presidential Government,* ed. Hugh Heclo and Lester M. Salamon (Boulder, Colo.: Westview Press, 1981), 21-43.
7. Congressional requests for executive agency information may be blocked by executive privilege. See Bernard Schwartz, "Executive Privilege and Congressional Investigatory Power," *California Law Review* (March 1959): 3-50; Raoul Berger, *Executive Privilege: A Constitutional Myth* (Cambridge, Mass.: Harvard University Press, 1974); *U.S. v. Nixon,* 418 U.S. 683 (1974); and "Symposium: United States v. Nixon," *UCLA Law Review* (October 1974): 1-40. Also see the remarks of Rep. John N. Erlenborn, R-Ill., on executive privilege in *Congressional Record,* daily ed., July 28, 1983, E3835.
8. *Rulemaking Procedures Reform Act of 1986,* 99th Cong., 2d sess., S. Rept. No. 99-492, 2.

9. William West and Joseph Cooper, "The Congressional Veto and Administrative Rulemaking," *Political Science Quarterly* (Summer 1983): 286. The data cited in this study were compiled by Clark Norton of the Congressional Research Service, Library of Congress.
10. Louis Fisher, Government Division, Congressional Research Service, Library of Congress, information supplied to the author. Also see Elder Witt, "High Court to Clarify Sweep of Its Legislative Ruling," *Congressional Quarterly Weekly Report*, Dec. 6, 1986, 3025-3030, and Joseph Cooper, "Congress and the Legislative Veto: Choices since the *Chadha* Decision," in *Making Government Work: From White House to Congress*, ed. Robert E. Hunter et al. (Boulder, Colo.: Westview Press, 1986), 31-67.
11. Harris, *Congressional Control of Administration*, 284.
12. Quoted in Louis Fisher, "Annual Authorizations: Durable Roadblocks to Biennial Budgeting," *Public Budgeting and Finance* (Spring 1983): 38.
13. *Washington Post*, Jan. 1, 1988, A17.
14. *Workshop on Congressional Oversight and Investigations*, 199.
15. Michael Kirst, *Government without Passing Laws* (Chapel Hill: University of North Carolina Press, 1969), 37. See also William Rhode, *Committee Clearance of Administrative Decisions* (East Lansing: Michigan State University Press, 1959).
16. Holbert N. Carroll, *The House of Representatives and Foreign Affairs*, rev. ed. (Boston: Little, Brown, 1966), 172. A good example of nonstatutory controls involves the reprogramming of funds within executive accounts. Reprogramming refers to the expenditure of funds for purposes not originally intended when Congress approved the department's budget. Agencies secure approval for reprogramming from the appropriate House and Senate committees.
17. *New York Times*, May 12, 1983, B8. See also *New York Times*, Oct. 22, 1982, A16.
18. For studies of the General Accounting Office (GAO), see Thomas D. Morgan, "The General Accounting Office: One Hope for Congress to Regain Parity of Power with the President," *North Carolina Law Review* (October 1973): 1279-1468; Richard E. Brown, *The GAO, Untapped Source of Congressional Power* (Knoxville: University of Tennessee Press, 1970); John T. Rourke, "The GAO: Auditor ... Analyst ... Advocate," *The Bureaucrat* (Spring 1981): 43-49; Erasmus H. Kloman, ed., *Cases in Accountability: The Work of the GAO* (Boulder, Colo.: Westview Press, 1979); Frederick C. Mosher, *The GAO: The Quest for Accountability in American Government* (Boulder, Colo.: Westview Press, 1979); and Joseph Pois, *Watchdog on the Potomac: A Study of the Comptroller General of the United States* (Washington, D.C.: University Press of America, 1979).
19. Ellen C. Collier, "Foreign Policy by Reporting Requirement," *Washington Quarterly* (Winter 1988): 75.
20. *New York Times*, Dec. 31, 1987, A20.
21. *Congressional Record*, daily ed., Oct. 1, 1985, S1234.
22. *Los Angeles Times*, Nov. 16, 1987, sec. 1, 6.
23. *Congressional Record*, daily ed., Feb. 8, 1988, E190.
24. *New York Times*, Aug. 26, 1983, A14.
25. *Washington Post*, Jan. 21, 1988, A21.
26. *New York Times*, April 14, 1983, B10.
27. See, for example, Joseph Wholey et al., *Federal Evaluation Policy* (Washington, D.C.: Urban Institute, 1970); Joel Havemann, "Congress Tries to Break Ground Zero in Evaluating Federal Programs," *National Journal*, May 22,

1976, 706-713; "Evaluation: A Cautious Perspective," Public Policy Forum, *The Bureaucrat* (April 1976): 3-100; Robert T. Nakamura and Frank Smallwood, *The Politics of Policy Implementation* (New York: St. Martin's Press, 1980); George C. Edwards III, *Implementing Public Policy* (Washington, D.C.: CQ Press, 1980); and Harry S. Havens, "A Public Accounting, Integrating Evaluation and Budgeting," *Public Budgeting and Finance* (Summer 1983): 102-113.

28. John R. Johannes and John C. McAdams, "Entrepreneurs or Agent: Congressmen and the Distribution of Casework, 1977-1978," *Western Political Quarterly* (September 1987): 549.
29. See *Christian Science Monitor,* Aug. 5, 1982, 1.
30. *Roll Call,* July 5, 1987, 8.
31. *Congressional Record,* daily ed., June 8, 1983, H3737.
32. Jonathan Rauch, "The Fiscal Ice Age," *National Journal,* Jan. 10, 1987, 63.
33. *Washington Times,* Jan. 29, 1987, 1D.
34. Matthew D. McCubbins and Thomas Schwartz, "Congressional Oversight Overlooked: Police Patrols versus Fire Alarms," *American Journal of Political Science* (February 1984): 165-179.
35. *Workshop on Congressional Oversight and Investigations,* 5.
36. Ibid., 144.
37. Allen Schick, "Politics through Law: Congressional Limitations on Executive Discretion," in *Both Ends of the Avenue,* ed. Anthony King (Washington, D.C.: American Enterprise Institute for Public Policy Research, 1983), 166.
38. *Congress Speaks—A Survey of the 100th Congress* (Washington, D.C.: Center for Responsive Politics, 1988), 163.
39. See, for example, J. Leiper Freeman, *The Political Process: Executive Bureau-Legislative Committee Relations,* rev. ed. (New York: Random House, 1965); Randall B. Ripley and Grace A. Franklin, *Congress, the Bureaucracy and Public Policy,* 2d ed. (Homewood, Ill.: Dorsey Press, 1980); and Timothy B. Clark, "The President Takes on the 'Iron Triangles' and So Far Holds His Own," *National Journal,* March 28, 1981, 516-518.
40. Morris S. Ogul, "Congressional Oversight: Structures and Incentives," in *Congress Reconsidered,* 2d ed., ed. Lawrence C. Dodd and Bruce I. Oppenheimer (Washington, D.C.: CQ Press, 1981), 330. See also Morris P. Fiorina, "Congressional Control of Bureaucracy: A Mismatch of Incentives and Capabilities," in *Congress Reconsidered,* 2d ed., 332-348; Fiorina, *Congress: Keystone of the Washington Establishment* (New Haven: Yale University Press, 1977); and R. Douglas Arnold, *Congress and the Bureaucracy: A Theory of Influence* (New Haven: Yale University Press, 1979).
41. *Congress Speaks,* 163.

CHAPTER 11

A Dynamic Process

Anyone who views lawmaking in Congress as a precise, neat process of drafting, debating, and approving legislation overlooks the dynamic forces at work on Capitol Hill. It is not a static institution.

For better or worse, the interests, pressures, perceptions, and prejudices of members of Congress change rather quickly, a result, in part, of the election cycle, but also of other pressures and influences. The demands made by the presidency and the courts, international events, lobbying groups, and media disclosures are some of the ever-present forces that affect lawmaking. Congress, in short, is an institution in which procedures reflect and, in turn, perpetuate the messiness, openness, pragmatism, compromise, and deliberateness so characteristic of much American policy making. As House Energy and Commerce Chairman John Dingell once put it: "Legislation is like a chess game more than anything else. It is a seemingly endless series of moves, until ultimately somebody prevails through exhaustion, or brilliance, or because of overwhelming public sentiment for their side." [1]

Throughout this book, the point is made that at every stage of the legislative process a new winning coalition must be formed to carry a policy recommendation up the next rung of the legislative ladder; otherwise, its progress is jeopardized. And that coalition is ever changing, as the forces that mold it change. While coalitions are formed to advance legislation, others may form to tear it down. If opponents fail in one session of Congress they always can come back in the next to try again. As Senator Simpson emphasized:

> In politics there are no right answers, only a continuing flow of compromises between groups resulting in a changing, cloudy, and ambiguous series of public decisions where appetite and ambition compete openly with knowledge and wisdom.[2]

Despite its built-in—and frequently beneficial—inefficiencies, Congress's policy-making role is firmly grounded in the Constitution. It is true that the preeminent place envisioned for Congress by the authors of the Constitution has been modified by the growth of executive power in the twentieth century. But it is equally true that the constitutional separation of powers has preserved for Congress an independent role that distinguishes it from legislative bodies in most other Western democracies.

This book has focused on congressional procedures and rules because the mechanics of legislating influence the policy-making process. Procedural details and nuances have a crucial policy impact, and it is impossible to understand why certain policies are adopted and others are not without an appreciation of the rules governing the process. Substance, in short, can be shaped through procedure.

Congress's informal procedures and practices are often as important as its formal rules. For instance, neither chamber needed rules changes to permit lawmaking through "packages." Instead, the recent practice of relying on megabills to process much of Congress's annual workload is a product in large measure of legislative-executive, House-Senate conflict.

Moreover, no rules changes mandated that legislators must play both the "inside" game (maneuvering behind the scenes in Congress to pick up support for legislation) and the "outside" game (generating public support) to push controversial legislation through the House and Senate. "Being a good legislator means you have to do both," remarked Representative Gephardt. "If you are going to pass important legislation, you have to both deal with Members and put together coalitions in the country." [3]

The "rules of the game" are as important in illuminating the outcomes of the legislative process as they are in comprehending who wins at any competition—the presidential nominating system, for example. To use the presidential election analogy, it is difficult to appreciate electoral strategy in the general campaign without understanding the Electoral College or the campaign finance rules. Similarly, one cannot apprehend the behavior of members of Congress as participants in policy formation without a knowledge of the formal and informal rules and procedures under which they operate.

Congressional rules serve many functions: they promote stability, divide responsibilities, minimize conflict in daily decision making, legitimize decisions, and distribute power. Paradoxically, because the rules do distribute power they create tensions between those whose influential positions are protected by the rules and those whose influence is limited or threatened by proposed changes in the rules.

The substantial overhaul of congressional procedures that took place during the past two decades was in large part an effort by junior and newly elected members of Congress to correct perceived deficiencies and to gain more influence. When the two parties dropped seniority as the sole basis for deciding which members would head committees, they were not simply changing a selection procedure; just as important were the opportunities that were opened up for newer members to attain positions of authority.

This change, in turn, greatly affected members' relationships with interest groups and the executive branch. There are now many points of access for groups and individuals trying to influence congressional decisions. Changes in the rules can have broad impact outside Congress.

The thrust of these various changes (seniority, televising floor sessions, and so on) "has been toward greater egalitarianism and openness in the legislative process," observed Senator Byrd, "which we can all endorse." [4] However, when this changed decision-making environment is combined with external developments, such as the rise of wall-to-wall interest groups with the financial and technological capacity to create "instant constituencies" for or against issues, it is hardly surprising that congressional party leaders have difficulty in forging winning coalitions on complex and controversial legislation. "In a legislative body," declared Rep. David Obey, D-Wis., "we need more than good leadership; we also need good followship." [5] In today's Congress, the latter is often in shorter supply than the former.

With the emphasis on participatory democracy on Capitol Hill, Congress has devised a variety of innovative techniques to coordinate the internal distribution of power. Some of these include new "rules" from the House Rules Committee, multiple referrals, the reconciliation process, party task forces, and artful packaging of many proposals into one bill. In short, although Congress operates in a messy manner, it can develop coherent responses to public problems.

The effect of congressional rules and practices on policy outcomes has been demonstrated repeatedly in these chapters. The requirement for an extraordinary majority of the Senate to invoke cloture gives to a well-organized minority the ability to block passage of legislation desired by a majority. Civil rights legislation, perhaps the classic case, was repeatedly delayed in the 1950s and 1960s by the opponents' use of the filibuster.

On the other hand, the rules themselves may change in response to events or policy goals. Some rules are modified or ignored, while new ones come out of struggles over a particular problem. Cloture was made somewhat easier in 1975 by changing the size of the Senate majority needed to invoke it from two-thirds of those voting to three-fifths of the entire membership. In reaction, a long-ignored procedure was revived: the post-cloture filibuster. That tactic in turn led to two other changes (in 1979 and 1986) to tighten up the cloture rule. The mixed results and unanticipated consequences that attend some procedural revisions can even awaken second thoughts in members who originally supported rules changes. "I have, indeed, changed my views about the filibuster," said Senator Packwood. "I think if I had my choice now, I would go back to the two-thirds present and voting" requirement to invoke cloture.[6]

This book also has cited cases where an ostensibly procedural decision can be used to mask a policy objective. When members vote to table a bill, procedurally it appears as if they are merely postponing consideration of it. Nevertheless, such a procedure usually sidetracks the legislation permanently, while allowing members to say they did not take a position on the measure.

Important, too, are the differences in the way the two chambers operate. Each chamber functions under rules and procedures that reflect its basic constitutional design. A close examination of the differences as well as the similarities between the two bodies is indispensable to an accurate understanding of how Congress functions. Unlike those of the House, said Senate Democratic leader Byrd, the rules in the Senate favor the minority: "They were meant to favor the minority to prevent the majority from running over the minority. That is why there is a Senate. That is why this Senate ought to remain a Senate and not become a second House of Representatives."[7]

The most significant and enduring feature of the rules is that they usually require bills to pass through a labyrinth of decision points before they can become law. It is generally more difficult to pass legislation than to defeat it. These multiple decision points, coupled with weak party discipline, make necessary a constant cycle of coalition building—by means of the various bargaining techniques—to move legislation past each potential roadblock. The shifting coalitions, as noted earlier, combine, dissolve, and recombine in response to the widely varying issues and needs of members. Unlike in the past, when a few "barons" dominated legislative policy making, the greater decentralization of authority in today's Congress creates an environment in which scores of members have some—and often significant—bargaining power.

Coalition building is possible primarily for two reasons. First, members of Congress, who represent diverse constituencies, are not equally concerned about every item on the legislative agenda. Second, members pursue many objectives other than the enactment of legislation. They may seek reelection, election to higher office, appointment to prestigious committees, or simply personal conveniences such as additional staff or office space. These conditions create numerous opportunities for coalition building through the three types of bargaining discussed—logrolling, compromise, and the distribution of nonlegislative favors (primarily by the congressional leadership).

Another factor determining whether a series of majority coalitions can be built is the extent to which members are in general agreement that a law is required or inevitable on a particular subject. Members may have widely divergent views on the solution to the problem, but they usually will work to compromise their differences when dealing with "must" legislation.

A critical factor influencing the entire congressional process is time. As the two-year cycle of a Congress runs its course, every procedural device that can be employed has a policy consequence—either delaying or speeding up the processing of legislation. Frequently, as the countdown to final adjournment occurs, the bargaining process shifts into high gear. Bills that have been deadlocked for months are moved along swiftly as logrolling and compromises "save" bills in which members have a vested interest. Deadlines and threatened or actual procedural and policy crises, in brief, frequently activate the lawmaking process. Legislation stalled by opponents dies if not enacted before a Congress's final adjournment.

Congressional Procedures and the Policy Process has been revised during a period when Congress and the president devoted large amounts of time and energy to budgetary issues. In the face of soaring federal deficits, one issue seemed to dominate the congressional agenda: money. Members sought answers to recurring questions. How much will the program cost? Where will the monies come from to finance it? Which programs merit spending reductions or increases?

President Reagan, to be sure, accentuated this development by insisting on broad domestic spending reductions and tax cuts while demanding significant increases in military funding. From a procedural standpoint, legislators found that traditional lawmaking routines and the customary give-and-take that produce legislative compromises were thrown out of kilter by the emphasis on fiscal matters. But while Congress was forced to allocate more and more of its time to federal budgetary questions, its ability to deal with the changeover from a period of resource abundance to an era of resource scarcity proved to be extremely difficult.

Such internal and external pressures often compel legislators to engage in major introspective reviews of the institution's organization and operations. A concomitant feature of the legislative process, therefore, is that Congress from time to time seeks to change its rules and procedures to remedy specific problems, become more efficient, redistribute power, or affect policy outcomes.

And so the dynamic interplay between policy making and the rules continues. Precedents and practices are revised or abandoned and new ones established, often with great difficulty, in response to changing needs and pressures. "We always learn in this organization, even though we may think the rules are fixed and firm," observed Senator Packwood, "how the fertility of the minds of the Members manages to find ways to expand those rules."[8]

Congress's dynamism is assured by the regular infusion of new members, changing circumstances and conditions, and the fluctuating expectations of citizens. If Congress reduces or increases its lawmaking activity, it usually is not by accident but as a reaction to members' perceptions of what their constituents and the country want. For its part, the nation expects Congress to use its considerable powers and policy-making procedures to help resolve, or at least allay, the pressing issues facing the country as it approaches the twenty-first century.

NOTES

1. *Washington Post,* June 26, 1983, A14.
2. *Congressional Record,* daily ed., May 20, 1987, S6798.
3. Richard Cohen, "Taking Advantage of Tax Reform Means Different Strokes for Different Folks," *National Journal,* June 22, 1985, 1459.
4. *Congressional Record,* daily ed., Dec. 15, 1987, S18133.
5. *Congressional Record,* daily ed., Dec. 3, 1987, H10975.
6. *Congressional Record,* daily ed., Feb. 23, 1988, S1117.
7. *Congressional Record,* daily ed., Feb. 23, 1988, S1124.
8. *Congressional Record,* daily ed., Feb. 26, 1988, S1521.

Glossary of Congressional Terms

ACT. The term for legislation once it has passed both houses of Congress and has been signed by the president or passed over his veto, thus becoming law. Also used in parliamentary terminology for a bill that has been passed by one house and engrossed. (See LAW, ENGROSSED BILL.)

ADJOURNMENT SINE DIE. Adjournment without definitely fixing a day for reconvening; literally "adjournment without a day." Usually used to connote the final adjournment of a session of Congress. A session can continue until noon, January 3, of the following year, when, under the Twentieth Amendment to the Constitution, it automatically terminates. Both houses must agree to a concurrent resolution for either house to adjourn for more than three days.

ADJOURNMENT TO A DAY CERTAIN. Adjournment under a motion or resolution that fixes the next time of meeting. Under the Constitution, neither house can adjourn for more than three days without the concurrence of the other. A session of Congress is not ended by adjournment to a day certain.

AMENDMENT. A proposal of a member of Congress to alter the language, provisions, or stipulations in a bill or in another amendment. An amendment usually is printed, debated, and voted upon in the same manner as a bill.

AMENDMENT IN THE NATURE OF A SUBSTITUTE. Usually an amendment that seeks to replace the entire text of a bill. Passage of this type of amendment strikes out everything after the enacting clause and inserts a new version of the bill. An amendment in the nature of a substitute also can refer to an amendment that replaces a large portion of the text of a bill.

APPEAL. A member's challenge of a ruling or decision made by the presiding officer of the chamber. In the Senate, the senator appeals to members of the chamber to override the decision. If carried by a majority vote, the appeal nullifies the chair's ruling. In the House, the decision of the Speaker traditionally has been final; seldom are there appeals to the members to reverse the Speaker's stand. To appeal a ruling is considered an attack on the Speaker.

APPROPRIATIONS BILL. A bill that gives legal authority to spend or obligate money from the Treasury. The Constitution disallows money to be drawn from the Treasury "but in Consequence of Appropriations made by Law."

An appropriations bill usually provides the actual monies approved by authorization bills, but not necessarily the full amount permissible under the authorization measures. By congressional custom, an appropriations bill originates in the House, and it is not supposed to be considered by the full House or Senate until the related authorization measure is enacted. In addition to general appropriations bills, there are two specialized types. (See CONTINUING RESOLUTION, SUPPLEMENTAL APPROPRIATIONS BILL.)

AUTHORIZATION BILL. Basic, substantive legislation that establishes or continues the legal operation of a federal program or agency, either indefinitely or for a specific period of time, or which sanctions a particular type of obligation or expenditure. An authorization normally is a prerequisite for an appropriation or other kind of budget authority. Under the rules of both houses, the appropriation for a program or agency may not be considered until its authorization has been considered. An authorization also may limit the amount of budget authority to be provided or may authorize the appropriation of "such sums as may be necessary." (See also BACKDOOR SPENDING.)

BILLS. Most legislative proposals before Congress are in the form of bills and are designated by HR in the House of Representatives or S in the Senate, according to the house in which they originate, and by a number assigned in the order in which they are introduced during the two-year period of a congressional term. "Public bills" deal with general questions and become public laws if approved by Congress and signed by the president. "Private bills" deal with individual matters such as claims against the government, immigration and naturalization cases, land titles, etc., and become private laws if approved and signed. (See also CONCURRENT RESOLUTION, JOINT RESOLUTION, RESOLUTION.)

BILLS INTRODUCED. In both the House and the Senate, any number of members may join in introducing a single bill or resolution. The first member listed is the sponsor of the bill, and all members' names following the sponsor's are the bill's cosponsors. Many bills are committee bills and are introduced under the name of the chairman of the committee or subcommittee. All appropriations bills fall into this category. A committee frequently holds hearings on a number of related bills and may agree to one of them or to an entirely new bill. When introduced, a bill is referred to the committee or committees that have jurisdiction over the subject with which the bill is concerned. Under the standing rules of the House and Senate, bills are referred by the Speaker in the House and by the presiding officer in the Senate. In practice, the House and Senate parliamentarians act for these officials and refer the vast majority of bills. (See also REPORT, CLEAN BILL.)

BUDGET AUTHORITY. Authority to enter into obligations that will result in immediate or future outlays involving federal funds. The basic forms of budget authority are appropriations, contract authority, and borrowing authority. Budget authority may be classified by (1) the period of availability (one-year, multiple-year, or without a time limitation), (2) the timing of congressional action (current or permanent), or (3) the manner of determining the amount available (definite or indefinite).

CALENDAR. An agenda or list of business awaiting possible action by each chamber. The House uses five legislative calendars. (See CONSENT, DISCHARGE, HOUSE, PRIVATE, AND UNION CALENDAR.)

In the Senate, all legislative matters reported from committee go on one calendar. They are listed there in the order in which committees report them, or the Senate places them on the calendar, but may be called up out of order by the majority leader, either by obtaining unanimous consent of the Senate or by a motion to call up a bill. The Senate uses one nonlegislative calendar; this is used for treaties and nominations. (See EXECUTIVE CALENDAR.)

CALENDAR WEDNESDAY. In the House, committees, on Wednesdays, may be called in the order in which they appear in Rule X of the House, for the purpose of bringing up any bills from either the House or the Union Calendar, except bills that are privileged. General debate is limited to two hours. Bills called up from the Union Calendar are considered in Committee of the Whole. Calendar Wednesday is not observed during the last two weeks of a session and may be dispensed with at other times by a two-thirds vote. This procedure is rarely used and routinely is dispensed with by unanimous consent.

CALL OF THE CALENDAR. Senate bills that are not brought up for debate by a motion, unanimous consent, or a unanimous consent agreement are brought before the Senate for action when the calendar listing them is "called." Bills must be called in the order listed. Measures considered by this method usually are noncontroversial, and debate is limited to a total of five minutes for each senator on the bill and any amendments proposed to it.

CLEAN BILL. Frequently after a committee has finished a major revision of a bill, one of the committee members, usually the chairman, will assemble the changes and what is left of the original bill into a new measure and introduce it as a "clean bill." The revised measure, which is given a new number, then is referred back to the committee, which reports it to the floor for consideration. This often is a timesaver, as committee-recommended changes in a clean bill do not have to be considered and voted on by the chamber. Reporting a clean bill also protects committee amendments that might be subject to points of order concerning germaneness.

CLOTURE. The process by which a filibuster can be ended in the Senate other than by unanimous consent. A motion for cloture can apply to any measure before the Senate, including a proposal to change the chamber's rules. A cloture motion requires the signatures of sixteen senators to be introduced, and to end a filibuster the cloture motion must obtain the votes of three-fifths of the entire Senate membership (sixty if there are no vacancies), except that to end a filibuster against a proposal to amend the standing rules of the Senate a two-thirds vote of senators present and voting is required. The cloture request is put to a roll-call vote one hour after the Senate meets on the second day following introduction of the motion. If approved, cloture limits each senator to one hour of debate. The bill or amendment in question comes to a final vote after thirty hours of consideration (including debate time and the time it takes to conduct roll calls, quorum calls, and other procedural motions). (See FILIBUSTER.)

COMMITTEE. A division of the House or Senate that prepares legislation for action by the parent chamber or makes investigations as directed by the parent chamber. Most standing committees are divided into subcommittees, which study legislation, hold hearings, and report bills, with or without amendments, to the full committee. Only the full committee can report legislation to the House or Senate.

COMMITTEE OF THE WHOLE. The working title of what is formally "The Committee of the Whole House [of Representatives] on the State of the Union." The membership is comprised of all House members sitting as a committee. Any one hundred members who are present on the floor of the chamber comprise a quorum of the committee. Any legislation, however, must first have passed through the regular legislative committee or the Appropriations Committee and have been placed on the calendar before it can be heard by the Committee of the Whole.

Technically, the Committee of the Whole considers only bills directly or indirectly appropriating money, authorizing appropriations, or involving taxes or charges on the public. Because the Committee of the Whole need number only one hundred representatives, a quorum is more readily attained, and legislative business is expedited. Before 1971, members' positions were not individually recorded on votes taken in Committee of the Whole.

When the full House resolves itself into the Committee of the Whole, it supplants the Speaker with a "chairman." A measure is debated and amendments may be proposed, with votes on amendments as needed. When the committee completes its work on the measure, it dissolves itself by "rising." The Speaker returns, and the chairman of the Committee of the Whole reports to the House that the committee's work has been completed. At this time members may demand a roll-call vote on any amendment adopted in the Committee of the Whole. The final vote is on passage of the legislation.

CONCURRENT RESOLUTION. A concurrent resolution, designated H Con Res or S Con Res, must be adopted by both houses, but it is not sent to the president for his signature and therefore does not have the force of law. A concurrent resolution, for example, is used to fix the time for adjournment of a Congress. It also is used as the vehicle for expressing the sense of Congress on various foreign policy and domestic issues, and it serves as the vehicle for coordinated decisions on the federal budget under the 1974 Congressional Budget and Impoundment Control Act. (See also BILLS, JOINT RESOLUTION, RESOLUTION.)

CONFERENCE. A meeting between representatives of the House and the Senate to reconcile differences when each chamber passes dissimilar versions of the same bill. Members of the conference committee are appointed formally by the Speaker and the presiding officer of the Senate and are called "managers" for their respective chambers.

A majority of the managers for each house must reach agreement on the provisions of the bill (usually a compromise between the versions of the two chambers) before it can be considered by either chamber in the form of a "conference report." When the conference report goes to the floor, it cannot be amended, and, if it is not approved by both chambers, the bill may go back to conference or a new conference may be convened. Informal practices largely govern the conduct of conference committees.

Bills that are passed by both houses with only minor differences need not be sent to conference. Either chamber may "concur" in the other's amendments, completing action on the legislation. Sometimes leaders of the committees of jurisdiction work out an informal compromise instead of having a formal conference.

CONSENT CALENDAR. Members of the House may place on this calendar most bills on the Union or House Calendar that are considered to be noncontroversial. Bills on the Consent Calendar normally are called on the first and third Mondays of each month. On the first occasion that a bill is called in this manner, consideration may be blocked by the objection of any member. The second time, if there are three objections, the bill is stricken from the Consent Calendar. If less than three members object, the bill is given immediate consideration.

A bill on the Consent Calendar may be postponed in another way. A member may ask that the measure be passed over "without prejudice." In that case, no objection is recorded against the bill, and its status on the Consent Calendar remains unchanged. A bill stricken from the Consent Calendar remains on the Union or House Calendar.

CONTINUING RESOLUTION. A joint resolution drafted by Congress that continues appropriations for specific ongoing activities of a government department or departments when a fiscal year begins and Congress has not yet enacted all of the regular appropriations bills for that year. The continuing resolution usually specifies a maximum rate at which the agency may incur obligations. This usually is based on the rate for the previous year, the president's budget request, or an appropriation bill for that year passed by either or both houses of Congress, but not cleared.

CONTRACT AUTHORITY. Budget authority contained in an authorization bill that permits the federal government to enter into contracts or other obligations for future payments from funds not yet appropriated by Congress. The assumption is that funds will be available for payment in a subsequent appropriations act.

DILATORY MOTION. A motion made for the purpose of killing time and preventing action on a bill or amendment. House rules outlaw dilatory motions, but enforcement is largely within the discretion of the Speaker or chairman of the Committee of the Whole. The Senate does not have a rule banning dilatory motions, except under cloture.

DISCHARGE A COMMITTEE. Occasionally, attempts are made to relieve a committee from jurisdiction over a measure before it. This is attempted more often in the House than in the Senate, and the procedure rarely is successful.

In the House, if a committee does not report a bill within thirty days after the measure is referred to it, any member may file a discharge motion. Once offered the motion is treated as a petition needing the signatures of 218 members (a majority of the House). After the required signatures have been obtained, there is a delay of seven days. Thereafter, on the second and fourth Mondays of each month, except during the last six days of a session, any member who has signed the petition must be recognized, if he so desires, to move that the committee be discharged. Debate on the motion to discharge is limited to twenty minutes, and, if the motion is carried, consideration of the bill becomes a matter of high privilege.

If a resolution to consider a bill is held up in the Rules Committee for more than seven legislative days, any member may enter a motion to discharge the committee. The motion is handled like any other discharge petition in the House. (Senate Procedure, see DISCHARGE RESOLUTION.)

DISCHARGE CALENDAR. The House calendar to which motions to discharge committees are referred when they have the required number of signatures (218) and are awaiting floor action.

DISCHARGE PETITION. (See DISCHARGE A COMMITTEE.)

DISCHARGE RESOLUTION. In the Senate, a special motion that any senator may introduce to relieve a committee from consideration of a bill before it. The resolution can be called up for Senate approval or disapproval in the same manner as any other Senate business. (House Procedure, see DISCHARGE A COMMITTEE.)

DIVISION VOTE. (See STANDING VOTE.)

ENACTING CLAUSE. Key phrase in bills beginning, "Be it enacted by the Senate and House of Representatives. . . ." A successful motion to strike it from legislation kills the measure.

ENGROSSED BILL. The final copy of a bill as passed by one chamber, with the text as amended by floor action and certified by the clerk of the House or the secretary of the Senate.

ENROLLED BILL. The final copy of a bill that has been passed in identical form by both chambers. It is certified by an officer of the house of origin (clerk of the House or secretary of the Senate) and then sent on for the signatures of the House Speaker, the Senate president pro tempore, and the president of the United States. An enrolled bill is printed on parchment.

EXECUTIVE CALENDAR. This is a nonlegislative calendar in the Senate on which presidential documents such as treaties and nominations are listed.

EXECUTIVE SESSION. A meeting of a Senate or House committee (or occasionally of either chamber) that only its members may attend. Witnesses regularly appear at committee meetings in executive session—for example, Defense Department officials during presentations of classified defense information. The public and press are not allowed to attend.

EXPENDITURES. The actual spending of money as distinguished from the appropriation of funds. Expenditures are made by the executive branch; appropriations are made only by Congress. The two rarely are identical in any fiscal year. In addition to some current budget authority, expenditures may represent budget authority made available one, two, or more years earlier.

FILIBUSTER. A time-delaying tactic associated with the Senate and used by a minority in an effort to prevent a vote on a bill or amendment that probably would pass if voted upon directly. The most common method is to take advantage of the Senate's rules permitting unlimited debate, but other forms of parliamentary maneuvering may be used. The stricter rules used by the House make filibusters more difficult, but delaying tactics are employed occasionally through various procedural devices allowed by House rules. (See CLOTURE.)

FIVE-MINUTE RULE. A debate-limiting rule of the House that is invoked when the House sits as the Committee of the Whole. Under the rule, a member offering an amendment is allowed to speak five minutes in its favor, and an opponent of the amendment is allowed to speak five minutes in opposition. Debate is then closed. In practice, amendments regularly are debated more than ten minutes, with members gaining the floor by offering pro forma amendments or obtaining unanimous consent to speak longer than five minutes. (See STRIKE OUT THE LAST WORD.)

GERMANE. Pertaining to the subject matter of the legislation at hand. House amendments must be germane to the bill being considered. The Senate requires that amendments be germane when they are proposed to general appropriation bills, bills being considered once cloture has been adopted, or, frequently, when proceeding under a unanimous consent agreement placing a time limit on consideration of a bill. The 1974 budget act also requires that amendments to concurrent budget resolutions be germane. In the House, floor debate must be germane, and the first three hours of debate each day in the Senate must be germane to the pending business.

HOUSE CALENDAR. A listing for action by the House of public bills that do not directly or indirectly appropriate money or raise revenue.

JOINT RESOLUTION. A joint resolution, designated H J Res or S J Res, requires the approval of both houses and the signature of the president, just as a bill does, and has the force of law if approved. There is no practical difference between a bill and a joint resolution.

A joint resolution generally is used to deal with a limited matter such as a single appropriation.

Joint resolutions also are used to propose amendments to the Constitution in Congress. They do not require a presidential signature, but become a part of the Constitution when three-fourths of the states have ratified them.

LAW. An act of Congress that has been signed by the president or passed over his veto by Congress. Public bills, when signed, become public laws, and are cited by the letters PL and a hyphenated number. The two digits before the number correspond to the Congress, and the one or more digits after the hyphen refer to the numerical sequence in which the bills were signed by the president during that Congress. Private bills, when signed, become private laws.

LEGISLATIVE DAY. The "day" extending from the time either house meets after an adjournment until the time it next adjourns. Because the House normally adjourns from day to day, legislative days and calendar days usually coincide. But in the Senate, a legislative day may, and frequently does, extend over several calendar days. (See RECESS.)

LEGISLATIVE VETO. A procedure permitting either the House or Senate, or both chambers, to review proposed executive branch regulations or actions and to block or modify those with which they disagree. The specifics of the procedure may vary, but Congress generally provides for a legislative veto by including in a bill a provision that administrative rules or action taken to implement the law are to go into effect at the end of a designated period of time unless blocked by either or both houses (even committees) of Congress. Another version of the veto provides for congressional reconsideration and rejection of regulations already in effect. The Supreme Court on June 23, 1983, restricted the form and use of the legislative veto, ruling that it is an unconstitutional violation of the lawmaking procedure provided in the Constitution.

MAJORITY LEADER. The majority leader is elected by members of the majority party. In the Senate, in consultation with the minority leader and other senators, the majority leader directs the legislative schedule and serves as party spokesperson and chief strategist. In the House, the majority leader is second to the Speaker in the majority party's leadership and serves as the party's legislative strategist.

MAJORITY WHIP. In effect, the assistant majority leader in either the House or Senate. The majority whip helps marshal majority forces in support of party strategy and legislation.

MARKING UP A BILL. Going through the contents of a piece of legislation in committee or subcommittee, considering its provisions in large and small portions, acting on amendments to provisions and proposed revisions to the language, inserting new sections and phraseology, etc. If the bill is extensively amended, the committee's version may be introduced as a separate bill, with a new number, before being considered by the full House or Senate. (See CLEAN BILL.)

MINORITY LEADER. Floor leader for the minority party in each chamber.

MINORITY WHIP. Performs duties of whip for the minority party.

MORNING HOUR. The time set aside at the beginning of each legislative day for the consideration of regular, routine business. In the Senate it is the first two hours of a session following an adjournment, as distingusihed from a recess. The morning hour can be terminated earlier if the morning business has been completed.

Business includes such matters as messages from the president, communications from the heads of departments, messages from the House, the presentation of petitions, reports of standing and select committees, and the introduction of bills and resolutions.

During the first hour of the morning hour in the Senate, no motion to proceed to the consideration of any bill on the calendar is in order except by unanimous consent. During the second hour, motions can be made but must be decided without debate. Senate committees may meet while the Senate conducts morning hour.

MOTION. In the House or Senate chamber, a request by a member to institute any one of a wide array of parliamentary actions. A member "moves" for a certain procedure, the consideration of a measure, etc. The precedence of motions, and whether they are debatable, is set forth in the House and Senate manuals.

ONE-MINUTE SPEECHES. Addresses by House members at the beginning of a legislative day. The speeches may cover any subject, but are limited to one minute's duration.

OVERRIDE A VETO. If the president disapproves a bill and sends it back to Congress with his objections, Congress may try to override his veto and enact the bill into law. Neither house is required to attempt to override a veto. The override of a veto requires a recorded vote with a two-thirds majority in each chamber. The question put to each house is: "Shall the bill pass, the objections of the president to the contrary notwithstanding?" (See also POCKET VETO, VETO.)

PAIR. A voluntary arrangement between two lawmakers, usually on opposite sides of an issue. If passage of the measure requires a two-thirds majority vote, a pair would require two members favoring the action to one opposed to it. The names of lawmakers pairing on a given vote and their stands, if known, are printed in the *Congressional Record*.

POCKET VETO. The act of the president in withholding approval of a bill after Congress has adjourned. When Congress is in session, a bill becomes law without the president's signature if the president does not act upon it within ten days, excluding Sundays, of receiving it. But if Congress adjourns *sine die* within that ten-day period, the bill will die even if the president does not formally veto it. The Supreme Court in 1986 agreed to decide whether the president can pocket veto a bill during recesses and between sessions of the same Congress or only between Congresses. The justices in 1987 declared the case moot, however, because the bill in question was invalid once the case reached the Court. (See also VETO.)

POINT OF ORDER. An objection raised by a member that the chamber is departing from rules governing its conduct of business. The objector cites the rule violated, and the chair sustains the objection if correctly made. Order is restored by the chair's suspending proceedings of the chamber until it conforms to the prescribed order of business.

PRESIDENT OF THE SENATE. Under the Constitution, the vice president of the United States presides over the Senate. In the vice president's absence, the president pro tempore, or a senator designated by the president pro tempore, presides over the chamber.

PRESIDENT PRO TEMPORE. The chief officer of the Senate in the absence of the vice president; literally, but loosely, the president for a time. The president pro tempore is elected by the full membership of the Senate, and the recent practice has been to choose the senator of the majority party with the longest period of continuous service.

PREVIOUS QUESTION. A motion for the previous question, when carried, has the effect of cutting off all debate, preventing the offering of further amendments, and forcing a vote on the pending matter. In the House, the previous question is not permitted in the Committee of the Whole. The motion for the previous question is a debate-limiting device and is not in order in the Senate.

PRINTED AMENDMENT. A House rule guarantees five minutes of floor debate in support of, and five minutes in opposition to, amendments printed in the *Congressional Record* at least one day prior to the amendment's consideration in the Committee of the Whole. In the Senate, while amendments may be submitted for printing, they have no parliamentary standing or status. An amendment submitted for printing in the Senate, however, may be called up by any senator.

PRIVATE CALENDAR. In the House, private bills dealing with individual matters such as claims against the government, immigration, land titles, etc., are put on this calendar. The private calendar must be called on the first Tuesday of each month, and the Speaker may call it on the third Tuesday of each month as well.

When a private bill is before the chamber, two members may block its consideration, which recommits the bill to committee. Backers of a recommitted private bill have recourse.

The measure can be put into an omnibus claims bill—several private bills rolled into one. As with any bill, no part of an omnibus claims bill may be deleted without a vote.

PRIVILEGE. Privilege relates to the rights of members of Congress and to the relative priority of the motions and actions they may make in their respective chambers. The two are distinct. "Privileged questions" deal with legislative business. "Questions of privilege" concern members themselves.

PRIVILEGED QUESTIONS. The order in which bills, motions, and other legislative measures are considered by Congress is governed by strict priorities. A motion to table, for instance, is more privileged than a motion to recommit. Thus, a motion to recommit can be superseded by a motion to table, and a vote would be forced on the latter motion only. A motion to adjourn, however, takes precedence over a tabling motion and thus is considered of the "highest privilege." (See also QUESTIONS OF PRIVILEGE.)

PRO FORMA AMENDMENT. (See STRIKE OUT THE LAST WORD.)

QUESTIONS OF PRIVILEGE. These are matters affecting members of Congress individually or collectively. Matters affecting the rights, safety, dignity, and integrity of proceedings of the House or Senate as a whole are questions of privilege in both chambers.

Questions involving individual members are called questions of "personal privilege." A member rising to ask a question of personal privilege is given precedence over almost all other proceedings. An annotation in the House rules points out that the privilege is derived chiefly from the Constitution, which gives a member a conditional immunity from arrest and an unconditional freedom to speak in the House. (See also PRIVILEGED QUESTIONS.)

QUORUM. The number of members whose presence is necessary for the transaction of business. In the Senate and House, it is a majority of the membership. A quorum is one hundred in the Committee of the Whole House. If a point of order is made that a quorum is not present, the only business that is in order is either a motion to adjourn or a motion to direct the sergeant-at-arms to request the attendance of absentees.

READINGS OF BILLS. Traditional parliamentary procedure required bills to be read three times before they were passed. This custom is of little modern significance. Normally a bill is considered to have its first reading when it is introduced and printed, by title, in the *Congressional Record*. In the House, its second reading comes when floor consideration begins. (This is the most likely point at which there is an actual reading of the bill, if there is any.) The second reading in the Senate is supposed to occur on the legislative day after the measure is introduced, but before it is referred to committee. The third reading (again, usually by title) takes place when floor action has been completed on amendments.

RECESS. Distinguished from adjournment in that a recess does not end a legislative day and therefore does not interrupt unfinished business. The rules in each house set forth certain matters to be taken up and disposed of at the beginning of each legislative day. The House usually adjourns from day to day. The Senate often recesses, thus meeting on the same legislative day for several calendar days or even weeks at a time. (See ADJOURNMENT.)

RECOGNITION. The power of recognition of a member is lodged in the Speaker of the House and the presiding officer of the Senate. The presiding officer names the member who will speak first when two or more members simultaneously request recognition.

RECOMMIT TO COMMITTEE. A motion, made on the floor after a bill has been debated, to return it to the committee that reported it. If approved, recommittal usually is considered a death blow to the bill. In the House, a motion to recommit can be made only by a member opposed to the bill, and, in recognizing a member to make the motion, the Speaker gives preference to members of the minority party over majority party members.

A motion to recommit may include instructions to the committee to report the bill again with specific amendments or by a certain date. Or, the instructions may direct that a particular study be made, with no definite deadline for further action. If the recommittal motion includes instructions to "report the bill back forthwith" and the motion is adopted, floor action on the bill continues; the committee does not actually reconsider the legislation.

RECONSIDER A VOTE. A motion to reconsider the vote by which an action was taken has, until it is disposed of, the effect of putting the action in abeyance. In the Senate, the motion can be made only by a member who voted on the prevailing side of the original question or by a member who did not vote at all. In the House, it can be made only by a member on the prevailing side.

A common practice in the Senate after close votes on an issue is a motion to reconsider, followed by a motion to table the motion to reconsider. On this motion to table, senators usually vote as they voted on the original question, which allows the motion to table to prevail, assuming there are no switches. The matter then is finally closed and further motions to reconsider are not entertained. In the House, as a routine precaution, a motion to reconsider usually is made every time a measure is passed. Such a motion almost always is tabled immediately, thus shutting off the possibility of future reconsideration, except by unanimous consent. Motions to reconsider must be entered in the Senate within the next two days of actual session after the original vote has been taken. In the House they must be entered either on the same day or on the next succeeding day the House is in session.

RECORDED VOTE. A vote upon which each member's stand is individually made known. In the Senate, this is accomplished through a roll call of the entire membership, to which each senator on the floor must answer "yea," "nay" or, if he does not wish to vote, "present." Since January 1973, the House has used an electronic voting system for recorded votes, including yea-and-nay votes formerly taken by roll calls. When not required by the Constitution, a recorded vote can be obtained on questions in the House on the demand of one-fifth (forty-four members) of a quorum or one-fourth (twenty-five members) of a quorum in the Committee of the Whole. (See YEAS AND NAYS.)

REPORT. Both a verb and a noun as a congressional term. A committee that has been examining a bill referred to it by the parent chamber "reports" its findings and recommendations to the chamber when it completes consideration and returns the measure. The process is called "reporting" a bill.

A "report" is the document setting forth the committee's explanation of its action. Senate and House reports are numbered separately and are designated S Rept or H Rept. When a committee report is not unanimous, the dissenting committee members may file a statement of their views, called minority views and referred to as a minority report. Members in disagreement with some provisions of a bill may file additional or supplementary views. Sometimes a bill is reported without a committee recommendation. Adverse reports occasionally are submitted by legislative committees. When a committee is opposed to a bill, it usually fails to report the measure at all. Some laws require that committee reports, favorable or adverse, be made.

RESCISSION BILL. A bill rescinding or canceling budget authority previously made available by Congress. The president may request a rescission to reduce spending or because the budget authority no longer is needed. Under the 1974 budget act, unless Congress approves a rescission within forty-five days of continuous session after receipt of the proposal, the funds must be made available for obligation.

RESOLUTION. A "simple" resolution, designated H Res or S Res, deals with matters entirely within the prerogatives of one house or the other. It requires neither passage by the other chamber nor approval by the president, and it does not have the force of law. Most resolutions deal with the rules or procedures of one house. They also are used to express the sentiments of a single house, such as condolences to the family of a deceased member, or to comment on foreign policy or executive business. A simple resolution is the vehicle for a "rule" from the House Rules Committee. (See also CONCURRENT RESOLUTION, JOINT RESOLUTION, RULES.)

RIDER. An amendment, usually not germane, which its sponsor hopes to get through more easily by including it in other legislation. Riders become law if the bills embodying them are enacted. Amendments providing legislative directives in appropriations bills are outstanding examples of riders, though technically legislation is banned from appropriations bills. The House, unlike the Senate, has a strict germaneness rule; thus, riders usually are Senate devices to get legislation enacted quickly or to bypass lengthy House consideration and, possibly, opposition.

RULES. The term has two specific congressional meanings. A rule may be a standing order governing the conduct of House or Senate business and listed among the permanent rules of either chamber. The rules deal with duties of officers, the order of business, admission to the floor, parliamentary procedures on handling amendments and voting, jurisdictions of committees, etc.

In the House, a rule also may be a resolution reported by the Rules Committee to govern the handling of a particular bill on the floor. The committee may report a "rule," also called a "special order," in the form of a simple resolution. If the resolution is adopted by the House, the temporary rule becomes as valid as any standing rule and lapses only after action has been completed on the measure to which it pertains. A rule sets the time limit on general debate. It also may waive points of order against provisions of the bill in question, such as nongermane language, or against certain amendments intended to be proposed to the bill from the floor. It may even forbid all amendments or all amendments except those proposed by the legislative committee that handled the bill. In this instance, it is known as a "closed" or "gag" rule as opposed to an "open" rule, which puts no limitation on floor amendments, thus leaving the bill completely open to alteration by the adoption of germane amendments.

SENATORIAL COURTESY. Sometimes referred to as "the courtesy of the Senate," it is a general practice—with no written rule—applied to consideration of executive nominations. Generally, it means that nominations from a state are not to be confirmed unless they have been approved by the senators of the president's party of that state, with other senators following their colleagues' lead in the attitude they take toward consideration of such nominations.

SEQUESTRATION. The cancellation (or withholding) of budgetary resources pursuant to the Gramm-Rudman-Hollings Act. Once cancelled sequestered funds are no longer available for obligation or expenditure.

SPEAKER. The presiding officer of the House of Representatives and the overall leader of the majority party in the chamber. The Speaker is selected by the caucus of the majority party's members and formally elected by the full House at the beginning of each new congress.

STANDING COMMITTEES. (See COMMITTEES.)

STANDING VOTE. A nonrecorded vote used in both the House and the Senate. (A standing vote also is called a division vote.) Members in favor of a proposal stand and are counted by the presiding officer. Then members opposed stand and are counted. There is no record of how individual members voted.

STRIKE FROM THE RECORD. Remarks made on the House floor may offend some member, who moves that the offending words be "taken down" for the Speaker's cognizance, and then expunged from the debate as published in the *Congressional Record.*

STRIKE OUT THE LAST WORD. A motion whereby a House member is entitled to speak for five minutes on an amendment then being debated by the chamber. A member gains recognition from the chair by moving to "strike out the last word" of the amendment or section of the bill under consideration. The motion is pro forma, requires no vote and does not change the amendment being debated.

SUBSTITUTE. A motion, amendment, or entire bill introduced in place of the pending legislative business. Passage of a substitute measure kills the original measure by supplanting it. The substitute also may be amended. (See also AMENDMENT IN THE NATURE OF A SUBSTITUTE.)

SUPPLEMENTAL APPROPRIATIONS BILL. Legislation appropriating funds after the regular annual appropriations bill for a federal department or agency has been enacted. A supplemental appropriation provides additional budget authority beyond original estimates for programs or activities, including new programs authorized after the enactment of the regular appropriations act. (See also APPROPRIATIONS BILL.)

SUSPEND THE RULES. Often a time-saving procedure for passing bills in the House. The wording of the motion, which may be made by any member recognized by the Speaker, is: "I move to suspend the rules and pass the bill. . . ." A favorable vote by two-thirds of those present is required for passage. Debate is limited to forty minutes and no amendments from the floor are permitted. If a two-thirds favorable vote is not attained, the bill may be considered later under regular procedures. The suspension procedure is in order every Monday and Tuesday and is intended to be reserved for noncontroversial bills.

TABLE A BILL. A motion to "lay on the table" is not debatable in either house, and usually it is a method of making a final, adverse disposition of a matter. In the Senate, however, different language sometimes is used. The motion may be worded to let a bill "lie on the table," perhaps for subsequent "picking up." This motion is more flexible, keeping the bill pending for later action, if desired. Tabling motions on amendments are effective debate-ending devices in the Senate.

TELLER VOTE. This is a largely moribund House procedure in the Committee of the Whole. Members file past tellers and are counted as for, or against, a measure, but they are not recorded individually. In the House, tellers are ordered upon demand of one-fifth of a quorum (forty-four members in the House, twenty members in the Committee of the Whole). The House also has a recorded teller vote, now largely supplanted by the electronic voting procedure. (See RECORDED VOTE.)

TREATIES. Executive proposals—in the form of resolutions of ratification—which must be submitted to the Senate for approval by two-thirds of the senators present. Treaties today are normally sent to the Foreign Relations Committee for scrutiny before the Senate takes action. Foreign Relations has jurisdiction over all treaties, regardless of the subject matter. Treaties are read three times and debated on the floor in much the same manner as legislative proposals. After approval by the Senate, treaties are formally ratified by the president. Unlike legislative documents, however, treaties do not die at the end of a Congress but remain "live" proposals until acted on by the Senate or withdrawn by the president.

UNANIMOUS CONSENT. Proceedings of the House or Senate and action on legislation often take place upon the unanimous consent of the chamber, whether or not a rule of the chamber is being violated.

Unanimous consent is used to expedite floor action and frequently is used in a routine fashion, for example, when a senator requests the unanimous consent of the Senate to have specified members of his staff present on the floor during debate on an amendment.

UNANIMOUS CONSENT AGREEMENT. A device used in the Senate to expedite legislation. Much of the Senate's legislative business, dealing with both minor and controversial issues, is conducted through unanimous consent or unanimous consent agreements. On major legislation, such agreements usually are printed and transmitted to all senators in advance of floor debate. Once agreed to, they are binding on all members unless the Senate, by unanimous consent, agrees to modify them. An agreement may list the order in which various bills are to be considered, specify the length of time bills and contested amendments are to be debated and when they are to be voted upon, and, frequently, require that all amendments introduced be germane to the bill under consideration. In this regard, unanimous consent agreements are similar to the rules issued by the House Rules Committee for bills pending in the House. (See RULES.)

UNION CALENDAR. Bills that directly or indirectly appropriate money or raise revenue are placed on this House calendar according to the date they are reported from committee.

VETO. Disapproval by the president of a bill or joint resolution (other than one proposing an amendment to the Constitution). When Congress is in session, the president must veto a bill within ten days, excluding Sundays, of receiving it; otherwise, the bill becomes law without the president's signature. When the president vetoes a bill, it must be returned to the house of origin with a message stating the president's objections. (See also POCKET VETO, OVERRIDE A VETO.)

VOICE VOTE. In either the House or Senate, members answer "aye" or "no" in chorus, and the presiding officer decides the result. The term also is used loosely to indicate action by unanimous consent or without objection.

YEAS AND NAYS. The Constitution requires that yea-and-nay votes be taken and recorded when requested by one-fifth of the members present. In the House, the Speaker determines whether one-fifth of the members present requested a vote. In the Senate, practice requires only eleven members. The Constitution requires the yeas and nays on a veto override attempt. (See RECORDED VOTE.)

YIELDING. When a member has been recognized to speak, no other member may speak without permission from the member recognized. This permission is called yielding and usually is requested in the form, "Will the gentleman yield to me?" While this activity occasionally is seen in the Senate, the Senate has no rule or practice to parcel out time, other than in unanimous consent agreements.

Selected Bibliography

CHAPTER 1. CONGRESS AND LAWMAKING

Berman, Daniel M. *In Congress Assembled.* New York: Macmillan, 1964.

Bibby, John, and Davidson, Roger H. *On Capitol Hill.* 2d ed. Hinsdale, Ill.: The Dryden Press, 1972.

Burnham, James. *Congress and the American Tradition.* Chicago: Henry Regnery, 1959.

Davidson, Roger H., and Oleszek, Walter J. *Congress and Its Members.* 2d ed. Washington, D.C.: CQ Press, 1985.

Galloway, George B. *The Legislative Process in Congress.* New York: Thomas Y. Crowell, 1953.

Goehlert, Robert U., and Sayre, John R. *The United States Congress: A Bibliography.* New York: The Free Press, 1982.

Gross, Bertram M. *The Legislative Struggle.* New York: McGraw-Hill, 1953.

Jones, Charles O. *The United States Congress.* Homewood, Ill.: The Dorsey Press, 1982.

Kozak, David C., and Macartney, John D., eds. *Congress and Public Policy.* 2d ed. Homewood, Ill.: The Dorsey Press, 1987.

Luce, Robert. *Legislative Procedures.* Boston: Houghton Mifflin, 1922.

_____. *Legislative Assemblies.* Boston: Houghton Mifflin, 1924.

_____. *Legislative Principles.* Boston: Houghton Mifflin, 1930.

_____. *Legislative Problems.* Boston: Houghton Mifflin, 1935.

McCubbins, Mathew D., and Sullivan, Terry, eds. *Congress: Structure and Policy.* Cambridge: Cambridge University Press, 1987.

Orfield, Gary. *Congressional Power.* New York: Harcourt Brace Jovanovich, 1975.

Parker, Glenn R., ed. *Studies of Congress.* Washington, D.C.: CQ Press, 1985.

Ripley, Randall B. *Congress: Process and Policy.* 3d ed. New York: W. W. Norton, 1983.

Vogler, David. *The Politics of Congress.* 5th ed. Boston: Allyn & Bacon, 1988.

CHAPTER 2. THE CONGRESSIONAL ENVIRONMENT

Baker, Ross K. *Friend and Foe in the U.S. Senate.* New York: The Free Press, 1980.

Bauer, Raymond, et al. *American Business and Public Policy: The Politics of Foreign Trade.* New York: Atherton Press, 1963.

Blanchard, Robert O., ed. *Congress and the News Media.* New York: Hastings House, 1974.

Bolling, Richard. *House Out of Order.* New York: E. P. Dutton, 1965.

____. *Power in the House.* New York: E. P. Dutton, 1968.

Chamberlain, Lawrence H. *The President, Congress and Legislation.* New York: Columbia University Press, 1946.

Cigler, Allan J., and Loomis, Burdett A., eds. *Interest Group Politics.* 2d ed. Washington, D.C.: CQ Press, 1986.

Cook, Timothy E. "House Members as Newsmakers: The Effects of Televising Congress." *Legislative Studies Quarterly,* May 1986, 223-226.

Cooper, Joseph, and Mackenzie, G. Calvin, eds. *The House at Work.* Austin: University of Texas Press, 1981.

Davidson, Roger H., et al. *Congress in Crisis: Politics and Congressional Reform.* Belmont, Calif.: Wadsworth, 1966.

Dodd, Lawrence C., and Oppenheimer, Bruce I., eds. *Congress Reconsidered.* 3d ed. Washington, D.C.: CQ Press, 1985.

Edwards, George C., III. *Presidential Influence in Congress.* San Francisco: W. H. Freeman, 1980.

Fenno, Richard F., Jr. *Home Style: House Members in Their Districts.* Boston: Little, Brown & Co., 1978.

Hasbrouck, Paul. *Party Government in the House of Representatives.* New York: Macmillan, 1927.

Hechler, Kenneth W. *Insurgency.* New York: Columbia University Press, 1940.

Hess, Stephen. *The Ultimate Insiders: U.S. Senators in the National Media.* Washington, D.C.: The Brookings Institution, 1986.

Hopkins, Bruce R. "Congressional Reform: Towards a Modern Congress." *Notre Dame Lawyer,* February 1972, 442-513.

Huitt, Ralph K. "Democratic Party Leadership in the Senate." *American Political Science Review,* June 1961, 333-344.

Jacobson, Gary C. *The Politics of Congressional Elections.* Boston: Little, Brown & Co., 1983.

Johannes, John. *To Serve the People: Congress and Constituency Service.* Lincoln: University of Nebraska Press, 1984.

Jones, Charles O. *The Minority Party in Congress.* Boston: Little, Brown & Co., 1970.

King, Anthony, ed. *Both Ends of the Avenue: The Presidency, the Executive Branch, and Congress in the 1980s.* Washington, D.C.: The American Enterprise Institute for Public Policy Research, 1983.

Moe, Ronald, and Teel, Stephen. "Congress as Policy-Maker: A Necessary Reappraisal." *Political Science Quarterly,* September 1970, 443-470.

Ornstein, Norman J., ed. *Congress in Change.* New York: Praeger, 1975.

——, and Mann, Thomas E., eds. *The New Congress.* Washington, D.C.: The American Enterprise Institute for Public Policy Research, 1981.

Peabody, Robert L. *Leadership in Congress.* Boston: Little, Brown & Co., 1976.

Plattner, Andy. "The Lure of the Senate." *Congressional Quarterly Weekly Report,* May 25, 1985, 991-998.

Price, David. *Who Makes the Laws?* Cambridge, Mass.: Schenkman, 1972.

Ripley, Randall B. *Majority Party Leadership in Congress.* Boston: Little, Brown & Co., 1969.

Sabato, Larry J. *PAC Power.* New York: W. W. Norton, 1984.

Schlozman, Kay Lehman, and Tierney, John T. "More of the Same: Washington Pressure Group Activity in a Decade of Change." *Journal of Politics,* May 1983, 351-377.

Starobin, Paul. "Pork: A Time-Honored Tradition Lives On." *Congressional Quarterly Weekly Report,* October 24, 1987, 2581-2594.

Wayne, Stephen. *The Legislative Presidency.* New York: Harper & Row, 1978.

CHAPTER 3. CONGRESSIONAL BUDGET PROCESS

Ellwood, John William. "Congress Cuts the Budget: The Omnibus Reconciliation Act of 1981." *Public Budgeting and Finance,* Spring 1982, 50-64.

Fenno, Richard F., Jr. *The Power of the Purse.* Boston: Little, Brown & Co., 1966.

Fisher, Louis. "Annual Authorizations: Durable Roadblocks to Biennial Budgeting." *Public Budgeting and Finance,* Spring 1983, 23-40.

——. "The Authorization-Appropriation Process in Congress: Formal Rules and Informal Practices." *Catholic University Law Review,* Fall 1979, 51-105.

Haas, Lawrence J. "Unauthorized Action." *National Journal,* January 2, 1988, 17-21.

Hartman, Robert W. "Congress and Budget-Making." *Political Science Quarterly*, Fall 1982, 381-402.

Keith, Robert A. "Budget Reconciliation in 1981." *Public Budgeting and Finance*, Winter 1981, 37-47.

Havemann, Joel. *Congress and the Budget.* Bloomington: Indiana University Press, 1978.

Ippolito, Dennis S. *Congressional Spending.* Ithaca, N.Y.: Cornell University Press, 1981.

LeLoup, Lance T. *The Fiscal Congress.* Westport, Conn.: Greenwood Press, 1980.

____. "After the Blitz: Reagan and the U.S. Congressional Budget Process." *Legislative Studies Quarterly*, Winter 1981, 37-47.

Lindsay, James M. "Congress and the Defense Budget." *Washington Quarterly*, Winter 1988, 57-74.

Penner, Rudolph G., ed. *The Congressional Budget Process after Five Years.* Washington, D.C.: The American Enterprise Institute for Public Policy Research, 1981.

Rauch, Jonathan. "The Appropriators." *National Journal*, July 12, 1986, 1708-1712.

Rivlin, Alice. "The Need for a Better Budget Process." *The Brookings Review*, Summer 1986, 3-10.

Schick, Allen. *Congress and Money.* Washington, D.C.: The Urban Institute, 1980.

____. *Reconciliation and the Congressional Budget Process.* Washington, D.C.: The American Enterprise Institute for Public Policy Research, 1981.

____, ed. *Making Economic Policy in Congress.* Washington, D.C.: American Enterprise Institute for Public Policy Research, 1983.

Shuman, Howard. *Politics and the Budget.* 2d ed. (Englewood Cliffs, N.J.: Prentice Hall, 1988

Stockman, David. *The Triumph of Politics.* New York: Harper & Row, 1986.

Wander, Thomas W.; Hebert, F. Ted; and Copeland, Gary W., eds. *Congressional Budgeting.* Baltimore: Johns Hopkins University Press, 1984.

Wildavsky, Aaron. *The Politics of the Budgetary Process.* 4th ed. Boston: Little, Brown & Co., 1984.

Wilmerding, Lucius. *The Spending Power.* New Haven, Conn.: Yale University Press, 1943.

CHAPTER 4. PRELIMINARY LEGISLATIVE ACTION

Abram, Michael, and Cooper, Joseph. "The Rise of Seniority in the House of Representatives." *Polity*, Fall 1968, 35-51.

Bowsher, Prentice. "The Speaker's Man: Lewis Deschler, House Parliamentarian." *The Washington Monthly*, April 1970, 22-27.

Cooper, Joseph. *The Origins of the Standing Committees and the Development of the Modern House*. Rice University Monograph in Political Science, vol. 56, no. 3, Summer 1970.

Davidson, Roger H., and Oleszek, Walter J. *Congress against Itself*. Bloomington: Indiana University Press, 1977.

Davidson, Roger H.; Oleszek, Walter J.; and Kephart, Thomas. "One Bill, Many Committees: Multiple Referrals in the U.S. House of Representatives." *Legislative Studies Quarterly*, February 1988, 3-28.

Deering, Christopher J., and Smith, Steven S. *Committees in Congress*. Washington, D.C.: CQ Press, 1984.

Eckhardt, Bob. "The Presumption of Committee Openness Under House Rules." *Harvard Journal on Legislation*, February 1974, 279-302.

Fenno, Richard F., Jr. *Congressmen in Committees*. Boston: Little, Brown & Co., 1973.

Fox, Harrison W., Jr., and Hammond, Susan Webb. *Congressional Staffs*. New York: The Free Press, 1977.

Goodwin, George. *The Little Legislatures*. Amherst: University of Massachusetts Press, 1970.

Hook, Janet. "Parliamentarians: Procedure and Pyrotechnics." *Congressional Quarterly Weekly Report*, August 22, 1987, 1951-1954.

Kofmehl, Kenneth. *Professional Staffs of Congress*. 3d ed. West Lafayette, Ind.: Purdue University Press, 1977.

Kravitz, Walter. "Evolution of the Senate's Committee System." *The Annals*, January 1974, 27-38.

Malbin, Michael J. *Unelected Representatives: Congressional Staff and the Future of Representative Government*. New York: Basic Books, 1979.

Price, David E. "Professionals and 'Entrepreneurs': Staff Orientations and Policy Making on Three Senate Committees." *Journal of Politics*, May 1971, 313-336.

"Private Bills in Congress." *Harvard Law Review*, vol. 79, 1966, 1684-1706.

Shepsle, Kenneth A. *The Giant Jigsaw Puzzle: Democratic Committee Assignments in the Modern House*. Chicago: University of Chicago Press, 1978.

Sinclair, Barbara. "The Role of Committees in Agenda Setting in the U.S. Congress." *Legislative Studies Quarterly*, February 1986, 35-45.

Wilson, Woodrow. *Congressional Government*. Gloucester, Mass.: Peter Smith, 1885.

CHAPTER 5. SCHEDULING LEGISLATION IN THE HOUSE

"A History of the Committee on Rules." Committee Print, 97th Cong., 2d sess. Washington, D.C.: U.S. Government Printing Office, 1983.

Albert, Carl. *The Office and Duties of the Speaker of the House of Representatives.* H. Doc. No. 94-582, 94th Cong., 2d sess., 1976.

Brown, Lynne P., and Peabody, Robert L. "Dilemma of Party Leadership: Majority Whips in the U.S. House of Representatives, 1962-1982." *Congress & the Presidency,* Autumn 1984, 179-196.

Chiu, Chang Wei. *The Speaker of the House of Representatives since 1896.* New York: Columbia University Press, 1928.

Cooper, Joseph, and Brady, David W. "Institutional Context and Leadership Style: The House From Cannon to Rayburn." *American Political Science Review,* June 1981, 411-425.

Drew, Elizabeth. "A Tendency to Legislate." *New Yorker,* June 26, 1978, 80-89.

Froman, Lewis A., and Ripley, Randall B. "Conditions for Party Leadership: The Case of the House Democrats." *American Political Science Review,* March 1965, 52-63.

Hardeman, D. B., and Bacon, Donald C. *Rayburn.* Austin: Texas Monthly Press, 1987.

Jones, Charles O. "Joseph G. Cannon and Howard W. Smith: An Essay on the Limits of Leadership in the House of Representatives." *Journal of Politics,* September 1968, 617-646.

Mackaman, Frank H., ed. *Understanding Congressional Leadership.* Washington, D.C.: CQ Press, 1981.

Matsunaga, Spark M., and Chen, Ping. *Rulemakers of the House.* Urbana: University of Illinois Press, 1976.

O'Neill, Thomas P., Jr. *Man of the House.* New York: Random House, 1987.

Ripley, Randall B. "Party Whip Organizations in the United States House of Representatives." *American Political Science Review,* September 1964, 561-576.

"Scheduling the Work of the House." H. Doc. No. 95-23, 95th Cong., 1st sess. Jan. 4, 1977.

CHAPTER 6. HOUSE FLOOR PROCEDURE

Alexander, DeAlva Stanwood. *History and Procedure of the House of Representatives.* Boston: Houghton Mifflin, 1916.

Arieff, Irwin B. "House Floor Watchdog Role Made Famous by H. R. Gross Has Fallen on Hard Times." *Congressional Quarterly Weekly Report,* July 24, 1982, 1775-1776.

Bach, Stanley. "The Structure of Choice in the House of Representatives: The Impact of Complex Special Rules." *Harvard Journal on Legislation,* Summer 1981, 553-602.

_____. "Representatives and Committees on the Floor: Amendments to Appropriations Bills in the House of Representatives." *Legislative Studies Quarterly*, Spring 1986, 41-58.

Clausen, Aage R. *How Congressmen Decide.* New York: St. Martin's Press, 1973.

Damon, Richard E. *The Standing Rules of the U.S. House of Representatives.* Ph.D. diss., Columbia University, 1971.

Ehrenhalt, Alan. "Media, Power Shifts Dominate O'Neill's House." *Congressional Quarterly Weekly Report*, September 13, 1986, 2131-2138.

Fleisher, Richard, and Bond, Jon R. "Beyond Committee Control: Committee and Party Leader Influence on Floor Amendments in Congress." *American Politics Quarterly*, April 1983, 131-161.

Froman, Lewis A. *The Congressional Process: Strategies, Rules and Procedures.* Boston: Little, Brown & Co., 1967.

Harlow, Ralph V. *The History of Legislative Methods in the Period Before 1825.* New Haven, Conn.: Yale University Press, 1917.

House, Albert V., Jr. "The Contributions of Samuel J. Randall to the Rules of the National House of Representatives." *American Political Science Review*, October 1935, 837-841.

Kingdon, John W. *Congressmen's Voting Decisions.* New York: Harper & Row, 1973.

MacNeil, Neil. *Forge of Democracy: The House of Representatives.* New York: David McKay, 1963.

Polsby, Nelson W. "The Institutionalization of the House of Representatives." *American Political Science Review*, March 1968, 144-168.

Rhodes, John J. "Floor Procedure in the House of Representatives." In *We Propose: A Modern Congress*, edited by Mary McInnes, 201-206. New York: McGraw-Hill, 1966.

Riddick, Floyd M. *The Organization and Procedure of the United States Congress.* Manassas, Va.: National Capitol Publishers, 1949.

Robinson, William A. *Thomas B. Reed, Parliamentarian.* New York: Dodd, Mead & Co., 1930.

Siff, Todd, and Weil, Alan. *Ruling Congress: A Study on How the House and Senate Rules Govern the Legislative Process.* New York: Grossman, 1975.

Sinclair, Barbara. "The Speaker's Task Force in the Post-Reform House of Representatives." *American Political Science Review*, June 1981, 397-410.

Smith, Steven S. "O'Neill's Legacy for the House." *The Brookings Review*, Winter 1987, 28-36.

CHAPTER 7. SCHEDULING LEGISLATION IN THE SENATE

Asbell, Bernard. *The Senate Nobody Knows.* Garden City, N.Y.: Doubleday, 1978.

Bone, Hugh A. "An Introduction to the Senate Policy Committees." *American Political Science Review*, June 1956, 339-359.

Clark, Joseph S. *The Senate Establishment*. New York: Hill & Wang, 1963.

Cohen, William S. *Roll Call: One Year in the United States Senate*. New York: Simon & Schuster, 1981.

Ehrenhalt, Alan. "Special Report: The Individualist Senate." *Congressional Quarterly Weekly Report*, September 4, 1982, 2175-2182.

Glass, Andrew J. "Mansfield Reforms Spark 'Quiet Revolution' in Senate." *National Journal*, March 6, 1971, 499-512.

Granat, Diane. "Inside Congress: 'Tuesday through Thursday Club.'" *Congressional Quarterly Weekly Report*, July 16, 1983, 1427-1432.

Huitt, Ralph K. "The Internal Distribution of Influence: The Senate." In *The Congress and America's Future*, edited by David B. Truman, 91-117. Englewood Cliffs, N.J.: Prentice Hall, 1965.

Jewell, Malcolm. "The Senate Republican Policy Committee and Foreign Policy." *Western Political Quarterly*, December 1959, 966-980.

Krehbiel, Keith. "Unanimous Consent Agreement: Going Along in the Senate." *Journal of Politics*, August 1986, 541-564.

Oleszek, Walter J. "Party Whips in the United States Senate." *Journal of Politics*, November 1971, 955-979.

Polsby, Nelson W. "Goodbye to the Inner Club." *Washington Monthly*, August 1969, 30-34.

Riddick, Floyd M. *Majority and Minority Leaders of the Senate*. S. Doc. 97-12, 97th Cong., 1st sess. Washington, D.C.: U.S. Government Printing Office, 1981.

Walker, Jack L. "Setting the Agenda in the U.S. Senate." In *Policymaking Role of Leadership in the Senate*. A Compilation of Papers Prepared for the Commission on the Operation of the Senate, 94th Cong., 2d sess., 1976, 96-120.

Webber, Ross. "U.S. Senators: See How They Run." *Wharton Magazine*, Winter 1980-1981, 37-43.

CHAPTER 8. SENATE FLOOR PROCEDURE

Bach, Stanley. "Parliamentary Strategy and the Amendment Process: Rules and Case Studies of Congressional Action." *Polity*, Summer 1983, 573-592.

Bailey, Christopher J. "The United States Senate: The New Individualism and the New Right." *Parliamentary Affairs*, July 1986, 354-364.

Beeman, Richard R. "Unlimited Debate in the Senate: The First Phase." *Political Science Quarterly*, September 1968, 419-434.

Burdette, Franklin L. *Filibustering in the Senate*. Princeton, N.J.: Princeton University Press, 1940.

Calmes, Jacqueline. "'Trivialized' Filibuster Is Still a Potent Tool." *Congressional Quarterly Weekly Report*, September 5, 1987, 2115-2120.

Carlisle, Margo. "Changing the Rules of the Game in the U.S. Senate." *Policy Review*, Winter 1979, 79-92.

Cohen, Richard E. "Marking an End to the Senate's Mansfield Era." *National Journal*, December 25, 1976, 1802-1809.

Drew, Elizabeth. *Senator*. New York: Simon & Schuster, 1979.

Evans, Rowland, and Novak, Robert. *Lyndon B. Johnson: The Exercise of Power*. New York: New American Library, 1966.

Foley, Michael. *The New Senate Liberal Influence on a "Conservative Institution," 1959-1972*. New Haven: Yale University Press, 1980.

Harris, Joseph P. *The Advice and Consent of the Senate*. Berkeley: University of California Press, 1953.

Hook, Janet. "Freshmen Challenge Reagan—and the Senate." *Congressional Quarterly Weekly Report*, January 16, 1988, 122-126.

Huitt, Ralph K. "The Outsider in the Senate: Alternative Role." *American Political Science Review*, September 1961, 566-575.

Keith, Robert. "The Use of Unanimous Consent in the Senate." In *Committees and Senate Procedures*. A Compilation of Papers Prepared for the Commission on the Operation of the Senate, 94th Cong., 2d sess., 1977, 140-168.

Mackenzie, G. Calvin. *The Politics of Presidential Appointments*. New York: The Free Press, 1981.

Matthews, Donald. *U.S. Senators and Their World*. Chapel Hill: University of North Carolina Press, 1960.

Miller, James A. *Running in Place: Inside the Senate*. New York: Simon & Schuster, 1986.

Reedy, George E. *The U.S. Senate*. New York: Crown, 1986.

Ripley, Randall B. *Power in the Senate*. New York: St. Martin's Press, 1969.

Shuman, Howard E. "Senate Rules and the Civil Rights Bill: A Case Study." *American Political Science Review*, December 1957, 955-975.

Sinclair, Barbara. "Senate Styles and Senate Decision Making, 1955-1980." *Journal of Politics*, November 1986, 877-908.

CHAPTER 9. RESOLVING HOUSE-SENATE DIFFERENCES

Bach, Stanley, "Germaneness Rules and Bicameral Relations in the U.S. Congress." *Legislative Studies Quarterly*, August 1982, 341-357.

Fenno, Richard F., Jr. Chap. 12 in *The Power of the Purse: Appropriations Politics in Congress*. Boston: Little, Brown & Co., 1966.

___. *The United States Senate: A Bicameral Perspective*. Washington, D.C.: The American Enterprise Institute for Public Policy Research, 1982.

Ferejohn, John. "Who Wins in Conference Committee?" *Journal of Politics*, November 1975, 1033-1046.

Gore, Albert. "The Conference Committee: Congress' Final Filter." *Washington Monthly,* June 1971, 43-48.

Manley, John F. Chap. 6 in *The Politics of Finance: The House Committee on Ways and Means.* Boston: Little, Brown & Co., 1970.

McCown, Ada C. *The Congressional Conference Committee.* New York: Columbia University Press, 1927.

Oleszek, Walter J. "House-Senate Relationships: Comity and Conflict." *The Annals,* January 1974, 75-86.

Paletz, David L. *Influence in Congress: An Analysis of the Nature and Effects of Conference Committees Utilizing Case Studies of Poverty, Traffic Safety, and Congressional Redistricting Legislation.* Ph.D. diss., University of California, Los Angeles, 1970.

Pressman, Jeffrey L. *House vs. Senate: Conflict in the Appropriations Process.* New Haven, Conn.: Yale University Press, 1966.

"Reform Penetrates Conference Committees." *Congressional Quarterly Weekly Report,* February 8, 1975, 290-294.

Rogers, Lindsay. "Conference Committee Legislation." *North American Review,* March 1922, 300-307.

Steiner, Gilbert. *The Congressional Conference Committee, Seventieth to Eightieth Congresses.* Urbana. University of Illinois Press, 1951.

Strom, Gerald S., and Rundquist, Barry S. "A Revised Theory of Winning in House-Senate Conferences." *American Political Science Review,* June 1977, 448-453.

Vogler, David J. *The Third House: Conference Committees in the U.S. Congress.* Evanston, Ill.: Northwestern University Press, 1971.

CHAPTER 10. LEGISLATIVE OVERSIGHT

Aberbach, Joel D. "Changes in Congressional Oversight." *American Behavioral Scientist,* May-June 1979, 493-515.

____. "The Congressional Committee Intelligence System: Information, Oversight, and Change." *Congress and the Presidency,* Spring 1987, 51-76.

Art, Robert J. "Congress and the Defense Budget: Enhancing Policy Oversight." *Political Science Quarterly,* Summer 1985, 227-248.

Craig, Barbara H. *Chadha.* New York: Oxford University Press, 1988.

Dodd, Lawrence C., and Schott, Richard L. *Congress and the Administrative State.* New York: John Wiley & Sons, 1979.

Edwards, George C., III. *Implementing Public Policy.* Washington, D.C.: CQ Press, 1980.

Fisher, Louis. *The Politics of Shared Power: Congress and the Executive.* 2d ed. Washington, D.C.: CQ Press, 1987.

Freeman, J. Leiper. *The Political Process: Executive Bureau-Legislative Committee Relations.* Rev. Ed. Garden City, N.Y.: Doubleday, 1965.

Harris, Joseph P. *Congressional Control of Administration.* Washington, D.C.: The Brookings Institution, 1964.

Henderson, Thomas A. *Congressional Oversight of Executive Agencies.* Gainesville: University of Florida Press, 1970.

Kaiser, Fred. "Oversight of Foreign Policy: The U.S. House International Relations Committee." *Legislative Studies Quarterly,* August 1977, 255-280.

Morrison, David C. "Chaos on Capitol Hill." *National Journal,* September 27, 1986, 2302-2307.

Ogul, Morris S. *Congress Oversees the Bureaucracy.* Pittsburgh: University of Pittsburgh Press, 1976.

Scher, Seymour. "Conditions for Legislative Control." *Journal of Politics,* August 1963, 526-551.

Schick, Allen. "Congress and the 'Details' of Administration." *Public Administration Review,* September/October 1976, 516-527.

Scicchiatano, Michael J. "Congressional Oversight: The Case of the Clean Air Act." *Legislative Studies Quarterly,* August 1986, 393-407.

Taylor, Telford. *Grand Inquest: The Story of Congressional Investigations.* New York: Simon & Schuster, 1955

CHAPTER 11. A DYNAMIC PROCESS

Bailey, Stephen K. *Congress Makes a Law.* New York: Columbia University Press, 1950.

Berman, Daniel M. *How a Bill Becomes a Law: Congress Enacts Civil Rights Legislation.* 2d ed. New York: Macmillan, 1966.

Bibby, John F., ed. *Congress off the Record: The Candid Analyses of Seven Members.* Washington, D.C.: The American Enterprise Institute for Public Policy Research, 1983.

Birnbaum, Jeffrey H., and Murray, Alan S. *Showdown at Gucci Gulch.* New York: Random House, 1987.

Eidenberg, Eugene, and Morey, Roy D. *An Act of Congress.* New York: W. W. Norton, 1969.

Franck, Thomas M., and Weisband, Edward. *Foreign Policy by Congress.* New York: Oxford University Press, 1979.

Oleszek, Walter J. "Integration and Fragmentation: Key Themes of Congressional Change." *The Annals,* March 1983, 193-205.

Redman, Eric. *The Dance of Legislation.* New York: Simon & Schuster, 1973.

Rieselbach, Leroy N. *Congressional Reform.* Washington, D.C.: CQ Press, 1986.

Sheppard, Burton D. *Rethinking Congressional Reform.* Cambridge, Mass.: Schenkman Books, 1985.

Smith, Steven S. "New Patterns of Decisionmaking in Congress." In *The New Direction in American Politics*, edited by John E. Chubb and Paul E. Peterson. Washington, D.C.: The Brookings Institution, 1985.

Sundquist, James L. *The Decline and Resurgence of Congress.* Washington, D.C.: The Brookings Institution, 1981.

Vogler, David J., and Waldman, Sidney R. *Congress and Democracy.* Washington, D.C.: CQ Press, 1985.

Whalen, Charles, and Whalen, Barbara. *The Longest Debate: A Legislative History of the 1964 Civil Rights Act.* Washington, D.C.: Seven Locks Press, 1985.

Wright, Gerald C., Jr.; Rieselbach, Leroy N.; and Dodd, Lawrence C., eds. *Congress and Policy Change.* New York: Agathon Press, 1986.

Index